A Flowershop in Baghdad

MICHAEL BANZET

Library of Congress Cataloging-in-Publication Data
Banzet, Michael S

A Flowershop in Baghdad: American Exceptionalism in Iraq

ISBN-10: 1478271299

ISBN-13: 978-1478271291

LCCN 2012950467
North Charleston, South Carolina

A V-1 Enterprises Original

Cover Photo, Courtesy U.S. Army
Cover Design, Mike Banzet
Text Design, Createspace
First printing, October 2012

Distributed by: V-1 Enterprises
Springboro Oh, 45066

Printed in the United States of America

Dedication

To my wife and children—part of everything good I do and everything good I am.
To my parents; if it weren't for them, I wouldn't be here. That's biological fact.
Also, they are the most wonderful parents a child could have.

THE IRAQIS

General Jasham: Head of Iraqi Military Training
General Abbas: Head of the IQAF A7 training division; my first advisee; Samir's older brother
General Akram: Head of IQAF A7 after Abbas
General Altair: Number two of the IQAF
General Aslam: Head of overseas training
General Abdul Khalid: IQAF training school commander at Taji
General Arhem: Base Commander of Taji, keeper of goats and pigeons
Colonel Kamil: Became Commander, Kirkuk Flying Training Squadron
Colonel Asad: One of the Four Amigos; best friends with Colonel Wahid
Colonel Wahid: One of the Four Amigos; promoted to head of IQAF A7 after I left
Lieutenant Colonel Nasser: One of the Four Amigos
Lieutenant Colonel Ahmed: One of the Four Amigos
Lieutenant Amjad: One of the Magic Eleven; the most outspoken
Lieutenant(s) Mahmood(s): Three of the Magic Eleven
Major Ghalib: One of the three Mission Sensor Operators (MSO)s chosen to attend stateside training
Lieutenant Alhasan, Alaa: The other two MSOs
Major Bashir: First Iraqi to attend KingAir training stateside.

Contents

1	Preface	1
2	How To Become A Superhero	7
3	The Journey Begins	11
4	An Officer Or A Gentleman	43
5	One Day In September	65
6	Around The World In 80 Days	71
7	Vip Transport	77
8	Prepping For The Mission, Whatever It Is	85
9	Nice To See You Too	103
10	Meet The Boys	131
11	Four Amigos	149
12	The Magic Eleven	161
13	Iraqi Officer Training	187
14	Flintstone Village	213
15	Imperialist Warmongers	225
16	Little Big Man	239
17	Cake, Anyone?	265
18	A Hero You've Never Heard Of	283
19	Finally, American Arrogance	301
20	A Flower Shop in Baghdad	319

I

PREFACE

The truly amazing thing about me is that, as a product of this amazing country, I am utterly ordinary. However, once I leave the borders of these United States, I start to grow in power and influence until I become someone who can do anything: feed the hungry, shelter the homeless, protect the weak, and clothe the shabby. I know the answers to everything and can get anything from anyone. Money and power pour from my fingertips, like a superhero with, well, money and power-type powers. I actually use to have a costume and everything. It said US Air Force, and on it, there were a set of wings and an aircraft maintenance badge. No cape, but I could fly myself around with only the assistance of an aircraft.

This book was written to share with you how I came to the startling conclusion that I am indeed a superhero. Only within the borders of the United States do I fade into a mere mortal with the same problems and issues as everyone else in this little country. I was stunned at the realization that *I* had a secret identity kept from myself. It's as if Clark Kent went to take a shower one day, realized he was wearing a funny skintight suit and cape underneath his staid suit and tie, and wondered, "Where did *that* come from?"

Essentially, it took a year on the ground in and around Baghdad, working with the Iraqi air force (IQAF) day and night, for this realization to dawn on me; and then, only after I came home did that niggling thought solidify into a full-blown idea, one that I have to share: superheroes walk in our midst. It's like that movie *They Live*, with "Rowdy" Roddy Piper, where many people who look ordinary are actually aliens. He could only see them in their true form with special glasses—really ugly glasses. I would like to give you the metaphorical glasses with which to see these people. They are really, really worth seeing. Your level of education or financial status don't matter—these men and women and their stories should bring a tear to your eye and a lump to your throat. From the safety of your bed, with the electric blanket keeping you at *just* the right temperature and pillows propping up your head, watching Letterman or Leno while you drift off to sleep, it's difficult to comprehend the difference in worldview and self-imposed responsibilities that these quiet men and women have adopted.

The differences are stark. One group runs to the sound of guns so that the other can roll over and snuggle in their blankets. Many, especially in this day and age of chosen service, view the military as a place to go if everything else is falling apart. Or, as some have said, if you don't do well in some sort of educational pursuit, you'll get "stuck in Iraq"[1]. I'd like you to consider a different view—a view that entertains the idea that the ones who have chosen this type of service are the best this society has to offer. They may not be the smartest, best looking, richest, or best connected, but you'd be surprised by the silent quality of these people.

There are many of them—all shapes and sizes. You may have them in your family and not know it. There are more than you might think. This country breeds them like flies. And their attitude is contagious. You'll see. I'll prove it to you. The essence of their heroism is the selflessness of the action. Taking action at great risk to yourself for a greater cause, sometimes as esoteric as "freedom"—whether it's for a platoon, squad, or, in the case of the Iraqis I worked with, an entire country—some folks see what needs

---

1 Tapper, Jake. Did Kerry Hand Republicans a November Gift? October 31, 2006. http://abcnews.go.com/WNT/story?id=2619383&page=1#.T-UUa_VFmH8 (accessed Jun 22, 2012).

to be done, and, without glancing left or right to look for someone else, proceed to do it—a decision not made in ignorance, but in full knowledge of the perils that abound.

To that end, I will not be using real names for the Iraqis discussed in this book. I didn't tell them that I would be writing a book, as I really hadn't a clue that I would be driven to do so. I don't want to put any of them at risk without their permission. Many of them wouldn't care, but I must err on the side of caution. These people are too valuable.

This book, then, will describe my experiences during my year in and around Baghdad, Iraq, from 2007–2008. I'd been over the skies of Afghanistan and Iraq numerous times before, having deployed many times (at four months a pop) in the preceding years, from the very beginning of Operation Enduring Freedom. Upon returning to the United States, I would get a week off, then continue to go on the road as a USAF mobility pilot, running folks back and forth to the desert, or running training missions in the States. So I've stayed busy since 2001 and, as of the writing of this book, accumulated some twenty-five hundred hours in the air, about five hundred of which are combat hours. I've had some pretty awesome experiences in that realm, too, but this book isn't about that. It's about my time on the ground in Iraq.

For many pilots, being on the ground is akin to being a male guest on *The View*: enduring the screech of a thousand nails on blackboards. Through amplifiers. Piped directly into your head. However, I must say, without reservation, that the year I spent in Iraq was the most important year of my professional life. No contest. I've never seen the might and thunder, along with the tenderness and patience, of a military organization focused on a people before. And I got to see it from their perspective. Not many have had that opportunity. I was truly blessed to be among those that have been at the epicenter of history in the making.

Now then, there is always a place in this kind of book where the author is *sure* you have a burning desire to know the minutia of what is, in the author's fevered imagination, a fascinating life, dripping with large lessons and bubbling with wisdom, humor, and outright handsomeness. There is no detail too trivial to *not* be memorialized in print. I'm thinking of calling it *My Life*. What, already taken? How bout *It Takes a Village*? Taken as well. Okay, I'll just end up telling you a little bit about me and my career, mostly to prove my superhero thesis. Remember, I take no pride in how awesome I've become—it came as a shock to me too. Out of necessity, then, the next couple of pages must describe a bit about me. Think of it as the backstory on how the superhero came to be. But without bats, gamma rays, or radioactive spiders. Especially spiders. I hate spiders. I think that within this background, it will make the superhero transition that much more amazing, and you may see just a little of you revealed, too.

I'll cite some interesting situations from my humble beginnings, and my meteoric rise to humble endings, but I promise you, this is not some self-flagellating exercise. These are the things that I thought back on as I went through the year of training Iraqis, things I had to ask myself over and over. "Why do we do things that way, and will it work here? Will some of it work here?" If you're not familiar with the air force, you wouldn't get some of the conclusions that I've drawn; so, even though the narrative may seem to be a self-licking ice cream cone, this is an attempt to condense twenty years of experience into the first part of this book.

The second half of the book was much more difficult to write. Many of those main accomplishments evolved over the same period. I wanted to follow the individual threads over their entirety, so the reader (assuming there are any) can get the impact of the vignettes standing alone. That was how they occurred to me. I tried to write it chronologically, but it became so confusing that I would forget what my point was. And I was there. So the second half of the book is really written as a series of closely related stories that probably took place in overlapping timelines. I've chosen to describe each thread in the rope individually, versus trying to describe the whole rope. Hopefully, you will still see the ties that bind us at the end.

I would like to thank many USAF folks—Col. Jim Buchman, Col. Jazz Armstrong, Col Brooks Reese, Maj. Denise Shea, and a host of others who helped my failing memory. I hope you like this; not enough people know what you do. Thousands of military folks are anonymously representing the people of this nation in dangerous situations. The lowest-ranking deployed E-1 has a greater impact than all the ambassadors at all the swell parties with all the swell people. Thank you for representing me as well as you do. To my Iraqi friends: You have always kept the faith. Thank you.

I would also like to thank my best friend (dude-wise) Chris. He's probably rubbing all over someone right now. Oh, that's because he's a physical therapist, not a politician. But he has been a better friend than I, so doesn't know what a silent, strong foundation he has been to me.

A special thank you to Garry and John. I can only imagine how hard this was. I hope to do him justice.

Again, in no way am I implying that I am any different than the thousands who passed before; I've just written down what I saw, and the conclusions that I've jumped to.

Plus, it's probably the most important thing ever—ever.

2

HOW TO BECOME A SUPERHERO

I think I was born in California; I'm not sure; I was pretty young at the time. But soon after, I was taken to Montana to a tiny little town called Marysville, an old mining town nestled in the mountains twenty miles or so west of Helena. Here, my brother and I (and eventually my sister) roamed all over this no kidding ghost town of the West. It was awesome. I got to ride my bike everywhere, hiking and wandering all over this landscape strewn with old mineshafts, mining equipment, and dangerous chemicals. I think it was my family's version of Darwinism. I don't have any idea how many brothers and sisters I started out with, so I really don't know how many were "selected out" of the gene pool, but I ended up with an older brother (Clint) and a younger sister (Jennifer). They are still my older brother and younger sister to this day.

I really loved that place, so we moved. We wound up a little closer to Helena, only ten miles from the Montana capital (one of the 57 states visited by Barack Obama in his run-up to the presidential election[2]). I got a motorcycle in an attempt to further test Darwinism and eventually almost succeeded in selecting the two Banzet boys out at once. We had twenty-eight acres of land and two motorcycles (one was my dad's) going at the same time. And had a head-on collision. On twenty-eight acres. Take a second and really think about that. A motorcycle is about a foot and a half wide from the front, and the two of us tried to occupy the same foot and a half of space at the exact same time, amid twenty-eight acres of land. Clint got a busted ankle, and I almost died laughing.

Thus having established my genius early on, and really starting to like being closer to town (only seven miles), we moved again—this time to Kalispell, Montana, a little piece of God's country in the northwest corner of the state. One of the most beautiful places on earth. On second thought, it's terrible: stay away. Vail is really nice. You should go there. So, Kalispell is where I attended Flathead High School, but more importantly where I met the most amazing person in my life. She had it all: stunning looks, sparkling personality, amazing body (a woman's!), and no taste in men. I struck immediately after three years, and because she is a woman of her word, Debra remains married to me to this day. I got the "better"; she gets the "worse." Eventually, and against the better judgment of many, I graduated and a few months later joined the air force.

Although I'd joined up, I couldn't get in right away, so I had a couple of jobs until I reported to basic training. They were remarkable in that I hated both of them. One was working for a window and door company, as a delivery guy. I was fired after failing to complete some deliveries, which is apparently an expectation of a delivery guy. They were cheapskates, however, and wouldn't invest in any sort of communications gear; after being sent out to construction sites that may or may not have had any street signs and wandering aimlessly for hours asking random folks if they would like a window or door, I would bring it back. Which the management did not expect. Clearly not my fault, but in truth, I couldn't conceive of doing that job for any length of time. Took no intellectual horsepower, only muscle. Kind of serf-like. I've always had a low tolerance for silliness, and that

---

2 Reuters. May 9, 2008. http://www.reuters.com/video/2008/05/09/obama-ive-now-been-to-57-states?videoId=82127 (accessed June 22, 2012).

place took the cake for short-term thinking and general cheapness. I knew I was marking time, and that probably didn't help. So at some point, they had enough of me returning with the exact same load that I had left with, and when I tried to explain that the address they had given me didn't flipping exist, they decided that my talents could be best utilized elsewhere. Anywhere else but there.

After that I got a job at the local newspaper: in the back, just shuffling the papers around. I was responsible for assembling parts of the paper, helping to bundle it, and getting it out to various delivery people. The Saturday night shift really stunk, as we didn't get done until Sunday morning. The people there were actually very nice and helpful, but I noticed something. I became aware of how people ended up becoming trapped in jobs that they never intended to be in. People were waiting for…something. Guys had been there twenty years temporarily, looking for something else. I didn't want that to happen to me. My life had become a circle of work, gym, and home to my parents' house. I was getting agitated, and I certainly wasn't super helpful around my parents' house. I didn't fit that mold. I had someplace to *be*. I had something to *become*. It finally came time for me to get to the air force and do something with my life, so I jumped on a plane, headed for the great state of Texas, where if the heat of summer doesn't kill you, then the heat of winter will.

3

THE JOURNEY BEGINS

I joined the air force because I had always wanted to fly; airplanes have always fascinated me. They are not, to me, mere methods of transportation, tools sculpted from metal, leather, and rubber, but personalities unto their own. A P-47 is different than a P-51; an F-15 is different than a A-10. A C-5 is different than a KC-10 or a C-17. For me, one of the most contemplative, sad locations on the planet is the "boneyard" at Davis-Monthan Air Force Base in Arizona. It's where the services put their aircraft for storage, disposal, or destruction. To me, it is a true graveyard. Spent bodies, exhausted after carrying their charges safely through war and peace, sun and storm, sand and salt, glint dully in the harsh sun—aircraft awaiting total destruction or partial dismemberment as one part at a time gets donated to keep another of their brothers aloft.

Aircraft are inherently sexy. The army and its tanks are lumbering giants, slogging through mud and snow to grab the enemy by the throat to make them cry uncle (hard when an armored fist is around your throat).

Not sexy. The navy and marine corps float around the ocean, waiting for someplace to land—in the marine corps' case, land and shoot someone. Definitely not sexy. But airplanes and airmen: dead sexy. Slipping the surly bonds and all that. Some folks are drawn to the attributes of the army, marine corps, and the navy, and that is their right: doesn't make it less wrong. Such misguided folks probably wouldn't fit in the refined society that is air force life. Every wing is a slice of the Hamptons; every squadron is an exclusive club with a velvet rope; every flight, a cigar library where, after the jets are launched, brandy snifters come out and the discussion centers around obscure topics like quantum mechanics and how the Château Mouton Rothschild Pauillac is just too "oaky." I couldn't wait to get started.

I reported to Lackland Air Force Base in Texas in August. Perfect weather for a Montana kid. I lost five pounds in sweat on the bus ride over. Made for a lovely start to my career. I'll skip the more mundane parts of the training, but my penchant for smart-ass'ness was not appreciated to the level I'd expected. I did fine but had a few memorable moments that left an indelible mark on me. One of my lessons revolved around a misunderstanding between me and my drill instructor (DI).

Suffice it to say that a DI does not appreciate an Airman Basic running around the dorm bay at night, wearing only his underwear and the aforementioned DI's "Smoky the Bear" hat while doing a spot-on impression of the DI to the other forty airmen (none of whom, by the way, could be bothered to say that the man had entered the bay and was watching from the doorway). The rest of that evening was a little fuzzy, but it involved some slamming doors, standing at attention (a lot), and demonstrating a lot of military bearing (as much as I was able to muster in underwear and one sock). I was hustled into his office; then Staff Sergeant (SSgt or E-5) Dugan screamed and hollered at me, using a tightly controlled anger, red coming in waves over his already ruddy face, gesturing and pointing out several flaws in my character, physical makeup, and future potential. Apparently, he had given this a lot of thought.

I had no idea how controlled he was until he flicked down the blinds of his office, possibly to leave no witnesses to what was to transpire next. I calculated that I couldn't run, as the floor was highly waxed linoleum, and I was wearing the one sock, which would cut my acceleration in half. So I had to endure whatever was coming next. What was next took me by surprise: SSgt. Dugan collapsed behind his desk in laughter, dropping into his chair, kicking the wastepaper basket to cover his laughter. He looked at me with tears in his eyes; apparently the tightly controlled "anger" was in fact barely suppressed laughter. He said something to the effect that I was to look properly chastised upon leaving and that he was going to do some more screaming and hollering—and that I should never do that again. I didn't. Because he never left his hat there again.

There was another incident that deserves special note, as it demonstrates a principle of warfare that was to come into play in the deserts of Iraq some twenty years later. Our basic training dorms were just about to be condemned and were infested with bats. Of course the USAF was very concerned that the newest members of the world's greatest air force were protected from rabid bats, so instructions were given that in the event that a bat were to get into the sleeping quarters, one of us should get on the intercom and call for help, while everyone else should pull the covers of the GI blanket over his head—just like you do if there is a monster under the bed. A blanket is impervious to monsters *and* bats, according to the USAF.

The first time a bat came squeaking into the dorms, we did just that. Our designated hero ran to the intercom, squealed for help, then dived into his bed; meanwhile, throughout the bay forty young men were busy burying themselves under the covers and trying not to giggle. I wondered if the Marines had this very same contingency plan. Probably not. Anyway, the DI came up and hustled us out of the room into the dorm across the hall, while they took care of this intruder. We were actually made to cover our heads and "evacuate" in an orderly manner. I hope, for our sake, that it was a giant bat that could rend a human into tiny shreds. Because otherwise this would have been silly. We had made the call around midnight and didn't get back into the room until around two o'clock, exhausted.

We resolved never to ask for help with this particular problem again. We were just going to have to take on these two-ounce monsters ourselves, no matter the risk to life and limb. We thought the odds were favorable: forty 180-pound airmen against one, two, possibly three bats; of course, if it was more than that, discretion would be the better part of valor, and the DIs would again find forty quivering humps on cots waiting for rescue. But the fateful night came when two of the flying mice penetrated our defenses and proceeded to raise havoc with the airman on duty. We had found the DI's weapon of choice for the last incident—an old tennis racket—so we were fairly well armed. One old tennis racket, forty airmen, and two light and lethal death rodents.

The call came at about two in the morning, and the guard spread word throughout that there were bats in the bay. We all grabbed giant flashlights and went into our carefully planned battle drill, all the while trying to maintain silence, as the DIs could listen in via intercom. The next hour and a half was like a rave in an insane asylum. All that was missing was some sort of techno beat; we were already in our "tidy whiteys" waving lights around. The flashlights illuminated the ceiling like London during the Blitz, except on fast forward, trying to catch and hold in their beams the tiny bodies of the intruders. Of course, this was almost impossible, as the bats were fast, and there were forty heads and eighty arms flailing around in the striped dark. The designated marksman (with the tennis racket) was not having a great night. I could hear the swish of the racquet strings followed, more often than not, by a fleshy thud, or more painfully, a crack of the racket connecting with an elbow or finger—but no bats. This went on for several minutes, with several relief marksmen stepping up to the task of swinging the racquet without hitting anyone, and, as a side benefit, hitting and killing a bat. Unsuccessfully. At some point, another weapon was discovered. Pillows. Everyone had one, and the consequences of a miss were less severe. Depending on the severity of a strike, and the relative strength of a bat body, it could render the weapon unusable, but it was thought to be worth the risk. With a larger hitting surface, the pillow assault went a little better, although the tradeoff for the larger sweet spot was a lower kill ratio in the event of a hit. Eventually, the bats succumbed to the superior firepower, tactics, and can-do spirit of these American fighting men, especially when kitted out with pillows and flashlights. Plus the fact that they had brains the size of an almond...the bats, I mean.

This incident showed that the brass at the top doesn't always need to know the specifics of the operation. It must be conducted in alignment with command guidance (no bats in the dorms) and in a manner congruent with all Geneva Convention accords. No bats were killed in the bathroom or while praying. However, we discovered that the least painful way for us to get bats out of the dorms (accomplish the mission) and still be bright-eyed and bushy tailed (command directive) was to affect the outcome for ourselves. Which we did. The first attempt was, as mentioned, a messy success. But we learned. And became steely-eyed bat killers.

There came another lesson during the battle of the dayroom, which again bore fruit later in my career. This battle took place much later in the training, merely a week or two before graduation. The many duties required in order to keep forty guys in fighting shape required the delegation of many duties, one of which was laundry duty. On this particular day, I was assigned to help with the laundry, which seems like a relatively easy task, though fraught with danger. The danger of "horseplay", also known as "grab-ass", had been briefed many times as the single most heinous sin in basic training. That was ominous foreshadowing.

The laundry was to be brought up in our C bags, the ubiquitous bags most associated with servicemen. They expand to about 3 feet long, looking like thick, crumpled green canvas sausages strapped to the backs of the individual GIs. In this case, they were stuffed with about fifty pounds of laundry each, and there were about forty of them. Our job was to get them into our dayroom for further distribution. There was about six of us on the task, and we dragged them up the concrete stairs into the dayroom. So far, so good. The dayroom was decorated with models of airplanes hanging from the ceiling and murals painted on the walls. One of the most striking murals was a space scene depicting a satellite battle. It was mostly black, with stars in the background and lasers zapping back and forth. We'd gotten quite a few bags into the room and were making good progress when things went awry.

Unfortunately, it was discovered that the laundry bags could be used as a weapon, by grabbing the straps at the top and just swinging it. It worked like a giant Downy-soft mace. Immediately after this discovery, the room filled with grunting and sounds of impact, the occasional sock and T-shirt flying about like soft, bleached shrapnel. And then it happened, like in a highlight reel, in slow motion. I remember a smaller kid, standing up like a skinny god, feet spread apart, C bag hoisted high above his head, in anticipation of hammering one of my impromptu teammates with a giant blow. A crazy light gleamed behind his thick GI glasses as he readied a hammer blow to another airman.

I had a bag in my hand and quickly swung it in a tight arc, releasing it across the highly polished floor. It hissed across the short distance, spinning—fifty pounds of lethal BVDs, primed for mayhem. I watched the kid's eyes (behind the bullet- and woman-proof glasses) track his impending doom, seemingly powerless to take any action to prevent impact. It hit both of his skinny little legs, while his bony arms wobbled under the weight of the now useless bag hovering over his head. The heavy bag slid through him, barely slowing down, knocking his feet out from under him. His stiff body quickly reached the horizontal, and then gravity took over. At that point, time accelerated back to normal, and he hit the hard linoleum all at once, arms still stretched above his head.

The crack as his face hit the floor shot through the dayroom; hostilities were brought instantly to a halt; bags suspended, then dropped. There was a moment of silence, then he turned over, purple with rage. Also a little bloody. He looked at me through crooked glasses, blood staining his teeth and smearing his cheek. He roared, "Banzet, you son of a bitch!" and then he rolled over, simultaneously kicking his scrawny leg. Right through the wall of the space mural.

This was bad. We only had a couple of weeks to go, and this was clear evidence of that hobgoblin of basic training: grab-ass. Severe grab-ass. With malice a forethought. A hole in the precious mural was grounds for recycling, which would return the culprits to an earlier class, thus extending the stay in basic training. Nobody wanted that, but yet there was a foot-shaped hole in space. First, we had to convince the kid not to rat us out, which was fairly easy, as he was complicit in the act and knew it. Next, we had to figure out what to do with the black hole. Many suggestions were considered, but the one that held the most promise was this.

We were to take a length of masking tape from a lint roller and make two passes over the hole to cover it. We didn't have any paint, but someone else suggested using one of the most readily accessible commodities in basic training: boot polish. That seemed to work okay, but applying polish to masking tape was a skill that we didn't have, so we invented the procedure as we went. It became nice and black, perfectly matching the black background, except for the pinpoints of white that were the stars. Someone suggested we use the laundry marking pen, and that too turned out to be a good solution. So we were set; with only a couple of weeks to go, the evidence of the horseplay had been erased—we thought.

As training came closer to an end, we started concentrating more on classroom briefs and following up with more informal sessions, often held in the dayroom. This was unexpected. Another unexpected aspect was that the boot polish only lasted for about a day, before it dried up, turned gray, and started to peel. We ended up appointing guys to apply more polish, following up with more "stars." Another guy was assigned to sit in front of the repair. We were all ready to create distractions if the DI's eyes lingered too long on the spot during the course of a brief. This happened several times, as our DI would be in the middle of talking to us, and a curious expression would flicker across his face, triggering an explosion of questions from the sides of the room. Even now, I think that he would leave the event thinking that this bunch of guys really "got it." Yup, we were super interested in...whatever. There were a few more instances packed into the remaining week or so, but we all ended up getting out of there on time.

Just prior to leaving, we were sent to a career counselor who tried to match our skills (demonstrated by taking the ASVAB) to a job that the air force needed. Mine was not what I'd expected. I strolled into the Non-Commissioned Officers' (NCO) office and sat proudly in the seat. I knew what I'd signed up for. I was going to be a "Tactical Aircraft Maintenance Technician"; —to me, the most important job in the air force. Pilots without crew chiefs were desk jockeys, cube masters, chair-borne warriors. I sat waiting for my chance to tell the SSgt what I had chosen to do, thus earning immediate accolades for my career choice. I would probably be carried out on the chair, with children throwing flowers at my feet. It was a reasonable expectation. The SSgt flipped through my records, noting this and that and then said, "There's some mistake here; what was it you wanted to do?" I puffed out my chest, sat up straight, and said, "Ma'am, I'm going to be a crew chief!"

I didn't get the reaction I'd expected, instead a furrowed brow and more flipping through the records. The clock ticked the anxious seconds away as I waited to discover what I had said wrong. The furrow deepened, as if she was arguing with herself, then finally she looked up at me, blurting, "But you're smart! You can do *other* jobs; you don't *have* to be a crew chief!" Yes, she said those words in italics. She offered up several other jobs, including a crypto-linguist, which wasn't even fun to say, much less make a career out of. I politely declined, intimating that airplanes were sorta important to the Air Force, and crew chiefs were sorta important to airplanes, so that's what I wanted to do. She described the Crew Chief's job to me, including terrible hours, working outside in all weather conditions, hazardous materials, and dangerous machines. I was sold.

After training ended, I was sent to Sheppard Air Force Base for basic aircraft maintenance training. It turned out to be a lot of long days, filled with marching to class early in the morning, trying not to nod off during the day, studying in the evening, polishing boots, and prepping for the next day. I always ended up having a lot of fun, but it was mostly because I was always touching and fondling the aircraft. In one hangar, there was an F-16, an A-10, and an F-4. I was in heaven. I was training with aircraft that defended this nation from everyone else in the whole world. And these were the planes that did it. And here I was, some kid from Montana, elbow-deep in the guts of an F-4, trying to figure out the hydraulic pump. For me, it was quite a leap. This was reality. I felt this really mattered, even though these particular aircraft would never fly again. That wasn't my fault, of course, as they were pretty beat up if they came to the training base to be sheet metal cadavers for the eager mechanics that poked and prodded inside them. But I still felt a responsibility toward them. That sounds stupid even as I type it, but it was the truth. Graduation came soon enough, and it was on to the next phase of training in the making of an F-4 crew chief.

I arrived at George Air Force Base for training as a crew chief on F-4Gs. This bent-wing warrior was my dream come true, and I was absolutely captivated by the smells and sounds of these old birds waddling down the taxiways, exhaust fumes pouring out of the old J-79 engines and rippling to the tarmac. Seeing the flames and feeling the noise in my chest as they hit burner and went hurtling down the runway gave me a feeling of satisfaction that I rarely encounter, even to this day. As a kid from Montana, I'd never even touched an actual, flyable air force aircraft, and here I was, making this hulking monster go. I grinned like an idiot the whole time. I came home drenched in JP-8, hydraulic fluid or 5606 oil, loving it. This was what I had been waiting for.

We learned the dangerous parts of the airplane—apparently anywhere on the outside or inside of the airplane. The cockpit could kill you. The auxiliary air doors could chop your arms off. The weapons pylons would slice you open. The exhaust would burn you to a crisp—a smelly crisp. Changing a tire would burn the hair off your arms. The noise would deafen you. Stuffing the drag chute would either pinch your arm or stick a fuel dump mast in it. I still have my scars, or *Phantom bites* that I earned. It was truly a beautiful machine.

When this aircraft was designed, there wasn't an allowance for maintenance. You had to fight the aircraft to make it go. For instance, part of the launch sequence involved pulling the centerline tank safety pin. When I was instructed on how to pull it, the conversation went something like this (and you have to imagine the J-79s blasting out their joyous screeching the whole time, and the instructor has taken off one side of my ear protection, so he can yell in my ear, while the engines idle immediately above my head).

Instructor: You see that door there?

Me: Yes, sir.

Instructor: Well, you have to reach in there and feel around for the safety pin, and then press with your thumb and pull with your hand.

"This hand?"

"Who gives a shit which hand—I don't care—just reach in there and do it!"

"How can I push with my thumb and pull with the fingers of the same hand?"

After an incredulous look and a moment of silence as he stared at me, trying to figure out if I was just messing with him or I truly didn't understand the evolutionary blessings that came with an opposable thumb, still with a wondering look in his eye and a slightly opened mouth, he silently held up his hand and made a standard "grabbing" motion with his thumb and first two fingers.

Oh.

I started to reach into the opening in the belly of the aircraft, which was covered by a hydraulically actuated door about two feet long and a foot wide, quivering under 3,000 psi of hydraulic pressure.

Instructor (shouting again): Hurry up, because if the generator drops offline for any time, these doors cycle shut at 3,000 psi. Don't be in there if that happens.

"I'm sorry—what?" My hand poised in midair, hovering below the dark opening that was starting to look just a bit ominous. "It will chop my arm off?" I was really starting to believe that pin could just stay in there, and if the jet had an issue where the pilot needed to punch the tank off, well, it just wouldn't go. The aircraft could crash, but then, the pilot had a whole ejection system installed just for that eventuality, and I really wanted to keep both arms. I looked around for any one- or no-armed crew chiefs, but it seemed everyone had the standard issue set of two, so I figured there had to be a way around this dilemma. There was.

The solution was a two-inch-by-two-foot piece of metal with a claw on the end of it. This was a tool that had been locally manufactured by the fabrication branch. The tactic was to stick the claw end into the door and latch it around the door actuator, so if it did cycle while you were in there, you would just crap your pants, instead of crapping your pants and losing an arm too. The instructor handed me this flimsy-feeling piece of equipment, and I shoved it in the door, frantically feeling around for the actuator to fit it around. I latched it on then swiftly grabbed the pin, pressed and pulled, and out it came. Victory, albeit short-lived. Apparently, there was a lot more to launching this monster than merely pulling this one pin.

There was a whole launch procedure, and the guys that were good could make it look like a ballet. A *com out* launch was something to behold, as the nonverbal communications between the crew chief and the pilot unfolded in an intricate play that took them through the entire checklist without a word. All the required checks, from the stability augmentation system to the tail hook checks, were gone through with no electronic emanations. I didn't know it at the time, but there was a purpose beyond looking awesome. A silenced launch would give an enemy listening to certain spectrums no clue that there was an F-4 launch in process. Were the enemy to gather this information, target arrival times could be extrapolated, leading to the enemy placing counter-air assets in the most advantageous position. Of course, I had no idea about any of that; it just looked really cool; the crew chief and the pilot in perfect synchronization; the pilot's head tilts to check an instrument, glances up just in time to catch the chief's hand signal that the flight control surface is in the proper position. The pilot's head snaps back down, checking readings, while the chief has repositioned and already checked the next item, to be in place when the pilot glances up again, this time to another side of the airplane. This was done daily, hourly, by the average Joes on the flight line. The ability to accomplish this was the standard.

After seeing this, I knew I had made the right choice. I was exactly where I was supposed to be. I wanted to have the absolute trust and comradeship that comes from being a well-respected part of the pilot/maintenance team; but that would have to wait until I proved myself. That meant working my way up through the ranks and skill levels. There were many tests that I would have to take in order to move through the 3-5-7 skill levels. I had to pass my Career Development Courses (CDCs) and get practical task exams as well. During this process, I would be under the constant tutelage of a supervisor. In short, there would be a huge investment by me and the air force before I would be allowed to become a "Dedicated Crew Chief", and have my name on the jet along with the pilot's.

I graduated from George AFB as an F-4 crew chief and was sent to Zaragoza Air Base, Spain, eager to become the best F-4 crew dog in the USAF. Upon arrival I realized that this would be a little difficult to achieve, inasmuch as there weren't, in a manner of speaking, F-4s in Spain. I went to a different shop, where I learned things about other aircraft, including the heavies that were stationed there on a semi-permanent basis. I learned how to rig a door on a KC-135; I learned wheel and tire maintenance; I learned crash recovery skills. I also went out to the flight line to learn inspections on F-16s, A-10s, F-15s, and any other fighter that came through. There was a standing agreement with my boss that I could be temporarily assigned with the F-4 units when they came down to practice at the Bardenas bombing range. I also made another agreement with my boss: if I did well on my remaining CDCs, I would be allowed to go to school in my off time. Usually, you had to wait until your initial training was done before you were allowed to go, but the boss said that if I scored above 90 percent on my first test, I could enroll in school.

I kept after the CDCs and scored a 96 percent on the first test, enabling me to attend college as well as continue in the career progression course. In addition to these exams, you were also tested on your general knowledge of the air force, from history and tradition to dress and appearance rules. This was called the Promotion Fitness Exam (PFE), and the study guide was usually one volume about an inch and a half thick. It was heavy sledding: the only parts I really liked were about the history and airplane stuff. How to get dressed properly, while essential, was not interesting to me. It wouldn't hit me how important dress and appearance were until much later.

I eventually finished all five volumes (each about an inch thick), and kept up with the PFE material. Because I was doing well in all aspects of my job, I was selected to try out for E-4, Senior Airman Below-the-Zone. This involved an intense grilling by a panel of five senior NCOs. They could ask you any questions from any part of the PFE; as I said, I really didn't care for about 80 percent of it, so I hit the books hard again. I was up against eight other airmen- a couple of those I wasn't really worried about, but these guys were all hand-picked from their respective sections. So I had to make my absolute best impression. I studied my fanny off, but only had a couple of days to prepare. We were to meet in one of the older conference rooms on the base, and at the appointed hour, we all showed up with the enthusiasm of a member of a firing squad. Just not the guys with guns.

I was scheduled to go about the middle of the pack, so my angst got to build for about an hour, and then the bouncer (I forget his real title) had me rap on the door. The normal entry sequence called for a smart rap at the door; then someone on the panel would say, "Enter," and the airman would march smartly to two paces in front of the panel, station himself in front of the chair, report, salute, and on the command to sit, sit down without looking. The folks in front of me had managed to pull that off without too much trouble. My entry into the room deviated from the norm a little.

In order to establish my authority early, I pounded on the door—hard. It rattled around in the frame for a couple of seconds, and the bouncer guy remarked that the door actually opened and stuff, so I wouldn't have to knock it down. (In my defense, the door *looked* fairly solid.) Sometime between my thundering hammer, the door rattling around, and the guy's remarks, the panel lead must have said, "Enter," but I didn't hear it. There was an eerie silence on my side of the door, and the bouncer and I eyed each other as the seconds ticked by. I raised an eyebrow, asking him in silence if he had heard anything. He shrugged. Thanks, I thought.

From the panel's perspective, there was a crash at the door and, after the command to enter, dead silence. They waited in silence, but nothing. Apparently they started to whisper among themselves, wondering if there had indeed been a knock, or if someone had run face-first into the door. Just as they were about to inquire as to the nature of the injury that they were sure must've been sustained, the doorknob slowly turned, and a slightly disheveled crew cut poked around the door.

"Umm, I'm sorry, sir, but did you say come in?"

"Enter!"

"Now? Or did you want me to close the door and knock again and start all over, or just come in and sit down, or just simulate closing the door and knock right now, or—"

"Enter!" (*Dammit* was implied.)

I scuttled around the door, regained what was left of my military bearing, marched up to the panel, saluted, gave the required reporting statement, and sat down flawlessly. I had never been so proud of merely sitting down before (in all fairness, it was an awesome sit). The rest of it was fairly standard; I actually did quite well, but did get into a couple of sticky situations concerning the questions. I was fairly smooth in the questioning, but again, my talent for shooting myself in the foot before anyone else could rose to the fore.

I managed to tell one of the questioning board members that he was misinformed—that is, wrong. He had asked a question about the first jet combat, and the PFE had stated that the first jet air combat had occurred in the Korean War between an F-80 Shooting Star and a MiG-15. In very Clintonesque language, I stated that that all depended on your definition of *jet combat*.

"You see," I held forth to the inquisition, "there were jet fighters flying around in World War Two—they just weren't ours. The Me-262 accounted for many bomber kills, and the ME-163 was a rocket-powered fighter, and the Germans even had jet-powered *bombers*, so if the question is merely the first jet air combat, then the answer is clearly in World War Two, but if you're asking about USAF jets, then the answer is Korea, although that would be factually wrong."

Again with the silence.

I get that a lot. This question was one of the last in the series (I'm not sure if that was by design). I smartly stood up and saluted, executed razor-sharp facing movements, and marched out the door—correction, marched to the door.

Exhilarated by my awesome recovery from the entry debacle, I marched smartly, at a high rate of speed, directly for the door, where I had one more chance to make a good impression on the panel with a smooth exit. I grabbed the knob, deftly twisted, and yanked on the door. And pulled myself into it, as it didn't move. It jiggered in the frame, not swinging open at all. I redoubled my effort twisting the knob, but although my hand was a little sweaty, I was pretty sure that I had the knob disengaged from the frame. I jerked again, this time slightly less smooth, a little more panicked. Nothing again, except maybe a few of the brown flakes of paint flittering down from the jamb. I became acutely aware of crew cuts and stern eyes boring into my back, but I had to give it one more try. Twist, then yank. Again with the rattle—the jamb even bending a bit this time—but I still didn't have an exit. I was still trapped in the arena. I sheepishly twisted my head around, back to the panel.

"Is this part of the test?"

One of the NCOs harrumphed his way out of the chair and clicked his way over to the door, twisting the knob and opening the door in one triumphant motion. At least I think that's what he expected to happen. He got the same result as I did. I started to giggle, silently, and of course, that just made it worse. The door was well and truly stuck. Apparently, the bouncer really secured it after my masterful entrance, and now the door was jammed. It took three of us to get it open again. The bouncer pushed from his side as I and the NCO tugged from the inside. As I exited the room, gently closing the door behind me, I know I heard giggling in the room. I scuttled out into the waiting area, where the next contestants waited. I could see the relief in their eyes, as they had seen my entry and exit debacles. They figured if they could just get in and out of the door without hurting themselves, they would be golden. I sorta figured the same as well. I was pretty confident in the question-and-answer portion of the interview, but I was worried about the part where I had basically said that they, and the source document for the air force testing system, were wrong; but other than that, it was smooth.

At the end of the day, I found out that I had won the coveted stripe. I guess honesty and earnestness count for something. Even then, as a lower-ranking airman, I was confident I could be honest about things. I was always told that even if you screwed up, if you were honest, it would be okay. At Zaragoza, I realized that the system I was working for was a good one, despite the fact that the individuals sometimes didn't make the cut. And throughout my career, I found that to be true. I have tested the theory a few times and came up more confident in my leadership every time. There are certainly dogs in the USAF, but the vast majority are folks that take their jobs seriously and do what they do for far greater reasons than a paycheck.

I transitioned through a couple of jobs and wound up in the best job on base for me: the crash recovery section, which also handled transient aircraft. This gave me the opportunity to handle aircraft from all four US services and many different NATO countries. I also became aware of how much impact the US had on other countries just by being there. We were always working with the Spanish air force, flying with them, helping with the maintenance, and so forth. For lack of a better term, they seemed to possess a sort of *reverence* for American military. If I were a writer instead of a pilot, I'd probably have a better way to describe it. And this was a so-called first world country, modern and sophisticated. I felt that we were expected to "know" things, just by virtue of being an American. And we usually did.

The general attitude among the Spanish people, in my admittedly small circle, was one of respect and admiration for Americans. I lived in a tiny town called Monzalbarba, and the local bar owners and some others adopted me, looking out for me, and trying (with limited success) to teach this Montana kid Spanish. I played soccer with the local kids, drank beer with the locals, and drank more beer with the locals. I remember only a few times being treated poorly, and on one occasion, that guy was subjected to a such a nonstop barrage of rapid-fire Spanish from the bartender that he ended up leaving the bar. Juanjo, the short, fiery owner and bartender, looked at me and stated, "Muy mal." Noting my beleaguered expression, Juanjo got right up in my face, grabbed my cheeks, and squeezed, while carefully enunciating, "Baaaad guy." He then gave a dismissive *pffft* along with a sharp sweep of the hand. Generally, we were treated very well, and the little kids couldn't get enough of the Americans. That's not to say there weren't people there who didn't want us there.

At one point we were warned that there would be a protest at the front gate by a group who wanted the "fascists out." They meant the United States, irony not being a strong point of whatever group was doing the protest. It was supposed to be a fairly well-planned-out event; they would come to the gate, wave flags and stuff, say that we were taking over Spain, and then leave. Apparently, these guys were professional protesters. So, we were to use the back gate when coming onto base that day. Unfortunately, I forgot which day it was to occur and had decided to take the front gate into work. As I approached the gate, I could see American flags and Spanish flags being waved about and a group of about twenty-five people clustered around the gatehouse. It sorta looked like a parade! I came puttering up in my white Seat (pronounced "Saaaaot") Fura, with a giant grin on my face; it's not every day that one gets to be part of a parade! Especially one conducted in a foreign language, in a foreign country! I continued driving slowly into the crowd, noting on the placards the individual words in Spanish that I knew, like *US*, *airbase*, and *out*. Still, it didn't strike me as too odd; everyone seemed to be having a good time, jumping around and chanting. People didn't seem to be angry at all, but at the same time, there is a fine line between shouting for joy and shouting for anger, especially if you're notso-hotso in that language.

I slowly approached the gate, inching through my newfound admirers. I came up to the Spanish gate guard (the Americans were respectfully distant), expecting to be let right in. With a pained expression, he looked down at me and whispered, "Por favor, please go away." Huh? I thought there must be some misunderstanding. "No, no, I have my pass, proof of insurance, everything. I work on the base!"

"Señor, we cannot let you in; these are people who are not wanting you here."

And then it struck me what day it was and what gate I was at. My face must've shown the sudden realization and whitened considerably. The guard relaxed and smiled, assuring me that I could go to the other gate, and they would let me in. The cacophony of the former revelers—now protestors—took on an entirely different tone, as I began to meekly back away from the gate, this time, downright worried that I was in the middle of twenty-five people who really didn't like me. I accomplished a sixteen-point turn in the one lane at the gate. The protesters couldn't have been nicer, especially when they realized that they had an actual American in the car, and right in the middle of their protest. There was a lot of laughter and patting on the car as I passed, carefully. The Spaniards had protested in the same cheery exuberance that they seemed to accomplish everything else, not too seriously, and in good humor. Sometime after I left and went around to the other gate, I heard the protest had gotten a little more serious and rubber bullets were exchanged. Exchanged for yelps of pain, I was thinking. But, as these were professional protesters, I think they came prepared for that eventuality; I don't know how else you would measure your success in a job like that unless you counted welts at the end of a long day of rabblerousing. But they were sure nice to me.

I did fairly well at Zaragoza, and was in fact picked up for a prestigious (to me) assignment to follow. I was told I would be doing something in Nevada—just not what. I'd really never had an assignment before, so I really didn't know how it worked. I was a little bemused as I was called down to the Colonel's office, not knowing if I'd done something wrong, and he asked (after a proper reporting statement) if I knew what a great honor this was. Although I wasn't sure what honor he was talking about, by quick deduction I figured:

    A. I was not in trouble
    B. There was "honor" involved
    C. For a low-ranking guy, any honor is a great honor

So I enthusiastically answered in the affirmative, deftly repeating the words back to him about what a great honor it was to be chosen for this great...honor. He looked puzzled, as if doing some sort of mental recalculation before looking at my records, which were splayed out in front of him, then scanning down my list of accomplishments. He informed me that I had been selected, based on my quick promotions and records, for an assignment to Nevada, although it was pretty vague exactly where and what I would be doing—and oh, by the way, would I accept?

Accept what exactly? Well, I guess I had the opportunity to decline the assignment and take a more normal one. But really, who would do that? I couldn't get ahold of my wife, so I couldn't ask her feelings on the matter, and I had to make the decision within minutes. So I said yes, and thus began the next phase of my career, as an NCO and a crew chief on a jet that this Montana man could never have fathomed.

I really didn't know what I was getting into, mostly because no one would tell me. It turned out that I was being sent to the infamous *uprange*, a term used to describe various activities that are sorta off the books in the Nevada range. Although I didn't know it yet, I was going to be a crew chief on the F-117A Stealth Fighter.

I went through all of the screening and security processes and then went uprange, working a four-day-on and three-day-off schedule. I became intimately familiar with many of the systems on one of the most secretive jets in the world. Soon after I got there and started my qualification and upgrade process, Desert Storm kicked off, and many of those around me deployed; but since I wasn't qualified to work on the jet in all task areas, I remained behind to work in the training squadron, the "White" 417th Squadron. Eventually, I became a qualified crew chief and went for the first time to the desert, working out of Saudi Arabia, sending jets like Shaba 833 (mine) into the night skies over Iraq.

Deploying to Saudi brought on a new intensity to the job. Things were more and more serious. Even though hostilities were over by the time I got there, Saddam still had a ways to go in the "I surrender" department. He just really didn't understand the ramifications of the actual words. "I quit" means something different in the Arab culture. Historically, it means "I quit until I can strike again." And he just wouldn't behave, so that meant that we had to keep reacting to the provocations over and over, which meant sending the jets out as if for war for every sortie, even though they brought back the ordnance almost all of the time.

I again was amazed at the tight community that developed. My pilot and I had our names on the jets, and I really busted my hump, along with others, to keep the thing flying and clean. I was so proud of that airplane, and I cared personally for the pilot. Major Doug C and Shaba were my reason for being there.

Due to the hard work and technical proficiency of my crew, I won some award for highest FMC rate, which meant my aircraft was "Fully Mission Capable" for the highest percentage of time out of the squadron. I know this because I was given a plaque and some certificate in front of the whole wing. Even in circumstances like that (austere), the organization made sure that lower workers were recognized, having programs for the Airman, NCO, and Senior NCO of the Quarter, along with the lower-ranking officers getting awards for similar issues.

At that time I really liked to poke fun at the newer maintenance officers. Some of them were just barely older than I was, and I felt "salty" with my four years under the belt. The USAF is very tuned to folks in the beginnings of their careers, as a reflection of the attitude of this country. You can rise as far as you want to. Your future is up to you. Your career is limited only by your behavior. But that's not to say there won't be hiccups along the way: for instance, while in Saudi Arabia, I became a car thief.

I remember it clearly: I had worked late into the morning, as when your jet flies at night, you generally do the heavy maintenance for the other aircraft all night long. I had been changing an engine in another squadron aircraft, so I was filthy, tired, and ready to get a quick workout in before I slept through the day. I was groggy and a little punch-drunk; the F-404-GE-F1D2 had been particularly uncooperative, so I already had a lot of angst to get rid of in the gym. The facility was actually across the base, so I had to acquire some sort of transportation. I asked around, and the only thing available was an old school bus that we used for crew transport. I chased down Shakey, the vehicle NCO, and he gave me the keys, admonishing me to bring it back with a full tank; he had noticed last night that it was unexpectedly low. Ah, foreshadowing.

I emerged from the aircraft hangars where we lived, slept, and worked, into the brilliant sunlight of a Saudi midmorning. It was still cool(er) at this time of the year, so I had a sweatshirt on, along with a tape player to work

28

out to. I squinted my way across the taxiway to the bus, not really paying attention to anything else. The ubiquitous security police (SPs) were sitting in their trucks trying to be menacing behind their aviator glasses, but that was normal. I did the cursory tire check and walk-around of the vehicle. I checked underneath for bombs, and as I walked around the front I check the numbers on the front plate against the numbers that I had on the keys. They didn't match. Crap! I walked back across the taxiway, into the giant hangars, and tracked down Shakey again. He was surprised that the keys didn't match, as we were only supposed to have one bus, but as he scrounged around, he did find another set, and these matched. I trotted across the taxiway again, under the watchful eyes of the supercop in the truck.

I accomplished the same sort of inspection and jumped in the bus, started it up, and began to strap on the belts. As I looked up, I was astounded to see the SPs truck come screeching to a halt in front of the bus, lights ablaze. I glanced into the rearview mirrors to see others taking position around the back. I thought that some Saudi terrorist had broken into the base and somehow was on or around the bus. I shut off the bus and slowly looked around. The SPs had jumped out of their vehicles, hands hovering over their pistols. There were two groups of them, and they all seemed to be rather serious. The lead one was about fifteen feet in front of the bus, and they were all looking at me. I was looking at them, waiting for them to take down whatever bad guy was in the old, dirty bus with me.

"Get down!" the lead cop shouted in his best "authority" voice, which was difficult, as he looked like he was about twelve and dressed in his daddy's clothes. Nonetheless, as a twelve-year-old with a gun, that changed the equation drastically. So I hoped that whoever he was shouting at would comply pretty darn quick.

"You! Behind the wheel; get down!"

Me? I didn't understand why, but okay, I thought, I'll get down. Difficult to do when you're behind the wheel, but I started to slowly figure out a way to fold myself under the dash. I'm fairly tall, around six foot two, but I was doing the best I could to fold myself into a two-foot-tall space. The SP realized, I suppose, that if I got down on the bus, he wouldn't be able to see me, so he shouted again, using Mr. Authority voice.

"You! In the bus…come out where we can see you, *then* get down!"

Uh oh. It dawned on me that they were very concerned about me. Perhaps there wasn't a Saudi terrorist on board the bus after all. So I unwound myself from the gearshifts and came down the bus steps, hitting the concrete and starting to walk toward the loudest SP. That freaked him out more. The hand dropped slightly toward the pistol, and that got my attention (guns always do). I stopped. I heard a "Clear!" from somewhere behind me, signifying that the other SPs were now sure that I was the only sweatshirt-wearing, air force–looking, possible terrorist that wanted a workout in sight. Of course they had been watching as I had run back and forth, inspected the bus, and done all the stuff that you were supposed to do as I readied for my ill-fated attempt to go to the gym, so there should've been no surprise how many of me there were. I had my wallet in one hand and my cassette player in the other, standing beside the old blue bus, and I started to lay down on the cement. But I didn't even do that right. Mr. Authority needed me out away from the bus.

"Walk slowly away from the bus toward me, then get slowly on your knees, hands up."

Okay, I can do that; but the last time I walked toward him, he crapped a kitten and got all twitchy. So I complied as best I could, being careful not to spook the guy.

"That's far enough!"

I started to kneel on the ground and raised my hands high. I still had my wallet in one hand and my cassette player in the other. That wasn't good either.

"Drop what's in your hands!"

I carefully placed my wallet and music box on the ground beside me, but I was starting to lose my sense of humor about the whole thing. My knees hurt. Concrete is, well, hard. I raised my hands back up and apparently, as a result of my change of attitude, had clenched my hands into fists. That, too, was unacceptable.

"Unclench your hands!"

I shouted back.

"WHAT are you DOING?" I still didn't have any idea what this was all about. All I knew was that I wanted to take a bus to the gym, had done all the things I was supposed to do, and now I was in the middle of a hostage crisis, with me being the hostage. I was really hoping for one of my supervisors to come out and save me. But none came.

Mr. Authority made a couple of radio calls, and soon a supervisor came up in a sedan. I remained on my knees on the concrete, fists studiously unclenched; it seemed like a long time to me. An NCO walked over to the young airman, and everyone ratcheted down from DEFCON 12 to something a little more reasonable, DEFCON 3. My knees were aching. The NCO soon came over and started to ask me what was going on. I said I was getting up now, and after that I would be happy to explain all I knew, which was nothing. After I explained my piece, the NCO explained why things went down like that.

Shakey had gone to some sort of production meeting the night before on the other side of base. It was dark when he left to come home, so he inadvertently got on the wrong bus. The keys for the bus that he had driven were in his pocket, while the keys for the bus he boarded were in the ignition. So he came home with the wrong bus and two sets of keys. The goobers whose bus it was decided that, even though it was pretty obvious what had happened, they would alert the SPs about a bus theft. No one asked the obvious questions: who would steal a bus on a highly secured base, and what would you do with it once stolen? So the SPs went out and tried to find the big, blue bus. And they found it outside of our hangars, where Shakey had left it.

At this point, they could have come into the hangar and asked questions about the bus and quickly discovered that it was a mix-up. Or, they could have noted where the bus was and notified the owners of its whereabouts and, job done, retired back to their normal posts watching the perimeter of the base. Instead, they chose a third option: a stakeout. The big plan was to monitor the bus and arrest the next person that got in it, which turned out to be me. As I became more and more incredulous that this was the plan, I could tell that the NCO was feeling more and more ridiculous as his explanation went on. He started to slow down the telling as he was looking for ways to make the SPs' plan more plausible. After he ended his explanation of how they arrived at that course of action, he then moved on to how I got involved, asked a few questions, which I mostly answered by saying, "I don't know." There wasn't much I could tell him. I had only been involved in this notorious bus-heisting ring for about forty minutes or so myself. He decided that I shouldn't be shot after all and let me continue on my way, confiscating the keys to the bus. I was livid.

I went in and told my supervisor, who also became livid. He was an E-8, a Senior Master Sergeant (SMSgt). Very few make it that high in the enlisted corps, as there is only one more rank above that, a Chief Master

Sergeant (CMSgt). Only 1 percent of enlisted folks make it to that level, so these two ranks are very prestigious indeed. Smart officers listen to these men and women, even though they outrank them. So, my SMSgt fired off a phone call to his counterpart in the SP unit. He didn't like the fact that one of his guys was treated like a criminal and couldn't understand the stupid plan the SPs chose to implement in the great bus caper. At the end of the conversation, I was told to report to this SP SMSgt.

When I arrived, he ushered me into his office and asked me to sit down, while he started talking. He apologized to me for the time I spent on my knees and the whole debacle. He took full responsibility for the actions of his troops and said that if I had any anger toward the troops, that I should direct it at him. I was an E-5 Staff Sergeant (SSgt) at the time, and Mr. Authority was an E-4 Senior Airman (SrA). He didn't want me to take anything out on his troops. Of course I wouldn't have anyway; I'm generally not a very vindictive person. But it struck me as another important brick in the foundation that was becoming my leadership philosophy. Always stand by your subordinates in public; beat the crap out of them in private. Also, stick up for your subordinates when they're right. Don't let others mistreat them. Let them do it to themselves.

Whatever silliness was not inflicted on me by the SPs, I was able to do to myself, and I had a small role in inflicting the most casualties our squadron ever took while in Saudi. The base seemed to be at the end of the USAF supply chain, so although we certainly got what we needed in the way of parts and things to keep us running as a unit, the niceties were lacking. Anything good had been stripped off of the C-130s way before they got to us. As such, about two months into it, we were feeling very deprived of goodies. We were all getting stuff from home that we would usually share, but that was in small portions, usually a box of cookies that was put out in the ops hangar.

But on one Saturday, the C-130 came in on its normal run bearing in its belly, not only tires and supplies, but at the aft pallet, a gift from the gods—an entire pallet of goodies. No cargo-cult behavior was ever more evident than on that day. We were jumping around and whooping it up. Many of us surrounded the helpless pallet, and like hyenas on a nature show, when the loadmaster's back was turned, we pounced and liberated the whole pallet of stuff. We took the pallet over by our other junk and waited for the Herc to depart, so we could finish off the fresh kill. The four fans o' freedom blew dust and sand all over us as it taxied out of the cargo pad.

We loaded up all the supplies into the trucks and headed off to the hangars, our contraband carefully loaded and untouched, as it went against our honor to hoard something we had stolen fair and square. We would make sure the entire squadron had some of our tasty victory. As we pulled up and unloaded, word had spread that we had some extra supplies, and there were eager folks ringing the asphalt circle as we worked. We had never had so much help unloading. The magical pallet came down, and under a well-ordered chaos, the restraining straps came off, unveiling the glorious Mars, Snickers, M&Ms, and other chocolates that were stacked in a leaning tower of gooey goodness. I personally scored several bags of M&Ms and several miscellaneous candy bars.

We all scuttled back to our holes, clutching our booty. I had tossed down a whole bagful of M&Ms and was working on another, when I happened to glance at the stuff I was shoving in my mouth. Instead of being the more normal yellows and greens, there were shades of gray. They still tasted okay, so I continued to shovel them into my yap. I figured they were some sort of "combat" M&Ms that they had made special for us. So I pounded down the rest of the bag and started gnawing on a Snickers bar, again in the same "combat" colors of the M&Ms. After that satisfying meal, I washed my face, went up to the sleeping room, sat down on the bunk, flipped on my pen light, and was going to do some reading before I racked out.

We slept in the hangar complex, in a room that was probably thirty feet long, and since it was supposed to be bombproof, it was pitch dark when the blast door was shut. It was the kind of dark that your eyes cannot adjust to. The door itself was about eight inches thick and very heavy. The entire room was filled with steel bunk beds, and I was in a lower rack in a corner of the room. There was usually an understanding of quiet rules in effect at all times, as all manner of shift workers were trying to sleep throughout the day. I stashed a couple of bags of M&Ms in my bag (against regs) and started reading *Starship Troopers* (awesome book; terrible movie).

I was knee deep in the philosophical discussions in the book, when a gurgle took place deep in my belly—nothing to be alarmed at, but noticeable. As the gurgling grew in frequency and intensity, like contractions, I began to get a little concerned about the state of affairs and mentally tracing the path that I would have to take to the bathrooms if it came to an emergency egress from the bedroom. I became aware that I was only peripherally reading the story, mostly scanning the words while the greater part of my concentration was on the digestive happenings going on two feet below my chin. The path to the bathroom was circuitous, at best. Plus, I would have to do it in the pitch dark, with only a tiny light to guide me. So I concentrated hard on Johnny and the Roughnecks as Heinlein's characters bantered about political philosophy and citizenship. But eventually, the gurgling in my belly began to be accompanied by more physical manifestations of something going horribly wrong in my guts.

Everyone has had the squirts before, to varying degrees: sometimes it starts slow; sometimes it starts fast; and sometimes it starts under the auspices of another form of bowel activity, but ends up a "shart." That's what happened to me. In the pitch black, I tried to relieve the pressure by carefully scheduling the release rate, but to no avail. The minute the decision was made to conduct any kind of activity below the belt, the die was cast. My eyes flew open, and I sat bolt upright. Things had just gone horribly wrong downstairs, unexpectedly so. I jumped out of bed, and of course, being on the lower bunk, suffered a much shorter outbound trajectory than I had hoped. I reeled back from crashing into the metal frame, blood starting to spurt from my forehead and other liquids threatening to spurt from another part of my body. One hand over the gash in my head, one hand holding the little flashlight, I had my flip-flops on and was moving at a high rate of speed through the bottomless black. Little yellow circles of person or bed or wall showed in my light beam as it bounced crazily along. I was accelerating through the maze of beds, heading for the blast door, when I cut a corner too close, absolutely crushing my toe and ripping off my left flip-flop. Because of the impending disaster threatening to inflate me like a Thanksgiving Day parade float, I couldn't slow down. I hit the blast door at a high rate of speed then pushed it open; the bathroom was just down the hall. I came out right in front of a buddy of mine and pushed past him into the stall. I barely made it to the stall before I exploded like a chocolate hand grenade. My gut hurt so bad I started to moan. I was in misery. And I soon had company.

Next thing I knew, the bathroom door flew open again, banging against the wall, as another stall flew open and another fanny hit porcelain, sounding like the entire tuba section of a high school marching band had been hit by a garbage truck. I was just about to comment, when the door flew open again, and another and another came hustling in, in various stages of distress. I knew we were swiftly running out of room, so I tried to shut things down and get out of the john. Not so fast. My shorts were just coming up when I was hit with another wave of intestinal breakdancing. I slammed back down on the porcelain and let loose again. The bathroom was awash in sounds and smells, none of them good. It was a bunch of jazz bands warming up at the same time. Loud bass notes, higher percussion rat-a-tats, and several vocal invocations of "good Lord!" Finally, I got out, just as another guy came running in, screaming about the "f——ing candy." And then it dawned on me.

The events of earlier that day came back, and like Encyclopedia Brown, I started to solve "The Case of The Exploding Bowels." I realized that the loadmaster had never really worried about the pallet of stuff we seemed to get for free, though they are generally a class of absolute professionals. They may be a little (a lot) rough around the edges, but loadmasters keep an eye on their stuff—unless it's stuff they want to get rid of. M&Ms really don't come in "combat" colors. I looked at my stashed bag, and sure enough, it had expired several years earlier. What appeared to be gray turned out to be really faded, zombified greens and yellows and blues. The chocolate bars also: I suppose real camouflage colors wouldn't sell real well; no one wants to peel back a Snickers bar wrapper to get, instead of delicious chocolate, a lumpy green thing. Gray is right out. People would think that the product was, perhaps, old.

I'm not sure where this particular pallet came from; it may have just been running around the system for eternity, lost in the logistics hub in southwest Asia, a snack food limbo. Eventually, someone got wise to the unique nature of the pallet and sent it on its way, for one last time. I'm not sure if the stops before us had smarter people than us looking this particular gift horse in the mouth, but we were so giddy to get these free snacks that we didn't. (New motto: always look a gift horse in the mouth.) So we got it out; many of the squadron fell on it like a rugby scrum, and within hours, those same brave folks were sitting, in various stages of dress, blasting out the 1812 Overture into porcelain horns. It went on for about sixteen hours, and I played several symphonies myself throughout the night. It was terrible. The only reason it didn't impact the mission was because enough of the force hadn't sampled the forbidden fruit and, by working a little longer and harder, were able to cover for those of us selected out of the gene pool for a day.

It was always like that. No matter what has happened throughout my career, never once, have people allowed personalities to affect the mission. Not once. I'm sure I haven't been the favorite of everyone I've come across, and I've not been fond of a few folks, but the tires always rolled on time, if it was within our power to do so. Some of that is the can-do American spirit, and some of it is ingrained through training and the desire to help other professionals accomplish their mission. I'm not sure if the slogans that corporate air force came up with ever had any impact on our desire to achieve. The whole "No One Comes Close" campaign was a little ill-conceived for a force that prides itself on precision engagement. The real slogan was not letting your buddy down. And the reason you can't let your buddy down is that the mission suffers. It was always clear to me that the two goals were aligned. The mission was always just understood.

After I came back from this deployment, I continued to attend school in my spare time. It was a priority of the air force to have everyone furthering their education, and encouraging folks to get a degree. Not everyone had the same desire, however, and I was always careful to maintain some sort of parity with my coworkers. If I took time off to attend school in the evening, I made sure I worked the day shift. If I missed work, I volunteered to work weekend duty. As I got closer to graduation, I became aware of a program called Bootstrap, where you would basically be on temporary duty to the school you were attending, only having to report back to work when school was out of session. This was another program that demonstrated a sincere desire by the USAF to give people all the upward mobility they would try for. It would accelerate one's completion of the degree, it was hoped. I decided to apply for Bootstrap, and my disdain for the cube-warriors in the support fields took root at the same time. It also gave birth to Banzet's theory of relativity, which has been proven over and over, and I will explain in detail later.

When I came back from the desert, I was still stationed at Tonopah, working my four-on and three-off schedule, which made it difficult to attend class. Furthermore, the unit to which I was assigned had been ordered into the "white" world and down to Alamogordo, New Mexico, and there wasn't a campus down there. This would indeed help me to make a perfect case for Bootstrap. Unfortunately the comrades that worked down at the education center at Nellis refused to help with my application. I could really only try to make my case on the phone and on Friday afternoons when I came home, back down to Nellis. Needless to say, this process didn't work very well. All these hardworking support personnel "supported" me by leaving early on Fridays, in spite of my entreaties to stay a little later. I simply couldn't get any accurate information. This was when Banzet's theory of relativity was formulated.

The theory applies mostly to government entities, although commercial activities are not immune. And it almost exclusively applies to office workers, the kind that come in late, leave on time, and take every second of allotted break time in between. It concerns the inversely proportional relationship between getting correct information to the relative distance the information was from the individual's desk. For instance, if I asked for information about my eligibility for Bootstrap, and that information was there on the person's desk, then the odds of me getting correct information was high. Short distance; good odds. If the book was within "rolling" distance of the person's chair, then my odds dropped markedly. If getting up from the chair was required, then my chances of getting good information dropped to next to nil. If there was another room to go into, then I needn't bother calling. Due to this phenomenon, it became clear that I had to actually get a day off so that I could go there on Friday morning. Again, my superiors were the most supportive and really pushed me to get this figured out. And they gave me the time to make it happen.

So I traveled to the education center, trying to get some straight answers to the qualifications questions that had come up about my Bootstrap application. I arrived at about 0900 hours, figuring that was the golden hour before breaks, lunch, and of course their getting off early to "serve me better." I showed up to ask this aged oracle to help clarify the qualifications for the program. She was a doughy, old, and sour woman. She was everyone I had ever seen behind the counter at the DMV. She was firmly ensconced behind her desk, and upon seeing me come in, she deflated. There went her morning—an actual customer. After ascertaining what I was there for, she rattled off a couple of requirements. I met the ones she mentioned.

"But you're not eligible for this program," she stated.

"Why? I meet the requirements that you've mentioned. How is it that I'm not eligible?"

"Your unit is leaving."

"So. You never said anything about that. Can I see the regulation that covers this?"

"No. You're not authorized to see it; you're not an education *professional*." Those words hissed out of her cracked lips like air from an overinflated bicycle tube. The disdain in her eyes washed over me, standing there in my faded, worn uniform. I got a little heated up.

"Ma'am, I've got a clearance higher than you can count; I'm on the dean's list, and I've been trying to get this information for about three weeks. I read at a minimum of the eighth grade level, which is what I think your regulation is written at, so I'm pretty sure that I don't need you to explain even the bigger words—unless you need me to explain them to you. I'm here with the full knowledge and permission of my Lt Col Squadron Commander, and the reason is to get the answers that this office seems to be unable to provide me over the phone, or when I normally come in on Friday afternoon. So what I will be requiring is the regulation—now—so I can see for myself exactly what the requirements are for this flipping program." I exhaled slowly and watched as, after shooting me icicles through her shriveled eyes, the overweight civilian waddled back to get the regulation, then oozed back to me, plopping the tome on the counter.

After picking up the big book, I came upon the requirements section. There were really only three. Without question I met them all. I pointed this out, but there was, again, apparently something I didn't understand about this simple regulation.

"You're not eligible because your unit is moving," she proclaimed.

"But that's not mentioned in this regulation. There are three conditions; I meet them all; *certeris paribus* I am eligible by the simple fact that I am not *not* eligible." I was dumbfounded. Why on earth was this lady being so difficult? I hadn't yet developed a theory on civilian employees of the government, but that would come.

"We won't know who to assign you to, so we can't make you report to anyone." But this was a subtle retreat from the previous position. Was that a glint of fear that I saw in one of those bleary eyes? A barely perceptible wobble in one of her chins? I pressed my advantage.

"My commander and my unit will take care of all that. All you have to do is process the paperwork that says that I am eligible for the program. My unit will take care of the rest."

More thoughts crossed her eyes, as the prospect of victory started to play out. She might be able to get rid of me after all. "You take care of everything else, and I will sign your enrollment. I won't assume responsibility for anything else though. It's all on you." She threw the offer out there, daring me to accept. And this sounded like a condition that I've asked for my whole life: get out of my way.

"Deal."

She signed the application with a flourish and sent me out of her office, eager to get back to her chair, and further decomposition.

I was ecstatic. I could really hit school hard now. It all paid off, and I eventually got my degree while stationed at Alamogordo. I received a bachelor of science, graduating cum laude. (Someday someone will tell me what exactly that means.)

About that time I made a really stupid decision, basically throwing a grown-up tantrum.

I told the folks that wanted to send me to Officer Training School to pound sand. Not in exactly those terms, but I told them since I couldn't become a pilot due to the USAF manning situation, I said that I didn't want to be an officer. As I mentioned before, I was very sure about what I wanted to do in the air force; money was not really an issue; I just wanted to do something important. And based on my experiences with the support culture, I couldn't take the chance on doing anything that wasn't connected to the flight line. I decided to remain enlisted, even though I had wanted to go to OTS, with the goal of becoming a pilot. If pilot slots weren't available, then I didn't want to be an officer.

So I pursued my master's degree with the same diligence that I had pursued the bachelor's, and while I sat in class, among all officers, I started to think about going to OTS again. I was really busting my hump on the flight line, sort of enjoying my job crewing F-117s, but again, craving that upward mobility. I started to think that I had more to offer the air force. Some of the officers thought so too. One in particular stood out. Lt. "Rusty" was our maintenance officer for the 7th Fighter Squadron, and after having asked me nicely several times to go to OTS, he began to really kick me in the shins about being a chicken. It seemed like every day I would have to answer some comment about being a dumbass for not going to OTS. It got worse after my scores for the ASVAB came back, and I did fairly well. After a lot more finger-poking, I decided to submit my application to OTS.

There was the requisite mountain of paperwork that passes for an application to fill out. I became convinced (later confirmed) that it didn't really matter what paperwork was filled out, only that there was enough of it. If your pile tipped the scales at enough weight, your case was approved. I thought about just submitting a New York phone book for instant approval for everything, but where's the fun in that? So again, I had the full backing of the command and started to get really excited about the prospect of going to officer training. I got the giant package approved and sent out. Now all I had to do was wait to see if I made the cut, about a 15 percent chance.

The selection day came and went, but I heard nothing. I knew that they notified all the non-selects, and I hadn't been notified. But neither had I been notified of any selection. My commander, yet another great man, started asking questions about my status, and I couldn't answer them. I called the education center; they couldn't tell me anything. I called the Air Force Personnel Center (AFPC), and they couldn't tell me anything. They claimed to have never seen it. I was at a loss. I had wasted a full selection cycle, and now I had to start over. Lt. "Rusty" wouldn't let me forget what a douche I was for not being an officer, and many others continued to encourage me. Unfortunately, I was probably most encouraged by all the small folks that would disparage me and taunt me for not having been accepted to OTS. Like all people of this type, these guys were the ones that lacked the courage to even try, much preferring to sit on the sidelines and scoff those that did. So I decided to start over.

Beginning at the beginning meant getting some fundamentals right. I wanted to know what a couple of my scores meant, so I would know if I was going to be competitive or not. I had taken a test called the PCSM, or Pilot Candidate Selection Method test, and had received a 99 on it. But I had no idea if that was a percentage or a raw score or what. I was determined to get to the bottom of this, and of course, after the local education center had no idea, I again called the bowels of AFPC, which I assumed looked a little like the Urik-hai factory in the *Lord of the Rings* films. I eventually was able to track down someone who knew something about that particular score, after about four transfers. I ended up talking to a master sergeant who knew all about it. I asked about the score, and he assured me that I had received the highest score possible, and then the conversation got interesting. While relaying the story of the missing OTS package, he stopped me suddenly, asking my name again. After I told him, there was a long silence.

"Well, I've got your package right here. It's in my dead file."

I was stunned. "Dead file? Why?"

His tone was guarded, as if he was readying excuses; remembering my helpless inability to affect the chairborne warriors over the phone, I had to tread very carefully indeed, although I was steaming. I gently tried to get a little more information from him as to why it was in the dead file, and why no one had tried to contact me or my commander. There was no way to rip into him as I wanted to: he had my file, and it could easily get lost again, maybe permanently.

My tactic, therefore, was to try to salvage the package and get it into the next board, which was in two days. So I tried to swing this guy around to my side. He explained to me that I had filled out one piece of paper incorrectly. It happened to be the application itself: on it, there was a section in which you picked the three jobs that you would like to apply for, unless, the small print informed, you were applying for a pilot slot; then you only picked one other. So I had picked pilot and one other. I tried to explain that I thought that I had completed everything in accordance with the instructions.

He became a tad more defensive. "Look, we can't call everybody over every little thing; we don't have time for that."

I tried again, explaining that perhaps—seeing as how this was my career—the massive AFPC organization could call people on the things that would cause their applications to be rejected at least.

No such luck. They did not call people—period. If there was a problem, it was a problem with *your* application and, therefore, not really *their* problem. And, they didn't make mistakes anyway—so there you go. As he explained. "Look, I've been doing this job for three years now; I think I know my own form. You just have to fix this one part, and you'll be good to go."

I tepidly offered that I was pretty sure that the form had told me to just fill out one more job, if I had picked pilot for the first.

There was some harrumphing as he shuffled my partially resurrected application, looking for the Rosetta sheet. "Ah ha!"

I could visualize him scanning down the document to the appropriate section, looking for the triumphant line.

"Oh." He'd hit the part that told him he had screwed me. "Hmm. Tell you what, why don't you fax me an updated sheet, and I'll plug it in and get your package over to the committee in a couple of days. The next board convenes in a couple of days, and I'd hate for you to miss it. So just get it faxed to me, and I'll make sure that I personally take it over. If there is a problem, then I'll just call you."

I was going to remind him of his earlier point, but there is a limit to even my stupidity. So he was going to take care of it. Wow, what a relief. He would personally take it over. If you can't trust the guy who just hosed you, who can you trust?

So I told my boss what had happened, and after I helped unscrew him from the ceiling, he signed the new application that looked exactly the old one. He, too, knew the powerlessness of the operators versus the chairborne corps, especially at a distance. The important thing to him was that the mission (getting the application in) was accomplished. Later, after acceptance, we could go kneecap the bastard. Of course we didn't. Apparently everything got turned in, and after a month or so, I found out that I had been selected for Officer Training School.

I left for OTS, for three months of silliness; we had a lot of prior-enlisted folks, which gave the cadre, made up of junior Captains and Lieutenants, no chance against us. We pulled some of the standard hijinks, but there were a couple of incidents that bear telling. They had everything to do with leadership—requirements of.

4

AN OFFICER OR A GENTLEMAN

The first thing in OTS that struck me as crapola was when we had a leadership class and the instructor, a Major, told the eager-beaver class, after showing a pyramid organizational chart, that "the important thing to remember is that you out-rank eighty percent of the Air Force." This sounded like music to the ears of fresh college grads, many of whom were ecstatic that they would be able to boss somebody around. They relished being able to tell folks what to do, and the other party, instead of punching them in the piehole (as probably happened to them in college), had to do it. What fun! Unfortunately, that was the exact opposite of what I thought about leadership. Those were danger signals to me.

Leadership positions are very lonely places, and command is serious, at whatever level. That's why, even in this training environment, I and some of the other prior-enlisted guys resolved to correct that attitude wherever we saw it, whatever our ranks. There were a few folks that we had to have earnest conversations in the hallway with about harassment and integrity. Sometimes nose to nose. And so, it was in this vein that I, in the middle of this Major's speech, felt compelled to raise my hand. Which is often a prelude to me getting a professional kick in the shins. He had just finished his comments on how we would outrank these folks and how cool that is, so I asked if I could add to his remarks. He said I could, so it was really his fault.

I started off by saying that he was looking at it exactly wrong. In truth, I felt that leadership was more like an inverted pyramid, with the guy at the bottom having *responsibility* for all those 80 percent on his shoulders. If Airman Snuffy kicks his dog, then the lieutenant will hear about it. If the lieutenant kicks his dog, then the captain will hear about it, and so forth. The essence of command is responsibility and the commensurate authority to act upon assigned responsibilities. The lower ranks are not an assigned ego boost section, and anyone who thought that way ought not to be at OTS.

I thought King Leonidas (of *300* fame) had it right: when, at Thermopylae, Xerxes boasted that he would kill thousands of his men to conquer Sparta, King Leonidas countered, "And I would die for any one of mine." Which he ultimately did. So I thought that to dwell on the outranking issue sent the wrong message, but apparently to this personnelist Major, I was way off base. I endured probably ten minutes of shin kicking about this being a teaching environment and that there was really only one teacher and that he had ten years of experience leading other, well, personnelists. Talk about the leading edge of the rear. This kind of so-called leadership reared its head constantly throughout my "education" there. Almost invariably by support personnel. Some of them seemed actually surprised by our alternate views on leadership. There is a vast gulf between indoor leadership and outdoor leadership.

After OTS, I was a bit disillusioned and eager to get back to the real air force. Unfortunately, I went instead to Air Education and Training Command (AETC) to learn how to become a maintenance officer. You would think, as a seven-year Technical Sergeant (about half normal time) from maintenance, that I would have a fairly easy time of this four-month Aircraft Maintenance Officer Course (AMOC). On the other hand, if you've paid any attention to this book and my proclivity for finding poop to step in, you would know that was not to be.

My problems really started during in-processing, as I found myself with a bunch of prior-enlisted folks there for the same course, including a buddy of mine from OTS, Mike. In our class of eleven, there were six or seven priors, several from the maintenance career field. I asked if there was any sort of accelerated course for us, as we'd had a great deal of exposure to maintenance over the years. I was told that there was a bridge course for already commissioned officers in other career fields who wanted to become maintenance officers. It took about three weeks. I said, "Great! I'll take that one." I was eager to *not* be gone for four months: my wife was at home with a three-year-old and a one-year-old, and I had just come off an enlisted career that encompassed being gone every week for two years, a deployment, and then Officer Training School. So I really had no desire to spend one more second than I had to away from them. Of course, this was not to be: the official policy was that, since I was going to be a maintenance officer already, I had to attend the long course. The accelerated course was only for those who had no experience in the maintenance career field. And that was the high point of the course.

Although bummed out, I wanted to make the best of the situation. I resolved to really try, as the supervisor of the course (a fast-burning female captain) assured me that while I had valuable "enlisted experience" (said with a sneer) this course would teach me the officer perspective. Okay. I was on board; as long as I was going to be learning new stuff, then I would try to make the best of it. Mike, my buddy from OTS, was in the same boat—if anything, even less happy than me, as he had more experience and was a higher rank when he left for commissioning. But we decided we would give it our best shot. We would also try to use our experiences to help the new lieutenants along. Unfortunately, my "best shot" was not appreciated by the course supervisor, and this became more and more evident throughout the course.

About day four (remember, this is a four month course), we were to have a briefing on the parts of an airplane, which is a pretty good place to start for new maintenance officers. Being able to identify a "wing" really helps the credibility of a maintenance officer when addressing the troops, as in, "Look here, men. The boss wants us to produce ten percent more sorties this month, and in order to do that, we need to ensure that there are at least two of these things—wings—attached to each airplane." That's much more inspirational than just saying these "thingies." So I was fully on board with the whole "identifying parts" of the airplane meme. Unfortunately, the instructor was gone for the day, so the course supervisor thought she would fill in and conduct the class. Unfortunately, she really didn't know a lot about the topic. After a few missteps, she kind of giggled and said that she really wasn't the expert, so we should bear with her.

This went against two fundamental concepts that I have about military officers. One is that if you don't know something, say so and get someone in there who does know something about the topic; and two, don't act like a giggly girl. I don't care if you are male or female; reverting to a prepubescent girl in times of stress is not a characteristic of a good combat leader. I decided that the new lieutenants needed to have the right information about the aircraft in question, an F-16. I really didn't want these lieutenants hitting the field with the wrong nomenclature about basic aircraft components. They didn't need to be handicapped straight out of the gate. So I raised my hand and said, "Ma'am, those are actually flaperons, not slats; that's something totally different."

The goofy grin immediately left her pinched face, and she replied something to the effect of, "Oh, is that so?" I said that I had only had two years of working on F-16 C/Ds, but Mike over there had tons of experience with F-16A/B models, so maybe I was wrong. Mike piped up with an affirmative, and that sealed my fate for the rest of the course. The whole time, she tried to make me miserable, but the staff became divided about me. Most of the older civilians and higher ranking officers liked having me and the rest of the priors in class, but this lady and her minions really wanted to make my time there a "learning experience." Which was not good for the home team. But in spite of the leadership there, the rank and file really pulled together as a tight team around me and Mike. They became aware of the BS that was going on with me and helped protect me, even the new lieutenants.

In a particularly funny case, I received the only "Letter of Counseling" (LOC) of my career about midway through the course. The LOC was supposed to be a correctional tool—a written spanking. I'd never had one in my entire enlisted time, and it turned out that this one would be the only one that I would ever need.

I had become a little more vocal as time progressed and I was stymied at every turn trying to accelerate or test out of any curriculum. I told whoever would listen that I already knew all of this material; indeed, it was how I had been promoted. I would've been a dunce if I didn't know most of it. Those protests fell on deaf ears, even though I always specified that the course was perfect for those who had no maintenance background—just not for me. Things got kicked up a notch when our class leader filled out a formal complaint against one of the instructors for his classroom demeanor. The next day I was called down to the supervisor's office. She had a witness there, so I knew that it wasn't going to be any kind of accolade or medal awarding ceremony. It wasn't. She asked me if I knew why I was down in her office. I did: it was because she had called me down there. Although I knew the answer to the question, I wisely kept it to myself.

She went on to tell me that I'd had a bad attitude and was being disruptive in class, and some of the faculty was complaining about me. I sat quietly, waiting for her to finish; I knew there wasn't any point in trying to argue. As she wound down, I asked her which faculty members had complained, as the ones that I'd had seemed to really enjoy me in class. In fact, most of them had asked me to assist in instruction as some point.

"Well, umm, I can't tell you who has complained; it wouldn't be ethical."

"But how do I know what behavior is incorrect if I don't know what specific behavior you're referring to? And I can't tell that, unless I know who has had an issue with me."

"Well, all of your behavior is bad."

"Really? ALL of my behavior? Including my perfect test scores and perfect projects?"

"Listen, you will not argue, lieutenant; you will read the LOC, and you will sign it. Understood?"

"Yes, ma'am." I read the LOC, and sure enough, within the text, there was a statement that I was a know-it-all. It didn't state that I *thought* that I was a know-it-all; it said that I actually *was* one. So there I had it. On official Air Force documentation. I was indeed as smart as I'd claimed, and more. I didn't just know maintenance; I knew it *all*! I started chuckling to myself, but not as silently as I'd hoped. Her birdlike eyes snapped to me.

"What's so funny?"

"Well, this LOC really just says what I've been saying for two months now. I know all the material that is being taught in this class. I never claimed to know it all, but I do appreciate the confidence. All I ever really wanted was to be given the opportunity to accelerate within the course, but you wouldn't let me do that. This LOC is as if I had written it myself. So thank you for that."

"Umm, well, sure, you're welcome. I'm going to keep this here in my desk drawer, and if we have any more problems, then I'll file it. Understood?"

I understood that I was in for a long two more months.

It was worth it. Because of my enlisted experience, along with a couple of others in the class, I became more and more valuable to the instructors; and I began getting feedback from them that I was being discussed at staff meetings. They seemed to enjoy having me there and were a little perturbed that I was being singled out merely for wanting to excel. There seemed to be a definite divide, with the captain and a couple of her minions on her side, and all the other instructors and attached staff on my side. Many of the classmates would come to the ex-enlisted folks to see what it was like in the "real" air force. But this made the captain and her crew resent us (me) even more. It came to a head when we had our final simulation. The fast-burning captain wanted to make an example out of me and ensure that everyone knew that I wasn't infallible. She thought she had just the vehicle to do it.

The simulation was our final practical exam, and it was built up to be the be-all and end-all for the maintenance course. They were very proud of this simulation, and I was a little curious as to how it would simulate a flight line. Basically it was a room that had a glassed-in box overlooking the room, where Caesar and her minions could observe the festivities on the floor and send out various situations to the computers that were placed around the room. These computers represented a particular specialty, like crew chiefs, hydraulics, avionics, fuels, and so forth. At every station two officers took action on whatever popped out of the printer. The printers were old-style dot matrix–types, so they made a lot of racket while they printed. So, if the puppeteers wanted to see the hydraulics shop do something, they would send a command to the printer, and the two lieutenants manning that station would have to solve the issue. For folks who had never done this before, I guess it could be fairly daunting. Mike and I were assigned as crew chiefs. I think the little Caesar wanted to really shove it in our face that she could force us into a mistake, so that she could lord it over us to the assembled VIPs that were in the glass booth with her. She chose…poorly.

There was nothing too spectacular about our little task. For the prior-enlisted guys, we'd been doing this very thing our whole careers. It was basically forms maintenance—didn't necessarily reflect reality at all. For instance, if there was a requirement for one of my aircraft (Mike and I were each assigned eight aircraft forms) to get an engine change, we had to enter the red X in the forms, along with some of the other jobs that go along with it. Then we ordered it in the supply system. All of that was entered into the computer, and this was reflected in the main computer in the little glass room where one of the staff kept track of the general situation for the whole sim. This enabled Caesar to direct the inputs. And there was a full colonel and the course supervisor watching her run the whole symphony.

The show started fairly mundane. Aircraft developed issues, and lieutenants scrambled around to fix them. Mike and I dutifully recorded the changes to the aircraft in the forms. We quickly realized that there wasn't any reality connected to the tasks. You would do things that you would never do in a real flight line. We quickly ran out of engines in the supply system (they were trying to force a shutdown of some of the sorties). So instead of shutting down, Mike and I started swapping engines.

This is usually the last resort on a maintenance flight line. It costs twice the work, and often, the part you are pulling out and installing on another aircraft breaks or has some sort of leak. But in this exercise it didn't matter. Soon, Mike and I were swapping parts left and right, carefully annotating the swaps in the forms, all legal-like, and then going back to BS-ing. The aircraft kept flying sorties long after they should've been grounded; this started to agitate Caesar, and not in a good way. Watching Mike and I relaxing infuriated her.

Soon the ratcheting sound of the dot matrix printers started sparking up all over the room. I looked up at the glass booth, and there she was, glaring at Mike and me. She had the expression of biting down on a lemon—covered in dog crap (I imagine, I've never actually seen that). The printer noise increased. In all the cubicles, printers were spewing out tasks or situations on paper, like a stock market floor hosting a ticker tape parade. The lieutenants were going crazy. Mike and I were doing something like this:

"Hey, looks like tail 531 has a hydraulic leak, and there are no more reservoirs left in supply."

"Here, take the one out of my squadron—435." I annotated it in the forms and on the computer.

"Okay, thanks; here's that brake assembly that you needed."

"Thanks." Type, type, type. "So what are you going to do tonight?"

"I'm going for a run, then probably go to dinner with Ryan and those guys; how 'bout you?"

"About the same; where are you guys going to dinner? Oh, look, another altimeter is broke; should we tell the back shop?"

"Well, take one from 833, and we'll turn this one into supply; then, when the part comes in, install it into my aircraft."

And so on. Meanwhile, printers were spewing paper all around us, and the glass booth looked a little like a backlit set of *Dr. Strangelove*: Caesar throwing her hands around, then checking the computer, then yelling something to her assistant, then leering at Mike and me. Meanwhile her audience began to have this puzzled look on their faces; something wasn't sitting quite right with them. But no matter what happened, Mike and I casually carried on the conversation while entering utter nonsense, although accurate nonsense. The faster things went wrong from the booth, the more relaxed we became. And the more agitated the little Caesar became, and the more eyebrows started to furrow into a permanent, hairy V. Something had to give, and after a couple of minutes, it did.

The lieutenants manning the Transient Alert/Crash Recovery section came over, said they had an input that Aircraft 133 had an in-flight emergency and asked what they should do about it. I looked at Mike and queried as to the tail number again. It was as I thought. Now, here was a problem I'd never seen before in all my years of maintenance. I took the forms and stood up and, after a short discussion with the lieutenants, walked over to the glass cube and tapped on the glass. The captain looked out over her glasses and sneered, "Well, what is it?"

"Ma'am, I've got a problem here that I've never encountered before, and I need your advice." The gleam in her eye sharpened, and she abruptly straightened up. The printers ceased clattering out their orders, and the young guy that had been feverishly entering scenarios looked up, thankful for a respite.

"Well, I'm glad at last that we have something to teach you, lieutenant; now perhaps your time spent here will be worth something." At this, the VIPs started to really look a bit uncomfortable. More eyebrow furrowing, like someone had passed gas at a funeral. You smell something going on, but you don't want to make a scene—yet. She continued, turning to the assembled audience. "You see, this lieutenant has brought a lot of experience with him and wasn't sure that we had anything to teach him. We've been struggling with that for most of this course, but now, I think, we've finally validated that this course is useful—*even to those that have a lot of enlisted experience!*" She continued on in this vein for a little longer, while I contentedly let her continue. After a bit, the gloating started to sputter to a halt. The lieutenants were looking on in anguish, not sure what the heck was going on. She took a deep breath and exhaled, "Now then, how can I help you?"

I'd brought up my forms and the computer printouts that reflected the forms, so she could tell (and I could prove) that everything in my forms was reflected in the computer system. It was.

"Ma'am, I've got an F-15 squadron that I'm responsible for; but more importantly, Mike and I are responsible for generating a wing full of sorties, so we have been working closely together making the wing mission happen. So, doing that has generated a lot of 'cannibalization' between our two squadrons."

"Yes, I am familiar with cannibalizations, lieutenant; what exactly is the problem?"

"Well, it's about this aircraft that the crash recovery guys brought to my attention as having an in-flight emergency, tail number 133."

"Well, what? I'm sure you know that aircraft have emergencies all the time. They are fairly routine, and we've had one in this simulation already; so, again, what exactly is the problem?" She had started to get a touch impatient with this dumb lieutenant.

"Umm, I know about IFEs (in flight emergencies) indeed; my first two years as a crew chief were spent in Crash Recovery in Zaragoza, Spain, and I've responded to many, many emergencies, including ones on F-15s like these. But, ma'am, I have to be honest, I have never, *never* seen an aircraft that is on ten-mile final, with an engine fire, without any engines installed in it. As you can see in my forms and on your computer, aircraft 133 quite clearly has been annotated as having no engines installed, as I've given them both to Mike's squadron: one in 824 and the other in 445. So, that explains, I guess, how it launched without us being aware of it—an aircraft taking off with no engines would be fairly quiet. But I must confess that I am still mystified how this aircraft got on ten-mile final, and exactly *what* is on fire on that miraculous aircraft?"

There was a long silence; then she scurried around, looking for a way out. The colonel started to laugh; then everyone started to chuckle, including her. Some of the stress that had accumulated over the course dissipated.

As a matter of fact, upon graduation, that same captain asked me, in front of the general, if I would come to the school and teach. I was stunned. I told her that I thought I would "fail to thrive" and would be better off in the field.

I did not graduate with honors; my know-it-all LOC took me out of the running. But I graduated. I was off to my first assignment as an officer.

I reported to a northwestern air force base as a maintenance officer for conventional and special weapons. It was truly a great experience, but again, there were many opportunities to learn from my leadership, both good and bad. The good was because of my immediate supervisor, another prior-enlisted captain, who, because of my enlisted background, gave me the weapons handling flight as my first command opportunity. These folks were known in the squadron as a bunch of roughnecks and ne'er-do-wells, who the rest of the squadron looked down on. I loved it. I was pretty much a hardass and really beat the heck out of them, because they had become lazy and sloppy during the tenure of my predecessor, who was really out of his element. I became known as tough but fair, and really brooked no crap from anyone. But we also had fun. A lot of fun.

One of my challenges, however, was to run interference from the squadron commander. He was honestly one of the nicest men I've met but, in my opinion, totally out of his element in command. My captain was also a full-time interference runner for him. The colonel was well-meaning but totally bumbling in the execution of his aims, and mostly because of his god-awful communication skills—as in, everyone understood what he was saying, but, somehow, people always left a conversation with him a little more confused than at the start of the exchange. He was a human countermeasures dispenser. It was so bad that I started to take out a little green notebook I had to write down some of the pithier things he said, just so I could keep them straight. I often did this in full view of him at the weekly staff meetings. I would pull out the notebook and, while everyone tried to keep a straight face, begin writing things down. If the colonel saw me, he would encourage me. "Did'ja get that, Banzet? Nice to see someone paying attention!"

After a while I had quite a collection of gems, including these inspirational aphorisms:

"Looking for an escape goat to hang."

"If you look good and all your people are doing well, then you are already three legs up."

"If you do this right, all your problems will be so much easier."

"I'll support you one hundred eighty degrees."

"The brightest card in the deck."

"Thinking off the top of my tongue."

"Sometimes you can tie them to a semi, and you still can't drag them to water."

"Eyebrows spinning around in my head."

"We're humping through humps."

These were just a few of the pearls that he dropped in front of us swine.

His actions could be just as puzzling. He fancied himself a mighty hunter and, as such, helped purchase a German-manufactured BB gun for use in the Weapons Storage Area. That isn't as unusual as it might seem. The pigeons would get into the bunkers and crap all over everything, and as poop is corrosive, many units would have an eradication program. He thought that a great motivational tool would be to buy a very expensive air rifle and award top performers the chance to go shoot birds with it. He was wrong, but he did love that gun. Once, he called and told me to get into his office ASAP, that there was something important to fix (of course, with nuclear, everything is important).

So I hustled up to the office; after reporting, we started to discuss some component failure, when in the middle of it, he stopped. He told me not to move and slowly started sliding in his chair toward a closet in his office. Since I had no idea what was going on, I was frozen, only moving my eyes slowly around the room in order to figure where this obvious danger was coming from. He continued achingly slow to the closet. "Sir, what's going on?" I whispered, but was rewarded with a sharp, "Hush." I started to sink to one knee, a little below the window line; as we were in an explosive storage area, I figured that if there was going to be a blast, I would be sliced into tiny chunks by the flying glass, so lower was better.

He finally reached the closet about the same time that I had made it to my knee. I still didn't have any idea what the crisis was, and the colonel was giving no clues as to the method of our impending death. As he made it to the closet, he slowly opened the latch and reached in. And pulled out the damn BB gun.

At that point, my confusion was complete. If we were about to be blown to smithereens by a weapons discharge, the gun wouldn't help. If there were terrorists about, we would be able to give one or two of them bee stings before being overrun, so it was of limited utility there. In short, I could think of not one emergency where the right course of action was to grab the nearest expensive German BB gun. But that's what we were doing. But, I was a lieutenant, and he was a colonel, so I took it for granted that he was doing the right thing. I was new to the officer ranks. He started to pump up the gun, slowly and quietly. I got to my feet, wondering what was going on—no longer worried, just irritated. He motioned me over to him, trying to use hand signals that he must've learned at the movies. He pointed out his window, at...something. All I saw were a couple of transport boxes and some trees. Eventually, I saw what had transfixed the colonel—a raccoon. The masked bandit was running around the base of the trees, doing raccoon-y things, which as far as I could tell, were not an immediate danger to us. I asked if he was going to shoot the raccoon. When he replied in the affirmative, I asked why. I don't remember the answer I got, but it probably didn't justify death. I needn't have worried.

The colonel, after sufficient pumping, slowly raised the fully charged BB gun to his shoulder and eased it out the open 1950s-era window. *Pfft.* The raccoon looked around as a piece of bark flew from the tree several inches above his head. The little guy was only about ten yards away and full grown; he wasn't like a midget raccoon or unusually spry or even wearing a little Kevlar vest, so he should've been mortally wounded. The colonel grumbled about the sights on this expensive German BB gun and grimly started slowly pumping the gun again. I made further entreaties for the little bandit's life, but to no avail. He continued pumping the gun, an awkward silence punctuated by a bicycle pump sound as the colonel reached the required number of pumps. He again brought the stock to his cheek, locking his steely eye through the sights. *Pffftt.* This time the raccoon looked around, wondering why little pieces of bark had started to spontaneously leap from the tree. After a second, he went back to scrounging for berries or whatever, leaving an enraged colonel fuming behind the nearly painted shut window.

This time, the pumping wasn't so gentle. *Psst pssst psst* in rapid succession. I don't think there was a limit this time; someone had to die. Either the raccoon, of a perforated hide; or the colonel, of an exploded German BB gun.

And possibly a lieutenant, of laughter. After the third trigger squeeze, after which neither the tree nor the raccoon jumped, the colonel had had enough. "Dammit, Banzet! One of your damned troops has ruined this rifle!"

"Yessir. Now, back to this nuclear equipment malfunction."

In spite of his quirks, he knew a lot about the nuclear business and kept me on my toes for the upcoming inspection.

In turn, I kept my NCOs on the ball, and they tuned the flights like a drum. In truth, once the senior NCOs knew that I wasn't a complete dork, had high standards, and believed in their authority, they really turned loose. For example, I had a Master Sergeant (E-7) come in complaining that a Senior Airman (E-4) wouldn't do what he said. I looked at him for a long second. "Well, do you want me to make him a MSgt, or you a SrA?" After they realized I was not a micromanager and I believed in their skills, they were perfect. They would've made sure that the unit did well no matter what. That is the NCO's cross to bear, putting up with young, puppy-like lieutenants, constantly smacking them with rolled-up regulations every time they pee on the floor. But with someone who believes in them, a unit just takes off. They became eager to demonstrate their competence. Eventually we got that chance.

The air force conducts a large, thorough inspection for units that have special weapons, called a Nuclear Surety Inspection, and it was always a really big deal. These were the kind of inspections that if the unit didn't do well, commanders got reassigned, and that made everyone unhappy. Basically, this inspection reissued the license to handle special weapons for another couple of years. It was fine with me that we would have a bunch of pros sniffing around our operations to verify that we were doing it right. That wasn't the prevailing sentiment, however. You were supposed to keep your head down and avoid eye contact, just like survival school. Just show the inspectors the minimum and move on. Kind of like when you get pulled over by the highway patrol, and they say, "Do you know why I stopped you?" I have never responded, "Dude, I was going so fast I'm surprised your radar gun even caught up with me" even if that's what I was thinking. I'm always VERY surprised that I've been pulled over, and I let the officer understand that he or she clearly has the wrong guy.

So it was that mentality. Say and do the minimum for the duration of the inspection, and the sooner the team left, the better. And that's where I came in. To screw things up.

I spent my time taunting the inspectors. I dared them to find anything wrong with my team. My young airmen had trained mercilessly under the famous Master Sergeant Opie and were primed for anything. I would sidle up to one of the inspectors standing beside one of my guys and say, "You know what? I bet Airman Smith here doesn't know a damn thing about that rifle he's holding. If I were you, I'd ask him some pretty pointed questions." You could just see the kid puff up, and when the inspector accepted my challenge, they would just get their eyes watered, and walk away mumbling incoherently about the skills of my guys. It happened repeatedly the first day. During the debrief that day, it came out that some smartass lieutenant was goading the inspectors, and my commander was apoplectic. To my credit, he didn't even have to ask who the offending lieutenant was. He came right to me and wondered out loud just what in the hell was wrong with me.

I explained to him the underlying logic, both that my guys were well-trained and proficient in all their tasks and that these weapons were too important to try to hide anything. I would rather be fired than have a weapon get loose or damaged or some deficiency exist that went unnoticed because the inspectors didn't catch some oversight on our part. I wanted the toughest inspection. He pondered that and reluctantly went off shaking his head. The next few days were a continuation of that theme. I was everywhere poking fun at the inspectors and offering up tidbits about where I thought the next "weak" link was, which of course, always failed to materialize. My guys always came through. The months of realigning the flight had paid off, and the weeklong inspection turned into a breeze for my bunch. But the tremendous success of these studs had an impact on my career in a way that I hadn't expected.

Upon the conclusion of the inspection, there is what's called an *outbrief* which sums up the findings of the inspection. In this case it was held in the base theater. The base commander, wing commander, and all the brass sit in the front row. I was in back, goofing around with my guys. A very formal speaker monotoned on about the results of the inspection and ratings for the various sections. My flight garnered the highest rating possible, and that announcement resulted in a major disruption in Mr. Excitement's presentation. My guys leaped up and high-fived, and started screaming out "AMMO" and other easily spelled identifiers. The front row turned as one, some of them disapprovingly, but most of them had a twinkle in their eyes watching these young guys celebrate their inspiring performance. And their goofy lieutenant was the most obnoxious of them all. We all settled down, and Mr. Monotone continued with his very exciting speech. He came to the part in the presentation where he identified the Professional Performers, an honor that the inspectors could, if they wanted to, award to up to 10 percent of the inspected population. The speaker started to name names, and sure enough, he called my teams and a couple of my guys. I was really pumped about that and was making all sorts of noise as the guys walked up to the stage, which was how I missed it when he called my name.

Apparently he had to call my name twice. My guys just started pushing me up, and I went up on stage, saluted, and came back down—no big deal. But you never know who's paying attention. And in the military, someone always is.

Eventually, the air force needed pilots, and my neighbor, who was a pilot, pushed and pulled me to put in my application for pilot training. I had taken the tests and scored really high, but was still tentative; I was comfortable as a maintenance guy. He verbally abused me until I went ahead and put in the application. The one bad thing was that we were a geographically separated unit from our parent wing in the south. That Wing Commander owned a wing of B-52s, so he had a whole bunch of unrated officers plus rated nonpilot officers right there who saw him daily. I was a dork munitions guy three thousand miles away whom he may have seen twice. I really didn't have a lot of hope that I would get selected. This guy usually only picked one person to attend these types of programs. But that's when another typical American thing happened.

I was sitting in the Red Cross giving blood, when the Wing Commander (a general) of the host wing walked in to give blood. He saw me sitting there and recognized me from both the NSI and some tours that I had given him through the weapons storage area. He came up to say hi and remarked that he looked forward to seeing my pilot training application. I reminded him that I didn't actually belong to him, and my package had to be routed through the base down south. He thought for a moment and then asked if I could come see him on Monday. I told him that I would (like I had to give it some thought).

I showed up at his office, at the appointed time, not really knowing what I was there for—a common theme in my career. I was ushered into his office where he presented me with a handwritten letter to my General, starting off with "Dear Andy..." (Generals can say that to each other, you know.) He went on to fill the letter with lies and other nonsense about what a great guy I was. I was flabbergasted. Instead of taking the letter and running, I looked that gift horse straight in the mouth and said, "Sir, may I ask you why you took the time to write all this down? I have barely met you, you've only seen me a couple of times, and yet you took the time to write this extraordinary letter. Why?"

Over his glasses, from behind his giant desk, he said, "Don't you give me credit for being smart? (To my credit, I *knew* not to answer that one). I did this because I know all I need to know about you. When you gave me tours around the Weapons Storage Area, everyone seemed at ease around you, and you seemed to know what was going on. Of course that was only one time. Then, at the NSI outbrief—and yes, I was there—did you notice what happened when your name was called? I didn't think so, as everyone was too busy celebrating, but *I* noticed a couple of things. One, your teams all ranked the highest, and the morale was through the roof; and two, when your name was called, I have *never* heard the enlisted cheer like that for anyone, much less an officer. That told me two things: you were able to make your guys perform at a high level, and you were able to do it in such a way that they loved you for it."

I stood there slack-jawed for a moment. "Jeez, Sir, you *are* smart!"

A couple of months later, I was selected for pilot training as the southern bases' number one choice. God bless America.

I moved my family down to Mississippi and engaged in the contact sport of pilot training for a year, graduating as a KC-10 pilot. Enough stuff happened there to fill another book, but that doesn't belong in this volume.

Although I'd deployed in other capacities as a maintenance guy, it was nothing like the operations in the KC-10. They were very fast-paced, and as pilots, you were in charge. And responsible. The rest of the crew, flight maintenance and others, depended on you to have the answers, or at least the plan. They would help, as they had a wealth of experience, but the sheer scope of knowledge was required of me was unbelievable.

For instance, on all airplanes, there is a *dash one*. This amounts to the owner's manual for the aircraft; in the KC-10, it was a three ring binder, about three inches thick. 8x10 style. Both sides. 10 pitch font. Not enough pictures. It was a LOT of information. It described how we mechanically worked the aircraft. Took care of the "what's this button do?" questions. I still asked them, though. (right McManus?) Sometimes, before I pushed it. *After* you push something you're not supposed to, it becomes the "Oh shit" button. So we've got this giant owner's manual that we had to have with us. But there was more.

I had to know everything in this big book that described the mechanical workings of the aircraft, and I had to learn another set of rules describing how to operate the airplane. After I got it all started and stuff, what to do then? The air force had helpfully provided guidance on that as well— a lot of guidance. There were "General Flight Rules" describing weather requirements, some field requirements, and equipment requirements. This one was only about one inch thick. But that still didn't get me flying around. For that I needed an instrument procedures book—a big one, in two big volumes.

That's where the "Instrument Procedures", volumes one and two came in. Need to know the descent rate calculations if you're thirty miles from the field, flight level 29 zero, doing three hundred knots? Those formulas were in there. (Answer: you're screwed). What is the calculation to turn your current airspeed in knots into time? In there. What are the myriad ways to enter a holding pattern—wait, what altitude are you at? 'Cause that matters. Oh, all of that was in there. For non-pilots: there are many, many ways to enter holding. The actual number is what is known as a "shit-load". But, of course there is only one correct way at a time. And if you do it wrong, you'll be violated. This is as bad as it sounds. Also, you'll need to know how to calculate a lead turn into a precision approach, so you can roll out precisely on course. How far are you from the navigational aide? How fast are you going? A lot of math. I hate math.

After those volumes got you up and running, you then needed to learn the FAA procedures to accomplish in the United States, and of course, for operating worldwide, you also needed more guidance to fly according to international standards (ICAO). So we got into those as well. And the best part was that you had to have all this knowledge at your fingertips all the time, all while moving at a minimum of one hundred twenty miles an hour, or else you become what is known in technical terms, as a fireball. Imagine knowing everything in your car owner's manual, all the laws concerning driving (not just the signs, the legislative language too) in your state, and having to pass a test on all that, while driving and not being able to stop.

So this was just operating the machine. When you added in all the mission specifics and employment of the machine, it became even more complex.

But there was another big machine there, made up of flesh-and-blood Americans. And this one never stopped, it never broke down, it never left you stranded. During my first mission qualification ride as a copilot, I became more aware of the giant organization that was the USAF. Here we were flying around, picking up cargo, people, and refueling aircraft with absolute precision. We could fly halfway around the world, crossing myriad time zones, and arrive at a particular spot in space within seconds of when we said we were going to be there. There was always an air force presence there, watching over us. Sometimes it was a bit overbearing, but we always knew, that no matter what, we would be taken care of, whether mission- or personnel-related. But that obscures the fact that there are a lot of cogs that drive this machine, all of them doing their part. The infrastructure required just to give good weather briefing is amazing. From satellites to HF radios to the highly trained weather folks at some remote location, this entire organization existed to make missions happen, by keeping me and mine safe. I always got decision quality weather information, usually more than I asked for. It wasn't always right, but, hey, the bad info was always served up with a smile.

Flying worldwide missions also really brought into focus the capabilities of the aircraft I was flying. The big ol' KC-10 was a real gentleman's airplane: very capable, with cargo capability and multiple air refueling stations, large offload capability, and generous seating. And an oven. It was a little one, but in the right hands (I'm thinking of you, Kelvin) some fairly masterful concoctions were served up. And, of course, some Weapons of Minor Destruction. The aircraft was huge and powerful; it could take or give gas, both through a boom system (air force) or a drogue system (navy). I didn't really think about what that meant until I actually got on the road though.

For example, on one of my first mission-ready rides, we flew to Singapore and picked up four F-16s that were returning home. We onloaded extra pilots, crew chiefs, and various other ground crew, then packed the rest of the plane with parts and support equipment. All told, we were very close to the 590,000-pound maximum takeoff weight. We took off with very little fuel: when you are trading mission equipment for fuel, well, we could always get more fuel in the air, but it's hard to put on cargo at twenty-five thousand feet and four hundred miles an hour. So I've heard; I've honestly never tried it. The aircraft commander (AC), Tony, was dragging me along the preflight prep, mission briefs, engine start, and all the things that make a mission go. I swear, I was two days behind him on everything. But he got me out to the runway without mishap, and after watching the four Vipers blast off into the damp morning, leaving steaming paths down the concrete, he looked at me and said, "You've got the aircraft."

Now, I was expecting this. I had flown the aircraft many times before and demonstrated proficiency in all aspects of this mission before. Just, not on a real *mission*. I echoed back, "I've got the aircraft." My heart leaped into my throat. I was absolutely giddy. This would be my first mission takeoff. I had to get everything right. Power application. Speed calls. Have the abort procedures running through my mind. What happens if we *do* abort; we'll have hot brakes for sure—what's the evac plan? What's the target pitch to—

"Are you going to make the aircraft move, or are you waiting for something special?"

Oops. Okay. "Pushin' 'em up..."

After takeoff, we soon met up with a trusty KC-135, which rolled out in front of us at while I was still thinking about the takeoff and the departure and all the other issues that are associated with a transoceanic event. The AC chuckled to himself and pointed out the aircraft in front of us. Scared the crap out of me. He'd already started the appropriate checklists to prepare to onload gas. So, he had me hold at fifty feet away from the tail, until the checklists were complete. Then I started creeping up to the precontact point.

And really, that was fine with me. Except they don't make fifty-foot booms. I had to get closer. So, with Tony's coaching, I crept forward and up, until I couldn't stand it anymore, hands with a death grip on the yoke, butt cheeks sucking up the cushion. But I still wasn't close enough. All the while, he was sitting there, calm as a cucumber, watching me sweat. He got me to relax a little finally. Enough to make the damn 135 stop wandering over my windscreen. Tony calmly talked me through all the visual references that I would use as backup to the "Pilot Director Lights" which provided the direction I needed to maneuver the two-hundred-foot-long aircraft into the eight-foot refueling sweet spot. At the top of the boom envelope, I would be sitting about fifteen feet from the boom operator. In the other airplane. At four hundred miles an hour.

That makes a person nervous. Not to mention that there were four other airplanes watching all of this, judging the new guy. After Tony's patient coaching and the calm confidence of the rest of the crew, I slid up into position as the boom, which was extended and down, elevated. I slid underneath and established position. The wind noise increased then decreased as I slid under the boom, forward under the 135. There was a thump; then the light came on: latched. I was grinning like an idiot. And fell off the boom. But I stayed in position and, with increased pressure on the number two throttle, moved slowly forward three feet to get back within the envelope. Latched. I grew to love that light. It meant that our two aircraft were connected, and fuel would be flowing down the boom into our aircraft's thirsty tanks. Which also meant US power projection. After delivering fifty thousand pounds of fuel into our jet, the 135 peeled off, and we continued on our way. Just another day at the office. After that, another very American thing happened.

I was relieved that we had made it through my first refueling; Tony had taken the majority of the fuel; he was the real pro. We did the post refueling checklist; then I decided to get up and head back to the cabin area. I opened the cockpit door and looked out at the seventy-five people in various stages of sleep. That's what you do during a long mission. Military folks are experts at catching forty winks wherever they can find them—or twenty, or ten. I immediately recognized Josh.

By this time, I was a first lieutenant, and I saw that Josh had pinned on master sergeant. We had both been technical sergeants together. He looked at me, and I looked at him. A grin just about split my face in two, and he started grinning too. I had always really liked and respected Josh; I had known him from my very first assignment in Spain, and the following one, uprange in Tonapah Test Range with the F-117A. He was a solid, dependable, likeable guy. Puerto Rican, I think—not that it mattered: in this country anyway. He was always quick with a laugh and slow to anger. Would help anyone with anything. I told him that there was good news and bad news. The good news was that he was going home; the bad news was that I was the one who was going to get him there. Which was a lie, of course; the cockpit area had just become safer and smarter since I was back here talking with him.

He was now a flight chief with the F-16 unit, and here I was ferrying him around the world. He congratulated me on my career moves; he was one of the few that had never scoffed at me for my goal of flying. He knew that anything was possible. I congratulated him on his promotion and increased responsibilities. To me, it demonstrated one of the other unique qualities of American military service: class mobility. It didn't matter where you came from, what color or creed. Your career aspirations and how you conducted yourself on a daily basis pretty much determined where you ended up. Obviously, not a perfect system, as here I was flying an airplane worth 30 million dollars, but overall it worked. The superiors generally took care of those below, and that included career grooming. It seemed that everyone wanted people to succeed, as long as it was done honorably.

5

ONE DAY IN SEPTEMBER

I was going through the normal qualifications of a KC-10 pilot and was still a copilot when, during a mission planning session, I watched a couple of planes hit the towers in New York. When the second one hit, we stopped mission planning. Nothing happened the rest of that day, but I do remember a strange comment that one of the copilots made after I had remarked that we were going to war. He looked at me and said, "Why? The people that did this are dead!"

I was flabbergasted by that thought process. We had just watched unknown numbers of people die, the citizens we were sworn to protect, and this guy thought we were done before we started. I just don't understand people like that. I reminded him that we are not in a vacuum. People are assessing our strength and the will to use it all the time. A nonresponse to this, and the people that planned it and the people that enabled it would encourage ever larger strikes, just like the Khobar Towers, the USS *Cole*, and the first World Trade Center bombing led inevitably to this. He wanted to adopt a "smoking gun approach." I reminded him that a gun only smokes after it's been fired. He was a liberal, though, and the use of logic was anathema to him. And yes, the military does have its contingent of liberals; I don't know why.

We soon started flying Combat Air Patrols (CAP) missions over both New York and DC. It was eerie, as air traffic control was almost silent and only military aircraft were airborne. To me, it was amazing. Again, a kid from Montana and here I was flying these missions over the focal point of the world. Obviously, there were a ton of other folks doing their part. Still, for many Americans, the sight of American aircraft up and flying was comforting, and I was honored to be a part of it. I've still got some footage of the smoking hole that was the center of the Western financial world.

So, for some time, we went all over the east coast, staying on station as the country slowly righted itself—a ship in the Atlantic shuddering off a giant wave. Slowly things began to normalize, but beneath it all, plans were being delivered and courses of action considered. Meanwhile, we continued to be the only air traffic in the sky.

I remember one mission when we were delivering an aircraft to Texas for depot maintenance. Normally, when you take off, there is a series of vectors, departures, and limiting altitudes that one has to meet. It's a very busy time in the cockpit. You are constantly checking in and out of different sectors and receiving directions to deconflict from other traffic; plus, there are usually smaller aircraft buzzing around in and out of communication, and in and out of our path. But this time, as we talked to the controller almost immediately after takeoff, he said simply, "Cleared direct, Kelly." That meant that we were basically cleared to fly directly to Texas, without following any of the routes or even our flight plan. Just. Direct. Because no one was in our way. Over the whole country.

As the weeks went on, President Bush promised that the people who knocked down the centers would be hearing from us soon. And, as more of our guys plussed up a couple of the locations we had in the Middle East, the shooting war in Afghanistan started. Since the air threat was nonexistent, aircraft operated with impunity, with only a ground threat to worry about. But that could be mitigated by both defensive systems and tactics. So the tankers were right over the fight from the beginning. It was a significant shift in tactics and application; more fuel closer to the target areas meant more loiter time for the fighters and bombers, thus, more thunder and lightning for the guys on the ground. I've often wondered if the army private knows the vast array of airpower that is available solely to allow him to do his job.

So while the first wave of folks were over in the fight, the rest of us stateside continued to feed the beast, flying supplies and manpower into theater. In between those missions, we continued to train, and incorporate lessons learned by our comrades in harm's way. I was still a copilot when the next wave to go was notified, so we had a couple of weeks of deployment training before we left. It was to be my first deployment as a pilot, so I was pretty excited. I wasn't sure what to expect however, and as I had two small children, I wanted to do something for them to demonstrate to a seven year old why I had to leave.

Due to our proximity to New York, I thought I would travel to the World Trade Center site itself. So we all piled into the car, and headed for the site, not quite knowing what to expect when we got there. It was night, and a little chilly; a mist of rain hovered in the city. We found a place to park, then walked a few blocks into the mist, hunching in our coats like four little turtles. There was a rope cordoning off the site, but a second lieutenant guardsman was, well, guarding it. So we went up to the rope and asked if we could get a little closer. He sternly told me that this was a federal crime scene, and I needed to leave and so forth. I think he was very excited to have a reason to carry his gun around. So, we moved down the street and came upon several NY cops. I said hello, and they responded right out of Stereotype 101.

"How you doin'?"

I explained my predicament again. I would be heading out to the desert and going after the guys that did this; I wanted to show my family why. They talked among themselves for a few minutes, in that Brooklyn brogue. I couldn't really understand what they were saying, but after a lot of what was to me grunts, gestures, and exclamations, the head guy looked at me and said , "Tell you wut; Frank hea'll take you down, you know? We'll stay here wit yer family, okay?"

Again, straight out of central casting, these bighearted guys said that one of them would take me down, but the wife and kids would have to stay with them. So one of them peeled off with me, and the rest stayed with my wife and children, coffee cups steaming the night air. My family was probably the safest in New York with these big guys surrounding them.

I continued down to the site, with a cop beside me. The dust was a thing, almost alive, swirling in the thick beams of light that striped the night air. Trucks had been brought in and were moving debris. It was noisy and it smelled funny. I looked at some of the other buildings, and there were giant chunks taken out of them. A giant bull in a china shop had been let loose. There were gouges and broken windows, missing beams, and everything, everything was coated in dust, and many folks were wearing masks. But in spite of the chaos, there was a serenity to the situation. Some terrible things had happened, but here were the industrious Americans, sleeves rolled up, getting stuff done. Some wail and throw themselves to the ground, but much of America, regular folks, well, they just get stuff done.

I stood and watched for a little bit, making sure to stay out of the way of the trucks, backhoes, and other pieces of machinery scampering like prehistoric ants back and forth, up and down, busily carting away the larger pieces. There was also a small group of people standing off to the side. These were the remains people, the cop allowed. In case they found something that needed to be assessed and "handled." Big steel girders stuck out like broken fingers from one of the buildings. It was just eerie; it was noisy, but it seemed muted somehow—probably the dust, swirling and mixing with the mist, turning into a light coating of mud.

We stood there for a few minutes, just watching. And something clicked—again. I was in the right place at the right time. As I turned to look at my new comrade, I saw his eyes glistening as he stared at the same scene that he had seen many times. He said that it always got to him, how this was a sucker punch, implying that he didn't mind a fight, but it should be a fair one. He just grabbed my arm, locked eyes with me, and murmured, "Payback." I agreed, stooped down, and picked up a small chunk of exploded cement. That was coming with me.

We went back to my family, who by this time were a little chilly. We thanked NYPD's finest and walked back to the car, talking about the meaning of the whole thing. The children asked a lot of "why" and "what did we do to them" types of questions. I explained that some actions didn't really have a good reason. And you couldn't argue with some people, because they couldn't be reasoned with. The guys that did this believed in the kinds of ideas that left no room for any other ideas—no room. If you didn't like their ideas, they would hurt you. For them, people like us were bad—just by living our normal lives, we were proving the untruth of their ideas. If you say something is bad, but everyone doing it is happy, healthy, wealthy, and wise—well, it sort of makes you look silly. That's what this was all about: a bunch of people hating others for their success and for not adhering to the same ideas. It's heartbreaking to describe the absurdity of that logic to a couple of little kids—or Democrats. But I was able to convince my children, so they would at least understand my upcoming absence.

6

AROUND THE WORLD IN EIGHTY DAYS

This became the first of many deployments. Generally, our crews went out for three or four months at a time. Again, the army and others usually go over for a much longer time, and I was eventually going to go over for a longer deployment, but these first few were for the shorter tours. The desert really chews up the aircraft, with the unbelievable heat and the fine sand working together to make a maintenance nightmare. The maintenance folks, as always, were the unsung heroes. I saw many crew chiefs' uniforms stained white in the middle of the day, as the salt is leached out of their bodies. But, due to these magnificent people, our aircraft always made the mission. Our aircraft generally staged out of a couple of different airfields in the Middle East. We'd been using one of them since Southern Watch, basically keeping the coalition aircraft on station.

During one of these deployments my past came back to haunt me. As I was walking across the 115-degree ramp, I heard my name called.

"Capt. Banzet? Capt. Banzet! Over here."

I squinted the sweat out of my eyes and glanced across the wavering ramp. The heat was a weight, a physical thing that stole your breath. When you walked outside, it was like hitting a wall, and yet the ramp was a buzz of activity, airmen and NCOs laboring under the machines, which baked in the sun and were hot enough to burn your skin. The watchful eyes of the senior NCOs ensured that no one went without water (or Gatorade) for too long and could spot oncoming heat exhaustion. I saw a shape coming out from under a KC-135, where apparently this guy had been servicing the lavatory—not a prime job, even for an airman.

He was absolutely drenched in sweat, dark stains outlined in white running down his entire front. I didn't recognize him. He sharply saluted, which was weird on the flight line—you usually only salute full bulls (colonels) there. But I gratefully returned the honor and, wiping my brow, looked him up and down, trying to place where I knew him from. His black boots, while dusted with the ever-present, well, dust, gleamed dully, evidence of careful polishing underneath. Of course, he was in his T-shirt, which was soaked, and his desert cammies had been stained in the front and the back with the sweat coursing down his torso. I looked closely at this young man who obviously knew me, but I just couldn't place him.

"Sir, it's me; it's Airman Sayers, you know, from back in the nuke unit. Remember, with that goofy Col—"

That was it; that was all I needed said; now it all came back. This guy was one of the airmen who was always on the line of trouble and success. He worked hard but made poor decisions. He was one of those that you cut a little slack on in order to watch him grow through the immature decision making process. The military seems to accelerate the maturation of these kinds of kids; of course, some never mature, and their careers are usually somewhat truncated. I was taken aback, to be sure, as his specialty was nuclear weapons, and there weren't any nukes out there in the desert base. But it was the same kid, slimmed down a lot, and he seemed to be very happy—more than what I'd remembered. So I asked him what brought him out here into the desert. Wasn't this a long way from the storage and handling flight?

"Well , sir, you were always talking about the mission. Mostly when we'd complain about hours or conditions, or just generally bitching. You would shut us up and talk about the crew chiefs and flight line people, how their normal days were twelve hours, and weekend duty, and being drenched in sweat and fuel and hydraulics. You always talked about how rewarding the mission is. How challenging it is. Soon after you left, things started to go back to the way they were before you got there, and, well, I cross-trained into aircraft maintenance the first chance I got."

I started to grin, remembering some of the talks that we had over some of the issues in that unit. A nuclear weapons unit has pristine work conditions and a very slow pace, as befits a nuclear weapon. But the pace and the comfort level had no equivalence to flight line work, and whenever I'd hear complaining, I'd really light into the whiners about what happens in the real air force. We weren't damn shoe clerks. Those are the guys in the blues all the time. And here was a kid that had listened to one of my rants and decided that he wanted to get to the front line of the fight. But I wanted to know how it felt now; was he happy with his terrible working conditions, long hours, fuel and hydraulic stink, and unforgiving machines?

In a word, yes. Actually two words. "Hell, yes." Sayers was positively gloating over how much fun he was having. He felt sorry for those poor saps back in the missile field, who would never know the joy of launching out a recalcitrant aircraft into morning skies and awaiting its "no codes" return. Or better, having one return with all sorts of problems and killing yourself throughout the night getting it ready again. The noise, the smells, the…

I'd looked over at the task he had been performing when he'd spotted me walking across the ramp. Sayers followed my eyes and smirked up at me.

"Yes, sir, I *am* pumping shit out of that 135. In 115-degree heat. It sucks. But I am having a ball! I just wanted to thank you for telling me about this world. I've never felt better about what I'm doing with my life. This is important. I'm also starting to get my education, like you said. Everything is going great, and I just wanted to thank you."

I felt a little lump in my throat, and I'd be lying if I didn't feel pretty damn proud of myself too—not for anything in particular that I'd done, other than just show this kid (and whoever else would listen) a different type of job satisfaction. Once he'd sniffed it, he had grabbed on with both hands. He was a newsmaker now. On the front lines of the world, enacting the policies of this great nation. One of its thousands of heroes.

So I had become one of many deploying to the desert. Mobility pilots tended to spend a lot of time on the road, and each type of aircraft had its peculiar ops tempo. The C-5 guys were terribly busy, on the road about two hundred twenty days a year; we were busy too, but our aircraft were more reliable, so we lost less time to maintenance problems. The C-130s were humping too; the four fans o' freedom blowing dust all over the Middle East. C-130 guys are special—that's all I'm saying. Other types of airframes had really high numbers as well, especially "high demand, low density" aircraft, like the AWACS. There was a lot of airpower over both theaters, and somebody had to make them all hit each other. It seemed like the closest calls I had were when the AWACS apparently forgot that they were in the middle of their scope. Zing!

It was during one of those deployments that another significant event occurred. Unfortunately, it happened on the heels of a tragedy.

A Marine C-130 had crashed in a big fireball on the Pakistani border, but no one knew why. We were being repositioned to provide fuel and a comm hop to any would-be rescuers. As we pegged the airspeed needle to the max airspeed carat, we were passed by two navy F-14s, wings swept back, zooming past us like we were taxiing. Some of their brothers were in trouble. They were racing to help. About the same time, USAF F-15Es came on frequency checking in, and they too were racing to the scene. Some of their brothers were in trouble. They were racing to help. We had extra gas, so we were going to be able to provide top cover for whatever was happening on the ground for a time, until relieved. A couple of minutes later, the F-14s had established an orbit over the site; the F-15s were arriving, and we were pulling on to the scene. We checked into the strike frequency and listened in to the conversation to figure out where best to establish. The army was already there, on the ground, helicopters thumping through every radio communication they made. Because some of their brothers were in trouble. And they had raced to help.

As usual, the armed forces of the United States were worried about civilian casualties. The army folks were steadfastly making sure that everyone knew that there were civilians on the ground, and no one was to engage anybody until they were cleared. And there was quite a list of folks that wanted to engage; the F-14s had come across our baskets a couple of times, and the mud hens had hit the boom a couple of times as well. The army had troops on the ground and were securing the site. In short, because the marines needed help, representatives from all services had descended on their need, like avenging angels. The night sky was filled with pain for any who wished them ill. And the ground was spoken for by staid superheroes in camo. In cockpits and on hillocks and in ops centers under flickering screens, American eyes squinted and scanned, looking out for threats as they were scrambling for any survivors.

Unfortunately, there were none. At the end of the day, the C-130 had crashed into the mountainside because of the challenging conditions of the landing site. Just another one of the "costs of doing business" in a wartime environment. But what got to me was the rush to help a fellow American. Service rivalries went out the window, and every American in the vicinity that could be spared came running. Like Americans do.

One thing Americans do *not* do is "air raid villages and kill civilians"[3] as some politicians have claimed. Let me demonstrate one of the missions that I flew in support of Operation Enduring Freedom.

We were fragged to support the northern area of Afghanistan, and about halfway through the mission, a giant firefight broke out. We quickly repositioned and hooked up with a B-1 roaring northward to support the festivities. We transferred the required fuel; then, as the Bone sped off with its belly full of boom, we flipped around to catch another aircraft going to that exact same area. This one, however, was a cargo aircraft, a fat-faced C-17 (Buddha, in the mobility community, as it was fat and round and everyone worshipped it). It had little in the way of defensive systems and a belly full of humanitarian rations. It was going to the same area as the B-1—a hot area. But it was going in driven by this American crew, to deliver life, not death. This was not the first time that the USAF had delivered Humanitarian Rations. You may have heard of the first couple of times. As crews were flying into harm's way to deliver food to folks who may or may not have been friendly to us, the international community and the left wing media (I consider that term redundant) were extremely critical of the fact that they were the same rations that I was eating—not necessarily Muslim friendly.

---

3 Pickler, Nedra: Fact Check; Obama on Afghanistan August 14, 2007. http://www.washingtonpost.com/wp-dyn/content/article/2007/08/14/AR2007081400950.html (accessed May 2012).

So, after developing the Muslim-friendly rations, more crews risked their lives to deliver another load of rations to try to keep strangers living through the winter. Unfortunately, some of these landed in an old Soviet minefield, and some folks got hurt retrieving them. Of course, that was our fault too. So we spent more time and effort to feed people that we couldn't tell were good or bad because we didn't want suffering. Let that sink in. The imperialistic, arrogant way that America raids villages and kills civilians is by dropping carefully selected food items on combat missions. Usually pushed out the back of a cargo aircraft by some young airman, being flown in by some young airman, because that's what Americans do.

At least the ones I know. I don't know many liberals.

7

VIP TRANSPORT

After I'd done four or so of those four-month tours and countless Temporary Duties (TDY)s in support of the desert missions, hauling cargo and aircraft across the globe and racking up an average of about one hundred sixty days away per year for four years, I decided that it would be fair to my family to take an assignment that kept me home more. So, in spite of the fact that it wouldn't be good for my career, I asked to take an assignment at Wright Patterson for a unit that was doubling in size, from a flight to a full-fledged squadron. A good buddy of mine was already up there and said that the flying was good, and the squadron was great! So we packed up our things and zipped on up.

I learned how to fly a C-21A Learjet, a slick little aircraft that could seat eight in the back and about one and a half in the cockpit. I am six foot three and about two hundred thirty pounds. It was like shoving two people into a single-hole Porta-Potty and heating the whole thing up to one hundred degrees, then accelerating it to two hundred miles per hour. This temperature was important, because the folks in back often froze. If it was superhot up front, and super cold in the back, then the *average* temperature was just fine. It was like a climatological testing chamber for VIPs, congressmen, generals, and the like.

Upon boarding the aircraft, we would shove ourselves through the bulkhead into the hot zone. The bulkhead was about two feet wide, or about six inches smaller than my shoulders. Plus, it was about four and a half feet tall, or about two feet shorter than I was. And right in front of that was the radio console and nav stack. So basically, I would jump in, seat everyone, and then stick my butt right in their faces as I squatted, turned my shoulders, leaned forward, and high kicked over the radio stack to hurl myself into the right seat. Which was already one hundred degrees. It was like being one of those Russian dancers, lurching, and high-stepping into the spa of a cockpit. Very confidence inspiring.

In spite of that fact, I liked flying it just fine. I ended up meeting lots of important people (truly important, not movie star important) and only rarely had any bad flights. I can't remember any passengers that were out-and-out rude; maybe there were some. But then, I didn't fly many Democrat politicians; their treatment of military people is legendary within the military community.

I got to meet some pretty awesome people and, as often happens, have a lot of fun. One of the best military ones was a lift that we had to go pick up an army general. I hadn't really paid a lot of attention to the manifest, but we were picking up the Commanding General, First Army.

We pulled up to the airport; I had the copilot jump out and wait for the Distinguished Visitor (DV), while I filed the next leg of the flight plan. Then I jumped back in, updated the navigation system, set the cockpit for engine start, and waited. The party pulled up, and the general got out. He was by himself, which was a little weird; usually, generals take a lot of minding, so they have majors and lieutenant colonels scurrying around like mice around a cat. It's actually kind of funny.

The copilot saluted, and I threw the switches to start the number two engine. It spooled up and started to stabilize. The copilot got the DV seated and jumped in. As he got all situated, I looked back to my right. The general gave me a slight wave and smiled. Seemed like a nice guy. But he looked vaguely familiar. And with that in the back of my head, I motioned to the crew chief to pull the chocks, and he marshaled us out of the chocks.

After an uneventful taxi and climbout, we leveled off and relaxed a bit. I couldn't shake the feeling that I'd seen him somewhere. I looked at the manifest to scan the passenger list. And the name snapped everything else into focus.

Lieutenant General Russel Honore. The guy that handled the Katrina press idiots. The "stuck on stupid" guy. I looked back, and he was just reading a book. Since we were all stable, I decided to break out the patented smart-assedness.

I just inclined my head a bit and said (in a slightly raised voice), "I swear, the controllers up here are just stuck on stupid."

Then I slowly looked back.

His head really hadn't moved, but his eyes rolled up over his glasses. Then a big smile started to break over his face.

"How are you doing, son?" he inquired in a raspy, gravelly voice.

He put the book down, and leaned forward and we just started talking. It was a bit difficult to carry on a conversation in that situation, because my primary duties were always ensuring the safe operation of the aircraft. Even though the copilot was flying, as the aircraft commander, it really didn't matter how the duties were divided up, the entire aircraft and everyone in it was my responsibility. In spite of those obstacles, we had a decent conversation. He talked a bit about Katrina, about how frustrating it was to deal with the reporters, and that was the genesis of the "stuck on stupid."

The media bias (Bush controls hurricanes!), rampant ignorance, and rabblerousing (They're eating people! I know because someone I don't know told me!) hadn't affected me personally yet—that would wait till Iraq. But it was still disgusting to behold. The media had come a long way from reporting "news". And General Honore had been trying to get them to stop being selfish morons, for just a few days, in order to help things out in Katrina's aftermath. In my opinion, he should have said to stop being stuck on selfish.

Our choppy conversation only lasted about ten minutes; I just told him how awesome I thought that was that he smacked down those smarmy little twits who were breathlessly trying to outdo one another with crap stories instead of trying to be useful. He was just a very kind man—like many of the senior leaders I've met. The real turds seem to cluster at the O-6, or one-star, level.

After my super awesome landing—a landing so smooth we had to open the door just to make sure we were on the ground—Gen. Honore gathered his things, and I helped him off of the aircraft. I shot him a snappy salute; he returned a razor-sharp one, then grasped my hand. He placed one of his commander coins in my palm. They are supposed to be special, but in this case, maybe he just had extras. I watched him go, smiling.

That was fun. But, funny, well, that's a different story.

One yet another trip, I was flying with a young, blond copilot I'll call "Dennis." He kind of looked like Dennis the Menace, so it's a good fit. He was one of those guys who wasn't chubby, just had a chubby face. He was tall, very blond-haired, and very fair-skinned. And he looked like a three-year-old. You just wanted to squeeze his cheeks when you saw him. Ahem. Not me; other people.

So I was flying around with this six-foot-tall three-year-old, and we landed at a pretty nice airport (I forget where). The Fixed Base Operator (FBO), where private planes load and unload passengers, usually have some sort of snacks and stuff around for the crews. This FBO was very nice, and the best part was they had Otis Spunkmeyer cookies. Dennis ran over to raid the glowing glass cube of heaven before we even checked in.

But his dreams were crushed—the Spunkmeyer vault had been raided. He had arrived at an empty tomb, with just the lingering smell of delicious chocolate chip cookies to assuage his pain. He looked back over his shoulder at me with the most disappointed look. He looked like a big, giant-headed baby that had just pooped himself and wanted to see if anyone had noticed. I, with my usual empathy, burst out laughing.

Still dying of laughter, I walked up to the lovely people at the counter to request fuel and start the other paperwork. I mentioned that my copilot would be pouting for the rest of the trip because the Spunkmeyer well was dry. The lady smiled and said that there were fresh ones cooking in the back; they would be done in a few minutes.

I relayed that to Dennis, and he was very, very inordinately excited. His big baby head was illuminated with visions of chocolate chip, macadamia nut, and other delicacies spinning around. With his green flight suit, he looked like the old stop-motion Christmas cartoons. I allowed that we wouldn't be heading out anytime soon; the VIP wasn't even there yet.

About that time, a gentleman walked in who sparked something in my memory. He was an older gentleman, probably seventy to seventy-five years old. In spite of having a shock of white hair, he strode in purposefully, energetically. I couldn't quite place him, as I walked over to Dennis to wait for our passenger. I pointed the gentleman out to Dennis and asked if he looked familiar.

Dennis wasn't budging from his Otis vigil, but he looked over at the guy; he didn't recognize him. I knew it was someone famous, but I just couldn't tell who it was. Then it clicked: John Glenn.

It was the first man in flipping space, John Glenn, walking through the airport, and we were going to shake his hand. I told Dennis.

"That is John Fricking Glenn! Let's go say hi."

Dennis looked surprised.

We had just started off when catastrophe struck.

The lady came out from the back with a pan full of fresh, delicious cookies. The smell of everyone's kitchen billowed out in front of the pan like a heaven-scented air freshener. And it stopped Dennis in his tracks. He hesitated and looked at the still-mobile Glenn and the round angel droppings that were being slid into their cozy little slots in the little glass case. His cherubic face twisted in agony. Job's decision was easy in comparison to Dennis's. He turned back toward the cookies.

"Are. You. Kidding. Me." I had stopped, but Mr. Glenn hadn't. This would be the only time we would get to touch a living astronaut. And I had no desire to touch dead ones, so if I wanted to press the flesh of a spaceman, this would have to be it. Dennis took a couple of unsure steps toward me and Glenn.

Now his face was racked with worry. If he made the decision to shake Glenn's hand, would someone get the cookies? Or at least his favorite ones? He cast a look behind him; the lady was sliding the last heaven biscuit into the slot. Dennis looked around at the competition. There were several people in the lobby, some talking to Mr. Glenn, but a couple of them were starting to mosey over to the box. Now Dennis began to take on a look that gazelles take on when they see several tan, tufted tails bobbing over the prairie grass. Panic.

I looked at him in disbelief. I just said, "Really?"

After a moment's hesitation, he took a step back toward the cookies, then another, and another. He was going for the cookies.

I was going for John Glenn. I approached the dapper older gentleman, and before I could say anything, he spotted my flight suit and stuck out *his* hand. I grabbed it, honored. I told him how great it was to meet him, and we made a tiny bit of small talk about flying or something. I'm sure we just talked for a couple of minutes, but it was awesome. I looked over at Dennis, and he had gone from the big-headed-baby look to Gollum.

He had liberated a couple of napkins and scored some very impressive kills on the newborn batch of cookies. There was quite a pile stacked on his napkin, and he was masticating a chocolate chip one as I watched. Against his pale skin, some smears of chocolate stood out like a sad clown. I just burst out laughing. John had an inquisitive look on his face.

I pointed at the creature crouching in front of the Otis shrine.

"That, sir, is my copilot."

Glenn took a second to assimilate that. A big grin came over his face, and he turned to me. "Well, young man, good luck."

We shook hands again, and he turned on his heel, stepped on my foot, and left. (My foot has travelled in space, by proxy.)

Dennis showed up mere seconds later. "Is he gone?"

I was laughing so hard I was dying. I told him to go look in the mirror. He went back to the cookie case to look at the glass and then saw the big smears of chocolate. His pale visage coursed to scarlet like a scared cuttlefish.

I gave him crap for the rest of our tour. In a historic moment, he got cookies, and I shook hands with an American icon, and my foot walked in space. By proxy. And I got cookies too.

The squadron stayed busy; I was putting in full days, as the payment for being home every night (mostly) was max crew duty days, about sixteen hours. We could land at many airports in the course of a day, so by the time we got home, we were exhausted. But we were home. My family started getting used to me being around, and everyone was settling in nicely. So it was time for a change.

I've mentioned that the unit was building from a flight to a squadron as a result of careful planning; however, about two months after I got there, as a result of more careful planning, the unit was told they were closing. I was a bit bemused, as one of the reasons for those aircraft to be there was to transport high-ranking DVs, of which Wright Patterson had a plethora. That hadn't changed, but Congress had decided they would force the USAF to halve their C-21 fleet, so the unit was slated to be closed, which meant that C-21s from Andrews AFB would be flying up to Wright Patterson almost weekly from Washington, DC, to take the high-ranking folks to Washington, DC. And back.

The unit struggled along in limbo; the higher-ranking folks took off for greener pastures, ultimately leaving me in charge. The process was slow, but eventually the doors closed. And I was left to try to find work.

Fortunately, HQ was right up the road, and I soon found myself working in the one of the many offices. It was terrible. I found a cubicle with my name on it located in the basement of the HQ building. Sadly. The basement itself stunk, and was moist. There seemed to be a vacuum that sucked the life out of people when they came into the building. If the body snatchers would have invaded there, the aliens would've left, disappointed in the host selection. Zombies had more joie de vivre, but then, zombies would have more of a reason to get up in the morning. They didn't have to go back into the basement.

That's not to say that the people weren't friendly—they were; but there was a palpable dimness in this type of building, like the lights weren't on all the way. Colors were duller in HQ, as if having been washed too many times. Things were permanently dusty. People were smaller, rounder: a particular form of *hominus cubitus* that seems to infect buildings of this type. Scuttling from here to there, usually with a sheaf of papers or perhaps a binder tucked under a tiny, flabby arm. Hustling to get to a meeting where discussions would center on synergies, paradigm shifts, enterprise views, and efficiencies. Anything but actual production or action. And there I was.

The office itself was full of nice people with a terrible job: to try and make sense of the congressional boondoggle that was the Base Realignment and Closure Act. There was constant stupidity foisted upon the air force by our betters in Congress. One of my projects was trying to move a centrifuge (or two) from Texas to Ohio. The problem was that the 'fuge was so old that moving it would ruin it, or it would be ruinously expensive, if we could get anyone to do it at all. Since it was so old, we could use the same amount of money and build a state-of-the-art centrifuge in Ohio, maybe for even a little less money. Made sense to me, but realignment law is very clear.

The money could only be used to transfer the *exact same* capability, which in this case was a thirty-year-old centrifuge. It specifically could not increase the USAF's capability one jot. Which, in essence, became a smart tax on the USAF. If we wanted to put a brand new centrifuge at the place that we were told we had to have one, instead of moving a decrepit and most-likely-broken-when-it-got-there one, well then, we had to pay for it. In the millions. And this type of thing happened over and over. We constantly fought to do the right thing, however, tilting at windmill after windmill. I could only stand a couple of months of this mind-numbing behavior, until I finally went to my boss, an O-6, and said that if it wasn't for my family, I would volunteer for Iraq. I'd already been away a lot over my career, so I didn't think it was fair for me to go looking for deployments; they'd found me enough over the years.

Less than two weeks later, he called me and asked if I was serious about the comment. I said that I was, and, like a green-clad genie, he granted my wish. I was heading to Iraq.

This was apparently a big deal. At the HQ, my boss's boss asked me to come to the office to sign the acceptance. The general sat me down and asked me if I was going to decline the invitation. Apparently, seven other officers had opted to retire or take the "seven day" option, which meant getting out. I thought that was chicken shit. I was eligible to retire as well, but I was taking a paycheck and wearing the green flight suit: it wasn't fair of me to turn something down 'cause it was scary. So I looked him in the eye and told him so. It went like this.

"That's chicken shit, sir."

So I signed on the dotted line and then started to figure out how I was going to tell my lovely wife. It was one of the toughest things I'd had to do.

After I got home that night, and put the kids to bed, we just took a walk around the block, holding hands, talking about the kids and the things that were going to happen over the next school year. I was really having a tough time with all of that. I had a lump in my throat and was getting pretty choked up about all these plans. My eyes started to water. I'd never really felt this bad; the kids were older now; the teenage years were going to be challenging. Couple that with the business that she was running, and I really felt terrible. As I broke it to her, she stoically asked how long, and where. I told her that it would be Baghdad, and for a year. Her beautiful face tightened. Her brown eyes glistened in the streetlights—I've always hated that. Her eyes just tear my heart out. She never asked me if I could get out of it; she knew I wouldn't even ask. As I held her in the velvet evening, I could feel her crying, and tears crept down my face. I gritted my teeth hard, stopping a breakdown altogether. I would miss them all terribly, even if whatever waited for me in Iraq didn't kill me.

8

PREPPING FOR THE MISSION, WHATEVER IT IS

So, when the air force decides that you are going to do something, first, it decides it needs to train you for whatever it is you are going to do. Whatever that is. It really doesn't matter *what* you are supposed to do when you get in theater, the USAF will train you on something. If you're lucky, then those two events may coincide; although, even if you're lucky enough to be trained for the job you're supposed to be doing, the odds are that, in the theater, they don't do the job "that way." So it's a crap shoot either way, except there are no winning rolls of the die. You'll get world-class training, but in something unrelated to what you're going to do. But the USAF gets points for trying.

So, after I signed the paperwork, all of my pre-deployment training was scheduled. For the first time, I was issued real combat gear, knee pads, goggles, knives, and so forth. In my previous deployments, we were just issued the M9 pistol, and that is what we flew with. We were really only going to engage the enemy if we survived the crash. Which, in the type of aircraft that we flew, was a long shot. More likely that we would be shoulder rolling at 100 mph in the midst of a giant fireball. But, just in case my awesome piloting (I'm being redundant again) skills were enough to reverse the laws of physics and thermodynamics, we went through the normal qualifications with the 9. Which probably wouldn't impress my Marine brothers, but it was good enough for us.

This time, however, I was issued an M4 with collapsible stock and Aimpoint red-dot sight, in addition to the 9 mm pistol. That was different, but okay. We first reported to the pistol range and went through the course. It wasn't really that challenging, especially if you were creative. By "creative," I mean that the target paper had several targets of various sizes, and you were supposed to put a couple of rounds in each, at each different range. The technique that I used was to "miss" the large targets at the close ranges, accidentally placing rounds into the smaller targets, saving the big targets for the farther distances. The little targets were supposed to represent bad guys, just farther away, so, in my head, they were still "far" even though the actual paper was "close." Of course, others might just think that it was "cheating."

I ended up shooting expert, but it really isn't that challenging, even without my special techniques. Most of us could qualify. However, there was a technical sergeant that caught my eye. And he was a precursor of things to come.

Two slots over from my shooting position, he seemed to warrant a lot of attention from the instructors. As we went through the shooting course of fire, we eventually quit with the practice fire and shot for qualification. That consisted of fifty rounds at various distances and shooting positions. I think you have to get forty-five rounds on paper with a certain number in the head and chest of the unfortunate paper bad guy. Since I shot expert, this made me a valuable asset in the off chance that the base that I'd be going to was attacked by fluttering silhouettes attached at the head to tracks that stop at five, fifteen, and twenty-five feet. I'm your man, General Custer.

But. The TSgt was surrounded by the instructors, murmuring about retesting. Apparently, Dead Eye had gotten nineteen rounds on paper. Out of fifty. Nineteen. Which meant that thirty-one rounds had gone whistling downrange. And some at some of those less than impressive distances, too. On the first course of fire, when the target is closest, you can either shoot the target with the pistol or reach out and do the old "got your nose" trick, thus confusing the bad guy into submission. I looked at him and said, "Nineteen on paper?" How on earth you can only get nineteen rounds on the whole paper I don't know. Unbelievable. When I asked how he had gotten so, um, "out of practice," he said that he had never deployed before. In thirteen years, he had never deployed. I was stunned. My whole career had been deploying. Mostly because we had been at various levels of war since 1991, whether or not the country acknowledged it. But there are some jobs in the USAF where you never really see the pointy end of the stick. I have my own feelings about that; I'm more of a *Starship Troopers* kind of guy. I think that everyone should fight. Or at least be able to. Nonetheless, after ascertaining that the only way this guy would be deadly with a pistol would be to put a bayonet on it, I appointed him the grenade guy.

We attended a few more courses on base then went on our way to Camp Bullis in Texas to attend the Air Force Combat Training Course. After getting transported from the airport in the obligatory buses, we drove and drove, arriving out in the scrub of Texas. Our location was perched on a hillock, with a couple of Quonset huts (the instructional buildings) at the top, a couple of water buffaloes (wheeled tanks for drinking and rinsing water), and some picnic tables for chow. Our living facilities were about one hundred yards down a little trail through scrub pine on a leveled plateau of the hill. About fifteen tents, each designed to house eight folks. With two Porta-Potties to house poisonous spiders, snakes, and scorpions.

Texas was supposed to replicate the climate of the Middle East, and it accomplished that for me, as it was hot with giant bugs; but really there is nothing that can accurately reflect the broiling heat and powder-fine sand of the Middle East. And the giant bugs *there* are angry. I've really only run into one of the infamous "camel spiders" once, and that was in the United Arab Emirates, but that was enough to prejudice me forever. They will never be on my Christmas card list. At Bullis, the bugs were more benign, even though they ran the gamut of nastiness, from scorpions to black widows to tarantulas. They just didn't seem as intimidating. One bad insect-related thing happened there though: I saw a tarantula in a tree—something I did *not* need to see. I didn't know they could do that; I hate spiders, and to learn that those giant, hairy messengers of Satan have the ability to drop onto my head from above, seemed a bit of overkill. In spite of the danger, grave danger (is there any other kind?), I arrived in fine fashion, ready for anything.

We got all squared away, in-processed, and bedded down. I was BS-ing a lot with some of the guys, and I was the last one to get into our tent. By then one of the high-speed captains had commandeered it and was busy reading the rulebook of tents (really). We had several enlisted folks in there, and they were bemusedly sitting on their bunks, hearing how the tent was to be set up: how many boots and what other items had to be stored where under the cots, and so forth. The captain looked at me, and his face melted, transitioning from a conquering hero visage into that of a sad clown in a microsecond. He was no longer king of the tent. But quick enough, he decided that he could still be the tent adjutant. He took a couple of steps toward me, thrusting out the tent rulebook, saying, "Here you are, sir, the rules of the tent; we can just move your cot over here, in accordance with the regulation."

I should have been flabbergasted, but I had dealt with Air Force Education and Training Command (AETC) several times in my career, so this was totally expected. I took the offered rulebook, scanned through it and and tossed it on the cot that I was standing next to. More specifically, I tossed it on the floor. "I'm good right here, and you're good right there, as are the rest of you. Keep your stuff neatish, and if anyone gives you any grief, send them to me, because this rulebook is pretty chicken shit." I'm pretty sure I looked just like Patton as I said it. But it wasn't enough. The captain decided to give it one more go.

"We could get into trouble if we don't do what the book says. We're supposed to arrange our cots like this and our stuff like this," he said, gesturing around the tent.

"Okay, let's follow that logic, shall we? Let's pretend that these NCOs and company grade officers (CGOs) don't know how to get dressed or clean up after themselves. Let's pretend that neither you nor I give a crap and let them pile this place high with junk. And then someone discovers it. And tells us to clean it up. What will we do?"

"Why, we'll have to clean it up."

"Right; so we're in no danger of a new typhoid epidemic, then. Furthermore, I have every confidence that the fine men here in this tent need no babysitting from either of us. If they do, then I will be happy to babysit the one that needs it. Once. Until then, we will act like grownups. AETC deals with the least common denominator, so they write these kinds of books to keep the baby birds from shitting in their own nests. There are no baby birds here. So we will relax and try to max out the brain cells in learning what is important to deploying to a warzone, not where the socks go in the tent diagram. And don't worry, Captain, if I get relieved as tent commander, we will put everything back lickety-split. But, we don't need to make our own lives tough when AETC will do it for us."

And so we went to sleep.

When we got up in the morning, after chow, we headed over to the instructional facilities to see what we were in for. I was pleasantly surprised to find that there would be a real emphasis on learning local phraseology and rudimentary Arabic, along with cultural sensitivity. This was a large chunk of the training time allotted to us. This was indicative of the mindset we had going in. We were going to really relate on an equal footing to the Iraqis we would be working with. This was a distinct choice, and one that had a cost, one that I would become more familiar with after a few months in Iraq. The choice was made to not be the conquering hero, but the friend trying to give a down-and-out buddy a hand up. This was a choice, I think, mostly driven by a politically correct mindset. We really didn't want to say that we were superior, or "better" in any way; therefore, we could not tell the Iraqis with certainty *how* to do things, but had to gently prod them along, trying to align them with our objectives while not really telling them they were *wrong* so much. It was to be a collaboration, then, and not very directive. That policy and its weakness would be fleshed out later.

In order to help with that process, they had some Iraqi civilians, recent (within the past few years) immigrants to the United States spend hours speaking to us. There were two women and a couple of older guys. Our squad got a middle-aged woman who was raised in Iraq and had emigrated about fifteen years prior.

She was something. About five foot three and dark haired, she was a very buxom woman—and was about ten pounds heavier than she thought she was. One of my squaddies remarked that she was ten pounds of love stuffed into a five-pound sock. She was a thoroughly modern woman and relayed to us that this was really the norm in Iraq. Her shirts were usually tight (by default), and her jeans were also very tight, as if she'd gotten dressed and then swallowed a life raft. But she always had a twinkle in her eye and was constantly downplaying how important these very strict customs that we were learning were. While the USAF was twisting itself into knots trying to be inoffensive and proper, she constantly spoke of how beautiful Iraq was and how educated the people and how Saddam had ruined the country for a long time. Iraq was generally a very secular nation but had been wrenched hard into a fascism backed, when convenient, by a violent religious core. She fondly remembered evenings walking along rivers, restaurants, and dancing, then having to leave the country as Saddam ascended.

She also remarked over and over on how careful the Americans were to try not to offend anyone and said that we were just "that kind of people." In all her travels (and travails), she had come to love this country and our people. And marvel at our capacity for kindness. Here we were prepping for duty in a combat zone, and we were spending days learning the proper body language for polite conversation. And a few words here and there to humanize ourselves to the Iraqis. In order that we could help push, pull, and cajole them along into a democracy that was responsive to its people and a responsible member of the international community.

At one point, she was really in rare form in a teaching session, being very effusive in her quest to shove a few words of Arabic into our "limbic" brains (as a semifamous comedienne would say), when I noticed that her zipper in her aforementioned overworked jeans had worked its way down. All the way. Being very polite, I mentioned it to as many people as I could. Everyone loved her, so no one wanted to be the one to embarrass her in front of the twenty-five or so people in my group. So we all sat there looking anywhere but at her, as she went into detail about how to say "hello" in Arabic (*mar' hubbub?*). Eventually, mercifully, she ended her segment and sent us on a break.

I walked up to her and, sotto voce, said, "Could you tell me the Arabic word for 'zipper'?" Her dark brow furrowed.

"Zipper? Like the lighter?"

Everyone in the world, it seems, is familiar with the Zippo lighter. Another subtle way America is taking over the world, I suppose. But I clarified. "No, a *zipper*, like in a pants zipper, as in a 'your zipper is all the way down' kind of zipper." She looked puzzled for a few minutes then rattled off a bunch of Arabic.

After seeing the bemused expression on my face, she asked me if that's what I was looking for. As this was taking way too long to explain politely, and people were trickling back in, I just had to go for broke. "No, ma'am, your zipper. Your zipper is all the way down and has been for quite some time. I'm just trying to tell you to check your zipper."

Her face slowly went from puzzlement to shock, as it dawned on her what I was getting at. Her eyes widened in horror, and she let out a very impressive stream of curse words—doubly so, as it was in two, maybe three languages. But then she reached for the zipper. The zipper itself had formed into a severe Y shape as the serious expansion pressures pulled mightily on the teeth. The poor woman had two strikes against her when it came to correcting the problem: one, the ten pounds of love in a five-pound sock issue; and two, she couldn't see her zipper to fix it anyway. She looked like a wrestler trying to grasp a turnbuckle while putting two bald-headed men in a headlock. I was dying laughing. She had both hands trying to pull the zipper up, but that action squished and thrust upward the squishy part of her front and threatened to defeat the whole "looking down to see what I'm doing" part of the equation. I was staring in awe at the contortions this woman made just to zip up her pants. It was marvelous.

She would be awesome again, only this time a little later in the program as she stood on stage and lectured the entire group of about one hundred thirty folks. I was in the second row or so, and she was up on stage this time. And sure enough, the zipper worked its way, slowly, inexorably, a tooth at a time with every gesture. Snickers started sprinkling themselves throughout the audience, as more and more folks started watching. It was like watching a Christmas gift unwrap itself. Mercifully, before the zipper reached the bottom, she brought her translation topic to a close for a break again. I met her as she descended the steps and asked her to remind me again of the Arabic word for "zipper." She looked at me; an eyebrow dipped; then both rose in horror as she realized she was again the victim of a stealth pantsing. This time, I learned entirely new cuss words and how to apply them.

We saw her a couple of more times as the course wound down, but she seemed to have established a mechanism for dealing with the errant zippers that all her pants came equipped with—skirts. I never again saw her in a pair of pants. On those occasions that we did see her, she continued to go out of her way to emphasize the extraordinary level of concern that the

USAF was taking to make sure that we were equipped to interact with the Muslim culture wherever we found it. She personally thought it was a bit much, as the Iraqis were much more tolerant than we were led to believe and rather secular. She was prescient in that regard and right about many other things as well. I was able to use her training in good stead, although on a fairly limited basis. It was enough.

While all that learning was going on, we had to deal with some paradigm shifting of our own. There were quite a few pilots attending the course, with other support officers mixed in. As may be imagined, we were a little out of our element in this environment. So, when we were taught the basics of patrolling, it felt more like playing army. Of course, many USAF officers felt like I did. If I was ever in charge of a bunch of folks on the ground in combat, it would probably not be patrolling—it would be after things had gone horribly wrong. But, if the worst were to happen, we could at least go down swinging. Till someone who knew what the hell they were doing got to us. There is a reason army officers and NCOs practice a lot and are the experts on this activity. I wouldn't want someone landing my plane because they had a few Microsoft "Flight Simulator" hours, even if they *did* stay at a Holiday Inn Express. I'd prefer some practice.

So, we decided to practice patrolling for an afternoon (which I'm sure is the same amount of time the ground forces do). We were trying to get from point A to point B, while on the lookout for IEDs and telltale signs of enemy activity. One of our fearless leaders was a lieutenant colonel scientist, and he was leading the patrol behind us. As we strolled down the gravel road, under the baking Texas sun, in our full gear, we heard the trainers asking politely, "Sir, what are you doing?" I looked back to see what the commotion was all about, and here was this guy, off the road, rooting through a garbage dumpster. His weapon was slung over his back, and the rest of his patrol looked on uncomfortably.

"I'm looking for IEDs, of course," came the cheerful reply.

"Sir, you don't go *looking* for them; you try to *avoid* them. If you manage to spot them in the course of a patrol, you note them and call the experts. Which, respectfully, is not you."

"Oh."

But we continued patrolling, dropping to the ground, and calling out "contact right" or "contact left" or "hey, what did the guy say?" as the trainers called out scenarios. Now, that's not to say some of us didn't know what we were doing; we had a couple of USAF cops with us. I barely saw their faces though; I mostly saw the tops of their helmets, as they were mostly looking down, shaking their heads in disbelief. There was an undercurrent of seriousness to the exercise, but it did seem a little silly. None of us was going to any job that required, even slightly, leading or participating in a patrol. But the USAF wanted to train us on stuff, so by God, we were going to get trained on stuff. And they heard that there was patrolling going on, and so we should do that.

When the USAF doesn't know what to do, it settles for making you miserable. For instance, the compound was spread out with several rows of tents about one hundred yards from the main metal buildings that we held classes in. As the stormy season hit in Texas, on a few nights, rain and lightning blew through. The powers that be decided that the lightning was so bad that we all had to crowd into the classrooms in the Quonset huts for the evening. And of course, in order to do that, we had to grab our metal-framed cots and carry them over our heads through the one hundred yards of trees and lightning to the metal-framed huts. Benjamin Franklin was a piker when it came to our electrical experimentation. We all arrived at the hut, got everything laid out, and an hour later, we were told to tromp back, as the storm had passed. Looking back, I saw this line of bobbing aluminum cots, winding their way through a downpour in the pitch black, illuminated not only by the tiny lights folks had with them, but the flashbulbs of lightning. It looked like nothing so much as ants stealing your patio furniture. The next night was a repeat, up to the point where they told us to return home again, but we mutinied and stayed through the night. There were a lot of positives that came out of the camp, though. For one, we never went anywhere without our weapons, and that was a good primer for later in Iraq. We also became very familiar with the Porta-Potties and the things that could lurk in there, waiting for a tasty butt cheek to show. We all drank from a water buffalo and ate MREs, along with a catered mess, which wasn't too bad. But it was most effective in easing those of us not used to handling guns (e.g., the grenade guy) a jumpstart before we had to do it for real.

We got a jumpstart on our driving skills as well. We would all pile into the HMMVs and practice convoy driving and snatching disabled vehicles. That entailed roaring up beside the disabled vehicle, grabbing either the stowed tow rope or the metal tow bar, jumping into the seat of the disabled vehicle, and getting yanked out of the threat area. Here I discovered the opportunity to have a little more fun.

After doing it a few times in the heat of the day, in full body armor, although no ammo or anything, some of the folks were getting cranky. There was one technical sergeant, in particular, who was prone to hissy fits and had already bloodied an E-8 SMSgt's (Senior Master Sergeant) forehead by dropping the butt of his M4 on his noggin while performing an extraction. The Senior laughed it off, but this young man really got rattled. The TSgt was in his early thirties, round, ruddy faced, and potbellied. And he was really having a tough time. He was out of shape anyway, and the heat and stress were really getting to him. He was likeable, but his light bulb body gave no confidence in his physical abilities, which seemed to be maxed out just carrying all the gear. This led to irritation; he seemed to be about ready to explode. The guy just wouldn't stop complaining and whining about the conditions, the stupid instruction, the stupid this, and stupid that. His ruddy face was flushed, with his official Harry Potter glasses askew, perched on his sweaty nose. Everyone knows someone like that, I suppose. Like a porcupine, he was prickly. And everyone knows what you do when you see a porcupine; you poke it with a stick.

So I took it upon myself to help "be" the stick. He jumped in the "extraction" vehicle I was piloting. He was supposed to ride shotgun in the HMMV, while I roared up and skidded to a stop; then he would leap out, hook up the tow strap, and jump in the disabled HMMV, and I would yank him down the road. That was the plan. I had helped to prep the disabled HMMV by adjusting the seat. Under the watchful eyes of the instructors, I carefully adjusted the driver's seat all the way up, so that there was only about twelve inches between the steering wheel and the seat itself. Having helpfully prepared the way for my erstwhile comrade, I walked back to the rescue vehicle, idling in the heat. I hopped in, hit the gas, and roared up to the starting point of the exercise. The TSgt was still breathing heavily from the last excursion, but I pumped him up, telling him that we were going to set a new record for the day. Then, I got the signal from the instructors that the exercise was about to commence.

Upon the go signal, I punched the throttle, and the HMMV lurched forward, careening toward the disabled vehicle. Upon arriving at the scene of the pretend carnage, I hit all the right signals, beeping the horn as I blew by the disabled vehicle, grinding to a stop a good twenty-five yards past the casualties. I looked over, dust billowing into the HMMV, settling on to us, and shouted, "Go go go go!" He hunched his shoulders, took a deep breath, and with an explosive chuff, kicked the door open and leaped out.

"Aw, shit!" He had seen how far I had overshot. So I jammed the vehicle into reverse and started pacing him back into the billowing clouds of *cummulo dustus* toward the disabled vehicle. He was puffing through the roiling clouds of dirt, cursing every step, as we drew closer to the incident. By now, the rivers of sweat had turned into muddy tracks, like he was crying ink. The tears of a clown, indeed. I got into position and skidded to a halt, while he ran back to wrestle the snatch rope out of the front bumper. The M-16 rifle slung over his shoulder continued to fall off of his shoulder, interfering with the manhandling of the rope. I stole a glance toward the onlookers and noticed that everyone was laughing their fannies off. But the rumbling of the HMMV engine, boosted by me revving it, drowned out the laughter, so the young man struggling with, well, everything, didn't hear it. He was too busy fighting with the M-16. Which in turn was fighting with the snatch rope.

As this epic battle progressed, I was doing everything I could to help. Mostly by shouting "Hurry! Hurry!" and romping on the throttle, which produced not only noise, but a thick black smoke that mixed with the epic amounts of dust swirling between the two vehicles. I'm sure this helped in some way. He finally got the snatch rope in place, and as I tightened up the slack in the ropes, he sprinted (for him) around the driver's side door, which hung open, propped there by the ever helpful instructors. He gathered himself for a mighty leap into the seat of the HMMV, envisioning, no doubt, a triumphant landing in the dusty seat followed by a tremendous yank, rolling away from the cheering throngs. Reality intruded about midway into that sequence as he launched himself at the door opening like a fat kid at a dropped ice cream cone. He arced gracefully through the air, the Stay Puft Marshmallow Man draped in body armor and an M-16 soaring into the HMMV. And came to an abrupt halt halfway in, jammed in between the seat and steering wheel like Pooh in his hole after a honey binge.

I couldn't believe it. It was better than I had imagined: the poor guy was stuck at about the chest, his torso almost horizontal, but his lower half pistoning helplessly, his boots scrabbling at the gravel but failing to propel him forward. Of course, with his arms pinned, he couldn't go back either. So he was stuck. Although I couldn't hear, the onlookers stood swaying in the heat, clutching their stomachs in laughter. But I did hear the TSgt scream, "Godd——itt!" and then cut loose with all the other dirty words he knew. Which were many. One of the instructors grabbed him by the vest and yanked him out. His head swiveled around on his tiny neck, like a very angry lollipop, glaring at the assembled observers; then he tried again to wedge himself back into the rig. Since he hadn't adjusted anything, it was the same net effect, only slower. And funnier. In a series of short jerks, he was able to squeeze himself about a third of the way into the seat. He was totally focused on getting in the seat and was overlooking the obvious solution of adjusting it. Just wiggling and wiggling, trying to get into the seat. Like watching the birth of a huge, lumpy baby, only in reverse.

Finally, I shouted out to adjust the seat, and he squirted right in. A great cheer went throughout the adoring throng, as we were ready for the "snatch" portion exercise. Once in, however, he just sat there, breathing heavily, head down, hands in lap. The dirt and dust were flitting throughout the cab of the vehicle, sparkling in the sunlight. Like a thousand little similes glowing in a metaphor. Everything seemed to be muted and restful. Until I hit the end of the tow rope.

The disabled vehicle jerked forward into the cloud of black smoke left by the intense acceleration. Just before he entered the dark, roiling mass, I saw his hands fly up by his helmet, as everything reacted to Newton's law. A body at rest tends to get the crap jerked out of it when yanked by a HMMV driven by a malevolent pilot. Or something. The position of his hands meant that they weren't on the wheel, so I let off the gas, and sure enough, the snout of the HMMV poked through the smoke so I could see the occupant, hands now grasping the wheel, dirt-streaked face carved into a grimace, hunched over the wheel like a vulture gripping a particular tasty piece of carrion.

I lurched to a stop; the tow rope bunched up in front of the disabled vehicle, and it rolled forward to a stop. In the cab of the running HMMV, I couldn't hear the onlookers, but it was evident that they were dying laughing. I shut the machine off and walked back to the disabled vehicle, eyes locked on the TSgt, who, by now, had his helmeted head down, exhausted. I twisted the handle down to unlock the door and looked at the young man. "We need to talk."

We ended up finding a place to chat while other exercises continued. I explained that there would be a lot of times when stuff would really hit

the fan, and there were a lot of folks, both young enlisted and young officers, who would be looking to him for guidance, especially amid chaos. No
tantrums. Man up. I let him know that I had never seen any NCO act that
way. The thing that an officer looks for in the midst of chaos, is a solid
NCO. A good officer and solid NCO make an unbeatable team. I ended
the conversation then went to the senior master sergeant who was fuming
angry at the guy.

He was a Security Forces NCO who really had his stuff together; he
mentored all of us all the way through the training. He was also the guy
that Harry Potter had thumped on the head with the stock of his M-16. I
really loved this guy—a tiny, mustachioed, ornery spider monkey of a man.
Although, in truth, I really don't know how ornery spider monkeys get.
Bob was a quintessential NCO and a total pro at his job. I let him know
that I'd already talked to the kid and suggested that he keep that in mind
as he tore him a new fanny. He went steaming off and took a walk with the
technical sergeant. I think it took, as we didn't have any more problems
with the guy, and later, in Iraq, he turned in a solid performance.

The bottom line in the training that we endured was that it was not at
all about killing and warfare. In fact, very little of it was devoted to anything offensive: we barely got to even shoot our weapons. But we did get a
day with our M-4s, and I had a ball doing that, as it was the first time I had
ever used a red-dot sight. A really amazing piece of technology, it's a sight
that has a holographic dot in the scope. I don't know how they do it, but
the dot is immune to parallax, the thing that happens when you shut one
eye, then the other, causing whatever you're looking at to jump back and
forth. So you shoot this thing with both eyes open, keeping your peripheral
vision intact. Put the dot on target and squeeze the trigger. Point and click.
But that wasn't the only fun part.

My firing buddy was hilarious. An old prior-enlisted (like me) captain,
Gordo was one of the funniest guys I'd ever met. He was fairly short, so
I could just see the top of his helmet in the firing pit next to me on the
line. His Southern drawl hid his sharp intelligence, and his sense of humor
served in good stead not only in training, but later in Iraq as well. We got
along great. But he was having a little trouble.

He was sort of short, but his body armor was sort of tall. And his helmet, although technically the right size, just seemed too big, so there was
a lot of extraneous movement every time he would try to get into any sort

of firing position. The end result was that he looked like he was lying on an ant hill; he would shoot, adjust, shoot, adjust, adjust, adjust. It was little better when we got into the prepared holes. Since we were on an army course, they were first rate—concrete bunkers with built-in firing steps. Built for sort a tall folks. So, most of what I saw was a wobbly helmet bobbing up over the top, loosing off a few rounds, and sinking back down, only to reappear a few seconds later and repeat. It could have been strategy, but I don't think so.

The weapon that he was issued was a GAU-5, an old version of the M-16 that offered full-auto firing. Everyone else had three modes: safe, single, and burst. Safe meant no firing, single meant one round at every trigger pull, and burst shot three rounds for every trigger pull. Gordo's weapon had safe, single, and "Katy bar the door" (full auto). Gordo really had to be careful when pulling the trigger, lest he let loose all thirty rounds in the clip. At the same time, the rest of us were content with three rounds at a time. The range officers were constantly hovering around his bunker, "helping" him.

The best position was the prone position, where the targets popped up at fifty, one hundred, and two hundred yards. So, Gordo lay down, his grown-up armor forcing the too-big helmet down over his eyes—by "eyes," I mean face. So this particular drill went like this. His body armor collar forced the back end of his helmet up, pushing the front end down over his nose. So he would arc his head back as far as it could go, smash the collar down, and tuck the back of the helmet under it. He could only stay in this position for a few seconds as the equipment struggled to return to its rightful shape. The slightest movement and it all sprung back, turning him into a turtle with a too-big shell.

Gordo would get everything balanced just so; the target would pop up, and he would squeeze off a round, the jolt of which would set the armor free. Immediately, he was covered by his shell, virtually invisible, also blind. Then he would have to reposition and repeat, by which time the target had cycled and was back down. He quickly got frustrated, and so, in a move that generated enough cool points to last the rest of the training cycle, he made a fateful decision. He flicked the selection lever to full auto.

Now watching him became even better; he went through the same pregame routine, but when he pulled the trigger, even though he immediately retreated into his armored shell, his weapon let loose with a *braaaaaaap* and sent bullets downrange. He usually got the first couple of rounds on target, but the next several ended up sending up gouts of dirt farther down the field, sometimes impacting next to the downrange targets. I was giggling my fanny off; thank goodness I wasn't shooting at this time. On the first occurrence, the range officers' (air force NCOs) heads perked up, noting the more-than-three-round burst coming from my section of the field.

Meanwhile, Gordo had reappeared from his armored shell and readied himself for another fusillade. The unfortunate target popped up, menacingly preparing to advance on our position from one hundred yards, so Gordo responded by shredding the vegetation around it, denying it cover I suppose, so someone who could see could actually shoot the target. As the ten rounds leaped from the gun to bury themselves in random patches of earth (any one of which could be hiding an insurgent), I saw that the range officers had now fixated on our own little Middle-Aged Mutant Ninja Turtle, had gathered in a pack, and were heading for Gordo. By the time the next target had been narrowly and repeatedly missed, the NCOs were all standing over this little captain, just shaking their heads. Range officers cannot afford a sense of humor, but these guys were sorely tested.

I did hear something about "suppressive fire."

That was the only weapons firing that we did in the entire two weeks, because the aim of the course, in spite of its name, was really not about "combat" as much as relationships. As almost all of us were going to the Coalition Air Force Transition Team, it was about interacting with the Iraqis. Some were going to Afghanistan, so they had some more ancillary training before they went. But the training encompassed first aid and buddy care (where we actually stuck each other with needles; it was a bloodbath), how to talk and act around the Iraqis, and getting comfortable with various weapons. That's not to say that they neglected any combat training; there was the aforementioned patrolling and range work, but a large part of the training was devoted to the connecting of people in order to get the end state—a peaceful Iraq, one person at a time.

As the training drew to a close, the cadre actually had arranged a surprise visit from a couple of young Iraqi officers who were in the country for training. It was then that I first understood the kind of danger these young people and their families were courting for choosing the side of civilization in their home country. It seemed to me that there was a lot of secrecy associated with the visit, as I overhead their minders discussing routing home.

Again, I was surprised that there were dangers, even here in the United States, for these young men. They came in part to say thank you and also to give us a final prep as to the societal conditions on the ground. They wanted to personally thank us for what we (the United States) were doing and were about to do. So we met these two fine young men.

Abdul and Malik were part of an effort that brought screened members of the Iraqi military to the United States for training and, frankly, exposure to West. A great deal for the Iraqis, except for the fact that they became hunted when they returned. For the barbarians we were fighting, the successful return of these people, who had actually been to the great Satan and returned with very positive experiences, was a most dangerous weapon, aimed at the heart of their lies and hatred. They were very matter-of-fact about the chances that they stood upon return. Knowing that the United States couldn't be everywhere, they would be exposed and vulnerable until the situation resolved itself in Iraq. This hit home as they relayed the story of an officer who came to the United States and did very well in all the training, really getting it. Upon return to Iraq, however, he was discovered as that highest order of traitor—an educated, Western-friendly military man. He was hunted down and executed. It was only later, in Iraq, that I learned the rest of that horrible story.

This was the kind of threat that Abdul and Malik were going to be operating under; a daily guessing game where their lies and deceptions had to keep suspicion off of their activities, or they and their families would pay, in the most final fashion. Exactly like the heartache that Alec Baldwin and the Dixie Chicks had to live under in George Bush's America. But here they were, and they made sure that we knew that they were under no illusions about what they were going back to. As they were talking, Malik looked at Abdul, and they paused for a moment.

"We think that at least one of us will make it," he burst out enthusiastically. Abdul blushed, adding that they really both hoped to live, so it wasn't that they wanted to die or anything, but they were trying to be realistic. But it seemed like they really were just being matter-of-fact about the whole thing.

Some of their talk focused on the cultural differences between the Arab and Western worlds, for instance man-kissing. To me, it's always been a bit of a contradiction. Many men in that part of the world strive to be almost hypermasculine, backed by their religion. But after a lot of chest pounding and brandishing of knives or guns, the manly man would think nothing of gently holding hands with another dude as they walk along. And a standard greeting is an exchange of kisses (on the cheek, thank you; I'll never make that mistake again). Sincere ones, too. They look like those fake Hollywood kiss-kiss things you see, but these kisses are fraught with meaning. It would, later, become my honor to receive several man-kisses, but at this stage, it was still a little "Queer Eye for the Really Straight Guy."

The speeches became pretty informal, and the guys wanted a volunteer (victim) to receive the inaugural man-kiss. I was pointed out as a perfect candidate. I was *pointed out*. Just to make that clear. I stood up to advance my culture, straightened my shoulders, and made a dive for the guy's mouth. Malik saw my aim point and wrenched his head away, narrowly averting a clash of civilizations. Our lips hit each other's cheeks, as they are supposed to do, and then the other, this time under Malik's firm guidance. It was a success. I was blushing profusely and was glad it was over. Until Abdul started his bomb run. This time it went much smoother, and the kissing went off without a hitch.

Until Bob showed up. The senior master sergeant came flying out of nowhere, clad only in his PT gear, which consisted of thin (too thin) shorts and a T-shirt. He came screaming in, leaped into the air like a spider monkey, and landed on my hip, wrapping his scrawny legs about my waist. He then proceeded to man-kiss the hell out of me. Mustache and all.

It was time to leave.

9

NICE TO SEE YOU TOO

The C-17 belly was dark, only illuminated by the small windows and the persistent green light usually used for paratroops. Which we were not. In this case, it meant that we were approaching Baghdad International Airport. Most of us were sleeping, having endured about three days of travelling to get to Al Udeid, where we got on a C-17 headed for Baghdad. A few miles out, the light turned red, indicating that we should get our gear on. That was like wrestling one hundred of your best friends in a tub of molasses filled with large dinner plates. In a sauna. The C-17 can be configured for about one hundred very friendly troops, or about fifty people who don't like each other very much. I'm sure we had over one hundred people on the flight. We had depressurized, and the A/C couldn't keep up. So it began to be very warm in the belly. As the red light came on, there was this slow-motion thrashing about, in airline seats, of fairly large, sweaty men (and women!) struggling to put on these bulky vests and helmets in preparation for landing.

The vests themselves weighed about twenty pounds, even without anything in them. They were unwieldy, to say the least. There were two ceramic plates, each, depending on the size of the vest, just large enough to make you realize how much of you is *not* covered by armor. In my case, each plate was about fourteen inches tall and probably twelve or so wide. So, those went into pockets in the front and rear of the vest (later models had further protection on the sides too). This left about five feet of me not covered by armor, some parts of which I'm quite fond of. Then we had the added benefit of the gear and helmets, plus whatever carry-ons we had. So, we were all trying to strap into the tiny airline seats and trying to figure out how to find the seatbelt buckles, buried somewhere under all that gear. While searching for mine, I accidently became way too familiar with the staff sergeant next to me. I apologized and decided to risk whatever dire consequences awaited those of us who were not strapped in.

The aircraft started its tactical approach into the airport, which included some tighter turns than most folks were used to. I had been a tactics officer, so I wasn't surprised at the maneuvering, tracking along in my head as we went through the twists and turns and rapid descents. But like most pilots, I hate riding in the back. Some of my companions didn't enjoy the maneuvering at all, and coupled with the heat, I really expected to see some liquid yawns. Eventually the twisting and turning stopped, and the aircraft established itself on short final. The loadmasters were in their positions to spot Man Portable Air Defense missiles (MANPADS), but their efforts were not rewarded, as we made it down without incident. The tires hit the runway with a thump, and that marvelous machine rolled to a stop.

The ramps dropped, and we stepped into the liquid heat of July in Baghdad. I immediately started melting but shuffled into the line, dragging too many bags and guns and everything onto the concrete. We were hustled off of the ramp, as they had been hit by rockets the preceding couple of days and were trying to get everyone into cover. The standard procedures then took over; folks were culled out by their owning organizations. Some army guys got peeled off, then some of the navy folks, some civilians, and as our ever-shrinking group got closer to the blessed air conditioning of the building, a couple of air force units took the people they were expecting, so our bunch was whittled down to about thirty folks. While walking to the shimmering, white metal, prefab buildings, I looked around, and evidence of our efforts in the war was everywhere.

There were several bunkers, each with evidence of newer repairs, Americans living and working in aircraft shelters that had been bombed by the Americans that had come before and evicted the previous tenants. There were some parts of Iraqi aircraft around that had been discarded from the old air force; all the way across the ramp, there were probably fifteen or so commercial aircraft, including a 747, and Russian transport aircraft just sitting in the dirt. In no particular order, just aircraft smashed into and under each other in various states of disrepair. That's what happens when that guy with the orange wands is not there to guide you into the gate when you fly commercial.

We ended up dumping our gear in the dust and shuffling onto the benches that filled the small building we had navigated to. Our sponsor came and started calling out names and who was going where. By and large, I was with many of the folks that I had attended Camp Bullis with. One by one these folks were called; all were to be assigned to Coalition Air Force Training Team (CAFTT) in some capacity. Gordo, of full-auto fame, would be heading way up north to be a maintenance advisor at Kirkuk. The little lieutenant colonel with the huge laugh, Chuck would be staying here. Some were to be staff, performing the normal functions of a headquarters, and some of us would be advisors, interacting with the Iraqis on a daily basis. My name was called; I would be staying at Camp Victory as the advisor to the Iraqi air force training command (A7).

That was great news for me, because, darn it, if I was going to be in a combat zone being rocketed or mortared or shot at, I didn't want to get hit while creating a Powerpoint presentation on the effectiveness of changing font sizes on the war effort. Or while on the toilet. About the same thing really, except that work on the toilet is more productive than work on PowerPoint. So I was pretty happy to be going to the main mission. By luck, it also kept us out of the headquarters staff, as they were in the Green Zone, close to the embassy, and under constant mortars and rockets, while we would be at Camp Victory, a giant sprawling encampment about ten miles away.

They finished up the in-processing and got us settled in for the night, about forty of us in a tent. There was a Camp Bullis reunion again, with a lot of familiar faces. At that point a truck came around and dropped off the rest of our bags. Mine consisted of a couple C bags (about two feet by two feet by three feet), an A bag (a cylindrical bag about four feet long, diameter of about eighteen inches), and a regular midsized piece of luggage. They had mostly military gear in them, changes of uniform, chemical warfare stuff, quite a few books, and some personal gear. It was pretty heavy, but my computer and stuff had also made it through, so I was pretty happy to get it all unloaded. Soon enough, there were piles of gear at the end of each cot all the way down the tent. There was a work party of third country nationals (TCNs) refilling the sandbag berms that were about four feet high surrounding the tents, but nothing else seemed to be going on.

No one really knew what to expect, but so far, it was a pretty normal deployment for me. Except for a couple of pillars of smoke that were building on the horizon. Car bombs. So that was unusual. But the heat was Middle East standard, which is "standing on the top rack on broil while someone throws sand in your face" hot. The only thing to do was to try to get used to the idea of the heat, not to try to stay cool. So we hung out in the tent most of the time; we would only be staying until the billeting folks figured out a trailer for us to stay in. Because they had to match you up with someone of similar rank, it might be a few days in this temp tent or rather quick—it just depended on your rank. But most of us were on the same schedule and were in the same unit, so it wasn't a big deal. A couple of other folks came in, in transit from somewhere, but only stayed for one night.

I got lucky; my number came up fairly soon. I only ended up staying two nights, as a vacancy opened up in the trailers about half a mile away. I was pretty excited and wanted to get settled in; plus I had tormented my tentmates enough. I already mentioned my penchant for smart-assedness. One of the folks that we were replacing, a captain named Jesse, came by with a pickup and offered to assist me in moving my stuff. I put on my vest and helmet and then went to grab one of my A bags. I started to lift it and stopped. Or was stopped. The damn thing weighed a ton. I couldn't believe that I had packed so much crap and that I had already forgotten how heavy it was. But, being a man, I certainly wasn't going to let the rest of the guys see my pain. So I gritted my teeth and hefted the bag up, sweat immediately beading up on my forehead as I staggered to the plywood door. Jesse held it open for me, and I passed through, toward the pickup idling in the dust, actually feeling the canvas straps of the bag lengthening my fingers as I went.

I got to the truck, dropping the bag with a thud. I repositioned with both hands, and with a spine-compressing heave, I got it into the truck.

After I stopped crying, I composed myself and went back inside to repeat, sweating like a Democrat on a witness stand. On the third trip, Jesse grabbed the last one and immediately went through all the same emotions that I had. The rest of the tent was strangely silent, as the guys all lounged around in various stages of disinterest. But Jesse let me know in no uncertain terms what an extraordinary packer (so to speak) he thought I was. But he gamely dragged the overstuffed bag to the now groaning truck and wrestled it inside the bed. I followed the bag, and we went bouncing across the compound.

The compound I was headed to was about ten acres of rutted dust, covered by gravel. And rows of trailers. The trailers that we stayed in were like shipping containers, about thirty feet long, divided in half, then subdivided, so each half had two folks in it. For some of the enlisted, there were three in each half. But to call them shipping containers implies a certain amount of strength. There wasn't. They were a thin, metal-walled sandwich of foam. Basically to keep the heat out. You could puncture it with a ball point pen. So my abode would be a garden shed with a roommate. I was immensely grateful as I knew that many folks were stuffed in tents and other arrangements. Some had it better, some had it worse, but the American military has an innate ability to make anything home.

Jesse homed in on my trailer, 14C, and backed the truck in. My roommate wasn't there, so we just started to unload my gear, going through the same pain, except this time Jesse smartened up by deciding his task was getting the bags from the middle of the truck bed to the back of the truck bed, so I could more easily unload it and carry it the twenty feet to the door, then up the four wooden steps to my room. Sure enough, after I staggered back, there he would be, big smile on his face, my outrageously heavy bag sitting ominously on the tailgate. The bag of Damocles. Sweat was actually spurting from my head now, like a punctured water balloon (many would say that is an apt description). Thank goodness the heat vaporized the sweat upon exit, so I merely looked like Thomas the Tank Engine, dressed in a funny greenish suit, puffing back and forth between the truck and the trailer. Eventually, I got all of my belongings into the trailer, thanked Jesse, staggered back inside, peeled off my sopping blouse (no, not a girl shirt—the outer garment in a military uniform; but a lovely lace thing would've been much cooler, thanks), and collapsed wetly onto the stained, dusty mattress.

So, Baghdad in July; and this was going to be my home for the next year or so. A dim fluorescent light hung directly over two wall lockers (made of stuff that wished it could be cheap particle board) set up in the middle of the floor, which created a wall for a smidge of privacy. A fine, tan dirt (a substance more substantial than dust) coated everything and made everything sand-in-your-swimsuit gritty. The air conditioner was stuck in the wall, positioned above the wall locker divider, where it sent small dirt devils scampering over the top of the conjoined wall lockers. It had seen better days; the front sagged tiredly off the case, and the motor chuffed along like Chitty Chitty Bang Bang with emphysema. The small army of dirt devils carried the cool air along the filthy top of the divider, to spill into each side, carrying a stale, hot scent with it.

The carpet was layers of several parts of old rugs, kind of like a geological dig, where the more layers I peeled back, the more I revealed the lives of those who had lived here before me. Apparently, they were all filthy. So I took a deep, albeit guarded, breath and decided to get settled in. I grabbed the nearest A bag and, with my last bit of strength, dragged it toward me. I opened up the flap, grabbed the heavy metal zipper, and ripped it down, exposing a torn plastic shopping bag. I didn't remember packing anything like that; I groaned. After all that effort, I had grabbed the wrong bag.

But on further inspection, I found my nametag, so that couldn't be it. I walked over to another of my bags, verified the tag, and ripped it open. And found another torn shopping bag. Now, I'm no Encyclopedia Brown, but something was amiss. I gingerly opened up the shopping bag. Apparently, I had been shopping for sand. Some—that is, all—of my tent-mates had put some of the sandbags from the wall around our tent in my bags. About four for each bag, which added about one hundred pounds per bag. I burst out laughing. Now I truly had a mission. Find out who did this and make them pay. A lot.

After I unloaded an entire desert ecosystem out of my bags, I looked around the trailer and started to put all my belongings away. It was then that I noticed the bullet hole through the trailer, both sides, about chest high. It was thoughtfully filled in with silicone to keep the larger bugs out. I was starting to get an inkling as to the randomness of death here. I would get the full picture later. I sat and thought a bit, the A/C unit rattling softly in the background, blowing slightly cooled dirt devils down my filthy neck.

So here I was, in Baghdad, Iraq.

This was one of the situations that had occurred to me several times in my career. I found myself in the epicenter of a major happening on the world stage. Obviously, there were thousands of others, doing far more dangerous work—running convoys, providing security, patrolling—but I was going to play a part too. Whatever schemes the politicians and their cronies come up with, the implementation always comes down to the individuals in the field. Like me. Like Jesse. Like whichever bastards had filled up my luggage with sand. And like them, I was going to do my level best. I wasn't sure how I would react when I was shot at. I wasn't sure how I would interact with the Iraqis, and I wasn't sure exactly what I was supposed to be interacting with them about. But I was sure about this. The flag on my uniform would not be sullied by any action I might take here. Whatever happened, I would make sure that no one would think less of the United States because of me. Some may call that simpleminded. Some may not be proud of their country; indeed, some may even say that it's " a country that is 'just downright mean,' we are 'guided by fear,' we're a nation of cynics, sloths, and complacents." [4]

But they don't know what I know. They don't know who I know.

One of the people that I would soon get to know was my group commander. We all had to get our in-brief to welcome us in and discuss the rules of engagement for our tour. This was something that happened in every deployment I'd ever been on, but this one would be a little different. We would have to be bussed over to the Green Zone from Victory in an up-armored RV, right out of *Stripes*.

It was called a Rhino, and it was piloted by a couple of army guys. It ran like a little bus line. There were three runs a day, and we were signed up a couple of days before. The time was classified, so the best you could ask for was morning, noon, or night. The night before, a classified message would be released, and you'd find out your specific times. Then you showed up fifteen minutes earlier in order to process and load.

You could not load unless you were fully dressed out, including vest, helmet, gloves, goggles, and throat protectors. There were a couple of other pieces of gear that were designed after the vest, in response to the emerging

---

4 Lauren Collins March 10, 2008. The Other Obama. March 10, 2008. http://www. newyorker.com/reporting/2008/03/10/080310fa_fact_collins?currentPage=all (accessed June 24, 2012).

improvised explosive device (IED) threat. The deltoid armor protection (DAPs) were basically layers of Kevlar that were attached with Velcro into place on your shoulder, protecting from the outer shoulder to outer elbow; and another piece, side armor protection (SAPs) went inside the vest and protected your sides, which the armored plates didn't do. These added a few pounds and eliminated any possible cooling from ambient air.

So, about fifteen of us mustered into the parking lot in the July midafternoon sun. It was about 115 degrees, but it was a dry heat, so that made it seem like a balmy 114. In short order, I was drenched, actually feeling the sweat soaking through my pants, making for interesting stains on my uniform. I wasn't the only one though; all of us were melting, one bead of sweat at a time. A herd of incontinent turtles waiting for a bus. The first we saw of the Rhino were the two HMMVs that preceded it in the convoy. They were the gun trucks, each sporting a machine gun, either the big M2 .50 caliber or the smaller M240. Although, to me, there is really no such thing as a "small" machine gun. The HMMVs came swooping in to the parking lot, then a couple of Rhinos, then some more gun trucks. The whole procession rolled smartly to a stop; the heavily armored doors creaked open, and about twenty-five sweaty, dirty, tired-looking people of various status came out. There were of course quite a few army folks, and additionally navy and marine corps personnel, civilians (appropriately covered in armor), and British armed forces came staggering off the bus.

The crews were soaked as well. The troops on the gun trucks dismounted, took off their copious armor, and began stretching backs, limbering up stiffened joints, and trying to grab some shade. The ubiquitous water bottles were out, and the soon-to-be-familiar crackle, as they were finished and crushed, began to echo across the compound. The unrelenting heat had pounded them through the inadequate A/C units, which failed to halt the slow cooking in the crew compartments. The men and women in those turrets kept watch over their charges, the two slow, vulnerable Rhinos, filled with people they didn't know, in spite of the searing heat. The primary targets of any sniper and most exposed to IED shrapnel of any crewmember—they maintained second-by-second vigilance over all of Route Irish, one of the most dangerous thoroughfares in Iraq.

After a short respite, the crew brought out a clipboard and started shouting out the names of the folks that made the list, as oftentimes there were too many people to fit on the Rhinos, so they would be bumped.

We grabbed all our gear (checking to make sure there were no stowaway sandbags) and shuffled into a pile by the door. After my name was called, I snapped my chinstrap and got onto the Rhino. It was absolutely stifling inside and full of dirt and dust. There were about twenty-four seats in the vehicle, two columns of two seats. I wasn't sure where to sit, but I used a seating methodology that I'd never considered before.

I tried to consider the odds of getting hit by either an IED or a rocket-propelled grenade (RPG) and where I wanted to be sitting in the event of either one. I thought it more likely to be an IED attack, as in this heavily patrolled area, it would be harder to set up an RPG ambush; plus there was the proximity to the event for the bad guy. You can be nicely concealed for an IED attack, but if you shoot an RPG, you're left standing with a smoking pipe on your shoulder, not too far from the folks you just shot at. And if those guys are US Army or Marines, you don't have long to contemplate the tentative nature of your position. So, in the case of an IED, I had some more decisions to make. Should I be on the inside left row of the bus, as that would be the side farthest from the blast? Not if we were hit by an explosively formed projectile (EFP), as that really scatters after it hits the target; the farther away I was from the wall, the greater the chance to get shredded as the shrapnel and super-heated metal tore through the cabin. The fragments come out in a cone from the point of impact, so farther is not necessarily better, especially since the cabin was only about six feet wide.

If we got hit by a standard artillery shell or pile of explosives, then the farther away, the better. But I figured with all the help the Iranians were giving the insurgents in EFP tech, we would probably get hit by that. I also calculated the forward or aft position, but I had no way of knowing whether the triggering device would be manual or another method. So that placed the expertise of the trigger man in the equation. A good one will trigger the bomb at the right time, gutting the middle; whereas someone who hasn't had the necessary job training will hit at the extreme aft or forward, as his timing would be off. But the army was doing a great job of thinning the ranks of the bad guys, so I was going to bet on a new-bie. I collapsed onto a seat on the left side, toward the middle.

After everyone loaded up, a young army private jumped into the driver's seat, whirling his body armor on in a fashion that spoke of his familiarity with the process. His supervisor stepped onto the bus, spoke a few words to him concerning the latest intel updates, and became a flight attendant on the world's worst airline.

"Ladies and gentlemen, if you could all get seated, please; welcome to the Rhino. I am Specialist Franks. Transit time for this run should be around forty minutes. In the event of contact, this vehicle will be the casualty collection point (CCP) for the convoy. Can I have two strong volunteers for stretcher duty?"

Violating a long military tradition, I raised my hand to volunteer, as did a colonel toward the back.

"Okay, you and you," he said, pointing his dirty finger at me and my new stretcher buddy. "There are medical kits at the fore and aft of the vehicle; use those and not your personal med kits."

He turned his attention back to the captive audience.

"If we are hit, exit though the door on the side or in the rear, whichever is the farthest from the contact side. If we are on our side, you can utilize the door in the roof by turning the two handles inward and pushing outward on the door."

No mention of *why* we would be on our side.

"If the roof exit faces the contact side, it may not be the best exit, so consider the rear exit. Form up on the noncontact side, provide suppressive fire, and wait for rescue. The gun trucks will establish a perimeter; follow their direction. Fire extinguishers are located here and here in case of fire. There are spare arm and rib protectors in the overhead, and you must have them installed. You will not be required to put on your goggles and gloves until we go red passing the checkpoint. Please remember to wear your throat protectors."

This orientation was way better than just pointing out the exits and demonstrating the complexities of the belt buckle. So, we all squished into the seats, and after a couple of minutes the truck commander (TC) got confirmation that the route was green. Good to go. The young driver gamely tried to lever the big vehicle into gear and, after a significant amount of grinding and lurching, got us moving. The HMMVs accelerated ahead, the gun barrels pointed skyward. Then the two lumbering Rhinos, followed by the two other HMMVs. We twisted and turned through the small roads, making our way to the perimeter gate. As we exited the base, we all put clips in our weapons, put rounds in the chambers, and put on our eye protection. Then, just like that, we were outside the wire.

Now, I know that there were a lot more dangerous places to be in Iraq, in July of 2007. There were countless army and marine troops scattered all over the country, taking huge risks day in and day out, but this was pretty good for me. I started going through all the actions I would take if we got hit in the front or in the back or flipped on the side; just like in pilot training, I was chair flying the actions that would keep me and my buddies alive in the event of, well, an event. The bus twisted and turned, accelerating and decelerating, on and off of roads, in and out of the concrete barriers that were everywhere.

From my vantage point, I could hear the radio transmissions over the convoy net, the constant information flow washing from the front to the rear, calling out suspicious activities or just opportunities for mayhem that kept cropping up.

"Vehicle on overpass, passing right to left...vehicle right side, stopped...two individuals, left side, ten o'clock."

Each callout was a possible ambush. But mostly, since 95 percent of the population was friendly, the calls identified friendly civilians. I saw several vehicles filled with families, driving the opposite way, as the barrels of at least two machine guns tracked slightly behind them. I was in bunker down mode. There wasn't much I could do in the event of an attack. Just take it and hope I was functional enough to repel any further attack. But the young men and women in the turrets—they were responsible for keeping the attack from happening. They were keyed to make those split-second decisions with lifelong consequences every day, all day. I couldn't imagine the intensity of thought for responsibility like that. And they were constantly reacting to the new information passed over the net.

There seemed to be only one voice that floated out of the radio speaker, but all the others in the convoy reacted to it. I could see two heads swivel as one when "vehicle left" came out. The second and third HMMV gunners would cover that aspect and then immediately snap to the next callout. It was an amazing display of synchronization and discipline. And all under an unrelenting sun.

Meanwhile, inside the bus, it was a rolling, dirty sauna, and I was wrapped in a Kevlar towel. My goggles had fogged up, with the sweat pooling up in the lenses. Our driving crew was constantly making adjustments, as we veered from one side of the street to the other, depending on threats. Of course, even where there were no obvious threats, there were threats.

The insurgents had become proficient (with the help of their friends the Iranians) in hiding IEDs in everything from dead animals to foam made to look like pieces of guardrail or rocks. The HMMVs had some obvious countermeasures, things that were supposed to trigger a certain kind of bomb, and there were other technologies to help with other aspects of defense. But the Rhino really had nothing except its svelte good looks and the ability to take a punch.

Eventually, we made it to the green zone. Another series of road blocks, the outer ones, looked like couch cushion forts writ large, manned by the Iraqis. These were not a whole lot of fun to pass. The guys manning the guns looked sketchy to me, dirty and tired looking. Some of the guys behind the guns looked not as friendly as I would have hoped. Of course, it may have had something to do with being in the worst place in Iraq—the middle of the fight. It also looked like the bunkers were built using the whatever-is-lying-around method. For an initial impression, this book had a pretty tattered cover.

We passed a couple more Iraqi checkpoints then started coming up to the American-manned ones. It's hard to describe the gratitude I felt just seeing those smiling GI faces. They all seemed to at least wave in recognition of other GIs rolling into town. As we hit the main checkpoint, the convoy lurched to a stop; we all had to file out and clear our weapons. You stuck your barrel into the clearing barrel (a fifty-five-gallon drum filled with sand), dropped the clip out, then racked the slide, bringing out the round in the chamber. Then with the slide held back, the driver or the TC would verify the chamber was clear, at which point you could release the slide, flipping the selector to safe. At that point, you could be cleared back onto the bus.

After everyone got back on board, we started rolling again, this time to the Rhino yard, the central so-called bus station there in the green zone. There were probably fifteen speed bumps, big ones, in the short trip to the yard, and every time we hit one, it had to be at a really low speed (which, I guess, is the point), and the heavily armored bus lurched alarmingly from side to side. I'm not exactly sure what the point of having speed bumps in a warzone is, especially inside the base, but it seemed to me we were in the greatest danger of tipping over during this time. That would've been embarrassing. But I couldn't see where we were going as inside the outer perimeter, we were surrounded by T-walls—big, gray, cement walls about ten to fifteen feet high, a foot thick, and about six feet wide. They looked like upside down *t*s, as the base spread out to about four feet thick, so the whole thing could stay up.

The streets were lined with these things, so that the whole base was a series of corridors, the bus like a giant, tan rat in a gray maze, searching for the cheese. They were a great idea, as any rocket or mortar that came in would be substantially contained. Of course, if you were in the blast radius and not on the other side of the wall, then you probably wouldn't appreciate the distinction. I'm sure these things saved many lives, including some friends of mine. But they did cut off visibility except for very tall buildings. We could see several large palaces, including the embassy off in the distance. Several of the giant palaces had been redecorated by the airpower of the US military, mostly specializing in instant skylight installation. So we really couldn't see where we were going until we actually turned into the opening in the long, gray walls.

We pulled into the yard after going through one more checkpoint, really just a long cable stretched across the road. This one was manned by a guy from Triple Canopy, one of many security companies that operated there. He was from Fiji, as were a large number of the Triple Canopy men and women. He was dressed in khaki pants and shirt, with a ball cap on his head, a combat harness, and folding stock AK-47. He gave a big smile and dropped the cable, waving us into the parking area. The HMMVs went first; then the Rhinos pulled under a shed, stopping in the shade. The trip took about forty minutes, and I think it covered about ten miles.

I stepped out onto the pavement. All of us newbies were pretty excited to be there; after all, this was the famous Green Zone. Like I said in the beginning of this tome: one of the amazing things about being an American military guy was that we could, at any time, be in the epicenter of world events. Where I disembarked was about a half mile from the embassy. A bunch of the folks we were replacing were waiting in their Chevy Tahoes. They helped us load up all our gear, and then we set off again, bottoming out over the speed bumps as we made our way to the temporary sleeping facilities.

Behind the embassy was a trailer with a civilian who was in charge of handing out the bedding. I shuffled through the line and got my garbage bag of bedding, consisting of a hideously flowered sheet and a matching thin blanket. I think mine had a giant parrot on it. But the fact that there was bedding implied that there would be a bed in my future. Which was good, as we had been on the move pretty consistently for about a week and a half. I had spent one night in my trailer in Camp Victory and the rest in some sort of temporary shelter. So I was ready for some sort of bed. After we signed in, we walked around the embassy to another set of really big tents on the other side. There were about four temporary tents—huge, probably one hundred feet on a side. We were each assigned a tent, and as most of us were in the same tent, it would be like old home week, but without the sandbag trick.

As we approached, it was hard to miss the great wall of sandbags that outlined each major building. There were also little concrete shelters made up of some mini-T-walls with a couple more over the top. It made for a shelter about five feet high, four feet wide, and eight feet long. I was to find out later that a lot of people could fit into those little shelters. The sandbag walls were made up of green nylon sandbags that absolutely got eaten up by the sun. Many of the walls were deteriorating, the bags frayed and the sand spilling out onto little dunes by each wall. That's not to say that the walls were no good; the outer sandbags were gone, but there were still a couple of rows standing. I hoped they were enough to stop whatever they were built to stop. Our little group threaded through the entrance and opened up the wooden door into tent number one.

It was dark and amazingly cool; across the floor were scattered probably sixty or so cheap little cots, with the gaudiest mattresses on them you'd ever seen. Perfect matches for my newly acquired bedding. On several of these cots were exhausted army or marine corps members, even at this relatively early hour, asleep on the raw mattress. Their dirty gear and well-worn weapons were piled neatly at the foot of the ten-dollar beds. Worn boots sagged quietly by their owners. The sleepers mostly were in their uniforms, as they too were in transit, not necessarily homeward. More likely, they were just passing through, rejoining a unit. Still, I stopped and considered for a second. At the risk of not sounding like the manly man that I am, I was unexpectedly touched. A lump leaped to my throat, and I furrowed my eyebrows, as I do when I want to blubber. These were young kids, in their early twenties. One would expect them to bounce up and go play football in the empty lot (no, not touch—these aren't liberals) or roar up and down main street in a junky car. Or play beer pong. But their gear bespoke a deeper purpose to these young men. It's funny how a uniform covers up skin color; these were just young Americans, who had put their lives on hold, left the most prosperous country on earth, and were now lying, exhausted, curled up on a gaudy, thin mattress, covered by a thin blanket in a tent holed by shrapnel, getting paid next to nothing to risk their lives. Because they felt their country needed them. Because they wanted to make a difference.

We all quietly put down our gear and threw our sheets over the mattresses, and went off in search of food. After walking around the embassy again, we came upon another sandbagged building, this one by an Olympic-sized pool. Saddam sure liked his pools. And now we were using them. We gawked for a little bit then proceeded into the chow hall. Dining facility. Whatever. It actually didn't do the place justice to call it a chow hall, as it was really very nice. Of course, we were right next to the embassy, so the facilities might be expected to be better, but in truth, I would find much better places at other far-flung bases later in my tour. We walked through the double doors and came upon a sizable spread. Burgers, dogs, and all sorts of short-order delicacies stretched down the left side, while in the middle was a formidable salad bar with all the fixings. To the right were the entrees, everything from macaroni and cheese to roast beef, plus a cold cut bar. In short, it was clear we were in danger of starving. Indeed, everywhere I went that entire year, the dining facilitates were absolutely top-notch. So we washed our hands (an enforced ritual) and went to chow down. The servers were all contractors, many of them from the Middle East or far afield, even the Philippines. Army folks in uniform were running around as quality assurance folks, and I can tell you that I never had a bad meal. Of course, if I had, I would have simply put it back and gotten something different.

After a delicious meal, we headed back, this time cutting through the embassy. The building itself was huge, one end of it being dedicated to the embassy, and the rest, to the myriad functions of a giant armed effort. Men and women in various uniforms and civvies wandered up and down the halls, scurrying in the way bureaucrats do. There were military folks from everywhere—Britain, Poland, Japan, Tonga (yes, Tonga)—plus bevies of civilian contractors. All the halls were marble, and the walls were covered in pillars and frescos and God knows what else. Even with all the beautiful materials, it still looked shoddy. There were some nifty paintings, usually of rockets and horses, and lots of other things that generally didn't go together, like *Dogs Playing Poker* writ large. There were a couple paintings with blanks in them the size of Saddam's head. Overall, it was like a giant double-wide decorated in late-Liberace.

The best thing that I found in the whole place was not only another little eatery, but a Green Bean espresso place. Over the course of my year there, the Green Bean probably took my firstborn's college fund. It was always staffed by TCNs, and I always got some sort of triple espresso. There were Green Beans everywhere; no matter where I went, there would always be one, and most of the time there would be some sort of line. The Green Bean in the palace was located in a giant room that held a bunch of chairs, tables, and sofas. It was a game room and relaxation room, and a couple of concerts were held there too, by bands made up of whoever was hanging around that could play an instrument. You'd be surprised at the talent. I would stack up a bunch of GIs over Hollywood for talent any day.

So I became familiar with the Green Bean, and all was well. So far it had been an uneventful deployment. After a coffee with my buddies, I made my way back to the giant tent, collapsed on the thin mattress, threw the blanket over my head, and went to sleep.

Morning came early, and by "morning," I mean rockets; and by "early," I mean 0300. The warning horns bellowed, and I rolled out of bed like a pro. Onto my gear, which hurt. Since I wasn't sure what was happening, I just rolled on my armor and helmet, and stayed put. There were two schools of thought on indirect fire attacks. Some folks thought that you ran to the bunker as fast as you could, and others thought that if you rolled into your body armor and hit the deck, it was safer. I became a proponent of the latter. I became convinced that if it was your time, then you were hosed, so don't die tired. After a contractor was killed in a bunker via a direct hit, I determined that the rocket or mortar would have to come to me; I wouldn't go running to it. So I stayed put. The rockets hit somewhere else, and we all went back to sleep, although you tend to be a good listener after the first rocket attack of your life.

The official morning came early—that was for sure. Not only had part of my brain been switched on to hear the raid alarms, but troops were coming and going at all hours; and in spite of the real effort to be quiet, there was always some noise. Plus there was a snorer. Nothing can incite a burning hatred for someone you don't know like a snore. I wanted to set him on fire. Eventually, little watch alarms started beeping sporadically around the tent, and moaning and groaning, with the creaking of cheap beds, followed in short order. As a group, we all shuffled into the bathrooms, which were cheap trailers that either had shower stalls or rows of toilets. In the morning it was a popular place to be, as everyone in the world was trying to crowd into the facility at the same time. You were supposed to be taking combat showers: you wet down, turn off the water, soap up, then rinse off. Most guys made an honest effort to do it; water was at a premium because it often had to be trucked in, then pumped into large tanks. But it was wet, so it worked.

After the shower, especially if it was busy, you then stood around and tried to look noncommittal and disinterested, as naked and seminaked dudes wandered around the trailer while you jockeyed for a sink to shave. Men have perfected this noncommittal technique; you could be showering two feet away from someone, not saying a word, apparently totally oblivious, then when its safe, like shaving, you are totally surprised to see your long lost friend, like he just appeared out of nowhere. Eventually we got all scrubbed up, because we were going to meet our new group commander, and we certainly wanted to make a good impression.

It was a beautiful day as we walked to the CAFTT compound. The sun was shining and there was a light breeze. There wasn't a cloud in the sky, but it wasn't oppressively hot, yet. The colors were a bit washed out, it seemed to me, an overexposed film that I was stuck in. It was just so bright! There were palm trees lining the streets, a bit bedraggled and torn. There were a couple of blackened stumps. It must have been a beautiful drive before the war; when you are a ruthless dictator, you can spend money any way you want, and no one gets to complain. It was hard to imagine just how lush it must've been because of the giant, gray T-walls that were basically just outside all the sidewalks, forming the long gray corridors that we had become familiar with on the Rhino ride in. In the middle distance, a couple of palaces loomed, one with several direct hits from my buddies. At the end of the block was a shelter, usually large enough for about ten folks to fit in. I became very aware of the distance to the shelters; it was one of the survival techniques you developed, always updating your position in relation to the nearest shelter. But halfway down the block, there would have been no way you could reach either bunker in time, so would just hit the dirt.

At this early stage, we didn't even have to wear body armor outside. The threat condition (threatcon) we were in mandated that the armor had to be within ten minutes of where you were. You always had to have a weapon on, of course, but we didn't realize how free we were then. After an eight-minute walk to the compound, we got to another gate, this one manned by yet another foreigner; this time, security would be provided by a young gentleman from Uganda. Because when you think security, you think: Uganda.

This young's man name happened to be Peter, a passionate Christian and one of the nicest gentlemen I had ever met; indeed, all the Ugandans were very nice and respectful. We trooped through the exit then to the clearing barrel; we were responsible for providing our own clearing official. You stuck your weapon into the barrel (filled with sand), dropped the clip (if you had one in), and pulled back the slide. After verifying that the chamber was clear, you could proceed. Over time, it became a ritual before entering any building.

We filed into the building that was the heart of the coalition effort. The army, navy, and marines all had presence here, and the place was swarming with all of the coalition partners, military and civilians. The military folks were all mightily generating PowerPoint presentations as if their lives depended on it. I once again thanked the Lord that I would not be here, in the heart of the bureaucracy, but elsewhere, doing I didn't yet know what. What surprised me the most was the presence of Iraqis in the large room. Many of them were US citizens and had come back to help, but there were Iraqi nationals scattered around in civilian clothes as well. One thing I picked up on was the large number of Christian crosses that were dangling from many of the women's (and some men's) necks. There were all stylishly dressed in the latest, but well-worn, fashions.

One large man, about six feet two and fifty years old, an Iraqi by way of Chicago, came up to me with a broad smile and a large belly, sticking out an enormous hand and saying, "Welcome!" It was clear that English was a second language, but he spoke well through a heavy accent. The ring of hair around the very shiny head defied gravity, forming what looked like a science fair project in a third grade expo. It didn't stop at his ears, either. I think he had more hair coming out of his ears than around that little ecosystem orbiting his head. But that smile was enormous, and the large, dark eyes glittered with humor. Hadi would become a valuable ally for me in the war. Not all warriors in this cause were young men with guns. We had many that were old men with pot bellies, no guns, wearing armor that was too small or too big, helping in whatever way they could to assist us in relating to the Iraqis we were here to help. It was fitting he was the first to greet me.

After Hadi and I chatted for a minute, we were all herded into the conference room. Apparently, we were in for a full day: there was going to be the boss first, then some in-processing. As we all arranged ourselves around a long conference table, I took stock of who was here with me. Again, it was an amazing cross section of America. There was the little, bespectacled Maintenance Officer, Lieutenant Colonel Chuck, who was with me in Camp Bullis. There was Randy, a giant Texan C-130 driver, upon whom body armor and helmets looked straight off a GI Joe action figure. Denise, one of the few females with us, a personnelist by trade, who would become a real asset for the team. Most of us were captains or majors, with a few lieutenant colonels. We waited nervously for the big man himself to arrive, and finally the aide came in and snapped to attention.

"Ladies and gentlemen, the Commander!"

We leaped to our feet, anxiously seeking out our leader, a large, confident, and gifted orator, who commanded the room and exuded the confidence of a full-bull colonel—a proven combat leader. Maybe he was behind the short, chubby guy who just walked in.

Unfortunately, he wasn't. Apparently our CO was to be the less physically fit of the Pillsbury Doughboy brothers. The colonel was a short man, about five feet four, but dapper, he imagined, his feet shoulder width apart and hands on hips, his flight suit wrinkle-free, but not from ironing. I mentally added blinking lights at his elbows, and *poof*—instant Buzz Lightyear, almost to scale. His carefully coiffed hair topped a shiny, plasticky face. He had that quick, small step of those who want other people to know they are in a hurry. He strode into the room and waved his hand down in a "be seated" gesture. My first impression wasn't all that good, but he hadn't said much yet; I was sure that would change things. After all, the air force spends a lot of time teaching people how to speak to audiences, and a full colonel would have had more training than most.

It turned out that he had read all the things the air force had to say about leadership and decided to avoid any of them in his welcome speech. He did say he was glad that we were here. Sort of. He started off by saying that he was sort of a hero, by helping put out a fire on an aircraft that had come in during a rocket attack. Then he moved on to say that he was most definitely a hero, possibly a role model for Audie Murphy. After briefly covering how awesome he was, he moved on to cover how non-awesome we were. I couldn't believe it. It was the first time in more than twenty years that I had ever had anyone tell me I sucked, although I wasn't singled out—the entire group was below standards.

He started by saying that there were many of us who were passed over, and many were non-deployers, but in spite of that fact, we were expected to do our best. Our "best" was understood as *not-so-much*. He went on to discuss how disappointed he was in the quality of the folks he had assembled around the table. I personally hadn't seen that in the group that I was with; after all, many of them I had gone through Camp Bullis with. I looked to see how everyone was taking this most unusual of pep talks. Brows were furrowed, mouths were pulled down, and heads were being scratched. It was clear that I was not the only one mystified. We were all waiting for some sort of punch line. The colonel allowed that he would still probably do well, even without the best folks around. We just weren't supposed to screw up the progress that had been made to this point.

Eventually he did discuss the mission; we, the advisors, would be interfacing with the Iraqis, carrying out the wishes of the CAFTT, and prodding them along the right path. He did allow that HQ understood that Iraqis had their own timeline and the going could be slow, but we were making progress. Of course, the implication was that we *had been* making progress. We degenerates would probably screw it up and start the war all over again. He described the tenuous position of the air force general, Kamal, a Kurd who, it seemed, was out of favor with the Iraqis, but was one of the "good" guys, so we were stuck with him for the near term. (In truth, there were a lot of initiatives that had been started and were showing promise, but we didn't hear a lot about them; we would have to wait for our in-brief back over at Victory for that.) He mentioned that the Iraqis were flying more missions, and the formal schooling aspect was staggering to its feet, but he spent a lot of time emphasizing the headquarters functions and how the USAF would be functioning over here. I expected a lot more emphasis to be placed on the advisor roles, as that was the reason I was here. But he seemed to be discussing a stateside operation, with the only twist being that occasionally ruffians would shoot, mortar, and rocket you. The advisor role was only discussed as an afterthought.

The speech itself was mercifully short; of course, there are only so many ways you can say "you suck," and he had exhausted his thesaurus. The whole thing probably took about ten minutes or so, but was disproportionately memorable. One of the things seared (like my secret missions into Laos, Cambodia, and Trenton, New Jersey) into my memory was his closing statement.

I have the impression of him standing there, glaring balefully over his glasses, hands still resting on his hips, staring each one of us down. I distinctly remember the extra folds of pale flesh spilling out over his T-shirt and scarf. It looked like his head was resting on a delicious stack of fat sugar cookies. Which was what made his closing remark even more precious.

"Remember: just because you are going to be busy is no reason to neglect your professional commitments. You are still a member of the US armed forces."

He fixed his beady little eyes on some of the assembled group, glaring like an Oompa Loompa with a bowel problem.

"That means that some of you need to get to the gym."

With that, our group commander spun on his tiny heel and strode out of the room. We leaped to our feet, called ourselves to attention, and then, as we got ready for the next briefer, started buzzing about what the hell just happened. No one had ever seen or heard anything like that, especially in the kinder, gentler air force. We wondered what could've inspired that sort of a speech. The colonel was obviously a political animal, so I couldn't figure out what he could've been up to. At least we were confident in the fact that there couldn't be a stranger briefing in the rest of the afternoon.

Then came the intel brief. This was to be the weirdest briefing ever. Not depressing, like the colonel's, but just flat-out weird. It was also where I made a big mistake and managed to look like an ass.

Intel folks are a strange sort of cat. The good ones know that a lot of the information they pass on is dated and not really top-secret material. Of course, they do occasionally have really good stuff. And smart folks listen to them when they start to talk. The good ones know the limitations of their product.

The bad ones treat everything like its top secret and act like they are certainly the smartest folks in any given room. Operators usually dismiss these guys, sometimes to their detriment. Because of the incessant "crying wolf," you can easily miss the nugget of info that you should've listened to.

I don't think that the first type of intel officer has much use for the latter, either. This guy was definitely the latter.

He came in, a walking contradiction. He was definitely of Asian descent, short and trim, but he sported an awesome walrus-like mustache, like a big German, and completed the ensemble by wearing the military-issue glasses, like a big dork. These glasses are lovingly referred to as BCGs, or birth control glasses. No child has ever been conceived while either party was wearing BCGs. He wore his M9 on his side and shouldered his M4, which he had "decorated" with sand-colored grips and a giant flashlight, which I assume came in handy when he was reading his comic books late at night. He threw some rolled-up maps on the table, introduced himself, and started to speak.

At least he didn't start off by saying how much *we* sucked. He started off by saying how the *Iraqis* sucked. In his opinion, they were incredibly untrustworthy and thoroughly penetrated by bad guys. He allowed that so far he had kept the folks outside in the cubicles from knowing that he was an intel officer. So far, he had me fooled as well. But he went to great lengths to describe the extent of his psyops against what were essentially our allies. So, there was the element of surprise thing. And after five minutes with Colonel Flagg of CAFTT, the enemy would have returned him to the front gate, a la "The Ransom of Red Chief." But he rambled on, talking how he basically had a secret identity and only here, behind closed doors, could he reveal his true persona. But, he wasn't just a master of disguise; he was also a weapons master. And he would let us in on that skill too.

He described how he would practice drawing his pistol in his hooch at night, quick drawing right there. But first, he showed us an alternate way to clear his weapon, namely by opening the slide and sticking his finger into the opening. The fact that he still had all his fingers is proof that God needs amusement. So he took his pistol out, racked the slide back, and stuck his finger down through the slide into the magazine well. And stood staring at us as if to say, "Impressed?" He then holstered it and redrew. After a few more iterations, he thought that we got it. We did, but not in the way he thought. At some point, I figured he would have to get into the intel portion of things, as I was a little curious about the proximity of my hooch to some of the hot spots, like Sadr City. Well, I wasn't disappointed.

He then said he would explain the current situation. He unrolled the rubber bands, then the maps, and laid them on the table. He then started talking and pointing. Keep in mind: we were all seated around a twenty-foot-long conference table, and he was at one end of it. So when he looked down in front of himself to point out all the bad spots and activity, no one else could see what he was talking about. The true genius of this particular intel guy was demonstrated in full color. I actually got up and walked over to where he was, in order to see what the heck he was talking about, because it may as well have been a paint-by-numbers of his favorite action hero (probably Green Lantern) for all the good it was doing us.

I could tell he really didn't like me looking over his shoulder, compromising any intel he was trying to brief. But soon, others got up and walked over to where we were to see if they, too, could get a peek at his intel. Finally, he got the hint and picked up a corner of the large map (about three feet square) and held it up with one hand, while trying to point out areas of interest with his official intel pointer (a mechanical pencil). That worked about as well as one would expect. The paper rolled over itself, obscuring his pencil, and, indeed, his whole arm had disappeared into the curl of the paper. Eventually, he had enough and, in a fit of pique, threw it down onto the table again, so he could use his favorite forum—the forum in which no one could see what he was doing.

I did, however, in spite of his efforts, peek at the map. Someone had taken a lot of time and effort to color in some red areas, areas with names like Sadr City, which seemed to be awful close to where I would be sleeping. Seemed to match the bullet hole in my trailer. I said something to the effect of "Jeez, Sadr City is that close?" which elicited a glare from the mustachioed man. Or maybe he wasn't looking at me at all; it's really hard to tell with those glasses. He may have been staring at a person in the next room, through the wall. But he did mention that we were surrounded by bad guys, including those in the other room.

At that point I'd had enough; I went and sat in my chair, just looking at this guy. It was embarrassing to see. After his pretend gunplay and his worthless briefing, I just wanted him gone. Professionally, I just wanted him gone. There are too many consummately professional intel folks out there to have this guy ruining their name. Mercifully, he ended, and as he scooped up his raft of papers and shuffled out the door, I shouted, "See ya later, intel guy!"

He came storming back in, furious and red faced.

"Who said that!" he yelled, glaring at everyone.

I said that I did.

"Now, I've been compromised!" he hissed, spinning on his heel and storming out.

I told his back that I was sorry, and I meant it. I later said it to him in private. I shouldn't have let his rampant stupidity make me stupid as well. Operational security (Opsec) was always a consideration, especially here. But I had had it with his unprofessional manner and his continual running down of the Iraqis as untrustworthy and unworthy in general. I was taught in our briefings and all through my life that people are good if you know how to plug into their system. Our challenge would be to find out how to relate to the Iraqis, understand their value system, and try to bring them along with us. We had consciously discarded the "conqueror" mindset, so we would have to try and pull them along. I felt that the better we understood them, the better we could do that.

Yet here was this guy, tucked into his little world, surrounded by Iraqis working in cubicles right next to him, and he was so paralyzed with fear that he had to make every one of them a bad guy, so he wouldn't have to relate to any of them. Who knows how much intel he missed. Those Iraqis lived downtown and probably heard quite a bit. Had this knucklehead been more approachable, he may have been able, in casual conversation, to pick up subtle cues that may have had operational payoffs. As it turned out, I probably got more intelligence value from my guys (Iraqis I worked with) just by shooting the breeze with them. But I hadn't met them yet; at that point I was just mad and disappointed in our outlook (if this same vision was shared by the leadership).

It wasn't. The first viewpoint, however, that of the chubby colonel, remained strong through the last briefing as our in-processing came to a close. I believe it was the next day when we actually received our initial briefing by the general in charge of CAFTT.

General Dice was a very thin guy of medium height, with sunken cheeks, wire-framed glasses, and a receding, fuzzy sort of hairline. He looked quite a bit older than he actually was, unless he and Jesus were actually racquetball partners. As I looked at him, I started to smirk; I just kept envisioning him on a porch somewhere yelling, "Get off my lawn, dammit!" Or better yet, being unmasked in a Scooby Doo episode, lamenting that he "...would've have gotten away with it, if it hadn't been for you meddling kids!" He just had that sort of face. He was also very much in love with himself. He mentioned that he worked out all the time and was in really good shape. Having thus started off modestly, he decided to turn up the heat.

Although not a hero on the ground, like the colonel, he was, perhaps, the best pilot ever. He could fly around the world in a C-17 (although he was probably just using the aircraft so the other pilots wouldn't feel inadequate; I've no doubt he could levitate) and arrive over his target within two seconds of when he said he would. This was a metaphor that we would hear ad nauseam over our time in CAFTT and would become the standard by which all things would be measured. It would be used to make the other party feel bad about their accomplishments, or lack thereof, often used to deride a struggling timeline. As in, "You know, I can run around this building twelve times and arrive within one picosecond of when I said I would, and you can't even get the Iraqis to buy uniforms for themselves." That sort of thing. So the general's words inspired us throughout our entire tour.

Other words inspired us as well. This guy was a dark raincloud looking for a silver lining to snuff out. Again, I really didn't know who he was talking about, but he kept hammering home the fact that many of us had been passed over and that our careers were not like his. Now the colonel's briefing started to make sense. He had gotten it from this guy.

So, we were once again subjected to a barrage of backhanded compliments, front-handed insults, and two-handed malapropisms. The gist of the welcome briefing was that, while he was glad we were here, he would be even more excited if it wasn't exactly, well, us that had arrived. Kind of like when the in-laws show up. You're glad they are there, but wouldn't you be happier if it was Publishers Clearing House with a four-foot-long check? So he managed to work his way through his disappointment by relaying how hard he had worked to get us all here. Only that seemed to magnify his disappointment in who showed up. He summed it all up like this: "I expected to have the top ten percent of the air force come here. Instead, I got you."

Again, I looked around the table and tried to spot the obvious rejects. I didn't see any, but I hadn't looked at records or anything. The bright and shiny folks that he was expecting seemed to have better things to do than get their hands dirty deploying and stuff. How are you supposed to get promoted when you are three thousand miles away from the ass you need to kiss? But here we were, so he decided that he would be able to "mold this

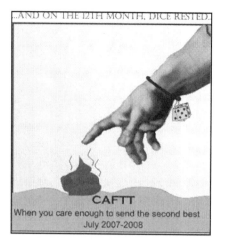

...AND ON THE 12TH MONTH, DICE RESTED.

CAFTT
When you care enough to send the second best
July 2007-2008

raw clay into a useful body," or something along those lines. "The B team" was mentioned more than once. This part stuck with me and would end up on a couple of patches I designed for our team. But, like most military members, I decided that in spite of the awesome leadership that I seemed to have, I would be kicking ass and taking names at...whatever. I still didn't know what the hell I was doing here.

He did answer that question, generally, in what I thought was the best part of the welcome speech. He actually got into the details of what CAFTT was all about. He seemed to be a little more switched on to the advising side of the house, in stark contrast to the colonel before. He seemed to understand the depths of the "stunting" to the Iraqis that had gone on for thirty years. The slow progress was directly related to trust and responsibility, of which the Iraqis had very little for each other. He did allow that the Iraqis definitely had their own timeline, and the process by which they got things accomplished was very different than ours. In fact, I would find out that it was almost a perfect inversion. He seemed to genuinely like the Iraqis and empathize with their plight, but at the same time, we had definite goals to accomplish via the Iraqi air force in the relatively short time we were going to be here. And that would be a challenge, but he seemed to be very aware of it.

I ended up really respecting the guy quite a bit for this. In spite of his penchant for back-patting himself, the use of silly, often wrong metaphors, and inspiration by degradation, he was a true believer in the mission. I think he was the right guy at the right time for the mission. Once, he called me and another guy into his office to make sure that we understood why he was doing something. And then he asked what we thought about it and encouraged our honest assessment. He certainly didn't have to do that. He also had a pretty good feeling for the Iraqis and really tried to pull them along. Definitely a good man to have in our corner to start this part of the adventure.

His predecessor had restarted the Iraqi air force, maintaining a loose organization and a vague roadmap of where to go. The Iraqis had started up with about forty guys in a couple of smoke-filled rooms with one or two computers that may or may not have worked, as power winked on and off. I think there were about eight chairs for all of them, three chairs in front of the computers, in the pictures that I saw. As Dice took over, he added a lot more organization and definite goals. The Iraqis grew as well, slowly, adding some more personnel and aircraft. They had started with three ancient C-130s, a few CH2000s, Seeker ultralights, some donated Comp Air kit planes, some Hueys, and some grounded Mi-171s.

It wasn't much to go on; as it stood, the IQAF had about three hundred people, and the average age was about fifty. Apparently, we had raided Florida and grabbed anyone in black socks and sandals who was eating at a buffet at three in the afternoon to start the new Iraqi air force. Dice allowed that it probably wasn't the A team from the Iraqi side. It began to dawn on me that we were going to have our hands full. But, I hadn't met a "real" Iraqi yet, so I didn't quite know what I had in front of me. As Dice ended our whirlwind of briefings and welcomes, he became a little more relaxed, but still, he insisted that while he was glad to see us, he wasn't that glad to see *us*.

Well, nice to see you too.

10

MEET THE BOYS

After that uplifting couple of days in the International Zone (IZ, same as Green Zone), we reversed the process and came back to Camp Victory to meet our immediate boss, a British officer, Group Captain Farmer. I had never really worked with the Brits before, other than in the air, but they were a big part of the large coalition, covering everything from administrative support to active combat. A lot of policy wonks were there as well. In my short trip in the IZ, I was constantly asking our minders, "Who are they?" There were military, civilian, Japanese, Polish, Australians, Georgians, Tongans (yes, Tongans) all bustling around. Let's not disparage these folks: no matter the size of the contingent, these people were there in a combat zone. Oh, and media and liberals; I would've never guessed the diversity of the help that Iraq was getting if I had only read the media accounts. A lot of the smaller countries seemed to be pulling internal security (gate guards, etc.). And for all you snickering about "safe behind the walls": rockets, mortars, and poorly aimed gunfire specialize in that sort of environment.

I'll demonstrate that in the following pages; so wipe that smirk off your face.

We eventually made it back to our trailers at Camp Victory and reported for our first real day of work the next morning. After a 1.1-mile walk from my hooch, we arrived at the CAFTT advisors' trailer. The trailer was in the shadow of yet another palace, currently inhabited by the Air Component Coordination Element (ACCE). This USAF two-star handled advising the commanding general of Multi-National Force–Iraq on aviation matters. So there were plenty of brass there. Even though we weren't in their unit, they treated us pretty well because we were all airmen.

What made the place especially valuable was that it had real bathrooms, about five or six no-kidding bathrooms decorated in modern Liberace. This was one of the small things that we don't think twice about here in the comfy States, but having a private place to take a dump is a luxury. We only had one incident, with a colonel who decided that we weren't going to use their bathrooms, because they were for the general and the general's staff (namely, him). That lasted one day. The general found out about it and directed that, from now on, we would all crap on this guy's desk. Okay, maybe not, but the general made it clear that, as fellow airmen, we were to be taken care of. Like always. That colonel was probably intel. So we were really happy with our neighbors.

The previous tenants had set a pretty poor precedent. This building had allegedly been inhabited by one of Saddam's daughters and her husband. According to the rumor mill, this was the son-in-law who left Iraq for Jordan, spilled everything he knew about various weapons programs, then returned after Saddam promised to forgive everything. (I'll hold my breath while you guess how that turned out.) A couple of days after they returned, the daughter divorced her husband (which should have been a sign), and the day after that, the "traitor" was killed in a gun battle by mystery gunmen. I'm guessing the wedding gifts also had to be returned. It was said that the Iraqi authorities really investigated hard. But in the giant game of Clue–Iraq, Pre-Invasion edition, there was really only one answer, ever: Saddam henchmen, in the sandbox, with an AK-47.

The interesting part was that there was a reddish discoloration on the steps to the palace that was said to be the blood of the dead, which had seeped into the stone. I guess it could've been true. The whole Camp Victory complex had the aura of death all over it. Which was weird, because it was a fairly scenic place. There was water everywhere, with manmade lakes surrounding us, palaces of various sizes and shapes dotting the horizon. Depending on your connection to Saddam, your lakeside property in Baghdad may actually have had a lake by it. Then of course, you would have needed a houseboat to put on it. Which there were—houseboats of various sizes and levels of floatation ability (some were more sunken than others) rested in these lakes. Some serious money was spent on this giant playground. Sort of a stimulus package from Saddam.

Our trailer was right on the shore of one of these little lakes in a gravel parking lot. The IQAF directorates each had a trailer, making about seven trailers that surrounded us, along with their operational "headquarters," a little stone building that the number two man in the air force worked in. There were two Porta-Potties to service all the trailers (including ours). The IQAF HQ had a real bathroom, but it was constantly broken and wet (with what I didn't care to find out). That's why the short trek to the palace was so valuable. The rest of the little gravel square was occupied by big, tan Chevy crew cab trucks, purchased by the Iraqis, and a couple of private cars as well. So, in a gravel-filled lot about sixty yards by sixty yards, most of the IQAF headquarters was working its way into the modern era.

The group captain had a genuine smirk on his face as he welcomed us into the trailer. The trailer itself was a lot bigger than the one I lived in. It was constructed of the same material as my hooch—foam covered by really sturdy tinfoil, the kind you could totally wrap a big sandwich in. When you walked in the cipher-locked door, you were immediately confronted with a wall of body armor and helmets. A little to the left was the doorway that beckoned into the boss's office, which was about ten feet by ten feet. To the right was the big common room stuffed with about ten desks, computers, and a constantly changing number of chairs. So this was the office.

Group Captain Farmer was my first exposure to the dry humor and pragmatism of the British airman. He was about five feet six and had a face that seemed to be designed for grinning. He always had a twinkle in his eye and a quick wit. I think he was a navigator in the United Kingdom, but he was the lead advisor here and, as such, was constantly working with General Altair, the number two guy in the IQAF, while our number ones, Dice and Kamal, tackled their roles in the IZ.

One of the first things we noticed was a black armband he was sporting as he greeted us. I was a bit worried about what that meant at first until he explained to us that it was a symbol of that dark day in British history: July 4, 1776. Since it was about the ninth of July, he was still in a period of mourning. Suddenly, the hand-lettered sign on his door made sense. This was the office of the " Colonial Oppressor". I knew immediately that I was going to like this guy. What a welcome relief to the greeting we had received from our own. He occupied a critical position in our chain of command, mainly running interference between the "corporate" USAF, on the other side of Route Irish, and the "field", here. I wasn't sure about the dynamic between the two organizations, but Group Captain Farmer seemed to do a pretty good job holding them at bay, evidenced by the esteem the guys already here held him in.

I knew that we had the right kind of leadership when soon after I got there I discovered that the guys had taken a picture of him in a cowboy hat and placed it on one of those sites that personalizes coffee cups, T-shirts, and other articles of clothing. The "other articles of clothing" was the most interesting. I was happy to know that in the event I wanted to get my wife a special little something for Valentine's Day or something, I could get some skimpy little panties with his grinning, cowboy-hatted visage on the only piece of cloth attached to the string parts. Which would really spark up the bedroom.

Of course, if he was a butthead or something, no one would have even cared to do that. They loved him, and on Fridays, they would darken the little office and watch *Black Adder* on the projection screen. Sometimes in body armor. This was where people wanted to be. He had done such a great job of building the team of Americans that they would choose to be at work in their very spare free time.

Farmer sat everybody down; space was at a premium as we were here in full strength, along with most of the current team. So the room was packed; equipment was strewn everywhere; everyone sat, slouched, leaned, and scrunched into all the available spaces. He welcomed us aboard, cracking jokes and littering his speech with Briticisms. It was obvious that the team here was tight; subtle references to things that had happened brought appreciative chuckles throughout the assembled troops. Our mission became a little clearer as he discussed the history of the effort, the challenges posed, and the team we were working with. He discussed in detail the Iraqis, their organizational weaknesses and their strengths. Unfortunately the list of weaknesses was much longer than the strengths.

One strength was, unfailingly, that they loved their country and were taking huge risks to get it back.

It was during this part that I started to understand what a monumental task we had ahead of us. The Iraqis had been thoroughly destroyed. Not by us—we removed the catalyst for the destruction. Under the thumb of Saddam, the way to survive was to distance yourself from any responsibility, crave authority, and lie. The opposite of the values that we try to instill in our military members. When objectives are at the whim of a dictator, there is no point in trying to think long term; you exist on short-term tactics. You don't want to be brilliant (doctor, military member, politician, or fill in the blank), as that's dangerous. You also don't want to be a dumbass (doctor, military member, politician, or fill in the blank), as that's dangerous. You want to have lots of power, but you certainly don't want any responsibility.

Now, we had a group of people, most fairly old, fiercely patriotic and brave, but a few utterly without a sense of responsibility. This was the mixed bag that we were to be working with. Most of you reading this will be in your thirties or forties; how would you like it if a fresh-faced bunch of kids (we were much younger than them) came in and told you that the way you had lived your life was totally wrong (I'm excluding parents in this of course; you've been told this by your kids for decades). Unless those folks were armed, you may be inclined to just punch them in the face. And if they didn't handle their advising just right, then as soon as they left, you would be going right back to what you used to do.

And that's exactly what we couldn't allow to happen. Too much American blood and treasure had been spent on this operation. As I grew into the job, I would come to realize that another, equally important currency had been spent—the blood of Iraqi patriots. I just didn't know them yet.

As the group captain continued on his briefing, the dreaded PowerPoint presentations came out, and we were introduced to various buzzwords that we had to bend and shape to what we would actually be doing. It wasn't easy, but the group captain seemed to have it all under control. Twice a week Farmer would make a trip over to the IZ (or "I zed" as the Brits called it) and brief our status to the CAFTT brass. It certainly didn't sound like things were moving fast enough to warrant twice-a-week rides over Route Irish. Our job was to give him something to brief. As he went through the

PowerPoint presentation, he showed the dazzling array of arrows, boxes, and animations that represented the progress of the IQAF. This was in comparison to the entirely different set of arrows, boxes, and animations that represented the USAF expectations of the IQAF.

The entire set of rules seemed a bit odd to me. We were to understand the "different" ways Iraqis accomplished objectives, but we still gave them objectives with our timelines. These objectives were ostensibly signed off and agreed to by the IQAF leadership, but the impetus for these objectives really came from our side. Which was understandable, but I was wondering how this was all going to play out. I could see, by all the various lines on the presentation with red marks (never good in a briefing), where the progress was versus where it was supposed to be. I hadn't met our counterparts yet, so I had no clue as to their thoughts on this methodology, but it just seemed like the rules were incompatible. We would set the goals and timelines, while they would get it done with their methods and with their resources. The thing that popped into my head was these were folks who we had just been absolutely destroyed—in large part because of their training and tactics. And since we were working with many of the folks of that same generation, without a very firm hand, I just didn't see how that was going to work.

We spent a little more time discussing what was expected of us, interspersed with a couple of stories reinforcing the stakes that we were dealing with, for us and the Iraqis. One of our guys, a maintenance lieutenant colonel who Chuck was going to replace, was in a Rhino that had been hit by an IED a few weeks before. Apparently, he was all snuggled down, right over the rear wheel well, when the IED went off. He said that it wasn't calibrated right or something, and the full force of the explosion ripped right under his feet, travelling along the axle. The cabin itself wasn't penetrated, but the vehicle was disabled. My tactics instructor had once said that in combat, even aerial combat, survival comes down to feet and seconds. I thought that was a bit of a stretch at first, but here it was written in scarred, smoking metal. But not scarred, smoking flesh: all because of an emplacement team that set the IED a foot too close to the road or angled it a degree too low or the Rhino was too close to the explosion or the trigger man didn't wait for the right kind of target. Feet and seconds.

It was bit tougher for the Iraqis. We were eventually told the rest of the story that was alluded to in the Camp Bullis days regarding one of the

Iraqis that had been identified by the Americans as the right kind of leader to take the IQAF to the place they should be. Articulate and smart, with a Western mindset, he emerged relatively unscathed by the Saddam regime and was selected to go to the United States for language and officer training. He completed all his courses in an exemplary fashion. Then he came back. At some point, the savages that we were at war with caught him in some misstep: someone saw him coming home via the wrong route, someone on base compromised him, or one of his children said something to someone who then said something to someone. The tiniest mistake from anybody in his family would have doomed him. And it did.

One evening when he got home, they were waiting for him. With his wife and children. The jihadists then demonstrated their honor. After raping and killing the children and working their way up to the wife, they finally killed this shining star. They cut his head off with a rusty pocket knife and threw it out into the street. It was a warning: don't work with the Americans. Especially not in the new Iraqi military. The men who worked with us generally stayed on base all week; thus, their families were downtown and basically unreachable. It took a long time to get through the checkpoints, so they couldn't make it home in a hurry. We made sure that they didn't have any weapons on base and that they only had certain kinds of cell phones. All for good reason, but the impact on those that followed the rules could be fatal.

So, that was the environment that I found myself in. There was plenty of humor and shenanigans (often supplied by yours truly), but it could instantly turn deadly serious. I knew that the folks I was with were dependable and honest. I had that luxury. The Iraqis didn't.

I was introduced to the guy that I was to replace, and I instantly knew that we were going to hit it off. Not that we needed to, as he was a Lieutenant Colonel, and I was merely a Major, but a turnover goes more smoothly if it is conducted by folks that genuinely like each other. Lieutenant Colonel Buchman was a tall guy, around six feet, sporting a desert flight suit and a sad face. Maybe that was because he was a nav. They are always sad because they aren't pilots. Either that, or he was constantly hearing the world's worst joke in his head. He had dark, deep-set eyes, a large nose, and a soft voice. He may be the most patient, nicest man I've ever met. I would learn later what a perfect fit he was for this job—the most stressful and emotionally taxing job I've ever had.

Jim had responsibility for advising the A7, or training division general. I hadn't really thought it through, but I was privileged to be involved with this particular division. Of course everyone thought that they were advising the most important division, but training—training is where all the ingredients come together: people, equipment, mission. Everything is a function of training. And it looked like I was getting in on the ground floor. Jim explained to me the organizations that had been stood up so far; he rattled through it all with encyclopedic precision. He knew precisely how many people were in what classes, and where. He quietly spoke about the goals that we had for the IQAF, and again, I was impressed with myself. I had managed to land in the most important aviation advisor job in Iraq. As the training went, so too would go the Iraqi Air Force. We (already I was considering "we" to be the advisors and the IQAF—I went native early) only had about three hundred folks, spread out over four bases and flying only four types of aircraft. They quit flying the Comp Air after a fatal crash took the lives of four US airmen and one Iraqi pilot, and the Mi-171 (a variant of the venerable Mi-17) helicopters were grounded. So that left a small cadre of planes and people to train, build (not rebuild, this was different), fly, and stay alive when they weren't at work.

At this time the training division was working at three training locations: an English language lab in a little compound at the Baghdad International Airport called New Al Muthana (NAMAB), an Officer Training School at Taji, and a Military Training School at the Iraqi Military Academy at Rustymaya (IMAR). And that was it. Not much to build an air force from. Taji's role was to be similar to our Officer Training Schools (OTS), a fairly quick way to make lieutenants. There is a lot of disdain for the "ninety-day wonders," but the United States can pump out pretty darn good officers in ninety days. But that's the United States.

IMAR was about twenty minutes as the Huey flies to the south of us, and it was based on a military academy first started by the British in 1924. It was back in business, now pumping out Iraqi army cadets, and a little sliver had been carved out for an IQAF presence. It certainly wasn't very big, but this was supposed to replicate the training that a four-year military academy stateside would give to a high school graduate, only in about half the time. The Air Force Academy of the Desert.

Taji was to the north, and would be the OTS of the Iraqi IQAF. Jim relayed that the Iraqis weren't super keen on the whole 90 day wonder thing, but we had managed to convince them that there would be a good product at the end of the process. We would be inducting college graduates into an intense English language training program, and when they passed that, sending them to Taji.

The English language training (ELT) would take place at NAMAB. Squirreled away in a small part of the Iraqi base at Baghdad Airport, this was the English language lab that every cadet would have to go through. One of the really smart things that General Kamal, the IQAF commander, had done was commit all Iraqi officers to learning English. As English is the language of aviation, and many of the books and maintenance manuals that he was using were in English, this made good sense. Additionally, I think there was a bit of a prestige thing going on; all the cool kids speak English. It was also a good way to break with the repressive traditions of the past and serve as a safeguard against radicalism. If a person speaks English and travels to the West for training and mentoring, then it's a little harder to believe some of the more outrageous things that are said about the Great Satan. If you can hear for yourself speeches and policies, then you'll see what a good and decent country we are. (Unless you listen to Democrats. Then you get what Saddam would've approved of.) The best way to control a population is isolation. With the information flow across the globe these days, if you speak English, you have access to very different points of view than what extremist regimes would like—the opposite of isolated. For these brave military students, English would be the key to understanding the West, without the editorial of an imam. This would be expanded on in one of the best speeches I hadn't heard yet, by a little general that I hadn't met yet.

So Jim continued on his little whiteboard, diagramming all the relationships among the various programs and with the larger mission. CAFTT was a little microcosm of what was happening with the navy, in small numbers, and the army, in huge numbers. NATO was involved mostly with the army, it seemed; because we were so small, some folks didn't even know that we existed. This was a blessing in disguise, because as I got more involved in the NATO efforts, I was glad they were overlooking us. Right—keep "helping" the army. We only had about eighty people in any sort of pipeline; the army had thousands. But, just like in the States, it's a little harder to make an airman than it is a grunt. The standards were higher, but we had to make sure that those expectations were tempered with reality. And speed. As Jim went on, I started to see the delicate balancing act we were involved in, and it went to the heart of what makes a society function, and ultimately would be the ticket out of Iraq for combat troops.

Our goal was to get the Iraqi military stood up as fast as possible, with the caveat that it had to be the right kind of military—one that was respected and dependable. Some societies lend themselves to that sort of thing, some do not. It depends on the values of the society at large. That's why our military is the way it is. It's a reflection of our larger societal values. What I was to discover was how difficult it can be to build a value-based military arm when many of those values were absent in the society at large. Or worse: when the imposed values are in contradiction to the values prevalent in the society at large. I hadn't made those connections yet, but the challenges that Jim was describing were part of the overall equation that would determine our success there.

Jim continued on for a few more minutes, putting the details in perspective, fleshing out all the efforts that had been attempted up to that point. As my eyes glazed over, he finally looked up from his diagram-filled board and said the words that would alter my life: "Well, do you want to meet the boys?"

Hell yes, I did.

We gathered up our things, grabbed some papers, and headed for the door. It was the first time I had ever been to a meeting while carrying a pistol. In retrospect, I wish I would have known earlier in my career how much more smoothly being armed makes meetings go. All the other interminable meetings I'd attended would have actually been useful had I been packing. We stepped out into the afternoon sun and walked the twenty yards to the A7 trailer. The trailers themselves were on risers, so we took a couple of wooden steps up to get in. All of the trailers were surrounded by mini-T-walls (like a regular T-wall but one-eighth the size). So while the trailers were elevated, the walls to protect them were shrunk. I'm not sure what calculations went into that equation: the walls were about five feet tall, and the trailers had been elevated about two feet, so the bottom three feet of you would be protected while in the trailer. For me, that was a gap of about a foot between the top of the T-wall and the bottom of my body armor—that's a pretty critical foot.

In spite of the "grave" danger (is there any other kind?) Jim opened the door, and I readied myself for my first look at the men who, until a couple of years before, had been ready to kill me. Well, the first look had to wait, as cigarette smoke billowed out of the door in ever-expanding roils. For a second, I thought that the building might be undergoing a large but tightly contained fire. Jim plunged in, the clouds curling around him, but I hesitated, and as I stood on the step for a second, a voice from within the billowing clouds spoke. It was just like Moses at the burning bush, I imagine: a disembodied, deep voice speaking from within the opacity. Except in this case, instead of getting your future career briefing, it was a joyous "Jim!"

"Hello, hello, hello!" A deep booming voice set off a cacophony of higher, smaller voices all chattering at the same time. I waited for Jim's voice to ensure that he hadn't been snuffed in the gloom, and when I heard his nasally reply, I held my breath and took the plunge. I emerged on the other side of the plume to see a trailer that was about ten feet wide by thirty feet long. It was divided into two major sections: immediately to my right, a partition and door that contained the office of the general, and to my left, the rest of the trailer was open. There were four despondent desks in the open part, along the right side of the wall, with about five and a half chairs. The desks were covered in papers and ledgers with some discolored computers jostling with overflowing ashtrays to stay on the desktop. There was a minifridge on the left side of the wall, under the windows, which looked out over the mini-Ts onto the back of another trailer. On the fridge were an electric teapot and a Lipton's black tea box beside a little dish with water and a couple of spoons in it. Farther back along the left wall was a battered, tan filing cabinet, the top piled high with even more ledgers and papers. Next to the cabinet was an actual Iraqi.

Actually there was a whole bunch of them. But since they were very animated and my eyes were burning, I had trouble getting an accurate count. I saw Jim surrounded by guys shaking his hand and wildly gesturing as if they hadn't seen him in a long time. To my knowledge, he had been there yesterday. I stood quietly for a second, my mind racing back to Camp Bullis, trying to cover all the rules that we had been taught for greeting. Was it the right hand over the heart? Was I supposed to man-kiss? A hug? What to say? Was it *marhaba*? How about *as-salaam alaikum*? There were so many ways to get this initial impression wrong. Because after all, these were rigid ideologues who very easily took offense; plus they were angry and resentful and dangerous. I knew this because the mainstream media had said so. While I stood there looking like a robot that had run down, Jim introduced me. And here they came.

I was probably the world's worst ambassador at that time, as I was being swarmed by five friendly, well-meaning Iraqis, and standing there like a dope. I was trying to place my hand over my heart (a sign of sincerity) at the same time that they were trying to shake it. I recovered, then tried to hug, and got jammed in the chest by an outstretched hand. I was getting ready for a man-kiss and starting to roll into one's outstretched arm only to realize that he was just clapping me on the back. I finally just stood still, in hopes of avoiding an international incident, which was clearly brewing. About that time, as I was out of airspeed and ideas, came a great, deep, booming laugh. Everything sort of subsided, and the two guys that were closest to me kind of turned. The booming laugh belonged to a short (maybe five foot four), squatty guy toward the back; he looked exactly like someone who would laugh like that. He was "portly": his "chocolate chip" uniform was stretched to the maximum so that between the buttons in his blouse were little parentheses through which you could see his T-shirt. He had a giant shock of thick, black hair and the giant, obligatory mustache. His dark brown eyes were big and piercing. He walked up, and noting that I was going through spasms of random etiquette, he thrust out a huge hand. I finally got it right and offered mine.

I'm not a small guy, but I felt like I had just stuck my hand into a meat glove. His giant paw engulfed mine, with the other hand following suit, until my right hand seemed to be truncated at the wrist. A brief flash of fear went through my head, as I was in a trailer full of bad guys with my gun hand effectively disabled. In retrospect, I guess that was the right reaction to have; I still didn't know these guys, and there were plenty of sketchy characters in the Iraqi military. But at that moment, my fear felt like a bit of a betrayal. I was here to help these guys, and I was worried about them killing me. Of course Jim, grinning like a Cheshire cat in jet jammies (he wore his flight suit; I rarely did) helped ease my mind. I hadn't thought about it from the Iraqis' perspective yet.

"Hello, my friend; I am Asad. I am pleased to meet you."

His deep voice matched the grin and the smiling eyes, and Asad seemed genuinely pleased to make my acquaintance. His English was very good, and he seemed very confident. I had studied the Iraqi rank insignia, and as near as I could tell, he was the equivalent of a colonel. It was a little hard to tell, because each uniform seemed to be of the "whatever I had lying around that morning" variety. Asad was dressed in the aforementioned "chocolate chip" cammies that were in use during the first part of Desert Storm; some of the other guys wore green French-designed flight suits; another wore an American flight suit; and the other guys wore a later variant of the desert cammies, the kind that had the soft pastels instead of chocolate chips. So it was a little tough to ascertain exactly what ranks I was surrounded by.

So I said, "Salaam alaikum." This seemed to make a small impact on Asad; his mouth twitched into a grin, and he gave the appropriate response; the giant hands relaxed their grip. He told me that he was an engineer—an aircraft engineer. I was a bit puzzled by the nomenclature, but as the conversation progressed, I was able to ascertain that he was an aircraft maintenance officer. I told him I was too. He beamed a huge smile and then said, conspiratorially, "You must be very smart then, no?" I would disabuse him of that later. He then mentioned that he was very valuable, mostly because he was the only one who could type.

Another man approached—this one a tall, bald guy, no mustache (!), and more of the big, brown eyes. He used to be thin, but now, as middle age had come and gone, a small, round belly filled out his French flight suit. He gripped my right hand while beating the crap out of my shoulder with his left. Some people would say that he was just clapping me on the back. But they weren't there; it was a beating. Apparently it was all in good humor as his face split into a toothy grin, beaming as he said, "Hello, hello, hello. Welcome, my friend; I am Kamil!" He was easily as tall as I was and seemed to radiate goodwill. He had a soft voice, but the guys seemed to listen when he talked. I got the impression that he was respected in this room. He also looked to be a colonel equivalent. He was a pilot, having logged hours in many different types of aircraft, including the F-1 Mirage and then trainers, the L29 and L39. Since I was in my Airman Battle Uniform (ABU) (like I said, I rarely wear my jet jammies), he assumed I was something else, not a pilot. We didn't get too far into that conversation when another man stepped up.

From the side of Kamil came a smaller man, balding, slight of build, and also in a French flight suit. He didn't have any patches on at all but did have the epaulets of a colonel. His boots were untied and the flight suit unzipped to about his navel. If he had just been mugged, no one would be able to tell. His remaining hair was unkempt; his voice was gravelly from way too many cigarettes. He came up to me, stuck out his hand from the pushed up sleeves on his flight suit, and said, "Hello, Major." My initial impression of him as a mess was blown away in a heartbeat as I looked into his twinkling eyes and felt them assessing me. There was hardness to those eyes, and intelligence gleamed behind the flint. "I am Colonel Wahid." His English was a little more reserved than the others but still perfectly understandable. He seemed to be a little shy, but something told me there was a lot more than met the eye with this one. He too was a fighter pilot, flying just about everything that the Iraqis had, including the Mig-21, Mig-23, and Su-24. In fact, I seemed to be surrounded by fighter pilots. Dammit.

Next came a tall, younger (mid-forties) Mig-21 pilot, sporting another French flight suit, a shock of gray spiky hair, and, yes, a giant moustache. This guy looked a lot like Saddam, except there was a kindness in his slate-gray eyes; he had a quiet, demure manner. He extended his arm out and, with a shy grin on his face, murmured, "Hello." His name was Ahmed. I was a doofus and mispronounced it "Aukmed." He was too kind to correct me then; indeed, it would be many weeks before he would correct me, and even then, it was only when his buddy, Nasser, prompted him to do so. He would prove to be one of the nicest men I have ever had the privilege of meeting.

Nasser I met next: jet black hair, push broom mustache poking out from a largish nose, protruding chin and darting eyes. Standing about five feet five, he looked like a little, tanned Super Mario; but he was almost painfully shy, fidgeting a bit as he shook my hand in a powerful grip. He too was dressed in a flight suit, but this one was impeccably put together: the pilot wings adjusted just so, and the lieutenant colonel epaulets clean and straight. He spoke in very precise, clipped words with a somewhat high, nasally voice. He had been a colonel in the old IQAF and had volunteered to come back in order to "help".—a very selfless man. He explained to me that he was an F-1 pilot and that his friend, Ahmed, had driven a truck. He saw the look of panic on my face; could I have misunderstood so badly what his buddy did? I stammered that I thought he flew the MiG. Nasser burst out laughing, then went into classic pilot mode, using his hands to demonstrate the relative turn radius of the two airframes. He didn't know a ton of English but made sure that every word was precisely enunciated. It sounded like a radio that you are quickly turning on and off, catching about every third word—kind of like HAVE QUICK out of sync. But from it I realized he was just dogging on his friend for flying a heavy fighter bomber instead of a quick little fighter like his. Fighter pilots never change.

I was running out of Iraqis to meet, but I still had yet to meet the boss. There was another guy who had come in from the little room on the right, which I had assumed was the general's. This was a very small little guy, probably about sixty years old, with unkempt, gray hair and a huge mustache. He had eyebrows so big he could dust things just by being surprised. He was clad in the chocolate chip cammies, with the blouse unbuttoned most of the way down and a dirty T-shirt underneath. The dirty shirt was struggling, but failing, to contain a giant poof of gray chest hair that was exploding like a fur grenade from his collar. He had very small features and a skittish manner, like a hairy little squirrel in a room full of cats. He stuck his hand out, almost setting me on fire, as he was holding the most rancid cigarette I've ever smelled. I actually knocked the ash off of it with my hand, as he drew back, switched the cigarette to the nonshaking hand, and tried again.

"Hello, hello, hello, Major. How are you, Major; I am fine, and I am Samir, and I am happy to meet you; it is very good to meet you, and I am Samir, and I am happy to meet you, and I am Samir, and hello and happy..." I'm actually not exactly sure of what else was said. But I gathered that I was a major, he was Samir, and he was happy to meet me. It turned out he was actually the Iraqi general's little brother. He was the only other one who was not a pilot; he was an "airplane director," which I later interpreted to be an air traffic controller. He was a very nervous little guy. A little later I would find out why.

As we made small talk, the boss showed up. General Abbas came in from outside, as he had been attending a meeting in their little building across the parking lot. He was a short man, with gray hair and a big mustache, in the chocolate chips again. The lower pockets of his shirt were bulging with something. You could see a little resemblance between Abbas and Samir, but Abbas was much more confident and presented a military bearing. He stuck out his hand, and I gripped it and shook. Again, the "Hello, hello, hello," and the effusive goodwill poured out. He pulled Jim and me into his office, where he began to talk about the United States and how great it was. It was the first of countless times that the "occupiers" would be referred to as the "friendly side" by the "occupied." Abbas had an interesting vocal quality: if he wanted to emphasize something, his voice would lilt upwards. He also would get very excited and repeat his yesses, as in, "Please, Banzet, you want some tea and crackers? Yes, yes yes yes yes." This would be followed, regardless of my response, by a machine-gun blast of Arabic, at which point one of the guys (almost always Samir) scrambled to get some tea on and, once complete, get some sort of biscuit or cracker to go with it and deliver it to us.

So that's what happened; midway through his speech on America, he asked if we wanted tea, and true to my training, I said heck yeah. Who wouldn't want hot tea when its 110 outside? Especially if it comes in cups that have never been washed! So Samir went scrambling off and plugged in the teapot, spooning sugar into the little cups in preparation for the hot tea. The rest of the guys were scrambling around trying to find something else to bring in to us, their own personal snacks and whatever was in the little fridge.

In just a very short time, we had lots of different goodies shoved at us, and shortly thereafter, the piping hot tea arrived replete with the Lipton's bag and a solid foundation of sugar settled on the bottom. That's when I discovered why the general's pockets bulged so. They were stuffed with crackers. Abbas reached into his pockets and grabbed a handful of crackers, placing them on the little blue-gray glass saucers that held our tiny cups. Crackers and parts of crackers anyway.

Abbas explained that he always had to eat things because he had "sick blood," so he had to constantly have a supply of munchies wherever he went. While he was explaining, Jim leaned over and whispered that he had diabetes, while Abbas continued on talking about the progress that had been made and what was ahead for A7. But all I saw was a big, gray squirrel pulling stuff out of his pockets and then, two-handed, nibbling on his crackers. He really looked like Merlin from the "Sword and the Sorcerer" when he changed into a squirrel. Again, sort of a typical moment for me: I was in this momentous occasion at the focal point of our efforts here, and I was trying mightily to stifle a terrible case of the giggles because I had transposed this Iraqi general with a five-foot-tall, camouflaged, cracker-eating, chain-smoking squirrel.

But I eventually got over that and started to listen intently to what he was saying, and the smile started to fade from my face and heart. As Abbas continued to describe the state of the efforts, he inadvertently veered into the situation outside the wire. Most of the guys here lived on the base for differing amounts of time. Some stayed for two weeks; some left every four days. It was very difficult to get on and off base for the Iraqis, including a lot of time spent standing in line at the entry control points (ECPs). And that was dangerous.

The insurgents watched the lines, looking for folks that were part of the new Iraqi armed forces. It was apparently okay to work for the Americans as a laborer or, of course, as a spy, but a member of the new IQAF was marked for death. So were their families. And this, relayed Abbas, was what happened to their middle brother. Someone found out that he was actually working with the Americans in the wrong capacity and shot him to death on a bridge. Abbas was thankful, however, that the bad guys acted too quickly and didn't patiently wait for the brother to go home to his family, because as yet, they were unharmed.

That explained, then, the younger brother's nervousness. He was terrified, waiting for the other shoe to drop. But Abbas, whether due to bravado or true bravery, declined to show any fear. He calmly went on and on about the training and how Jim was very helpful and how the friendly side helped so much; but he spoke very little about the dangers that awaited his staff or their families.

We had been in his office for quite a while, but he felt that he would gain important prestige if *he* introduced the guys. So even though the buzz had died down in the other room, he brought us back out to begin introductions again. We started with his brother, whom he dismissively introduced as "Samir" and then moved on. Samir, clung to my hand, pumping it as if we hadn't just met thirty minutes before, and tried to engage me in conversation, about anything: where I was from, how I liked Iraq, was I married, and so forth. I was trying to be as polite as I could, but I needed to catch up to the boss, so I sorta got caught in a tug-of-war for my hand. I eventually disengaged myself and caught up to the now-impatient Abbas. He was standing in front of Asad, who was sitting down at his desk, his ample belly now freed of his blouse; an overtaxed T-shirt accomplished the restraint. He was busily mashing his sausage-sized fingers one at a time onto the ash-filled keyboard in front of him.

Abbas, in his singsong voice, trilled, "This is Asad. He is very faaat; he is very lazzyyyy. He must run and get into shape, or I will kick him!" (I later learned that the term *kick him* generally meant "to fire someone," not physically kick.)

Asad calmly looked up at his boss, cigarette dangling from his lips, ash breaking then tumbling down his belly, finger poised above whatever unfortunate letter was going to be mashed next. He glanced at me, then with a twinkle in his eye, asked Abbas calmly, "Well...What do you want: typing or sport?"

I burst out laughing, as the rest of the guys broke up as well. Abbas reintroduced me to all the other guys, as we exchanged knowing looks and acted like we hadn't just met minutes before. I also heard about a couple other guys that weren't around that day: There was a mysterious Kareem "Sport," who was in charge of administering physical fitness tests for entry into the IQAF. I would meet him only once or twice. A couple of minor functionaries I would meet later, through happenstance, in the foreboding Ministry of Defense (MOD). But these, then, were the gentlemen I would be spending most of my time in Iraq with: Kamil, Asad, Wahid, Abbas, Ahmed, Nasser, and Samir would form the nucleus of the team that would help double the size of the IQAF in one year.

11

FOUR AMIGOS

So now, after all the administrative in-processing was done and I had been introduced to the guys, it was time to start the hard work of figuring out what exactly I was supposed to do about all I had learned. Nothing that I had been taught in my military training seemed like it was going to help me. All my training—except what I had undergone at Bullis—had been primarily focused on employment of weapons systems, how to lead and follow, and the administrative minutiae required (required?) to run a giant bureaucracy such as the air force. It looked, then, as if I would have to rely on the basic things I had learned as an American, not necessarily as an airman, to make me effective here: treat people well, start with honesty and respect, expect the best, prepare for the worst, and work hard.

For me, this meant getting the lowdown from Jim on the total current state of the Iraqi training system. So I would show up for work each morning; Jim and I would huddle in our corner desk, going over the figures that came effortlessly to him: how many people were in class 70, where they were, what phase of training they were in, and so forth. Then, we'd go through the whole drill with class 69. And so on. As I mentioned, Jim had this encyclopedic knowledge of them all. When I arrived, there were about four hundred folks in the Iraqi air force. They had established some training courses and some rudimentary recruiting, but it wasn't ticking on all cylinders. Jim knew that it wasn't enough, and the pressure to put more through was immense.

And that was the constant challenge: quantity versus quality. The old maxim that "quantity has a quality all its own" didn't really apply here. We had to have a minimum level of competence that many in the States take for granted, but here, it was compounded by war and decades of mistrust and duplicity as everyday givens. So how much time could we afford to invest in building an Iraqi airman in order to get the right level of competence and mindset? Not only were we trying to build competent leaders (and followers), we were trying to build that in an air force. Airpower is not only a complicated process to learn and master, it is more unforgiving of error. It is also an inherently English-language driven endeavor. So there were several strikes against our success before we even got up to bat. And our "bench" was pretty thin too.

We needed an educated person, knowledgeable of English, and brave enough to sign up for a public endeavor that made him (or her) an instant, persistent target of a couple of different groups. The insurgents were constantly hunting (and catching) members of the IQAF. The Iraqis were convinced that the Iranians were specifically targeting the IQAF, especially those members who'd flown missions against them in their war in the 1980s. They held a grudge. In addition, it was hard to even find out where to join. To be seen in one of the recruiting stations, which were under constant surveillance, could very well be a death sentence. We also couldn't just take the rural, farming kids, like the army could. In the poorer parts of Iraq, formal schooling was generally truncated early, and the schooling that a person did get was sketchy. That didn't bode well for the maintenance of a complicated weapons system or a C2 node or even command and control policies and procedures. No, we had to have a pretty rare combination of attributes for our trainees—the kind we take for granted in the States.

So we were racing against time, trying to build a credible air force that would keep a lid on the insurgents, inspire the general population to rally around the government, and eventually, provide a stabilizing force throughout the region. And all we had to do was teach them English, design a curriculum that wasn't too foreign, and establish an open and transparent moral order, while at the same time working with the existing old-guy network to nurture the young ones, keeping them alive long enough to graduate and then mentoring them while they came into the operational IQAF. Kind of a tall order for a couple of Americans and a few Iraqis.

In the meantime I got to know Jim and view his relationship with the four main Iraqis that he was working with. I knew that they liked him, as evidenced by the resounding welcomes we got whenever we showed up. And he genuinely liked them. Each day I would head over to the little, smoke-filled trailer to discuss the latest crisis, whether there was enough pay or water or food at the various sites for the students.

The first class, a small one, had graduated from the southern school (IMAR), and they were now in the system. Army inductees—they had been skimmed off the top of the class and sent to the air force start-up. The Iraqi air force was thought of as an elite service (in spite of the fact that toward the end Saddam was apparently unhappy with them), but it still took a lot of negotiations to make that happen. Out of the big compound at IMAR, which was a source of pride for the Iraqi army, a small chunk—a couple of buildings—had been carved out by the air force for their start-up course. These accessions were precious commodities, and to get the cream of the crop was a major coup. They were the product of a very rapid accession course, a lot of training in the British tradition of marching and such taught by Iraqi army instructors, overlaid with courses in our ethics and military discipline. But they were just the start of the pipeline.

Another group was getting ready to enter the training. They were college graduates who were going to be put in NAMAB to study English until their scores on the American Language Course Placement Test (ALCPT) scale met the minimum requirement: a 60 had been established as necessary to enter basic training, while pilot training required a 70.

A pilot training class hadn't yet begun, as they didn't have any trainer aircraft or Iraqi instructors. This was to be a real point of emphasis that we would push the Iraqis for; instructors of their own at all levels and areas of instruction that now simply didn't exist in any numbers. It was a real problem trying to get any; in addition to the risks mentioned above, there was a serious consideration that had to be addressed before bringing back mid- to senior-level former members of the IQAF—that is, Baath Party membership. Not only did the individual incur considerable risk in joining, the institution did too. Some of the folks trying to come back in were compromised or, at least, maintained allegiance to the old order. At the worst, they considered the new Iraqi air force members to be traitors and would actively pursue their deaths; at the least, they'd pass information on ongoing ops or American dispositions (where we were in the field, not whether we were cranky or not). Even folks who were on the fence could be lethal; if they got upset about anything, a casual conversation about who they were working with would spell death for that family. So Baath Party membership over certain levels was verboten, in spite of the sentiment that, according to Colonel Wahid, Baath Party membership was kind of a rubber stamp. Some used their membership in this club to get ahead; while some used their talents and ambition to get ahead, with membership being seen as a necessary evil. The trick was finding out who was who.

And that took time. Which we didn't really have. We had to get instructors in, and quickly. Our time horizon for getting the Iraqi cadre up to 20 percent was a couple of months. The Iraqis had a different timeline: however long it takes: it was their families and lives at risk if we got the wrong ones in. Our lives were at risk just being there, but we were fairly well protected by the heroes in the army. They were not; they lived in the neighborhoods and streets that the bad guys roamed with their beady little eyes watching for any hint of affiliation with the Americans.

So, as we went to see the Four Amigos every day, we'd hector them about getting more instructors into the pipeline, and they would, just as vociferously, say that they were trying, but it was a slow process. That was not welcomed in our morning advisor team meetings as we described the progress for the previous day. Our boss, the Brit, was very understanding and had a fairly pragmatic view; but the USAF folks in the IZ were a little more troublesome. And it wasn't Dice. The general, however brusque, seemed to understand what we were going through; it was the colonels in the middle, as it always is, who caused the most heartache.

We would have our charts and graphs, which showed no progress. This lack of progress would be carefully annotated and then captured in another briefing that would be generated to pass this report of no progress up the chain, where it would be briefed to the staff. Then the questions would come, along with the exhortation to try harder. Wash, rinse, repeat. No one liked telling the general about our tremendous lack of progress, but the Iraqis just couldn't move that fast. So we made up more charts; this time, we called them lines of operation (LOO) charts, with lots of arrows and colors on them in hopes that would help. Doing LOO charts had worked in all the academic exercises that the brass had been through. It was a complete mystery why it didn't work here.

"See, right here, this green arrow is '"Iraqi instructors" so the Iraqis should be getting "Iraqi instructors" because it's pointing, well, right toward progress."

"But they don't have any instructors because the security risks associated with rapid accession of men with unknown loyalties puts them and their families at risk, transforming an over-administrated, broken, slow process into a familial trust process, followed by countless, cautious interviews, followed by an over-administrated, broken, slow process. This looks like no progress, but it's just very, very slow progress."

"But this green arrow..."

And so on. The general was getting a ton of pressure from the top, rightfully so. As mentioned several times before (and will be several times after), this was a tightrope. We needed them to quickly take over the training and put more Iraqi faces on the military force, but too quickly would result in the waste of the sacrifices of the US men and women who had enabled them and us to get this far—and kill the most valuable Iraqis.

So Dice was walking a fine line. He was realistic on both fronts. But his minions were desperate to tell him good news (new that they had nothing to do with producing, neither would they live with the consequences of pushing too hard). You know that if you get to tell the boss good news, they associate that good news with you, no matter what.

That's why every time I briefed Dice, I rubbed his belly.

As we went through our daily meetings with the guys, I got to know them a lot better, and they, me. Jim and I were very different: he was a lot more serious, but both of us were fairly casual. Although I always referred to him by his rank, as I was his subordinate, I never felt restricted on what I could say to him. Of course, he was a really good guy, so it was easy to be respectful of him. Plus, it was important to show respect to him, regardless of his AFSC. The Iraqis put such a premium on pilots that we had to make sure they didn't dismiss anyone out of hand merely because they weren't zipper-suited sun gods. Except in my case, then it was perfectly acceptable.

We were going on the hunt for the elusive Iraqi instructor. To do that, we had to get the personnel director of the IQAF to help us out with the methods and up-to-the minute progress of the effort. But, because their data systems were destroyed, most of the records were captured on giant ledgers, which were kept in and on scratched, dented cabinets scattered throughout the musty basements in the MOD. So we first had to get access to those old, musty records. That meant heading over to the IZ, via Rhino, to meet Mr. Hadi.

Mr. Hadi was the personnel director for the IQAF, a retired army general who was being advised by one of the few females that we had with us. Denise was a real trooper, very confident, with a ready smile, and totally professional. She was able to work among the Iraqis without any trepidation; likewise, Hadi didn't have any hang-ups about working with her. And since he seemed to be well respected in the Iraqi military, I thought that he would be a critical ally to get to "want" to help us.

The whole Iraqi command structure was so fractured that it was next to impossible to look for a bottleneck organizationally (although there was significant efforts to map them), so I decided that I would try to attack the problem from a personal viewpoint. That meant networking with a lot of folks. This wasn't exactly new to the Iraqis, but they were a little hesitant to go too far outside their comfort zone, for some of the same reasons I've mentioned above. They especially didn't like going anywhere within their own chain of command. And that would show up later as a real problem.

As this would be the first time I had met Hadi, I felt I needed to bring a present. But I was pretty limited on what I could get. For some reason, I had a couple of Big Chief pencils, the ones that you get in the third grade that you wrap your whole hand around and scratch out *cat* on extra-wide, lined paper. Or maybe that was my senior year; I get mixed up. So I brought those.

We would meet one of the guys over in the MOD. I think Nasser came with us that day. Nasser seemed to be the guy that would travel to the external agencies with us the most. Asad would go with us in the compound where we worked in daily, but Nasser was the external guy. He felt a little more comfortable in the MOD, I guess.

So we arrived, blinking in the afternoon sun, in the Rhino yard of the IZ. Denise and Jim led off, as I hadn't been there before. I was wrapped up in my dusty body armor, helmet, equipment pouches, armed with my pistol. And sticking incongruously out of one of my 9 mil clip pouches were a couple of bright yellow Big Chief pencils. We walked through a couple of gates and onto the MOD grounds. Nasser was waiting there in his civilian clothes, a nervous smile on his face. He turned and set off for the front door. As we climbed up the steps, we paused at the door: there were quite a few posters plastered over the windows. I asked Nasser what they were, and he explained that these were "heroes" who had been killed in the last few months. One guy had been kidnapped right out of the MOD, then executed.

That made me feel just super.

The MOD was a huge building, about four or five stories tall and extending a couple of football fields in either direction. The inside was imposing as well, but the fake luxury was really starting to wear. In all of the buildings, there was sheen of faux opulence, as if Saddam was permanently tuned in to the Donald Trump decorating show but had to shop at a craft store to try to complete the look. So you had a lot of gold and marble things in various stages of falling off of the cement walls.

There was some wood on the walls, and the closer you got to power, the more wood there would be and the nicer the décor would become. But we weren't very close to power apparently; it was a bit run down, as we had come in through kind of a side door. Jim didn't like coming here very much, and I was starting to see why. The corridors were very dark, and quite a few Iraqis were milling around, some armed with variants of AK-47s. There were guards standing outside the doors of many offices, usually the ones with a lot of wood. So we were walking down darkened corridors, surrounded by a lot of armed soldiers of questionable allegiance, and all we had were our 9 mm pistols, body armor, and, for me, two really big, yellow pencils. But Nasser didn't even have that. He was just moving along in his civvies, without a thing to protect him.

We twisted and turned through several passageways, feeling more and more like I was in a Scooby Doo cartoon; disembodied eyes following our little procession through the haunted house, as the skewed electric lights flickered in tempo with the unreliable power generation. We reached the stairs, and as I started to go up the broad staircase to where I assumed the IQAF personnel director would be, I realized I was alone. I had assumed that the natural order of things would mean that the air force was on the upper floors. I was wrong. We were down. In the basement. In the moldy, scary Scooby Doo basement. So we made our way down the deteriorating marble stairs into the basement. This was a whole new level of uncomfortable. It was still dark, but now it was musty and smelly as well. As we moved through the ill-lit maze of ventilation equipment and plumbing, we saw offices and desks scattered throughout the space, wherever they could fit. Tired-looking folks in various stages of office-wear glanced up from their desks or appeared from the gloom, scurrying past with a sheaf of paper clutched in their hands. It was obvious to me that this was about as far from power as we could get, so I started to wonder if this Mr. Hadi could help us at all. Eventually, stepping over power cords connected to wobbly, dusty fans, and other office detritus, ducking under ducts and generally not touching anything, we arrived in the corner of the basement where Mr. Hadi had set up his empire.

It was a fairly small empire, just the corner of a basement with about eight to ten desks arranged as a moat, helping to protect the principle denizen. The lower part of the sweating concrete walls had a greenish tinge, as mold was a constant problem. But that didn't mean it was cool, by any stretch. Somehow the Iraqis had managed to mess with thermodynamics, violating the very laws of physics to ensure that it was hotter in the basement than it was upstairs. But the rattling fans did their best to ensure that it was all evenly sweltering by blowing around the moist, hot, smelly air.

We approached a wizened old man, snappily dressed in a faded sport shirt and tie. He was a skinny little guy, about average height for the Iraqis, but already it was obvious that he was totally in command of his element, however modest. We waited respectfully just inside the moat of office furniture, two giants in body armor (Jim and I) and one female, also sporting the latest in Kevlar fashion, and Nasser, in his casual Friday look. After a certain amount of discussion, Mr. Hadi dismissed the man he was talking to and looked at us as if he was seeing us for the first time. He didn't recognize Jim and I, but his already-lined face creased into a smile upon seeing Denise. In halting English, he said, "Hello, my good friend Captain Denise; it is good to see you. You have brought some more friends, I see."

Denise made all the appropriate greetings and turned to introduce us, Jim first. When my turn came, the frail old man clapped me on the shoulder, his dark eyes twinkling, looking for all the world like a grandfather greeting some poorly costumed trick-or-treaters. He gripped my hand in both of his, declaring that it was very good to meet us. I explained that we were here with the Iraqi training division, and introduced Nasser, who shyly nodded and made his respectful introductions. There was a slight pause, then Mr. Hadi barked out a couple of orders for someone to bring tea. He gestured at us to sit and then started rummaging through his desk for something. After a few minutes, he found what he was looking for and—with a triumphant "Aha!"—produced some chocolates. They hadn't fared well in the heat and I certainly didn't recognize the brand, but he was so proud of his treats that I just couldn't say no. Besides, I had learned it was bad form to turn down their offerings. I was always conscious of how much these snacks cost them and how much stock they put in making us feel welcome. So I picked the foil wrapping out of the candy and popped it in my mouth, surreptitiously getting the rest of the wrapper out of my mouth when Hadi wasn't looking.

Then I presented the Big Chiefs. "Sayyid, I brought you something as well. Many people that I talk to say that you are a big man in the Iraqi military. Because you are a big man, you deserve a big pencil. These are the biggest pencils that they make, and you should have them."

I gave him the pencils, with both Jim and Denise looking at me like I was the biggest dork. I was giving giant first-grade pencils to a very powerful man in the Iraqi military. Hadi wiped the looks off their faces, however, with the look on his. A beatific smile had come over his face as he grabbed the giant pencil in his diminutive hand. He held it upright in front of his face, like a tiny, wooden Excalibur. The look on his face was absolutely priceless. I mentioned that the pencil was also good for instilling discipline, by whacking people over the head. "That's why I wear a helmet, sayyid, because Colonel Jim"—rolling my eyes toward the erstwhile navigator—"hits me all the time."

Judging by Hadi's reaction, that was one of the three funniest things ever said in the history of humanity, and I'm not even sure what the other two things are. He just really enjoyed the thought of me getting hit over the head. A lot of people do, I'm afraid. Even though we had just arrived, and the rule of thumb was to just BS for thirty minutes or so before trying to conduct business, I thought that this broke the ice enough to try to get to the reason we were here.

I brought up that we had heard that there were about one hundred or so instructors waiting to come into the IQAF, and I wanted to know a little more about their whereabouts. It was very dicey trying to address any perceived deficiencies in someone's division or area of responsibility. So I couldn't just ask "…how come A-1 (the personnel division) was not getting the instructors we require" as that would trigger the avoidance response, and we would lose an ally before we started. So I kept it to just wondering where the instructors were. He immediately shouted out a couple of names, and in a couple of seconds a couple of guys popped up bearing giant ledgers. Each ledger had to have been 18 inches by 12 or so. Hadi grabbed one, and spun it around, so we could look at the…Arabic, in lines and columns. He started pointing out this line or that column as proof that they really did do a good job of getting Iraqi instructors. Nasser was fascinated, but then, he spoke and read Arabic. There were indeed about ninety instructors in various stages of accessions. Some were awaiting interviews, some were awaiting MOD approval; many had been approved, but had not returned calls.

Mr. Hadi allowed as that was due to the "security situation," which was a polite way of saying that many of these guys were scared to death, and something had happened in the interim that had caused their initial enthusiasm for joining up to wane. I never saw any of the guys berate or criticize those who decided not to join up; it was a personal choice that varied with all the families and situations. Mr. Hadi had placed his family in Syria, where he had relatives. He had lots of company in that regard. My four guys were about the only ones I knew that all had their families still in Baghdad. Most others had deposited them in Syria or Jordan, and a couple of folks put their relatives in Egypt.

So, it wasn't terribly odd to have guys that had previously expressed interest in joining back out as the stark realities of the reach of terrorism took hold. It just sucked for us. For all the chicken and egg arguments that have already been mentioned, until the terrorists felt that it was too dangerous for *them* to operate with impunity, it would be dangerous for *our* guys to publicly serve their country and their cause. So that was hurting us in this fundamental building stage. But Mr. Hadi, there in that dusky, sweltering basement, thought that the instructors would be coming to "help the friendly side" with the school.

I gently corrected him. "Sayyid, the friendly side is here to help *you* with the school. It's your school and your air force. Soon, we are going to leave; that's why it's important to have the right men instructing all the ones that come after."

He blinked in the silence, mentally slowing down my speech, translating on the fly. I was relieved to see, as he made it through my thought, a grin spread over his wrinkled visage.

"Yes, Banzet, it is our air force. You are right. We must *learn* from the friendly side. We are trying, but the security situation is difficult. It will take time. But we have one hundred instructors for you to use."

I loved the guy, but it was like arguing with a Democrat: facts versus intentions. Mr. Hadi was saying that we could count on these one hundred instructors because they *meant* to be available. I was saying that there is a significant difference between *meaning* to have a parachute on your back and *actually* having a parachute on your back. I wanted actual instructors that I could touch. Not that I would mind you, but we needed a physical Iraqi presence in the classroom.

But there are some bridges just a little too far to attempt on the first meeting. So, I allowed that it would sure be awesome when those one hundred readily available instructors would someday be in a classroom to do some instructing to this young force that was being built. He thought it was great that they had these one hundred instructors ready to use. Jim looked at me as if to say, "See what I've been dealing with." Nasser looked happy, but also shot me a knowing glance. Denise seemed to be happy I didn't poop on the floor in front of her advisee. So overall, it was a big success, with no real progress made. Which was a hard concept for me to get my head around before I went to Iraq, but not after. In Iraq, we would start to define "success" as not going backward, with "big success" meaning making discernible progress. And since I had given the head of the IQAF personnel division giant pencils, it was discernible progress—a "big success."

We left about the same way we went in, up through the labyrinth of pipes, wobbly fans, and sweaty people, up to the ground floor of the MOD. We established a trail formation much like the one we used when we came in: it provided a bit of security in these darkened hallways. The only person who didn't have someone watching his back was "Tail End Charlie," or "Tail End Mike" as the case was. I felt a bit silly, walking through these office hallways in full body armor, including helmet. Although I would also have felt silly taking a 7.62 round through the back because one of these guys had had a bad day.

We finally made it out of the building, blinking in the bright sun, and immediately started to sweat. We had a couple of hours to kill before taking the Rhino back to Victory, so we journeyed to the Green Bean coffee shop in the embassy. The smiling Tibetan served up our drinks while we gathered our thoughts. It was looking like building the IQAF was going to be a tough road for the allies. After my brief exposure to the Iraqis, I thought it may be difficult for them, too.

I didn't know the half of it.

12

THE MAGIC ELEVEN

Out of the chaos that was the beginning of the formal military education effort for the Iraqi air force, there emerged two main efforts: the OTS-like facility at Taji and the proposed four-year college (condensed to about two years) at the Iraqi Military Academy at Rustymaya (IMAR). We had stolen the first recruits for the IQAF from the Iraqi army graduates there, but we also had the first class that had been recruited straight from the Iraqi college system solely for the IQAF in training at IMAR. They were finishing up their marching instructions and weapons qualifications with the Iraqi army, after which they would come to the air force to get their language training up to snuff and go on to OTS at Taji. These were the first "pure" accessions brought in specifically for the air force.

Again, it's worth reminding the reader of the age of these young men. Most of them were around twenty-three years old. They had to sneak their way into the recruiting process and submit to a background check that could easily turn into a death warrant if seen by the wrong people. There was enough information in those documents to compromise the whole family. Most of them had joined without the knowledge of their families. One young man that I had the privilege to meet had told his father, but I found no one else among the students who had told anyone in their family what they were doing. It was dangerous for all involved. There were a lot of cover stories being spun, but with the fluidity in the work situation, families would believe that a young man had to travel up "north" to get work, only returning after an extended period of time. As long as there was money to help feed the family.

About this time, as if to reinforce the danger that the Iraqis were in just by attending our schools, K9, one of the advisors from the IMAR school, reported to us that the head of the Iraqi army facility that housed the IQAF school was stealing equipment, mostly computers, from the Iraqi air force. It was also recognized, unofficially, that this was a "bad" guy. The Iraqis didn't trust him at all but, with the constant threat of exposure, couldn't do anything about it. General Abbas explained that this was indeed a bad guy, but if the leadership from A7 were to confront him, they could all be compromised. So this was truly a job that only the friendly side could do. Jim wanted Asad and Wahid to come down, but they wouldn't be anywhere near any confrontation with the dirty general.

I gathered up another guy that worked on the headquarters side of the team, a big lieutenant colonel that I'll call Xerxes. He had a huge mustache, stood about six feet two, and had a Southern accent; he was perfect for the job.

This would be my first flight over Iraq in an Iraqi helicopter, and it would prove an eye-opening experience. It did start off a bit rocky. I was travelling with a couple of former generals and a couple of current lieutenant colonels, and I overslept.

I hate people who are late. It shows a lack of respect for whomever you are meeting. Also, it demonstrates a lack of discipline. So here I was, waking up in my hooch, my watch just sitting there, not beeping. With a hearty "Oh shit," I leaped out of bed and put on my office attire. By this time I was pretty good at whipping on all the body armor and stuff, but that was tempered by the fact that I was going to run and walk the mile to work, scrounge a truck, and then take the truck around the complex, covering about four miles and five or six checkpoints. And I was already late.

As luck would have it, it was a relatively cool morning, so at least I had that going for me. The mile to work went by fairly quick. The M-4 rifle was kept at the office, so at least I didn't have that hanging off of me. As ridiculous as those speed walkers look—hips swiveling, arms splayed out like they are square dancing forward—I looked like that, only up-armored. An up-armored speed walker.

I arrived at the work trailer in about eight minutes, hoping against hope that Jim and the guys would still be there. Nope, they had left on time. And Jim had a scowl when he left, according to the scuttlebutt. I was able to score a small truck, though, so I was still in the game. Since I didn't have any communications with the others at this time, I couldn't even verify they were still on the ground. The Iraqis said the helo had left though, so the mission was still a go. I just hoped the Iraqis would be late (at that time, a safe bet).

Spitting rocks from the tires, I zoomed out of our parking lot, across the speed bumps (don't know why they call them that, I never gained any speed upon hitting them), hit the pavement, and got started on my next challenge: the five-mile derby.

It was fairly uneventful, jumping speed bumps, passing big trucks on the wrong side, swerving off road, then becoming very polite and calm upon approaching a checkpoint. After passing the checkpoint, flooring the gas, drifting around corners, levitating over potholes, and then slamming on the brakes and ever-so-calmly approaching the next checkpoint. Dr. Jekyll and Mr. Earnhardt.

I hit the last challenge—that is, checkpoint—running about thirty minutes past takeoff. This was the entrance to New Al Muthana air base (NAMAB). This was the Iraqi base located just on the other side of Baghdad International's runways. They used the same runways. I wasn't sure if the commercial side was up and running yet, but the IQAF side sure was. They operated their C-130s and a detachment of the little CH-2000 aircraft out of there on a regular basis. The IQAF Hueys also went through there quite often.

In order to gain access to the base, I pulled into a corridor of cement T-walls, which guided me up to a cable that was stretched across the cement corridor. There was a two-tier security system in place to get through. First was a young "janood" toting an AK-47, sitting in a tactical, up-armored, white plastic lawn chair. I already had my plastic laminated NAMAB access card out and ready to go. He got up, smiled and waved at me, and ambled over to inspect my credentials.

I gave him a hearty *marhaba* (an informal hello), and he cleared me to go to phase two: an ancient gentleman in a little hut about fifteen yards farther along the cement corridor. In response to the wave and burst of Arabic from phase one, the old man came out of the little hut, blinking in the early-morning sun. I think his AK must have still been in the hut. Either that or he didn't have one, instead relying on some sort of ninja training so that he didn't need a weapon. But it was more likely that he just left it in the hut. He looked for all the world as if he had just woken up. He raised an acknowledging hand and dropped the cable to the tarmac. He waved me forward, and I bumped over the large speed barrier next to him. He waited till I went through, tiredly put the cable back on the hook, and went back inside.

As soon as I got out of sight, I hit the gas and, going as fast as I could reasonably justify, came rumbling past the little group standing outside the Iraqi terminal building. I had made great time, but I was still about thirty minutes late. It probably didn't help matters as the billowing cloud of dust settled gently over the little group of everyone who outranked me. I jumped out of the little truck, grinning (I do that a lot). I pulled all my gear from the bed of the truck, hoisted it on my shoulder and walked over to the dusty little group.

Jim looked pissed. His normally placid, kind face was scrunched up, and his jaw was tight. Xerxes didn't seem to be too bothered, and the Iraqis were just grinning their asses off. It was good news: the helo hadn't arrived yet, and the guys that had done everything right and showed up thirty minutes prior had now been waiting for an hour.

Meanwhile, as I walked up to the little, now dusty, group, I heard the distinct "wop wop wopping" of inbound Hueys. I started to laugh; my timing was perfect. I neared the group and offered my apologies. "I'm sorry gentlemen; my alarm didn't go off. I really apologize for my tardiness."

Jim was still mad but said dismissively, "That's okay."

Asad started chuckling as I was going through my apologies. I reiterated my sorrow at being late, but that just made Asad laugh harder. Even Wahid was chuckling now. I finally asked him what he was laughing about.

"Banzet, I don't believe you are sorry."

"What? I'm saying I'm sorry right now!"

"I don't believe you."

"But, I'm saying that I'm sorry! I'm sorry for being late!"

"I don't believe you."

Wahid jumped in. " Yes, Mike, I don't believe you too."

I wondered if there was some subtle Iraqi thing that I had missed to properly convey my abject sorrow at being late. Was I supposed to put my hand over my heart? Was I supposed to say some Arabic phrase before I apologized? What did I miss in my training that would allow me to properly show my deference and discipline?

Asad saw my mental gymnastics and thought he would clear it up. "Mike, do you want to know why I don't believe you?"

"Yes, Asad, please tell me." I made a mental note to take down whatever cultural nugget was going to come out, some subtlety that I could use to ensure that the Iraqis would take me seriously, and so I could truly communicate with them. I was ready.

"Mike," Asad giggled, " I would believe you are truly sorry if you weren't laughing while you said it."

Oh. Then they both burst into another round of guffaws, and Asad popped me on the shoulder and told me they were very happy to have me here. But, they cautioned, Jim was very upset. They didn't think it was a big deal, but Jim was mad. I told them that I would fix it. Just about that time, the Hueys settled, and the Iraqi door gunners came out to meet us, splitting us up and guiding us to the sides of the helos. I noticed there were Americans scattered through the two crews flying the birds.

I had resolved that if I was traveling by ground, I would only need to take my 9 mm pistol. If we were hit by something, not only would there be some pretty angry army guys with automatic weapons around me, but also, if some of the army guys were down, there would be plenty of guns. I felt this would not be the case when traveling by air. If I got whacked while in the helo, in the off chance that my magic flight suit did protect me from the fireball, impact, or what knocked us down in the first place, the chances that I would be on my own were pretty high. There were guns on the helo, but I didn't have much faith they would be usable. So I decided that if I was going to be traveling by air, I would include my M-4 and appropriate ammo, which meant all I could stuff in my ammo pouches. The guys we were fighting didn't take prisoners. I didn't intend to be one, for however brief period of time I would have my head on. Geneva convention and all that notwithstanding.

After both my guns, I threw on a backpack with some other essentials, so I was about as awkward as I could be as we waddled toward the Hueys.

The young Iraqi door gunner was standing outside the helo, making sure no one would walk into the tail rotor and become a pink mist or, worse, ruin the tail rotor. Then, like a column of up-armored ants, the first couple of folks disappeared into the open door. By the time I got there, clearly it was already full. There were already about twelve pounds of Americans crammed into a ten-pound helo. I hesitated, assuming I'd be placed elsewhere. I was wrong. So in I went.

The gunner went down the line of passengers, ensuring they were all strapped in, then strapped himself in to the outward facing seat, just aft of the co-pilot. He swung the gun into position, barrel carefully pointing up. I looked over at Xerxes; he flashed a mustachioed grin. I glanced back at the gunner; he seemed to say a few words to the pilots. The whine of the engine rose a couple of octaves, and the rotor disk started to flex upward. We were on our way.

As this was my first helo flight over Baghdad, I was on super high alert. I swear I saw gun flashes all over the place. Every broken bottle, every mud puddle was an AK-47. The gunner was calmly surveying the scene, but I was looking all over the place, becoming acutely aware of just how thin the doors really were. I wasn't confident they would repel a paperclip launched by a rubber band, much less a 7.62 round. This type of helicopter wasn't meant to take a punch; it was meant to haul folks around. The pilots were armored, but the cabin area didn't have a lot of protection, as weight is always a premium for any aircraft, more so for helicopters. Now in flight, the chopper didn't vibrate much, but the classic Huey rotor slap made for an interesting soundtrack to our journey. It was okay by me, because as long as that noise was being generated, so was power to the rotor. If it got quiet, I would really start to complain.

The flight didn't take that long, and as soon as I figured out that the gunner probably didn't need a whole lot of help, I took out my little camera and started taking video.

I remember being struck by how old the young gunner's eyes were; they looked weathered and weary. He was constantly shifting his gaze over his area of responsibility; it must have been exhausting, day after day, hour after hour. Just like the gunner in the HMMVV. I was again struck how my life and the lives of all those in the aircraft were in the hands of this young Iraqi, a total stranger who's only connection to me was that he had been trained and mentored by a fellow American. He saw me grinning at him and flashed a tired smile back at me.

We hustled over the city in our loose formation, two tan dragonflies darting across the pale sky—perfect targets, if one were so inclined. But, since we reached the outskirts of the IMAR perimeter without incident, I guess without incident, I guess no one was. The city was a mass of garbage and chaos: soaring, beautiful structures next to smoking garbage pits. It surprised me a great deal. According to the media, Iraq was pristine before we got there and ruined everything. I didn't see the kite-flying tournaments that we were assured went on there, but many times I did see self-propelled dust clouds twisting their ways over any flat, clear piece of land. Occasionally, these clouds of dust would break up into groups of little kids booting a soccer ball back and forth. Sometimes the little guys would wave, but most of the people who looked up didn't. The kids did though.

As we broke over the berms that defined the boundaries of the IMAR complex. The school itself was the southern tip of the area, so the helos tightened up and got into their landing formation. I saw the small bit of concrete that we seemed to be aiming for, and the Hueys made a sharp break to landing. The nose came up, killing the airspeed, and the aircraft started to settle to landing. As they squatted on the ramp, I untangled myself from the mass of crap I had brought with me, and Xerxes and I disembarked. We were met by K9 and hustled to his truck. As we piled into his truck (I went into the bed of the vehicle), the thumping increased, and I turned to see the Hueys lifting off, tail high, into the bright Baghdad sun.

K9 took us on a little tour of the base as I bounced around in the back of the little Toyota. This place had a lot of history—, ironically, British history. The Brits had a huge influence in the region, and it still showed up in various ways. The manner in which the Iraqis marched and saluted was a big nod to that heritage, which revealed itself as we bounced along.

A couple of platoons of Iraqi army cadets came marching by, guided by a senior cadet armed with a wooden stick—a symbol of immense prestige that projected instant authority. This young man saw us out of the corner of his eye, puffed his chest out a little farther, and barked his orders out a little louder.

I'm not sure what he was thinking, but he kept looking at us out of the corner of his eye. His face became sterner, and his stick became more active. Pointing here, gesturing there: a large requirement for instruction had apparently just been realized. That attitude rippled down the column; in turn, the marchers' chests puffed out, shoulders rolled back, and boots stomped a little harder onto the dusty earth. Orders were barked out louder still, and responses were crisp and tight. As we continued driving past, about twenty sets of eyeballs slid into their corners to keep us in view. We drove slowly in the opposite direction and past the cadet commander at a distance of about six feet. The young man's brow was furrowed, and he wore a scowl on his lips. He made a point of avoiding our eyes as the little truck slowly trundled by. His little group started to bend around the edge of a building, and I continued watching. Just as he was about to disappear behind the wall, the cadet commander looked my way. Time stopped as our eyes locked. There was a second pause; then his face split open with a giant grin. He raised the big stick in a salute. I waved back in reply, as he disappeared from sight. It was one of my most memorable salutes.

We finally came to a halt in front of what looked to be a fairly new building, at least from the outside. Apparently, the air force contingent had been given one of the newer facilities to conduct their classroom training, with other types of instruction (weapons, marching, etc.) being conducted by the Iraqi army. K9 allowed how that this basic training certainly had a place, as that was one place where they had Iraqi instructors, at least at the tactical level, where the cadets could see them. The training would be more effective if the Americans were part of the foundation, but not as visible parts. But we would take what we could get: Iraqi army providing marching and basic military instruction, with ethics and "air mindedness" being taught by the USAF advisors.

We jumped out of the truck and started to walk up the wide stairs into the building. There were a few USAF guys working on sandbags on the side of the building. They had been hit by some mortars a couple of days before and had some windows on the ground level blown out. There weren't any injuries, but apparently, it had indeed disrupted the lesson. I stopped and talked to one of the guys stacking the bags. He was a midranking enlisted guy from a personnel career field. He had been there about four months and loved what he was doing. He had never done anything like this, and in spite of the sniper attacks, rockets, and mortars, he really felt he was helping these young men see things from a different perspective.

He was one of the very few Americans these Iraqis had interacted with. And even though he wasn't trained specially for this, as an American military member, he was expected to succeed at his task, whatever it took. So he was assisting in English language instruction in his spare time, in addition to syllabus development and classroom instruction. Plus sandbag development. The heroes of the opposition were pretty fond of rocketing and mortaring the schools that their countrymen were learning the ways of the decadent West in. So there were a lot of sandbags and aid stations around the school. We were already trying to cram a lot of schooling into the kids' skulls in a short amount of time, and trying to learn English listening with one ear in the headphone and one listening for incoming rounds slowed things down a bit.

We had to meet the commander of the school in about an hour, so we had to leave the sergeant and continue our impromptu tour. We walked into a dimly lit entrance (sandbags over windows cut down on the ambient light) and looked for a place to set our gear down. Off to the side was an instructor's office where we could put our backpacks and stuff, but we wouldn't be leaving our guns; those would accompany us everywhere. After stowing our gear, I got a chance to look around a bit. Even though this was supposed to be one of the prestigious schools, it was that same sort of painted plaster over cinder-block construction that made for lumpy, weepy walls. Hollow-core wooden doors contributed to the general cheapness of the interior. A fine coating of dust blown in through the numerous blasted windows left evidence of activity everywhere.

We peeked into one of the classrooms and saw the combination desk/chairs that are ubiquitous in middle schools throughout America. The thing that struck me was that there just weren't very many of them. Those seats were being used by the future backbone of the Iraqi air force. And there were so few seats. This was another one of those moments, when the gravity of the situation hit me all at once. I was here, at the beginning of a new chapter for an entire nation. The first "pure" class had yet to graduate, and the hard work put in by those before me had positioned us for success. Some of the basic processes were in place, but the big drive to fill those seats was the subject of all the PowerPoint briefings that I'd seen. Here was the best evidence that America doesn't destroy, it builds. We had excised the tumor of Saddam, but the infection of radical Islam was all about, sniffing for weakness and striking where it found some. We were creating antibodies here. Ones that eventually would spread and make the whole region a safer, healthier place. If we could just get them to live that long.

The cadets themselves were in another part of the complex, learning to fire AK-47s with the Iraqi army, under the mentorship of the US Army.

This was okay with me, because this visit was really about confronting the base commander about missing equipment and corruption. The United States had spent a lot of money on local business, to refurbish this and other buildings, and the scuttlebutt was the base commander was getting a cut of it. The most heinous suspicion, though, was that he was involved in the disappearance of some cadets, and in general being a bad guy. Which was why our A7 guys felt uncomfortable coming with us to see the commander, instead, dealing with their peers stationed there. I was glad that I had the big lieutenant colonel with the big mustache along.

At the appointed hour, we arrived at the man's office. Xerxes, Jim and I were with K9 only, as we really wanted to minimize the number of faces this guy saw confronting him. If he was as dirty as we thought, it wouldn't do to make him mad and still have to sleep in close proximity to his power base. So K9 was pretty nervous and really wanted us to do all the talking, especially the talking that included words "You're a dirty bastard" and stuff.

I had my pistol and M-4, and Xerxes and Jim were similarly armed. K9 was just wearing his pistol. The Iraqis were not supposed to be armed, but sometimes, bad guys have been known not to follow the rules (something gun control zealots have yet to realize). So we were sitting in the anteroom with a couple of this guy's Iraqi assistants. The room was well appointed, a couple of fairly new couches along the walls with some fabric-covered frames standing in front of the walls themselves. These effectively screened the walls, creating a space to hide... something.

Unusually, there wasn't any tea offered up, and we were kept waiting for too long, I thought. My sixth sense started to tingle a bit, so I stood up, under the pretext of stretching my legs. I tried to nonchalantly look behind the screens, but I couldn't do it without attracting a lot of attention. Again, there was a delicate balance to be struck. We didn't want to come off as scared, which would equal more pushing and malfeasance from the bad guys, but I certainly didn't want to be dead either. We were trying to pretend that everything was all right and there were no suspicions, while I was getting ready for anything. I hadn't really been trained for gunplay at close quarters, but at these ranges, I wouldn't really have to be a very good shot. I would just have to shoot.

We all sat on the couches and talked with one another, while the Iraqis sat quietly. Eventually, another Iraqi came out and said that the general would see us now. I guess he had kept us waiting long enough to establish how powerful he was. K9 had told us this was his standard MO. He would constantly slip meetings or delay them so long they were of no use; very rarely did anything productive come of scheduling a meeting with this guy.

We were ushered in by the third Iraqi, the other two falling in behind us. We arrived in front of the man's massive desk, the two guys behind us sliding off to the sides, one of them joining the usher, who had slid off to our left. That made it four to three. The general was a heavyset guy, with typical Arab features: an aquiline nose, dark hair, dark eyes, and, of course, the ever-present mustache. He smiled; his eyes didn't.

K9 said hello, and introduced we three as people coming from head-quarters to talk about some things the school needed. In deference to rank, he introduced the colonels first, then me.

I slapped my right hand over my left breast. "Salaam alaikum, sayyid."

"Wa alaikum al salaam," he replied.

"Please, my friends, sit."

The layout of the room was very similar to the one we had just left, maybe a little bigger. The same type of screening was in front of the walls on the sides, and now, there were two Iraqis on our left and one on the right, plus the general behind the desk, facing us. There were two couches angled to form a loose V in front of the desk, which, if one were to sit in them, would place our backs to the door and the walls. That would not be me. There were four Americans and four Iraqis (that we knew of). We were pretty sure the Iraqis were not as clean as the driven snow, and we were not combat experts. Xerxes was an A-10 driver, Jim was a nav, I was a KC-10 driver, and I think K9 was a logistician or something. SEALs probably wouldn't be that impressed by our hand-to-hand skillsets. Or Boy Scouts either.

The general pretended he was outraged that we hadn't had tea yet and ordered it up with a great show of theatrical anger and indignation. One of the Iraqis ran out to get tea, but I expected he was leaving for some other, more nefarious purpose. While he was gone, neither Xerxes nor I felt comfortable sitting in the couches. That would put us in a terrible tactical position. It's hard to bust a cap in someone's butt from a seated position on a couch.

The disconnect couldn't have been more strident. Here I was in an edu-cational system, worried about an ambush. A real one, not an intellectual exercise. Where the loser was dead or in front of a video camera in an orange jumpsuit, not just embarrassed.

So, with me twisted into a pretzel sitting on one of the couches trying to cover the door, the pleasantries began. Xerxes thanked the crooked bastard for providing a place for the air force to train and for taking such good care of them. The noxious little turd was magnanimous, allowing that he was pretty awesome and a great guy to boot. I kept trying to figure out what was behind his desk and there were those fabric-covered frames off to either side of it as well. Plus I was thinking that I would feel better once the missing Iraqi showed up with the tea, hopefully without an AK-47.

After a relatively short exchange of pleasantries, K9 started steering the conversation around to the missing computer equipment. The general kept steering it away from that topic. We certainly weren't going to broach the issue that we thought he might have been behind the killing or kidnapping of our students, not now. We would start with the equipment piece. And that was what K9 kept hammering on.

"What has happened to our computers, sayyid?"

"They must be stuck in our warehouses."

"They were stuck in the warehouses for the last two months."

"Ah, paperwork is very hard to do, and it takes a long time."

"You said the paperwork was done the last two meetings we had."

"It is very difficult; plus, I don't think we have the computers."

"What has happened to the computers, sayyid?"

And so on.

Shortly after this exchange, it became clear that Xerxes didn't have a lot of patience. I was still waiting for the missing Iraqi to come back, but Xerxes was having none of it. There were guys that had a very tough time dialing back the American "cutting through the BS" trait, and he was one of them. He abruptly stood up, grabbed a chair, and flipped it around so it was in the middle of the little space in the center of the couch-desk-couch triangle. He then sat back down on it and said something like this:

"Listen, sayyid, I think you know where these things are, and you need to help us get them back. They are not your property, and the Iraqi air force needs them. If you are stealing things from us, we will find out, and we will be very unhappy."

I imagine my eyes got really big about that time. I was really concerned that we were not in a very defensible position if the unthinkable happened and we pushed the general into a corner where he thought the best option would be a noisy, high-caliber argument. I wasn't sure about K9's or Xerxes's handiness with weapons; I certainly hadn't done much air force–mandated training for close-quarters stuff. As I've mentioned before. If the United States were invaded by paper targets that stopped at distances of fifty, twenty-five, and five meters, the country would be safe with me. Given that I didn't think these two individuals had been through any secret Rambo training, I tried to soften the Xerxes's statements.

"Sayyid, we think the computers are probably lost, but I bet you can find them. The most powerful man in IMAR can find things that are lost."

The general continued to prevaricate, but a little less stridently. He acknowledged that there were some accountability problems with the air force, but he thought that maybe he could work through them to get the computers back. After a little bit more conversation along those lines, the missing Iraqi came back in. With tea. I could tell that K9 was a little more comfortable now.

I think the one-two was a pretty good combo. I hadn't realized I would be playing good cop to Xerxes's bad cop. K9 was happy to be the "I'm not causing any trouble for you" cop, because he had to live there. We were happy because the guy knew that we knew that he was dirty, but we had also given him an out, to be slightly less dirty.

We ended our meeting with good feelings all around. We had a definite time frame to get the equipment back, and no one was going to get knifed in the back. As we walked back to the school building, I mulled over that maybe I had been wrong all along about this guy. Maybe K9 was overreacting. Maybe Xerxes's threats were wholly unnecessary. Perhaps our very vulnerable students were safe after all, and the Iraqi army leadership was doing their best to ensure their success. Only time would tell.

Classes weren't in session, so we decided to just walk to where the students lived, joining up with a very happy Wahid and Asad on the way. This is when I would start to know this extraordinary group of young men, and thanks to the perfect timing of my deployment, I got to see most of them all the way through the process. We soon arrived at where the students were warehoused. That is a decent word for it, as the billeting arrangements left a lot to be desired, at least from our point of view. The facilities were constructed of a god-awful green sheet tin, with internally divided walls over bare concrete floors, dressed up as best could be by the young men that lived there for weeks at a time.

As we approached, I noticed a couple of jagged holes and broken windows. From mortars and neglect, but mostly mortars. There were sandbags piled up around the outside but not in a neat, effective fashion, just piled up. Overall, it looked like the green deserted building that you see in every movie where they finally figured out where they are holding the kidnap victims. Before the big shootout.

As Jim and I made our entrance, young Iraqi men came popping out of their living spaces, faces bursting into smiles as they saw that it was the Americans. They all came up and wanted to introduce themselves and ensure that I knew their names, and that they got my name correct. But Banzet was out. They just couldn't pronounce it. They would've broken their teeth trying. So they collectively settled on "Major Mike" or "Bonset." Once we got that straight, we proceeded with the tour.

We followed the gaggle of Iraqi officers in training through their living spaces. It really looked a bit like an indoor homeless shelter. There was the overarching space, which was quite big, that had been divided into smaller rooms by some concrete walls, but the predominant impression that I got was lots of tin. The tin was further divided by fabric and clotheslines. Very colorful sheets and blankets completed the "construction" of their little warren. The floors were raw cement, with the occasional rug and, in some cases, pillows. Of special note was a blue inflatable chair sitting in the middle of the floor.

There wasn't a whole lot in the way of creature comforts, as the accommodations were arranged by the Iraqi base commander with whom we had just exchanged pleasantries. So just keeping the cadets out of the sun was considered a win. Americans do have a way of taking care of folks in need, though, so if the cadets were ever in real need of something, that something usually showed up, often times via the personal dollars of the USAF members there. Just another way we terrorize brown people.

On this initial visit, the little group of eleven were very interested in meeting with the new Americans. I spent some time talking about my family and why I had come here in this capacity; why I was away from my family for a year. At that time, I didn't really appreciate the scope of the danger these guys were in, especially when they weren't under our care, but outside the wire in the red zone. Even as I slept under "the blanket of protection" provided by the professionals in the US ground forces, they were totally without cover when off of the complex.

They told me what happened when they tried to get home for the three- or four-day break they got every couple weeks. They would get paid, in cash (the Iraqis had no electronic money system, no checks or anything), and leave through the gate. They staggered their departures to avoid tipping off the vultures perched outside the gate there was prey afoot. Few had cars, so they would then hook up with their carefully prearranged rides with trusted friends. This was someone who knew they worked on base; some of the rides were trusted more than others and knew the truth. Sometimes these rides terminated at a bus stop, which added another removal from the base, where they would board a bus to their final destination. Or they would walk from the bus stop, to give the illusion that they had arrived via that conveyance.

Others had farther to go, and that involved checkpoints. Like everything else in Iraq at that time, some of these were more "official" than others. According to the cadets, closer in to Baghdad, the US Army would assist in manning the checkpoints, and thus, the cadets felt safer. But out farther into the rural areas, the Iraqi army took over, and the professionalism went down markedly. As did the trust. A young man travelling various distances with (relatively) large amounts of cash on him would have a very hard time explaining himself. There certainly were a lot of bad conclusions that even the most trustworthy of guards could reach. There were also several bad conclusions a corrupt gate guard could reach. Any of these could result in a shootout. As these guys relayed these situations, I could see the tension in their faces. I tried to imagine my stress if each commute I made could result in me being shot or kidnapped or robbed.

They all had to go through some form of that every couple of weeks. They couldn't stay on base forever, and most of them had to get their *floos* (money) home to their families, which drove them to take these risks. And they were real risks.

Some of the other students in the same area had been killed, kidnapped, or just disappeared. And with each one that disappeared, there was the gut-churning fear that the deadly dominoes would start to topple. Information would flow from one tortured soul to another until finally, when our student arrived home, yelling the Arabic version of "Hi, Mom, I'm home," there would be bloody strangers waiting instead. For another domino.

In spite of that, the students seemed to be very chipper, talking about their engineering prowess and the language challenges they were experiencing. There was a constant pull from one area to the other, as we would get invited to their living spaces, and someone would try to fire up some tea.

It was really very, very basic, but they were proud of their surroundings. They had done what they could with what they had; the electrical connections these men had come up with meant that using any electrical appliance had the potential to provide lots of entertainment value for the survivors. But the chatter never stopped. They would keep peppering Jim and me with questions about the United States and our families. We ended up adjourning to a classroom, where Wahid and Asad got to work.

They turned from the fun-loving guys that had accompanied us down there, to military professionals. Asad listened respectfully as Wahid spoke. It was very evident that Wahid was used to being listened to. The man was a natural-born leader, and it showed. The normally chatty students listened respectfully, and eyes turned from Asad to Wahid as one then the other made points about the Iraqi air force.

Of course, I didn't have a clue as to what was being discussed, as most of the conversation was in Arabic, but the students seemed to be paying attention. I did notice that, in spite of the attention paid to the two splendid Iraqi officers, the young men kept sneaking glances at me and Jim, as if to corroborate whatever the Asad and Wahid were saying. Of course, given that I didn't speak the language, I was really trying to match the inflections of the guys with my facial expressions.

After too short a time, we had to get to the landing zone for our helo back home. We said our goodbyes, clapped the smiling kids on the back, and started walking back to where we had stowed our stuff. We didn't have a lot of time before we gathered our gear, jumped into the back of the Toyota, and reversed the process to get back home. Sure enough, right on time, two tan insects skittered across the washed-out sunset to become Hueys settling on the ramp. We squashed our way in again, Xerxes folding himself up and me hurling myself into the cabin.

As we winged our way over the darkening city, we shouted over the thumping rotors about the events of that day. Overall, we both were satisfied with the way it went. I thought that the general wasn't such a bad guy; Xerxes thought he was, but that he had been stymied, at least for this round. I thought that I had been silly, being overcautious. I also thought Xerxes had pushed too hard; but it may have been the combination of me and Xerxes that made the general see things our way. We jinked and swooped around the mauve sky, the tan skin of the Huey blending into the night. It was a beautiful night, ripe for thinking big thoughts.

The baser human emotions were less fixed than I thought, perhaps. Maybe evil wasn't as ingrained as I thought. Maybe truly evil people just haven't had the right chance. I thought about the guys I was working with, the Four Amigos. To date, I had seen nothing but kindness and care from them.

They had married women from different Islamic sects (the Sunni and Shia that Joe Biden said couldn't live together in the same country). In fact, the quote from the Democratic senator, now vice president, was: "The idea, as in Bosnia, is to maintain a united Iraq by decentralizing it, giving each ethno-religious group—Kurd, Sunni Arab, and Shiite Arab—room to run its own affairs, while leaving the central government in charge of common interests" [5]. It's a good thing our guys hadn't read that article, or they would've gone home and divorced their wives, started a war within the office, and defected from the air force. The number one man was a Kurd, the number two a Shia, and it was a mixed bag after that.

They were kind toward Christians (story about that later) and did not even get agitated over the subject of Israel. Of course, this may have all been a front, but I just didn't think so. Little, timid Lt. Col. Samir had just wanted to live in peace and grow flowers. Yet he had been at war his whole adult life. He didn't even want to be in the military, but it was the best way to be protected in the Saddam regime. His older brother had recently been gunned down. His one remaining brother, General Abbas, had to watch over him, like an older brother should. He was constantly worried about his wife and children, as were all the guys.

So, if there was goodness in the Saddam air force, even while they as an organization were doing terrible things, couldn't there be goodness in this base commander? Was I wrong to be so mistrustful of the general and his motivations? I was starting to think that I had to trust more. Even though I wasn't as exposed as the students and staff were to malfeasance within the

---

5 GELB, JOSEPH R. BIDEN JR. and LESLIE H. Unity Through Autonomy in Iraq. May 1, 2006. http://www.nytimes.com/2006/05/01/opinion/01biden.html?pagewanted=all (accessed June 24, 2012).

Iraqi military, I was vulnerable in stages. Still, I wasn't worried about my family being hurt, and I wasn't worried about being kidnapped (much), and I didn't have much call to venture off the base and mingle with the public. Sure, I could get sniped or rocketed or mortared, and had, but the bad guys couldn't really get to me. So I had good reason to trust more, not less.

As a matter of fact, I was wondering if my Iraqi friends had made much ado about nothing. Maybe they were exaggerating the dangers they were enduring. Perhaps they were using that "danger" as an excuse to drag their feet and perform slowly. I was still relatively new, and I thought that maybe my underlying assumptions could use another look. So I looked again at the mission in a different light.

It turned out that it had been a success. A couple of weeks later, K9 said that the missing equipment had shown up. So I was proven right. My basic faith in people doing good things when given the chance was proven out. Xerxes was too hard on the poor guy. My students were in good hands, and I could rest easy that they were safe in IMAR.

A couple of months later, in a joint op, the army assaulted the school with the express intent of taking that general and his minions out. It turns out that the "general" was actually a colonel, and the reason he was in charge was because he had kidnapped the real general. The joint op blew locks off doors, searching for him and his rat-bastard cohorts. A USAF "personnel-ist" captain was shot in the firefight that ensued. They found the colonel hiding in a closet with a pistol. It turned out he was dirty as hell, and may have contributed to the death of at least one of the students. A noxious weed in this garden of oh-so-fragile young blooms. So much for my theory.

But, my theory of the hard work and dedication of the American "gardeners" was well founded. With the constant oversight and assistance of the staff at IMAR, and the rest of us providing top cover, the Magic Eleven made it out of IMAR intact and were instructed to report to their next phase of training: specialized English training at NAMAB.

As mentioned before, the Commander of the Iraqi Air Force had made the decision to mandate that English proficiency would be a prerequisite for an IqAF commission. This group represented the first group of IQAF cadets that would go through the whole syllabus, including the English proficiency hoop they had to jump through. That requirement did lengthen the time required to get a person commissioned, and the numbers of IQAF officers was of intense interest to the friendly side. So there was a lot of pressure to pump bodies through.

We gave them a couple of weeks to get settled; then Jim and I went over to monitor their progress. We told Bev we were coming, then jumped in a truck to head over to NAMAB. Bev was the person most responsible for ensuring the eleven young men received quality English language training (ELT) while at NAMAB. She was a tiny bleached blonde, about five feet tall, one hundred pounds, with an energy that belied her age. I was never rude enough to ask, but she had to be around sixty or so. Her sun-wrinkled face was always full of optimism and cheer. She loved those young men and was so dedicated to English language proficiency that, after spending all day with the students, she taught the old guys (current Iraqi officers) on the side, in the evening. All with a pistol hanging off of her waist.

I think she worked for the Defense Language Institute and had volunteered to be there. It wasn't her first time, either. She really had the right temperament for being there, doing what she loved. She was absolutely fearless and took no crap from anyone. That was exactly the tone that needed to be set for these young cadets. In a society that was full of sliding truths, these young guys soon learned that Bev was a stone wall. No one slid through her class. The minimum score was required to progress—end of discussion. She gave the older guys a lot more flexibility, as they weren't in a formal course and being too hard on them would discourage them, but the students got the hammer—the velvet hammer.

She brooked no nonsense from the young men but was an absolute she-bear when she felt her students were in jeopardy, and that venom was usually aimed at the bureaucrats that made life more difficult for her there. She was constantly fighting with the supervision back at DLI about re-volunteering in place, to continue the progress that she was seeing. But the rules said she would have to go home soon, whether or not she wanted to stay. So she made a lot of enemies stateside. The young Iraqi students, however, with all the vulnerability that surrounded them, ended up calling her Mom.

So, Jim and I had commandeered a vehicle and drove over to the facility one sweltering day, all armored up in our little Toyota-like pickup. We made it through the checkpoints and bounced over to the little U-shaped building that housed the future of the IQAF.

Bev had them all out of class in one of the common areas. Their classrooms consisted of a bunch of small, pressboard desks, in official fake-wood covering. On the little desks were a Rosetta Stone software box, some headphones, and some booklets to mark their progress. Overall, some fairly Spartan conditions for study. Kids stateside would be staging walkouts if they had to study in these conditions. Little did the Magic Eleven know, but soon enough, they would look back on these conditions as "the good ol' days."

The guys all swarmed around us. I made sure to shake each and every hand, and they were all smiling and laughing and trying out various phrases in English. It was chaos again, with everyone talking at once. After a bit of this, it settled down into a more somber tone. Pay was an issue again.

The Iraqis had no electronic funds capability, there was no type of checking system. You got paid in cash, and you paid for everything in cash. This was fine, as long as someone physically got the cash to you. And that was the problem: the bureaucracy hadn't caught up to the moves of the students yet.

As I understood the pay system, it depended on a complex series of ledgers and books that eventually got to the paymasters, who would apportion to the base commander a certain amount of dollars according to number of people, rank, and if there was any special pay involved. The base commander would then divide the physical piles of cash among his group commanders, who would send a pile down to the squadron commanders, and so forth. The potential for fraud was extremely high, giving our financial management specialists a lot to do.

It was also very slow, so any move to another installation resulted in a decent amount of lag time in which the individual didn't get paid. Of course, higher rank reduced the lag time appreciably, but our students were barely in the system at all. So they often didn't get paid for a month or two. Usually, the friendly side had to intercede on their behalf, always dragging the Iraqi comptroller with us when we went. In Iraq, when you were out of money, you were out—no loans, no credit cards. It was indeed dire circumstances for the students and their families if the money didn't show up. So that was a primary topic of conversation. But there was also a lot of concern about the difficulty of the English test and a bit of wheedling about the score required to move along in the system.

The minimum score required on the ALCPT was a 60 to get into the system and a 70 to go to OTS. In order to get into pilot training, you needed an 80. An 80 was pretty darn conversant. It had to be: flying lessons were going to be conducted in English. There was no time to explain what *gear down* means on short final.

Since Mom seemed to be pretty much a hardass, they thought they would give us a try. It was pretty funny looking back: they thought that the two big, burly men would be a softer touch than this tiny older woman. They were right; but on the scoring, we were absolutely inflexible. We had to be.

We took that subject a bit further in this group setting. We started talking about the unlimited possibilities that they had if they could just master English. If they were to master the English test, they could end up becoming pilots, travel to other countries, and participate in exchange programs. The awful George Bush, the unilateral unilateralist, had arranged it so that the poor Iraqis could only get training through the United States, as we were the only ones there.

Well, us and the United Kingdom. And Italy. Well, Germany, too, but they don't really count because they were always helping people. At least the countries in the region were stonewalling the efforts—well, except for the United Arab Emirates and Jordan. But I'm pretty sure everyone else hated us; the media said so. We were rushing to war; being all unilateral and stuff. I didn't have the heart to break it to the Japanese and the Tongans and the host of others previously mentioned that they really shouldn't be there, helping.

But at this juncture, I kept on hammering away to the possibilities that existed for those who studied hard and did well on the English exam. I was met mostly with blank stares.

The group informed me that they were engineers and, as such, would always be engineers. I asked, "What if you don't want to be engineers?" Well, they informed me, we are engineers; that's what we've been told we're going to be. I briefly recapped my career (which is why I spent a lot of this book telling you), and said that you could do anything that you wanted to do, as long as you met the requirements. It didn't matter where you came from or what color your skin was; as long as you were qualified, you had a chance. I specifically didn't talk about affirmative action, the concentration of racial and sexual bias. I thought it better to leave them believing that I came from a meritocracy.

There was a bit of silence.

There really was some confusion in the group. They were supposed to be engineers, and they certainly hadn't expected to be able to go anywhere else than Iraq. There were a few furrowed brows; I could almost see thought bubbles over their heads. Apparently, options weren't a common thing to have at your disposal in this part of the world. Yet, it was standard equipment in the world I just left.

But they started thinking.

We ended up talking about the visit to IMAR and the harrowing end to their tour there. They had known that the commander was a very bad man, but they couldn't say anything, or they would've been on the list of cadets that disappeared. They talked about how K9 and the friendly side were the saving grace that kept them safe. I guess they knew the work that was going on behind the scenes. I still have a tough time imagining the terror they felt and the uncertainty that must've coursed through their thoughts. The only people that they could trust were the conquerors.

The Magic Eleven continued to be at the top of our thoughts as we progressed through the daily grind. Their status was briefed at the highest levels, but they had no idea that US generals were interested in their progress. Some of the briefings that I put together ended up being folded, spindled, and mutilated, and winding up on the desks at the highest levels of US policy. The progress of the first genuine US-trained Iraqi air force officer cadets was of great interest to the highest levels of US military in Iraq. The actual students were preoccupied with their normal daily challenges.

Eventually the English test they so dreaded neared. Bev said that they were ready, but their confidence level was low. In this society, failure was forever. They didn't see it as a minor setback to be overcome, but a societal death knell. They had become so agitated that Bev called us up to come and talk to them.

So we followed the same procedure and wound up in a small classroom with the eleven worried young men. It became apparent that a couple of them had become the informal leaders, so we spent a lot of time talking to them.

One of the Mahmoods and Amjad were extremely well spoken and friendly, and tried to serve as a cultural bridge between us and the rest of the class. They were very worried about the upcoming test and the ramifications that it held for them. They had heard rumors that if they failed, then they would be sent to the army, and none of them wanted that. They started trying to negotiate the score downward in a replay of what they had tried at IMAR.

But this time it was pretty halfhearted. When we ended up explaining the need for firm standards, especially in aviation, Amjad raised his hand and nodded, admitting defeat without much of a fight. I felt as if he was put up to it by one of his less prepared classmates. So he felt that he just had to put it out there and had done so. Then Banzet said no, so what more was there to do?

We talked for a bit more in the group setting, then decided to take a little tour of the facility. We made it about ten feet because, as we broke up the formal group session, the guys thought they may have more luck conducting single ship runs. As soon as Jim and I turned around, we were both beset by individuals wanting to plead their case concerning the ramifications if they failed. They were certainly trying to hedge their bets.

Amjad had no such problems; he approached me and with a shy smile said, "Major, I think I am ready to take the test. I also think that I could maybe be a pilot, like you said. I would like to go to the UK and also America, so I have studied very hard."

Out of the eleven, he was the only one to express confidence in his passing the test and continuing on to OTS. There were lots of halfhearted assertions of the "maybe I will do well" type, but he was the only one who had said definitively that he would succeed. I did notice one other thing though. They all took the future state that we had described as more of a fact than some abstract concept, which they hadn't done previously. The possibilities of their world opening up because of both the new government and English mastery really frightened them, as they were now in danger of losing a whole world, even though six months ago it hadn't existed for them. They were terrified of losing a gift they hadn't received yet. That drove the "hedging" behavior. The possibility of becoming "anything" was now real to them.

There were a lot of worried faces in there that day, but between the natural optimism of Jim and I, when we left, most of them were looking forward to the test. I shook all of their hands, looked them in the eye, and told them that I knew they could do it. They still were carrying the daily stress of terrorists hunting them and occasionally not getting paid for a month or so, but I think we gave them some hope for the English test. If the Americans thought they could do it, then perhaps they could.

And a couple of days later, they did.

They all passed the ACLPT with at least the minimum passing score, and as they say in most military academies, if the minimum wasn't good enough, it wouldn't be the minimum. Jim and I immediately zoomed across the runway as soon as Bev called up with the good news. The first class for OTS was qualified to go. When we arrived, these kids had confident, face-splitting smiles and stood a little straighter and taller. That was another moment I wish you were there for.

I waded into the small crowd, shaking hands and slapping backs. This was the best part of my job. These kids were actually glowing with pride. They would be cleared to go to the formal OTS, located at Taji. This success made it easy to forget there was a shooting war going on, sometimes right outside the gate.

I got an abrupt reminder about this one evening, shortly after the graduation from English class but prior to them driving up to Taji. I was outside of my hooch when a giant firefight broke out outside the walls. I watched the tracers drift lazily up into the night sky then heard a couple of large booms. I couldn't do anything and didn't really think I was in too much danger, so I went in and got my little camera. I came back outside and, just as I brought it up and turned it on, several bullets buzzed by my head.

It really wasn't a *buzz*, but a low-frequency *whoosh*. I actually felt the puff of air as it passed. I handled it like John Wayne would. I started giggling. The first thing on my video segment of that event was me giggling, saying, "Holy poop, I just about had my head taken off by a bullet!" I may not have said "poop." If you expected me to dive for cover or do something smart, you have not been paying attention to this book.

I continued to shoot some video; there were more tracers, a couple more big explosions, and then, after a minute or so, sirens started to wail. The ambulances were rolling, and they were headed my direction. They blazed by and came to a stop about fifty yards behind me.

The bullets that whizzed by me hadn't missed after all. A young army man, who had been standing at the entrance to the gym across the road from me, had been hit in the chest and killed by that burst. The nature of our encampment (a vast "city" within a city) made it highly probable that any rounds (mortar, rocket, or rifle) that got lobbed over the walls would hit someone, whether it was a contractor, civilian, or US armed forces member, or a little group of young Iraq cadets struggling to learn English. And the bad guys didn't give a crap which one it was.

And our students went through the same thing, only magnified, when they had to leave the base.

They weren't safe anywhere.

13

IRAQI OFFICER TRAINING

We asked the Magic Eleven to gather up their meager possessions and venture up to the Officer Training School at Taji. My new principle, General Akram, who had replaced General Abbas, was ambivalent as to how they would get there. I was hoping we could transport them up there, but no such luck, they would be on their own. To me, even though the distance to be covered was not far, the cargo was precious enough not to risk any mishaps. But I was overruled.

When General Akram had arrived as our new principle, initially I was glad. He certainly talked a good game. It took me a bit to realize that he was totally full of crap most of the time and, although a good guy, really didn't have the stones to take the training of the IQAF forward. He was too comfortable where he was, so was really in the business of not making waves and earning a paycheck for all the waves he didn't make.

He was a small guy who compensated for that by having an outrageous ego. According to him, he was the IQAF number one pilot and had "trained approximately one hundred percent of the Iraqi Air Force" (with the utmost modesty). Of course, every time I heard something like that—similar to the IQAF commander's boast that he was in charge of training the old Air Defense Forces—I always thought, "How did that work out for you?" Akram was also quite a ladies man; indeed, if you could get past his looks and stature and abrasive personality, he probably was. He thought a couple of our team would be great additions to his miniharem (he had two wives); that was part of the special burden that the females among us had to bear.

The guys couldn't really stand him either, but they would do their best to operate in spite of him. He was a real pleaser, but if you knew him for any length of time, you knew that he was full of crap; still, that took a while. So he was able to wheedle some real perks for himself, the crowning achievement of which was a trip to America to attend some senior leadership course. Somehow, he passed the English training requirements to go; the guys were pretty sure there was bribery involved.

That was one of the benefits of longer tours for the Americans; we got a chance to get to know who to invest our time and money in. This paid dividends later down the road. We were actually able to see the performance of folks for an extended period of time, find out who among the Iraqis we could trust, and establish enough time for them to trust us. We could then get their real feelings on who truly were the "good" guys. By the time General Akram showed up to the division, the Iraqis were very comfortable with me, so it didn't take long for them to give me the lowdown on Akram: not a "bad" guy in the dangerous sense, but not one of the "good" guys that the Americans should put a lot of resources behind either.

On top of his incompetence, he annoyingly insisted that he was awesome. No matter what, Akram would blame failures on subordinates (or predecessors) and regarded successes, no matter how trivial, as his personal initiatives. Any similarities to members of the highest levels of our government are purely coincidence.

While everyone else was struggling to get to Taji, I thought it a good idea to have our best prospect, Amjad, come with me to the MOD to compete for an overseas training slot, preferably in the United States. A man named General Aslam was in charge of the whole overseas training division, and I thought it would be a good idea to have the general actually meet one of our young students—put a face to a name. And Amjad was a wonderful young man: tall, clear-eyed, confident, brave, and well spoken (in English anyway, I can't vouch for the Arabic part). A perfect example of the kind of young men coming through our course.

I had met General Aslam twice before and was really unimpressed. There were a few issues that General Akram hadn't wanted to address; he had said that Nasser could go with me to meet Aslam. Nasser had grimaced but had taken me along.

We had gone through the whole "Scooby Doo" house that was the MOD to get to Aslam's office. The trip was through myriad hallways and stairways, moving closer and closer to the offices of power, until we arrived at a little couch in front of a metal detector. Nasser got a pat down; I had to remove the clip from my gun. The Iraqi army soldier smiled at me as I went through. "Thank you, mister," he said.

I wasn't sure what that meant, but I said, "You're welcome." I think those were about the only English words that he knew. As I turned the corner of the hall, I slid the clip back in my pistol. Nasser saw that and smiled. I told him that I was his bodyguard, and I had to be ready. I think he understood.

We went through another well-appointed office and ended up sitting on a couch for a few minutes, waiting to see this guy. A nice little man in civilian clothes came out and asked if we wanted tea. He said that it would only be a few minutes before the general would see us. I was pretty sure that this was the power part of the meeting. He could make us wait. Nasser had given me the scoop on General Aslam on the way up.

Apparently he was married to the sister of an extremely powerful Iraqi, so was "unfireable," and performed like it. And since he had a tremendous amount of pull determining who would go to overseas training, he had become someone no one could afford to piss off. His favor would certainly smooth out the very difficult path to any overseas training position. His disfavor would render that path nigh impossible. His son had been selected, on pure merit, to attend a course in Italy, which he was currently failing, also on pure merit.

He sure had the hospitality thing down pat. After the requisite amount of waiting, as befitted a man of his stature, we were ushered into his office. I looked around the office at the décor: a small television showing some soap opera, a couple of wooden helicopter models, and several certificates from Americans that proclaimed what a great guy he was. He had an exterior office with a window overlooking Baghdad; I'm not sure in the current situation if that was a good thing or not, what with rockets and bullets flying all over at random intervals.

But it was fairly well appointed, and we had the tea and little cakes and chocolates. The little guy in civilian clothes seemed very proud to serve them. They were just little wrapped treats, but they were presented with a flourish that implied that in one of them was a golden ticket that would grant me access to a giant chocolate factory. Or something.

General Aslam was very slick. Even though I had intel on him from Nasser, I think I would've caught on to him pretty quickly. In the first ten minutes, he made sure we knew how powerful and important he was in relation to the overseas training. Then, there were some casual mentions of American flight suits and gloves and how nice it would be to have some of those. There was also the implication that he might need the friendly side's support to keep his son in training in Italy, because the Italians weren't treating him appropriately in the flying program there.

I think that meant they were holding him to standards. He also implied that the Italians were so unreasonable that he might be forced to transfer to another overseas training place. Knowing how precious each slot was to the Iraqis, I had a question for him.

"Sayyid, if your son doesn't succeed in Italy, shouldn't he come home? Then we can send other man to attend this important training."

"No, Major, my son will complete flying training in a very prestigious flying course. Then he can come home. If the Italians will not give him the right training, maybe we should tell them that we do not want their training."

I knew that the Iraqis had billions of dollars in foreign military sales (FMS) accounts. Basically, it worked like this: The Iraqis put all this money into a giant bank account (or accounts), because they were worried about corruption and thievery, so they wanted the Americans to manage it for them. And this money was used to purchase equipment, supplies, training, and so forth for the Iraqi armed forces. So this general was implying that he would somehow screw up the funds that were going to Italy for their training.

I wasn't sure if he had the juice to do that; it wouldn't have surprised me; some gentle whisperings in the right powerful person's ear, and all of the sudden, Italy wouldn't get as many training applications and attendant dollars. But that was classic shooting yourself in the foot. The Iraqis desperately needed quality, Western training in a safe environment. The issue was capacity. So they really couldn't afford to shut off any pipeline for training. And after all the diplomatic hoops were jumped through, there weren't tons of choices.

It didn't seem like this guy really cared about the greater Iraqi problem; I think he was looking for plunder. Some folks are so shortsighted that they will take and take from people today, betting that by the time there comes a reckoning they will either be dead or too far away to be held accountable. But enough about Democrats; this guy sucked too.

The theme throughout the whole meeting was one of General Aslam sniffing around, trying to ascertain an advantage for himself, even if it was only a pair of flight gloves. I wondered how many pieces of silver it would take for each slot.

After my first meeting with the guy, nothing in the intervening weeks would change the way I saw him. I was certainly playing the game, hoping that, by bringing young Amjad to him to show him the quality of officer we were producing, we would have an advantage on getting folks through the hoops.

So I was excited when the appointed day came that Amjad would accompany me to Aslam's office. Nasser had made the arrangements but, because I knew he hated this guy, I said that I could go on my own. He gratefully wouldn't be accompanying us on this trip. Amjad had spent the night in the area and allotted himself two hours to get through all the checkpoints and meet me at the guy's office.

I asked General Akram if he would like to accompany me on this trip to the MOD; he pretended to think about it. It turned out he couldn't make the time today—maybe tomorrow or the next day. I smirked; out of the corner of my eye, I noticed Asad jiggling too. He knew there was no way in hell Akram would go.

I gathered up Amjad and armored up to begin the walk over to the MOD. Amjad was very talkative and went on and on about English and the options that its mastery would give him. He was peppering me with questions about the United States and Britain. I asked him if he thought that he would graduate from our OTS. He smiled and said that whatever the Americans would be teaching, he would be learning. He informed me that he would be the number one graduate. He would then be attending pilot training, wherever. He had all the confidence in the world.

That started to fade a bit as we approached the MOD. Once again, I was struck by the irony that I was the one that was vouching for this young Iraqi cadet going through Iraqi military checkpoints. Amjad started to unconsciously drift closer to me as we started up through the dark corridors and through the stairwells. I was keeping a sharp eye out as we passed through the halls; I saw a lot of very curious stares. Amjad was getting some very searching looks, and it was making him very nervous.

It abated a bit as we made our way upstairs; it was better lit and felt a bit more secure. We went through the metal detector, with the "Thank you, mister" guy ushering us through. We wound up in the anteroom; the guy in civilian clothes came out and, with a flourish, presented the bowl of chocolates.

Amjad looked at me, and his look spoke volumes about the trust in the system. I of course grabbed several of the chocolates, popped one in my mouth, and gave Amjad a wink. It was okay. We weren't being poisoned.

We didn't have to wait too long for the meeting; we were soon ushered into the office.

General Aslam was regal, sitting behind his desk; he stood and spread his arms like a little, brown Jesus.

"Banzet, my friend, how are you today? Did you bring my gloves? Or a flying jacket?"

I strode up to him, shaking his hand, then touching over my heart as a sign of sincerity. "No, sayyid, I didn't; I brought you something better. I brought you Iraq's future! This is Amjad, one of our best cadets, and one that would do very well in out-of-country training."

Amjad took two sharp steps forward and snapped to attention, rendering a razor-sharp salute, British-style.

Aslam looked at him and casually returned the salute, then turned back to me. "Banzet, have you heard anything about my son? The friendly side must help keep him there. You must tell the Italians that they must be fair." He leaned toward me, conspiratorially. "I think perhaps they do not like Iraqi people. You must tell them that."

Ah, the race card—it knows no boundaries. And it's always used for the same reason: excusing abhorrent behavior: the worse the behavior, the more the card gets played. So Aslam, in an attempt to salvage a nonqualified, ill-prepared candidate (his son), was going to try to besmirch the Italians. I did point out that they still had quite a few other Iraqis in training there, and they were doing very well.

I'd forgotten that facts and logic are anathema to those who would play the card in the first place. He thought that perhaps the Italians were trying to get rid of his son because he was a brown Iraqi and the son of a superpowerful general, himself. I hid my disgust and tried to steer the conversation back to Amjad, who was still standing at attention.

I told Amjad to stand at ease and relax, and suggested he tell the general how the English training was going. Amjad started to talk in very fluent English about some of his experiences and some his classmates had been through and the hopes that he could continue his training in a Western (he said that specifically) country, so he could bring back all the experiences to Iraq.

Meanwhile, Aslam's eyes kept flickering over my equipment. I'd hung my helmet from my armor and had various doodads hanging off the other attach points on the vest. He would halfheartedly respond to some of the comments with a grunt or a noncommittal burst of Arabic, but I could tell my plan was failing miserably. I'd not accounted for the abject selfishness of the man in that office. He did whatever would keep him out of trouble and whatever would line his own pockets. In my opinion, he wasn't qualified to be in the same room as Amjad, much less making any sort of decision about his future.

The rest of the short meeting covered how important Aslam was and how we must make sure that he was happy. Amjad had lapsed into silence and just stood, eyes forward, hands at his sides. I could tell we were getting nowhere, and as I had stuff to do, plus, Amjad had to get off the base soon, I decided to wrap it up.

"Sayyid, I must go. I am very thankful that you spoke to us today. Now Amjad knows the most important general for his training." (I said I don't *like* bull crap; I didn't say I didn't know how to shovel it.) "I'm sure that he will remember this day for his career."

"Yes, Banzet, I am happy to see you. Can you remember the flight suit and gloves for me? Do you think you might have some for me?"

I said that I would try and looked over at the stone-faced Amjad. At my look, he came to attention, snapped a salute, and followed me out. I felt bad for the kid; I assessed that he was obviously very sad that the general didn't give a hoot about him personally. My assessment was wrong.

He was pissed. Almost apoplectic. As we made it out of the offices, through the anteroom and past the "Thank you, mister" guy, his face gradually became a purple color, and his jaw clenched till you could see the muscles pulsing under his skin. I started to ask what was wrong.

"Amjad, what is—"

"Stupid Iraqi man!" he exploded, interrupting me. "That general is the worst kind of Iraqi, and he is what is wrong with this country! He shouldn't be asking you for anything. He is embarrassing to real Iraqis. If he wants a flight suit, he should get it from the Iraqis, not beg the Americans for help. That is not what friends do. Friends don't beg. Iraq needs to be a friend to the United States, not a slave—to beg for things. We need to get rid of all those people; they are hurting us."

My plan, although failed in its primary objective, succeeded in an area that I didn't know I was testing. Amjad thought that Iraq should be partners with the United States, not a subordinate. And to do it on its own two feet, not as a petulant child taking money and resources while throwing the occasional tantrum. And if they got there with high-caliber men like Amjad and Speedy (whom you'll meet later), the United States would have a partner we could be proud of.

He continued his rant all the way back to the A7 trailer; as we got there late, only Akram remained, along with one of the newer additions to the staff. Akram nodded as I relayed the result of our expedition; he wasn't surprised. He said that at least Aslam wasn't angry at *him*. Maybe he had something there: Akram would have to engage Aslam more in the future, and maybe he was distancing himself from a friction point in order to be more effective in the future. Or maybe he was just a wuss.

But another problem had reared its ugly head in the interim. It was late in the afternoon, around 1600. Amjad was getting worried because he couldn't stay on base (he only had a day pass), and there was no one there to take him home when he did get off base. The most critical part was that this was the time that the bad guys really monitored the base gates, tracking who was leaving. Amjad was also going to be carrying some documents that would give away who he was and what he did for a living.

I asked Akram to help, and after a lot of back and forth, he said there was simply nothing to be done. Amjad had to go off base and catch a bus or something to where he needed to get to.

"Sayyid, Amjad is very worried that the bad guys will see him and stop him to ask questions. And you know that if they look at what he is carrying, they will be able to know what he does; that would be big trouble."

"Banzet, it is no problem; they cannot watch the exit all the time. They know that Iraqis are on base. It is okay."

"Sayyid, you sleep in your office."

"Banzet, it is different for generals."

Dammit, if Wahid were around, he would have taken care of the kid, but I was stuck with the task of telling Amjad that he had to leave. Amjad frantically called one of his friends that lived in the area. He could spend the night there. The tricky part, apparently, was that this was not one of Amjad's trusted circle. He didn't know what Amjad did for a living. But Amjad trusted him enough to risk the chance of exposure, especially considering there weren't many other options.

The kid lived within bus range, so the trick for Amjad was to get to the nearest bus stop, take it to another bus stop away from the base, and then take *that* bus to the friend's house. And he was terrified. I said I would walk him to the gate, and as we did, I tried to calm him down. He was shaking from sheer terror. Gone was the young man that I had met that bright morning; here was a kid who thought that in the next two or three hours he would most likely be dead. In a horrific manner.

He thought that he would be picked out of the crowd because he felt he was in the highest threat time to be seen around the base. Strike two was that he was of obvious military age and fitness. Strike three was that he was carrying incriminating evidence that would put lie to any cover story he had. He knew there was no strike four. I felt terrible that I had to throw him out there, but I couldn't do anything. Our procedures mandated it. The Iraqi air force were the ones that were supposed to ensure his well-being, but due to the indifference of the available leadership, they weren't.

As we approached the gate, he was shaking like a leaf, and his voice was tremoring. I was doing everything I could to lie to him and assure him that everything was going to be fine. I tried to make the case that the bad guys couldn't possibly watch everybody, and besides, according to our intelligence, the bad guys were really not clustering around the base anymore; they were trying things farther out. That was a total lie, but I tried to be convincing. It worked to a point. He was starting to calm down a little, but it was obvious that he was still worried.

He was fidgeting with the paperwork he was carrying, constantly rolling it up into a tube and then unrolling it. As we got closer and closer, his eyes never looked at me; they were constantly traversing what he could see of the buildings over the T-walls. Just before I had to pull up short and send him through the first checkpoint, I pulled him into a little alcove, where no prying eyes could see this young man getting a little extra attention from a USAF officer.

"Amjad, you are going to be fine. Be confident and steady, and you will be fine. Don't act scared. Be fearless. Just confidently keep moving to your destination. I will see you at Taji."

His young face was tense, and the papers were twisted up in his ever-moving hands.

"Yes, Major, I will."

His face belied his words.

"Amjad, look, I wouldn't let you go out there if I thought you would be in danger that the Iraqi air force's bravest and smartest cadet couldn't handle."

He glanced at me and gave a slight smirk, but, after a brief second, his eyes clicked back over to the T-walls and the Wild West beyond.

"Yes, Major Banzet, I am not scared. I am not worried."

Lying again. His eyes flickered back to me, smiling a bit distractedly.

I grabbed him by both shoulders.

"Amjad." At that, he was a bit startled. But, finally, his eyes locked on to mine, and he started to really listen. I smiled what I hoped was a kind smile.

"There are bad guys out there. But you are a good guy. And good guys always win. So I will see you in Taji in a couple of weeks, okay?"

"Okay, Major Banzet."

"Do you believe me that you will be all right?"

His eyes, now steady and calm, met mine. He softly said, "I believe you."

"Okay then." I stuck out my hand and shook his.

He inhaled, squared his shoulders, and turned to march out the checkpoint. From under the alcove, I watched him go until he disappeared into the crowd outside the second checkpoint. I was worried sick.

He arrived at Taji a couple of days later, not even the last straggler in.

The Magic Eleven had become the Magic Taji Eleven. At the time they arrived, the new school rooms hadn't been completed yet. A big building was being refurbished but had a few weeks to go. The Americans were really working overtime, trying to get the curriculum ready, figuring out where the students would live, where they would eat, and how they would get back and forth to class. But they had to deal with several interrelated layers of Iraqi and allied military command.

The constant variable was the Iraqi command structure, thanks to several competing factions from the Iraqi army to the IQAF commanders at Taji. Taji housed a couple of squadrons of Hueys and was slated to get the Mi-17s when they were certified airworthy. Plus, there was a huge Iraqi Army logistics presence and scads of different US Army units.

The Americans were constantly balancing, cajoling, prodding, and leading the Iraqis to take care of the students. The head USAF officer, Colonel Kim, was an F-15 driver that had managed to establish good relationships with the Iraqis, but his frustration meter was pegged at eleven. He, like me, clung to the fact that these Iraqi students were such good men that he was willing to endure the absolutely jaw-dropping juvenile games the Iraqi staff were playing with each other.

The Iraqi base commander didn't have authority over the school, but he had authority over everything else in that little slice of heaven. Plus, he had a flock of sheep right there on base, along with a flock of carrier pigeons of which he was justifiably proud, I guess. But these animals weren't going to take care of themselves, so he was prone to using our students to care for the animals, bring tea, landscape, and whatever else he thought of. The American instructors were constantly surprised to arrive to teach a class, find it empty, and discover the students were herding sheep. That would start a chain reaction of excuses and prevarications from the doofus in charge, forcing the Americans to confront the bad general about the students.

The IQAF A7 general at Taji, Abdul Khalid, or AK, was totally weak and scared of the base commander. But we were stuck with him, at least until the IQAF could get more qualified officers with the right outlook on responsibility and care of those under you. That was in fairly short supply in the region.

The bad general understood that as long as he didn't push things too far he would be able to do what he wanted with the cadets. Until the Americans showed up, then he would act contrite and claim that he really didn't know what was going on. But it played hell on the students.

I hadn't understood the magnitude of the dysfunction of the Iraqi command, and the telephone calls and e-mails that I got didn't really illustrate the difficulties that this childish, shortsighted behavior caused to the very people that could bring Iraq out of chaos and fear. Through the weeks that passed and the daily grind of staff work, it didn't really register. It was the difference between reading about a car wreck and being in one.

At our staff meetings, I would brief some of the difficulties the Americans were identifying up at Taji. Of course, that wasn't our only effort. There were ongoing recruiting efforts; Capt. Denise was busy handling those issues with Mr. "Big Pencil" Hadi: going slow was the norm there. There were constant payment issues; we had guys in finance working on that. We were filling in the next ELT class, successors to the Magic Eleven; I believe there were twenty-eight in that class and more behind them.

Added to that was the pressure for the piece de resistance for the current USAF general in charge of CAFTT at the time. General Dice had decreed that Iraqi initial pilot training would commence on October 1. That meant there had to be a physically qualified, English-qualified cadet graduated in time to start training up at Kirkuk, on aircraft that hadn't arrived in theater yet.

The specially modified Cessna 172s were being outfitted with diesel engines, and in the middle of the deliveries, there was a bit of a hiccup. One of the aircraft that had been fitted with the special engine had to make an emergency landing on a road in Florida, emblazoned with Iraqi air force markings. Anyone who thinks the internet is the place to find truth should've seen the theories explode about that fairly innocuous event. Among the best that I saw was that this single Cessna 172 was the vanguard of an invasion. From Iraq. With a four-place, single-propeller aircraft. One at a time.

But the aircraft *were* coming and would be in place in time to receive whatever young men had qualified for pilot training. The Iraqis had chosen the best possible commander for that first class: my own Colonel Kamil. That was a great choice; Kamil was everything one could want in a commander. He was kind and thoughtful, brave to a fault, and understood his responsibilities. He was struggling to get everything prepared up at Kirkuk, ensuring that when the cadets arrived, however many there were, they would have a place to live, eat, and train. There would be maintenance and logistics support for the aircraft and Iraqi pilots who could instruct, to our standards, in English. Huge challenges. But none of that mattered if we couldn't get anybody out of Taji to attend the course. The Diceman had decreed that October was the start of Iraqi pilot training, General Kamal had concurred, and that was that. We just had to produce them.

Buried in the slides that I produced for the briefings were words that clinically described some of the challenges those young men were going through at Taji, as a result of the bad Iraqi leadership there versus the tremendous leadership that awaited them at Kirkuk. Almost weekly, the childish behavior of the Iraqi generals would create a new crisis. Eventually, I convinced the rest of the A7 guys that some of us should travel up to Taji to check up on the Magic Eleven, to give a little encouragement, and try to see how things were going from their point of view.

We requested an Iraqi Huey to come get us, and in a couple of days, Jim, Wahid, Asad, and I jumped on board to fly up and check things out. It was kind of the standard plan; the Americans would get off and go with their counterparts for an hour or so, and the Iraqis would do the same with theirs. We would then meet up and continue together.

The flight there was spectacular, as always, zipping up the river at a couple hundred feet, boots hanging in the breeze, watching as the Iraqi door gunners waved with one hand, tracking targets with the other. I was waving like a lunatic to the people on the ground and watching them wave back. We zipped over the rows and rows of palm trees bathing in the warm, moist (river) air, amid the smell of palms and Huey transmission oil. I shot a glance at Asad. His broad face showed concern. He hated to fly.

We veered slightly west, cutting over several lush, green fields, small tractors bumping through the crops, black moving objects (BMOs) getting ready for the morning, moving livestock out of the pens for their daily routines. We flashed over the small river that was the southern border of Taji. The Iraqi door gunners, upon crossing the little river, stowed the RPKs, snapping the bolts back, pulling out the ammo belt, and stowing it in the mounted ammo can.

The two ships slid into trail, hover-taxied up the runway, and were marshaled into final parking. We got picked up by our respective groups, the Iraqis piling into one of their cars, and Col Kim stuffing us into his little SUV.

The first stop for us was an almost-finished schoolhouse to check out the progress. It was a two-story building that had been refurbished with dollars from the Iraqi FMS account. The plumbing had to be totally redone, and the electrical fixed; that had already been accomplished. There was a bit more electrical work to be done, but that was progressing.

At the same time we were touring the building, the commander was regaling us with the epic battle of wills between the various competing Iraqi factions. It was a rehash of the e-mails and phone calls that had generated the trip up here. By that time, the Americans were familiar enough with the Iraqi way of doing things that they believed us when we described the various fumbling around that we were contending with at the Iraqi HQ.

So we were trying to strategize as we walked around, but lacking the willpower from the Iraqi HQ, there really wasn't a whole lot we could do except continue pulling strings behind the scenes; in dealing with this generation of Iraqi leadership, that required a lot of string pulling. After we finished poking around the newish building, we all piled into the trucks again and went over to the current classrooms. We stopped in front of an old Iraqi antiaircraft piece in front of what looked like a small motel with a small, dusty, gravel courtyard. The facility was painted within an inch of its life.

Eight-foot walls encompassed the small courtyard, which faced the small line of motel-like rooms, about eight to nine of them. All the rooms were labeled, different areas of study denoted on the plastic-covered PowerPoint slide. It was a sweltering day, so we were keen to head into the classrooms, where we thought it would be cooler.

The guys opened the thin metal doors, with a clang, and we entered the dingy little classroom. There were several little desks sitting in neat rows, facing a screen, with a projector hung from the ceiling. An air conditioning system was mounted on the opposite wall. The walls had several "Air Force Power" posters hung on them (more on propaganda later) depicting various airframes that the air force produces in abundance. The walls also sported the various blisters and lumps from moisture under the copious amounts of paint. Walls with zits.

None of the machines were operating. It was dark, humid, and sweltering in that little room. In response to my questioning glance, the staff there explained that the Iraqi base commander had decreed that only four hours of electricity a day would be provided to the Iraqi school house. He had control of the amount of fuel that went to the giant diesel generators and, thus, the amount of air conditioning, and electricity available to the school.

And so it happened that in the middle of the 115 degree heat, in a bar-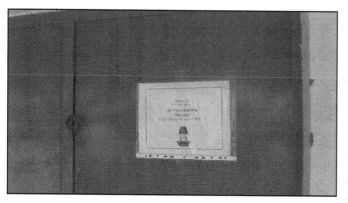ren section of the base, the students had four hours of electricity a day. The rule was to crank the AC as much as possible in the morning, trying to turn the students into sides of beef, then have them slowly thaw out after the power went out. Which happened around 1400, when the heat would be starting to reach its peak.

And when the power went out, the little rooms would become dark as tombs, so the flashlights and battery-operated lanterns came out, to continue instruction. Or you would open the door to let the light in, and the oppressive heat would follow. The cool air fled out, and the heat rushed in. Soon, the slabs of beef that were created in the morning would thaw out and start to cook. For about two hours, from about 1000 to 1200, the students were comfortable. By about two o'clock in the afternoon, everyone, staff and students, would be stripped down to sodden T-shirts and salt-stained waistbands.

Since PowerPoint was the method of choice for instruction, that died as well, so the teaching continued on whiteboards and notepads. When it finally got to be too much, the sweaty arms sticking to the papers and the sweat dripping into the eyes, the students were released for physical training. Not necessarily into the gym, I don't think there was one. I think it mostly consisted of soccer or running. Yes, in the same heat.

But at least at the end, there were nice cool showers they could take before repairing to the Iraqi dining facility, then more studying in their respective rooms. Really, just like I did in our Officer Training School, without the repressive heat and occasional mortar, rocket, and light machine-gun fire. I learned more about all of that a little later.

So Colonel Kim definitely had his hands full. As for the students, this high-speed guy couldn't say enough positive things about them. Against all the adversity, he said they had great attitudes and tried to see the best in all the shenanigans that the higher-ranking Iraqis were putting them through.

Our next stop was the barracks for the Magic Eleven. I hadn't yet been able to talk to any of them this time around, and I was really interested in talking to them. I thought they trusted me enough to tell me what was really going on. We took the 4-Runner to another nondescript, cinder-block building. Apparently the guys didn't know we were coming and were in the middle of their daily routine. We jumped out and walked into the common area. The flaking, painted walls formed a corridor with a bare cement floor. There were a couple of USAF posters hanging proudly on the ragged walls. The thin metal doors denoted a student dwelling. We took off our sweaty helmets and stacked our body armor by the door.

They didn't know we were there, so to rouse them, I yelled something stupid like, "Doesn't anyone study around here?" Heads started popping out of their rooms. Once again, I felt privileged to be where I was.

"Bonzet!" A kid whose name I didn't remember popped out of the room. He was one of the ones who was very sure that he wasn't going to pass the language test. In Iraq, it was much easier to expect the worst. You were often not disappointed. The arrival of the Americans had ruined a lot of that thought process for those Iraqis that weren't intent on violence and mayhem. Hope was possible with the friendly side. President Bush had brought hope and change to the Iraqi people.

After that initial yelp, the others popped out; eventually we were surrounded by eleven very enthusiastic young men. At this point, it was about two in the afternoon, so they hadn't been to dinner yet, but they had finished their exercising and showers and were hitting the books. Or at least trying to. It was dark in the building; the electricity had been shut off for the day. There was a little light coming out of the rooms on one side of the corridor, as the sun was starting down in its quest to become my wife's sunrise. It was bearable enough in the rooms, but everyone was in sandals, shorts, and T-shirts. They knew that the heat would keep building until night fell.

The whole gang was there: Mahmood, Amjad, more Mahmoods, and others. They were all smiles as they gathered around Jim and me, all talking at once. Colonel Kim kind of faded into the background, his tan flight suit blending into the walls; he had a satisfied smile on his face, a proud uncle watching his brood. I asked if I could see the palatial dwellings that these guys lived in. One of the Mahmoods motioned us into his room.

The high, small window in the room let in a little weak light; it was the sole source of illumination, so the room was quite gloomy. Actually, *room* doesn't quite give the proper vision; *cell* would be more appropriate. Mahmood's floor was bare, gray cement, with a couple of area rugs carefully placed. He had a small desk on the wall to the right of the doorway upon which rested a now silent computer. A pair of headphones were plugged into the computer for English lessons when the power was on. There were some English language books neatly stacked on the floor beside the desk, and that was it. His neatly made bunk was on the far wall, about six feet away. There was a small, pretend-wood wall locker, doors shut. Mahmood started the world's shortest tour.

"Major Mike, here is my room. Here is my computer on the desk. Umm, it works when the power is on; then I can study. Right now, I am reading these books." He gestured to the chair in the yellow beam of sunlight. "We can study for a few more hours." He smiled and gestured toward the pressed wood wall locker. "And that is my stuff." He seemed to be looking for something else to say, but there wasn't really any point: he'd covered everything about his lodgings in six sentences.

We chatted for a few more minutes, then wandered out into the common area. I asked how things were going—really. How was the IQAF treating them? I immediately was flooded with praise for the classroom instruction, how much they liked the teachers, and so on. Unfortunately, those were all Americans. So I pressed the group a little harder for the truth about the Iraqis.

Amjad spoke up, again assuming the role of spokesman for the group. All the earnest faces were gathered around, but Amjad stood out. He just had a bit more presence than the others, not loud or obnoxious, just a quiet confidence about him. He said, "Major Mike, there are some problems. I haven't been paid in two months. I don't have any money for food or to give my family." (I think his family thought he was working in the oil fields, so I'm not sure how he explained the missing paychecks). "I have to borrow money from family and friends."

This statement set off a round of "Me too's"; most of the people in that little group hadn't been paid. The pay failures were generally a result of the cumbersome Iraqi personnel system, which hadn't caught up with the moves yet. The generals didn't care, because it wasn't them. Any pay discrepancies for the IQAF generals were handled pretty expeditiously. It was really hard for the Americans to help because of the physical aspect of the money. It was just bags of cash and paper tracking—not a whole lot in the way of auditable systems. So while most of these young men hadn't been paid in a couple of months, the Iraqi system was still charging them for access to the dining facility and gymnasium (which we'd seen no evidence of). At this point, most of these eleven guys were paying for the privilege of being in the IQAF. But at least there were the amenities.

Amjad continued, "Many of us were sick for a very long time, too. We were very sick because someone poisoned the food in the dining hall. We have found lots of different things in our food, but mostly metal." I must've had a quizzical look, because the rest chimed in again.

"Yes, Banzet, we have found metal in the food. Metal shavings!"

I looked at Colonel Kim; he raised his eyebrow and gave a slight nod. It had happened.

Amjad continued, "And the water was monkey. Many of us got sick because of monkey water."

That one threw me. I had no idea what monkey water was. I hadn't seen any monkeys in Iraq yet, but I hadn't been everywhere, so I couldn't rule it out. Amjad saw my confusion and elaborated. "Major Mike, we got bumps from the monkey water! Lots of bumps from the monkey water and we got sick again. Vomiting and bumps!"

He pulled down the collar of his T-shirt, revealing remnants of what looked like boils on his upper chest. Once again, several of the enthusiastic young guys babbled their agreement and started demonstrating where they had these bumps as well. These young guy's clothes were starting to be pulled up, down, and off like a Madonna dance number. So, before it got too far, I held up my hands and raised my voice a bit. "Whoa! Hold on a second. First…clothes. On. Second, I see that you guys have some sort of boils. But where did they come from?"

Amjad saw that his explanation of "monkey water" had failed to inform me. He looked at the little group around him and held an English language huddle. As I was on the outside of the little group, I could only hear snippets of what was going on. I heard the word *monkey* a couple of times, followed by a burst of Arabic, then words like *foggy* or *cloudy*, followed by another burst.

Finally, a consensus was reached. The huddle broke up, and one of the Mahmoods decided he would take a crack at it. "The water. Our showers have foggy water in them. The foggy water causes us to be sick and to have these things." He indicated the boils. "We have to shower in foggy water."

"*Murky*! You mean murky water! Not monkey, muuuurky," I shouted.

That set of another cacophony of sound. *Muuurky* rolled off eleven sets of lips, over and over. They were looking at each other and saying "muu-uurky," then turning to another and repeating. It was one of the funniest things I'd ever seen. But they were so determined to learn English. Murky water was what was making them sick.

The Iraqi higher-ups placed very little value on sanitation, and these guys were suffering because of it. The American military considers the individual to be a weapon system and takes the necessary steps to ensure that it is operating at peak efficiency. Sanitation, food, and shelter are at the front end of any deployment. GIs don't go hungry. They may not like what they are eating, but as a rule, they don't go hungry. And they may not like the Porta-Potties or the taste of water from the water buffaloes, but they aren't drinking and bathing in fecal-flavored monkey water.

These guys were. One of the giant frustrations of the flight doc we had over there was trying to get the Iraqi medical folks to have a larger voice. So far, they just didn't have any purchase. In the big scheme of things, the Iraqis thought they had bigger things to worry about.

But risking losing training or, God forbid, a student to some preventable disease was the essence of shortsightedness. The senior Iraqi cadre seemed totally oblivious to how much had been given to get these cadets to this point. If Asad were there, he would have been shaking his head. Meanwhile, our flight doc was trying to assist them in preventing typhoid. In 2007, we were trying to prevent typhoid.

I snuck a look at Colonel Kim. He gave the same raised eyebrow and the same slight nod.

"Okay," I said, "other than the little things like food, water, and pay, are there any big problems?"

That brought a round of smiles.

"Major Mike..."

A little guy that hadn't said anything—ever, if I remembered right—timidly raised his hand. Everything about him seemed timid, but here he was, risking his life and putting up with so much crap; so *timid* is perhaps the wrong word. Unobtrusively may be a better fit. In spite of the lack of the proper adverb, he started speaking. "It is so very hot, Major. We cannot sleep outside, we cannot have fans that work, and we do not have air conditioning. We do not have lights, so that means we have limited study time. We stick to everything because we are wet all the time. I am very tired because it is very hard to sleep. That makes it harder for me to pay attention."

That sounded like more of the whining I was used to. He wanted to be more comfortable. I said something to the effect that I would see what I could do to make him more comfortable, but it was really up to the Iraqis. But sometimes, I allowed, you might be uncomfortable. Then he turned me into a jackass.

His eyebrows furrowed, and he said, "Major, it is not about my comfort; I want to study more. I want to learn all the Americans can teach me. All of those things that I said make it harder for me to learn. I could study into the night if I had lights, we could have longer days in the class if we had electricity, and we wouldn't miss class because we are sick if we had clean water. I want to learn more; I don't need to be comfortable."

It wasn't the first time that one of these five-foot-nothing young men made this six-foot-two, slightly older young man feel very, very small. At this point, they were probably about halfway through the course, with graduation looming ahead. And with the current Iraqi air force, we were having lots of problems with absenteeism, desertion, and overall lack of dedication—that was in the established cadre, who were all better paid, fed, and taken care of than these men.

Given that we were struggling with desertions in all aspects of the Iraqi military, smart money would expect to lose some, if not most, of these young men to frustration and constant, overwhelming, real danger. And like the bullets that barely missed my skull in Baghdad, Taji was a magnet for incoming as well.

As if to underscore that point, shortly before we had gone up there, one of the guys I deployed with (SMSgt Bob, the guy who embraced me like a rabid monkey during man-kiss training at Bullis) was nearly killed by a rocket. It blew through the thin walls of a building, striking a young army man inside. Bob, in a very different embrace, administered first aid as the young man died.

Smart money would not have had anyone enlist in the IQAF at all. Smart money would say that corruption, incompetence, and violence would carry the day over eleven young, vulnerable, isolated Iraqi men. The

Western press trumpeted every disaster, burying every success. These guys should have had no reason to think there was hope, much less a reasonable chance of success.

They had two things going for them. They were some of the most courageous men I've met, in some of the direst circumstances I'd known of. And they got to have daily exposure to Americans. The good, salt-of-the-earth ones. Not T.V. Americans. The ones who don't know the meaning of *can't*. The ones that run to the sound of guns, with brothers and sisters of all races right beside them. Those Americans.

And as for the Magic Eleven?

Not one quit.

Not one went on "strike".

Not one turned.

We didn't lose a single one.

As graduation loomed, the flight doc worked with the Iraqis, screening them for fitness for pilot training. The desert environment and substandard health care combined to cause a lot of dental problems and sinus issues. With the constant pressure changes involved in flight, those two issues were no-goes. We were hoping that most of the class would be fit for flight, but unfortunately, only four were medically qualified: Amjad, Mahmood, Mahmood, and, umm, Mahmood. The others were still healthy enough to be in the air force, but not aviation.

Plus, we had an additional requirement that they now had to score even higher on the ALCPT English test. They would be held to the same requirement expected of foreign students training stateside at the Defense Language Institute. This weighed heavily on their minds—another hurdle to get through. The Americans at Taji reassured, reinforced, and reinstructed, prepping them for the day of the big test.

A great indicator of the impact that the Americans had on them was the amount of effort the majority of the class that was not qualified for pilot training put into the language. They really didn't have a reason to push hard; they were already qualified as officers. The guys I had met at the beginning would not have tested again, as it was an opportunity for failure. These guys relished the challenge. 180 degree change in outlook. But, as the day approached, confidence was high that they would do well on the test. And when the pencil dust settled, 9 of the 11 scored over an 80. The other two were within two points.

That was a great day, and it was followed by several other great days. Soon after that, they graduated. We were able to hand out patches designed by General Akram and myself for the new Iraqi air force. My wonderful wife, who owns her own promotional products company, had them made up and shipped them to me in time for General Akram to hand them out at graduation. (Air force guys love patches.)

That happened in late September, just before the mandated IQAF flight training school was supposed to start. And Kirkuk was a long way away from Taji. General Akram just shrugged and said that the four students would find their own way up there. I again brought up the security issues, which Wahid agreed with. (I was including him all the time, in all conversations, in hopes he would eventually take over.) Akram gave a non-committal shrug and told Wahid to do something.

Wahid asked, "What about the helicopters at Taji? I will schedule them to bring down the four to us. Can you help get them to Kirkuk in a friendly side airplane?"

Perfect. I loved this guy. But he'd forgotten that his good friend Kamil was the commander of the Kirkuk flying training squadron. I mentioned that, and it was all the hinting it took. The Americans had prepped the battlefield on this one already. Lieutenant Colonel Snapper had his instructor pilots working long hours with Colonel Kamil's hand-picked pilots. In truth, they were really doing the heavy lifting up at Kirkuk.

They had designed syllabi, trained Iraqi cadre in the American methods of flying, checked out the aircraft (the infamous "invasion" Cessnas), and basically had everything ready for the new student pilots. They also operated the Cessna Caravan, a big turbo-prop that seats about eight. We were encouraging the Iraqis to use it not only for general light airlift, but a light-attack version as well.

So far, they just had the light-airlift version operating at Kirkuk, and as soon as the request went through for a plane to come to NAMAB to pick up the first four Iraqi student pilots, Snapper was ready to go.

The appointed day came. The four student pilots—Mahmood, Mahmood, Mahmood, and Amjad—were scheduled to touch their first helicopter and first aircraft on the same day, today. Richard (one of my British coworkers) and I waited on the ramp, looking to the northeast for a couple of little dots to appear out of the pale morning. The IQAF came through right on time. I'm not sure if they knew what precious cargo they were carrying, but I was nervous until the pilots brought the skids lightly onto the concrete.

I ran over to meet the guys. The Iraqi door gunner had very professionally stowed his weapon, unstrapped, and escorted the young lieutenants away from the aircraft. They were grinning from ear to ear and jabbering among themselves as they were handed off to me by the gunner, who stayed watchful until they were well away from the moving parts of the Huey. As I glanced through the front windscreen, I saw a grinning American pilot giving me the thumbs-up. Maybe they did know the nature of the cargo after all.

We gathered in a little group on the ramp, slapping backs; I kept saying, "I told you so," to the little four. Amjad was as confident as ever; one of the Mahmoods too; but the other two were quiet.

As we were standing there on the ramp, out of the blazing sun, right on time, appeared Snapper. I pointed out the aircraft coming in out of the sun.

"Mahmoods and Amjad, that (gesturing like Babe Ruth) is the airplane that is coming to get you. When Snapper takes off again, with one of you in the right seat, you will be starting the syllabus for the new Iraqi pilot training program. And when you graduate, you will be several of the most highly qualified pilots in the Iraqi air force. You will be able to do touch-and-goes, fly at night, and have instrument training."

They were looking at me like a dog given a Rubik's cube.

"Um...I realize that you don't know what a lot of that means, but I am telling you that when you graduate, you will be able to do things that only Iraqi colonels got to do, after they got a lot of flying experience. And you will do it as student pilots and then as brand new pilots."

They looked at each other, as Snapper turned off the active runway and started taxiing toward us.

I had the guys wait to meet him; the aircraft taxied up and shut down. I was grinning like an idiot but sneaking glances at the four. They had unconsciously huddled into a small group like gazelles sizing up a lion. I didn't blame them. It wasn't like they were some isolated Amazon tribesmen; they *knew* what an airplane was. But, I *know* what a rocket is. I would still be very pensive if someone hoisted me up and stuffed me into a little capsule on top, then started counting backwards.

This was much the same. They leaned their heads toward each other and were gesturing subtly, while still trying to maintain their cool. But that didn't work; Amjad caught me grinning at them, and his head split into a giant grin. It was so cool. Snapper and his Iraqi copilot got out, resplendent in their flight suits and obligatory sunglasses.

I was hoping to steer them to the Iraqi captain, because that's who we were trying to get them to emulate, but they wanted to meet Snapper first. The Iraqi captain was a very well-spoken, well-groomed young man, but when it came to meeting him or the American, unfortunately, they wanted to meet Snapper.

I needn't have worried. Snapper was masterful in steering them right to the captain.

"It's great to meet you guys; I've heard a lot of great things about you. On behalf of Colonel Kamil, I would like to welcome you to the first class of pilot training. Captain Faisel is one of our best instructors, and he will be taking care of you when we get back to Kirkuk."

Captain Faisel said a few words, but because they had to go refile a flight plan, he and Snapper walked off into the base operations building.

With a few minutes to kill, Richard and I walked them around the aircraft. Although a fairly simple aircraft, and certainly not in the same category as the jets Snapper usually flew (Vipers), to these young guys who had never touched or been close to a real aircraft, it was still pretty intimidating. We walked around it, pointing out flight controls and talking about what each surface did for the aircraft.

Elevators: when you pull back on the stick, the elevator comes up, the cows get smaller. Push down on the stick, the elevator goes down, the cows get bigger. That kind of expert instruction is what they got from yours truly. They would be getting better at Kirkuk. As we continued to walk around the aircraft, they got progressively quieter. I think that reality was sinking in: something they had never in their whole lives considered, until four months ago, was about to become reality.

One of the Mahmoods was mesmerized by the cockpit. The Caravan sits fairly high, and the door was open, so Richard had taken my little camera and got a great shot of Mo looking up into the cockpit. I walked up to him and started pointing out the various instruments and doo-dads that I look at when I fly. I don't know what they are, but I learned in pilot training to look at them, so I do. He was nodding his head and asking soft questions. I was encouraging him, saying that in spite of the intimidating nature of the displays, he would be trained so well it would become like reading a book. He agreed—certainly he could do it. After a bit more Q  and A, he went silent. I stood off his shoulder as the other Mahmoods and Amjad were still wandering around the tail. I quietly watched the back of Mo's upturned head. Seconds ticked by, and just as I was about ready to walk away, he turned and leaned back toward me so that only I could hear. "Major Mike..."

"Yes?" I tried to match his tone and volume.

A pause. Then, quieter yet, almost a whisper. "Sir..." His eyes locked onto mine. "Sir, can I do this?"

The vulnerability in those words arrowed right through my heart. The bluster and noise of the confident foursome was gone, and this young man, who had been through so much, was faltering. This hurdle seemed to be so high for him. And I said what you would have said.

"Yes, Mahmood, you can."

He looked back up to the cockpit, and into his future

Richard snapped another picture just at that moment. It was perfect.

About that time, Snapper and Faisel had come back out and were preparing to go. We loaded up the four, and I marshaled them out of the spot. The Cessna waddled along the taxiway, starting the first orientation ride of the Iraqi initial pilot training class. After coordination with the tower, we raced out to a taxiway and I whipped out my little camera. The Cessna spun onto the centerline of the runway; held for a second; then started to get bigger. The nosewheel came up as it passed, and leapt into the air. I saw some heads through the windows, and a wave.

Snapper did a big wing rock, and the Caravan winged towards Kirkuk with its precious cargo on the first sortie of the Iraqi Pilot Training Class. On October 1st.

Just like General Dice said it would.

14

FLINTSTONE VILLAGE

While all of that was going on, we settled into a routine. It was work six and a half days a week. The other half day was all mine. Of course no one told the raucous neighbors when my half day off was, so they didn't take off rocketing us. Pretty inconsiderate if you ask me. The best part was that I could sleep in a little on that day. I ended up reading lots of books, histories of Islam and the Arab peoples, counter insurgent warfare, and so forth. I think I read some fiction during that time as well.

Sometimes we would grab a vehicle, if available, and explore a little bit of the base. I wasn't as adventurous as some, but Jim knew of a couple cool places that he thought I'd like to see. If a vehicle was available, we could take it over to Camp Slayer (I'm not sure what went on there, but they had the coolest name) or some of the other camps on the other side of Baghdad International Airport from us.

Jim and I (and whoever else wanted to go) would hop in one of the old 6 Pax Chevys that the unit had, and we'd go bouncing through the vast complex that surrounded the airport. We would start from our trailers, cruising on a paved road for a bit, get off onto a dirt road, through some walls that tanks had run through, back onto another paved road, through a couple of internal checkpoints, back onto a dirt track by a canal, through another checkpoint, then, through an abandoned zoo (really), and so on. We eventually wound up on the southern end of the complex, the last couple of miles crossing various manmade lakes.

That's right. Lakes.

According to Jim, Saddam's stimulus package worked the same as many other stimulus packages: it stimulated those portions of the economy targeted by the folks ordering the stimulus, in this case Saddam. He had put in lakes and connecting canals, along with the corresponding bridges, passing by several variously sized palaces. If you were high up on the list of best buds, you got a corresponding-sized castle. Which, even if you were not on the super-cool list was pretty cool: I would certainly take a "small" palace on a lake.

I wasn't sure how much of the narrative I believed; I'm sure that Jim was relaying what he had heard from someone, who had heard it from someone. But, nonetheless, there they were. We skirted past several more while cruising through Camp Slayer, en route to a massive palace rising in the distance, all the while looking at the faux luxury that surrounded us: the small islands with small palaces connected by faded metal drawbridges. Apparently, we were going to a little complex in the same vicinity. As we got closer, we could see that there had been two distinct efforts made to work on the palace: theirs and ours.

From a distance construction cranes appeared, bent and broken. There was construction rubble around the entire complex. Holes ringed with soot appeared

in the roof, courtesy of the best skylight installers in the world: the United States Air Force. Walls were in disrepair; blocks of stone tumbled down around them like every Lego building I've ever built. The palace clearly wasn't finished; even the parts that were finished, we "unfinished." After countless dollars and multiple years, the giant palace remained unfinished, which made the name of this symbol even more ironic. Yes, we were headed toward the "Victory over America" Palace.

Saddam had named it a bit, umm, prematurely, after his smashing victory in the first Gulf War and his string of victories in the ensuring years of the no-fly zones, embargos, and resolutions. Quite a knack for irony, this Saddam fella. This huge building, within sight of probably five other large palaces and several smaller buildings, just in this one small area, was a pretty good indicator of the megalomania of Saddam. I would get to hear about the practical effects at a later date.

The complex looked across its lake at the reason we had come here. From a distance, it looked like a bunch of white mounds stacked on top of each other. It really looked a lot like a giant wasp nest or beehive. We rumbled on up in the old six-pack and came to a halt in front of it. It was a three-story playhouse. Apparently, Saddam had it built for his nieces and nephews or grandkids or whatever. It was a series of whitish, plaster-covered "caves" stacked on top of each other, sprawling for perhaps one hundred yards in either direction, and built up to three stories. There were palm trees planted all over the complex, and there used to be lights and stuff, which had since fallen down or been broken. There were little pathways and nooks and crannies in the lake. As a guess, there looked to be about thirty different little rooms, with many different themes. Some faced the lake, through which a kid could look out of the marble-floored room, through the oak-trimmed glass, onto the shimmering image of the giant palace.

Those kids would have been the privileged spawn of the upper echelons of the Iraqi ruling class: cronies, friends, and relatives of Saddam. According to the Four Amigos, there were a few levels in Iraqi society, and these children would have looked out of their little three-story playhouse secure in the knowledge they were at the top of the food chain. They may have been gazing out over that symbol of Saddam's might, content that they would be eating well, and maybe going for a yacht ride or a dip in one of the several pools that had been built into the manmade lakes. Winning the genetic lottery in Iraq was a good thing indeed.

Of course, now that kid would be looking through a shattered glass pane, nestled in a fractured oak frame, over a dirty, houseboat-filled lake, onto an image of a broken, blasted, and empty palace. This place certainly had seen better days. It had been stripped of anything useful, and the plaster façade had been broken through in several places to reveal the steel skeleton underneath. In some cases, you could see the entire three stories down to ground level.

There was a big electrical panel about midway up that had probably thirty different buttons on it; all the wiring had been cut away, but it looked like it controlled the watering (for all the palm trees suspended in the structure) and a ton of lighting. The place must've been something when everything was working.

It would've taken a ton of people to care for it though. Just cleaning the rooms would've been a chore. All the rooms had marble floors, and many had showers and bathrooms. Then there were grotto-type rooms down under ground level that, since we didn't have flashlights, we couldn't see much of. But Jim had come a couple of times before and knew his way around.

After taking the appropriate amount of stupid pictures, we finished exploring, jumped back in the six-pack, and headed for home, taking the opposite way around the lakes. We saw more of the same: sunken houseboats, small palaces, and little drawbridges; this time we were able to see a massive stone structure that served as a boat storage palace for all the yachts that Saddam had on this complex of landlocked lakes.

To me, it was incredible—a massive waste of resources for one man's pleasure. But the impact of the splendor really didn't hit home until sometime later, when I decided to take the guys out there to see it. They said they hadn't seen it before.

I piled Wahid, Asad, and Samir into the six-pack one day. It was always fun to watch Wahid and Asad spar back and forth. I've already mentioned that Asad was fairly rotund, and this meant that for him to get into the four-wheel-drive vehicle was, well, fun to watch. And the one who had the most fun with it was Wahid. Asad would swing his stumpy little leg up to the sill, but his belly would get in the way, resulting in gales of laughter and a verbal machine-gunning from Wahid. I think that Wahid was the only one that could, or would, give him so much crap. But if you've been best buddies with someone since you were five, that's your right.

After we had everyone in the rig, I asked them if they knew the way to the place. They looked at me in puzzlement.

"Mike..." Asad had his patient voice out, so I knew that I had missed something. "We were not allowed to even look at this place."

"We'd be shot! Bang!" Samir chimed in from the backseat, gesturing with a finger pistol. "You couldn't even mention this place; the police would get you," he squeaked.

Wahid's gravelly voice added to the fray, "Mike, Saddam had this whole area for his special uses. For us to fly over it in an air force airplane meant that we would get shot down or arrested when we landed. It was a very bad thing to do. We were not allowed to talk about this place, even in the officer's club."

That surprised me, twice. One, that this giant complex would be hidden in plain sight with the general population scared to even acknowledge something that was so clearly right *there*. And two, that this highly respected military aviator (Wahid) wasn't in the know. It made me feel a little better about Wahid; if he wasn't in Saddam's inner circle, then he must've been all right.

We certainly have our secret facilities; I was associated with the F-117 for long enough to know a little. But those areas are usually for military necessity. I believe that a government has to have its secrets. It's the nature of the secrets that reveals the nature of the government. National security is vital to any nation, just like household security is in my house. I don't suppose there is anything wrong with everyone in the world knowing my bank balance; after all, it's not like I've been taking campaign money from Freddie Mac or something. But I don't want everyone to, because of the possibility it would lead to more nefarious activity. So there are some secrets that should be kept, not necessarily because of their inherent value, but because of their leveraged value.

So, too, must a government strive to hide some things about itself that are perfectly legitimate. Its military, defensive, and offensive capabilities would be a good thing to keep to itself; that knowledge has inherent value. There may just be (liberals, cover your eyes for this part) nations or organizations or individuals that mean to do us harm—maybe even for no really good reason. (See chapter 5.) If those entities were continually unsure if their attacks would be successful or if there would be a supersized (this being America after all) ass whipping soon to follow, that would give most of them pause. Everyone in the military knows: winning an issue with political will is much preferable to winning on the battlefield. So those capabilities would be good candidates for secrecy. This was just a giant playground for Saddam; the fact that it was restricted from the general population, with severe penalties for violations, spoke volumes about the legitimacy of the project. It didn't have much to do with the national security of the Iraqi nation; it had everything to do with the willingness of a dictator to mortgage the future of his people for a playground. This was the way that he viewed his people: resources to be bled for his amusement. The entire population was paying "their fair share". I didn't know the half of it.

After realizing that these guys were going to be useless for navigating, I took off in the general direction of the Flintstone village. As we bounced along the roads, there was a constant stream of Arabic from the rest of the vehicle. One of the guys would point to a palace or a particularly ornate structure, burst into voice, sparking the other two into the fray, wildly gesturing and not-quite shouting. These outbursts would always end in Wahid sadly shaking his head, and tsk-tsk-tsking. I didn't really ask much of what they were saying; I was playing tour guide—in their city.

They got particularly excited about the houseboats, and Wahid really lost his mind when we drove by the giant dock building and saw the pools built into the sides of the lakes. I started to wonder if this was such a hot idea, because Wahid was generally a steady guy, I thought. I hadn't seen this level of anger from him before. Asad had a full-time job talking him down off the ceiling as we drove along. Samir was acting like Samir: expressing wonderment about the scale of the buildings, how the lakes were made, and so forth. He was like a kid at Disneyland.

As we finally arrived at the complex, I explained to them that this was the Victory over America Palace that Saddam had tried to build; they seemed to recognize the name. Apparently they were told that this palace was already complete—a monument to the greatness of the Iraqi people and the futility of the Americans' efforts. They didn't know that this wreck was that. That generated some serious head shaking and tsk-tsking. But they had never heard of or seen the "Flintstone village" before.

We rolled to a stop in front of the complex in a big cloud of dust. The ever-curious Samir was chomping at the bit to get out. At the risk of sounding a bit paternal, Samir always struck me as very childlike, and it was evident here. He was squirming in the backseat, looking at the honey-combed rooms with obvious enthusiasm, obviously very excited about the whole adventure, even though it was way outside of his comfort zone. He much preferred to be safe in the trailer with his older brother, the general.

Meanwhile, the other two kept up a conversation that didn't seem register with Samir.

Wahid and Asad were not having a good time, it seemed. I wasn't sure what was wrong, but (not for the first time) I felt that I was way outside the cultural loop. Like there was nothing in my experience that allowed me to connect with these two guys. I was missing something.

We dismounted the truck and just stood there, looking at the immensity of the project. Samir started to scamper off, busily exploring, while Asad and Wahid waited for me to start the tour. So, with the lake and the half-finished palace as my backdrop, I started telling them what I had heard about the place. As we started moving through the lower floor rooms, I noticed something that I had forgotten from my first trip—all the graffiti.

Americans are really good at establishing that we had "been here," wherever we go. Much of the writing was a particular unit or group that had been there. Some of it was concerning certain biological processes that were being wished upon Saddam, a few with accompanying graphics. There were quite a few love letters, short and sweet, declaring undying love for a girl back home. There was also some good-natured ribbing between services and guard, reserve, and so forth. Good stuff. I felt a bit weird, though—like we had desecrated something. I would never be one of those who pooh-poohs writing on bombs (yes, the PC police making sure that those 500, 1000, 2000 pound instruments of death didn't have any mean words on them) but it felt just a bit wrong.

The young men that wrote these silly things on the walls of this silly place had certainly paid the price of admission for doing so. But I still felt awkward looking at the graffiti in the company of the men who had been vanquished, and so thoroughly, too. Wahid's jaw kept flexing as we walked through the various rooms and I tried to explain what I knew of the place, which admittedly was only what I'd heard from guys who had heard it from other guys. But that was still more than what these guys knew about it.

After spending some more time on the ground floor, I took the guys up the little path to the top, which afforded a great view of the whole complex. We could look out over the lake toward the ruined castle and even take in a couple of sunken houseboats. As Asad, Wahid, and I looked out, Samir was orbiting around us, never too far away from what he thought of as safety, but still fascinated by the whole experience. He really looked like a five-foot-tall squirrel, scampering in and out of the honeycomb. But Asad and Wahid were in a different mood.

As we watched Samir pop in and out like a live whack-a-mole, I asked the guys what they thought. After a quick glance over at Wahid, Asad was the first to respond.

"It is very interesting. The engineering to do this is impressive, especially the electrics, and how the plumbing must have worked to water the trees; unless they had someone do it by hand. I thought that the structure was different, but the way that they did this was not very good." He looked at me with a wry grin. "When you have people working that are scared for their lives, they don't do very good work, like slaves, right?"

I supposed so; if you were scared to bring up any problems, those problems would go unfixed. I guess the thought was that if you could bury the issues, then be far enough away by the time it manifested itself, well, you were alive to see another day. This was another reinforcement of the WMD issue: if you had established such terrible consequences for any type of failure, then you wouldn't get accurate information. So my personal theory is that Saddam didn't know the true state of his own military, much less a highly technical program like nuclear weapon development. So, even if we had had perfect intelligence on what Saddam knew, or thought he knew, we still wouldn't have known jack about whether there was a nuclear program. We would just know what he had been told. Which was that "everything was going great, thank you very much, and we have many nuclear warheads, and they are all fine, and they are well hidden, and if you really want to actually look at one, Mr. Dictator-for-Life Saddam, well, I'll be happy to show you right after I get back from a trip that I've been planning to Jordan." Or something like that. This playhouse, to a much lesser extent, demonstrated that concept for Asad. He thought the whole thing was shoddy.

Wahid, it turned out, couldn't have given a crap about the workmanship. He'd been brewing on something the whole time we'd been walking around, and I was anxious to hear what he thought, if he would share it with me. He would.

"Mike, this place would cost many dollars, yes? Millions?"

I assumed that it had.

"And the palace over there"—gesturing at the Victory over America work-in-progress—"millions more, yes?"

I was pretty comfortable agreeing there, too.

"Do you know when these things were built, Mike?"

Upon my confession that I had no idea, he went on. "I think that these things were built during all the seasons; and during the seasons, things got very bad for us here in Iraq. Medicines and doctors became very scarce. In some parts of the country, food became hard to get. Not here, you see, but in some parts. But the seasons meant that Saddam would take all the medicine off the shelves so that the United Nations would see the Iraqis suffering and take off the seasons."

I looked quizzically at Asad for some help. I knew it was difficult for Wahid to speak English, and he was a bit self-conscious about it, so I was careful about asking for translating help too often from Asad. But I really didn't know what *seasons* he was talking about. As far as I knew, Iraq didn't have severe winters; the summers were hot, but they had always been hot, so I couldn't figure out what the seasons had to do with the United Nations or medicine or anything.

That look generated some Arabic back and forth, terminating in a quizzical look from Asad. He was struggling to find the right words to describe it too. It wasn't often that Asad couldn't find the right words; he was very fluent in English. But he started to describe the United Nations and when they keep people from buying and selling stuff to you. He just couldn't get to the right word.

Sanctions.

Wahid was talking about Saddam's reaction to the sanctions that were supposed to correct the dictator's behavior. Sanctions are the equivalent of being sent to time-out for dictators. It's a typical liberal tool. I want you to do something, but I don't want anyone to be able to say that I "forced" you. Plus, I want to be able to brag that I didn't have to use "force" or that I imposed my will on you. Because that would imply that I thought I was "better" than you, and in the liberal worldview, there isn't anything "better" or "worse," just different. You could also get a feather (fake: animal rights and all that) in your pointed little cap for "collaborating with the international community" so no one could say you were bossy.

It's perfect, really; you get a bunch of your friends together and vote, sometimes vigorously, for a dictator to change his behavior. If he doesn't, you vote really hard. Maybe craft a sternly worded memorandum to be read in front of your friends. When that doesn't work, perhaps there is a demonstration in order, of course conducted in the safety of your home country. What megalomaniac murderer could withstand that onslaught? What choice would that death dealer have but to change his behavior, especially if the sanctions would impact his people? He surely wouldn't want his people to suffer, *non?*

Unless.

What if this person, who has risen to the top of the pile based on how brutal he could be, *didn't care about the suffering of the very people he'd been repressing?* Well, the whole theory would go right out the window. If you couldn't persuade a person who had been killing, raping, and exterminating whole regions of his country—indeed raping the earth itself (ask the Marsh Arabs)—in order to achieve his aims, by writing several sternly worded memos (even on the best stationary, bold font, all caps), well, then I'm fresh out of ideas. Maybe if you did it for a long time. Just imagine how racked with guilt that guy would be. What's the worst that could happen?

Wahid sighed, and his rugged face stilled.

"Mike, when the sanc-tions"—he carefully enunciated the word— "came to Iraq, this is when Saddam built all this. The suffering was great for the Iraqis. While he was building this for children, he was also taking medicine off the shelves so that people would die."

I asked why he would do that.

He looked at me funny. "So he could show this to your TV and tell everyone that the people are starving because of you. But he is building these castles. He is not hungry. At each one of these palaces, there were people that had to serve three meals a day, every day, just so no one would know where he was at. That was at every palace in the country, Mike. He was never hungry, but many Iraqis were. And we just waited, because there was not enough to kill him. He got stronger, and we got weaker. So, for all those years, while we died, he built palaces and"—gesturing over the pale white mounds—"this."

Wahid's eyes got a little shiny. "While he was building this, he took the medicine off the shelves that kept my grandfather well. My grandfather died because there were no medicines that could help his blood sickness (I later narrowed it down to diabetes or something similar). He built from my grandfather's bones."

Samir walked up to us. Perhaps sensing the somber tone of our little group, he got slightly less bouncy as he approached. As the sun started to close on the horizon, backlighting the Victory over America Palace and bathing us in a soft, orange light, it was amazing to me how we four could look around us and see totally different things.

I saw evidence of the heart of America, wrapped in its might. I was standing there with my former enemies, looking at the obvious consequences of provoking the "sleeping giant," and mere months later we were spending blood and treasure lifting the Iraqis up until, in the future, they would support themselves.

Asad was looking at the technical aspects of the fruit of a poisoned harvest. The shoddy construction of the complex wounded his engineering pride and his thirst to get things right. He realized instinctively that this was the product of slaves, not free laborers. The Iraqis had been terrorized for years, and terror is not conducive to pride. Pride is a product of freedom and honesty, both of which were in short supply during the preceding years in Iraq.

Samir was looking at this through the eyes of a sixty year-old child. Although a member of the Iraqi air force for many years, he was not a man of war. He was a man of peace and simple pleasures: walking along the banks of the Tigris with his wife, planting flowers, raising children. He saw this in terms of children playing throughout this vast complex, blissfully ignorant of the turmoil and shadow behind its construction. He had been in and out of each little room, except for the scary dark ones. Life was simpler in Samir's world. Unfortunately, for most of his life, Samir couldn't live in his world. He had to live in Saddam's.

Wahid saw this in terms of cost. The cost to the Iraqis writ large, and to his family, personally. He would never get his grandfather back. As resources dried up, and Saddam was forced to choose between his people and his pleasure, he chose the way he always did. His people suffered and died, so he could carve out a series of lakes on which to put his houseboats that would be stored in the giant boathouse next to one of his many palaces. The international community watched and tsk-tsked about the distant suffering of a population. But Wahid was here. And painfully aware of the cost of the trades involved. His grandfather, as partial payment for a playhouse; but one grandfather was not enough. His story was one that had echoed throughout Iraq and was brought out in sharp relief here. A playground built of bones.

We ruminated in silence for a while and then, as if on command, all started to the truck at once. It was a somber ride back.

I never went there again.

15

IMPERIALIST WARMONGERS

It was hard to get used to the constant peril that our guys' families were in and who they depended on to keep them safe. As I mentioned previously, the guys that I worked with daily all had their families in and around Baghdad. Additionally, the new Iraqi air force members were a prime target for the bad guys. They were well aware of their families' vulnerability and the price for failure to conceal their activities.

The families were incredibly exposed. The guys generally didn't have their own vehicles on the complex and, of course, weren't supposed to have weapons. There was no way any of them could get off base quickly, as driving up to a checkpoint in any kind of hurry was a great way to get ventilated. So in order to get home to protect their families, they would have to get a ride to the checkpoints, slowly process through the nervous GIs (ours and theirs), then get a ride through traffic to their home. By the time they got home, it would be far too late.

All of the guys in the complex handled this differently: some hid absolutely everything from their families, some moved their families to a different country, and some told their families as few details as possible. The really vulnerable ones were the little kids. If they knew something about their father's real occupation and said, "My daddy is a pilot," in the wrong area or to the wrong kid, pretty soon there would be just another pile of disfigured bodies where the future of Iraq used to be.

So, everything my guys did was viewed through that prism. Many of them chose to sleep on base for the week, in order to minimize the number of times they went to and from the base. When they did leave base, they used varying routes and other tactics to throw off any tails that they had picked up. But they were all reachable by cell phone all the time.

If something happened, however, it wasn't like they could just call the police. In the low-trust society that Saddam built, the last person they wanted to show up was someone they didn't know. And the police were riddled with infiltrators, ne'er-do-wells, and thieves, all of whom, if they didn't actively hurt you, could certainly hurt you by loose lips. So to invite these guys into your home was at best a blackmail invitation, and at worst, murder.

Ironically (to liberals) the guys that I associated with felt safest in the company of the warmongering Americans. And not just us supercool air force–types: any American in uniform. Samir had asked me to come down to the gas station where he fueled up, so that the extortion and bullying at the pump would cease. When I pointed out that I was just one guy, and I only had two guns, he said it didn't matter.

"Banzet, all you have to do is be there in the uniform, and all the bad guys will stop. Everyone will behave. Can you come?"

No, I couldn't. It wouldn't be the first time that I would be invited off base, but it was interesting that the mere presence of an American would make people behave. I'm sure some of it had to do with the death and destruction that I could represent, but I felt it was more than that.

Everyone knows about America. We're a known quantity. I would have the honor of carrying the mystique of the nation that invents everything worth inventing, placed a man on the moon, sends rovers traipsing all over Mars, (to see the our flag, according to some Democrat Congresswomen), won both World Wars, feeds the world, and is the beacon of freedom to the planet. All on that little flag on my shoulder. That means something to people. Sure there are a lot of people who hate us; but that hate is borne of jealousy, not fear.

It's like the people that hated the erstwhile vice presidential candidate, Sarah Palin. Regardless of her politics, people on the left hated her. Hated an attractive, accomplished, powerful woman who seemed totally devoted to (and inspired devotion from) her family. Whatever her politics—I honestly don't know enough about them to ascertain whether she was a good or bad politician—she didn't seem to have a mean bone in her body.

Yet she seemed to inspire a visceral reaction by the very people who are supposed to champion the accomplishments of women and be on the look-out for any perceived slight of "womyn," anywhere, anytime. These same people sported "Sarah Palin is a C$$t" T-shirts and vilified her family. They called her every name in the book, and proudly so. So why would anyone hate her? Not disagree—hate.

Palin: "And that's how I would solve the energy problem, provide cars that run on unicorn farts, provide free education for everyone, invent bacon-flavored ice cream that helps you lose weight, and get us out of debt in two years. Are there any rebuttals or counter offers from my friends on the left?"

Random Democrat: "You're a bitch!"

And so it was with the United States, being lectured to by the Venezuelan president on freedoms, as he nationalizes the press and businesses. Being tsk-tsked to on human rights by such human rights stalwarts as Iran, fresh off executing a woman for meeting someone's eyes in a conversation. It's only a matter of time till we get lessons on finance from Uganda, honesty and openness from Russia, food production from North Korea, and the importance of courage from France.

But people know, deep in their bones, exactly what the score is. People don't hate Palin because she's awful. They hate her because they are: she exposes it merely by existing. The same for countries. Any comparison to the United States, whether implicit or explicit, and your country comes up wanting. And it's not because of any particular malice on our part. But, for these people and those countries, the kinder and nicer we are, the more infuriating it becomes.

At the end of the day and in the recesses of their souls, they know the score. We are a trustworthy, kind, and just folk. This was the root of

Samir's unusual request. People would respect me, the Imperialist warmonger, because they could. Despite all the propaganda from the terrorists and that from our journalists (I know, hard to tell apart sometimes), the general population knew the reality. They could trust me and my peers.

Decades of real world experiences with the American "grunt" had taught them that we are a good and just people, in spite of challenging circumstances.

For instance; one day I went over to the Iraqi trailer and it was pretty quiet. Wahid, Kamil, and Asad were in there and Kamil was regaling them with some stories, along with a stack of pictures. As I walked in, Kamil invited me over to take a look at the stack of photos that he had been showing to the other guys.

It was a pretty thick stack of faded 4x6 pictures of a young Kamil. Apparently, he had been quite an up and comer in the IQAF. There were several pictures of him in a red flight suit, lounging around with his buddies. I asked him what that meant, and he unconsciously straightened up; chest swelling just a bit.

"Mike, the red flight suit was given to the top pilot in all of Iraq".

There were a lot of pictures of him in the red flight suit. As I looked around the room, it was obvious that the other guys held Kamil in very high esteem. His dark eyes sparkled as he relayed the stories of him hanging out with his peers, goofing off and being young men with access to fighter aircraft.

Then, as he flipped through the stack, he came upon a photo, and hesitated as slight half remembered grin crept across his lips. His grin grew into a full smile as he plopped his index finger down onto the faded paper.

"That, Mike, was my car."

To me, it was a run of the mill Buick. It looked like a white 1980-ish Regal. It had been given to him by Saddam, as a reward for bravery in the Iran Iraq war. He had taken out a bridge or something that others had failed to. It was a reminder of greatness; the photos of that car transported him back, and the next few minutes, and the following many pictures were all about the car. Him by the car. Him and friends in the car. Friends in car, him out. Him in, friends out. Him in his red flight suit, and friends, leaning on the hood of the car. You get the picture. He had been transported to a different time by those pictures. He was king, a highly respected fighter pilot in a regime that worshiped the air force.

We were really laughing and pointing at the young Kamil when the next picture flipped. There was the frame of a car, rusted and burnt to a crisp. Kamil got somber, and immediately the tone in the trailer matched. Kamil's face took on a sad smile, and flipped another photo. This one was of just the VIN number, the rust lovingly rubbed off, captured in a carefully focused shot.

I asked what had happened.

"Mike, you blew it up".

He then relayed the story of a raid on a communications node that he was at during the first Gulf War. His car was parked outside and was blown to smithereens, then burned to a crisp by one of our bombs.

I kept forgetting that I was with guys that we had tried to kill several times and that there had been a real cost to them, in friends, family and possessions. After he relayed the story, the trailer got quiet. I didn't quite know what to say, but Kamil said it for me.

His big, dark eyes were liquid as he lingered on the picture, then looked straight at me.

"Thank you. Thank you for coming here, and giving us a chance."

I was so proud of the United States; all the time- and not because of its government, often times, in spite of it. The young men and women that were your (the reader's) face to the Iraqi people for so long had proven, in countless encounters over many years, that we are an honorable people. And it wasn't the State Department that made that happen, it was the average grunt.

I respected the hell out of those grunts and tried to do whatever I could to make them feel appreciated for their superb conduct under the worst conditions. One small encounter was seared into my memory like my numerous cross-border Laos incursions in my lucky combat hat. Oh, wait that was something else.

I had to go to the exchange for a pizza; my roommate Joe and I decided we would treat ourselves to a little bit of heaven. In order to get there, I needed to enter a checkpoint, showing my ID, and enter a series of T-wall islands. Several businesses had their own little island of T-walls: a patch shop; a little pieces-of-crap shop, and the object of my mission, the little pizza shop. It was just a trailer with an oven; I think there were five or six choices. But it was pretty darn good, and if I hustled, I could get it back to the trailer while it was still hot.

Dusk was falling particularly quickly, as the dust storms had started; everything was a burnt-orange haze. I could feel the dust going into my

nose and mouth, caking around my eyes, and getting in my ears. It tasted funny, like burned dirt. So the air was heavy as I arrived at the pizza place.

There were only a couple of folks in line ahead of me, but one was representing about twenty folks. Apparently, he was part of an army crew that was getting ready to go out on patrol. The other was an air force officer, whom I didn't know how much I didn't like yet. The young army guy started going through the list of his requests. He wasn't doing a good job. He stammered through a couple of items scrawled on a scrap of paper in heavy pencil. He was having a hard time getting through the list, mostly because it was hard to read. I studied him as he went through it.

He was in a dirty uniform, torn in high-stress areas, like the knees, and around where his Velcro patches went, with the ground-in dirt of hard wear; his faded uniform had clearly been around the block a few times. The army had gone to a lightweight uniform to deal with the heat and, apparently, had given up some durability to do it.

I glanced behind me, past the cable that denoted the parking lot where the rest of his crew was parked, about thirty to forty yards away. I saw young men and women walking around assorted HMMVs and the newer, more massive MRAPs. They were busy doing equipment checks, arranging the gear on the outside of the vehicles, and shooting the breeze. Through the orange haze of the drifting dirt, they moved like ghosts. But even at this distance, I could discern the slight differences in the darkness of the patterns of their uniforms. Either there were some new guys among them, or some had received new uniforms. I think it was the former, because the darker uniforms seemed to be getting some kind of instruction as they moved about the vehicles. There were some awfully young faces moving through the eddies of dust.

I returned my attention to the young man struggling through his pizza order. He was a bit embarrassed by the whole thing; the combination of the fading light, the hastily written order on the wrinkled scrap of paper, the swirling, drifting dust, and an air force lieutenant colonel in a flight suit looking on in disgust took him off his game. He finally got the order out but then realized he didn't have the money.

At this the snotty lieutenant colonel let out an audible snort and looked at me with a "can you believe this guy?" sorta look. He got nothing from me in return. I just met his gaze with a dead-eyed, "screw you" gaze. Respectfully, of course.

The young man cast down his eyes and murmured an apology to the colonel, which pissed me off even more, for his sake. The kid made an apology to the pizza guys and said he would be back in a bit.

I looked back at the group still milling about the vehicles. One small female was on top of one of the HMMVs, getting dressed in the fashion of the day. While young ladies back in the world have to make the agonizing choice of what heels go with what pair of socks, which in turn have to match their two-hundred-dollar, sparkly ass jeans of the week, this young lady had it easy: her Kevlar overpants went with everything. I'd never seen them before, but as the Iranians helped ship more sophisticated IED-making material into theater, our troops paid more of a price with their legs. So this young turret gunner was putting on the latest attempt to protect her from whatever shrapnel made it through the armor of the HMMV and started shredding the bodies inside.

I watched the back of the young soldier as he went over to the group to get more money, while the lieutenant colonel gave his precise order to the pizza guy. Well done, sir. After this, you can go back to your job in the embassy, sleeping under the blanket of protection that the guy you just looked on so derisively provides. I gave the lady my order and asked how much the order of the gaggle of soldiers was. It was about fifty bucks. I paid for that too, so they would start cooking them. It took a bit of time for the young man to finish gathering up the necessary dollars, so, as luck would have it, the butthead colonel was gone, and all of our pizzas came out at about the same time. This was another one of those times that I wish you could've been standing right there with me.

The young man came back clutching a fistful of dollars that he'd gathered from his buddies and was surprised to see the stack of freshly baked pizzas. It was heartbreaking to see his confusion as the pizza lady told him that that those were his pizzas and that they had already been paid for. He asked who had done it, and she nodded to me. My plan had been to get out of there before he came back, but as my stuff came out last, that didn't happen. Anyway, I knew what these E-3s, E-4s, and E-5s were making, so what was a big chunk of income to them wasn't as big of a deal to me. The young enlisted troop, dirty and worn, came up to me and tried to give me the money. I just started shaking my head. I told him something like this:

"Young man, you are about ready to go out on a nighttime patrol that will make the parts of Iraq that you roll through a little safer for a while. You are doing this while I am sleeping. You and your brave comrades will be in danger the whole time. You do this not because you are paid well, but because you are good soldiers. You have an impact on the Iraqis you meet, and since I work with them daily, I appreciate that. I bought you pizzas because I don't know what else to do."

Or something like that; that was the gist of what I said. I just wanted him to know how profoundly appreciative I was.

He was very excited and thanked me profusely. That's when it really got to me; he shouldn't be that appreciative of the small token that I had given him. His obvious sincerity and the unexpectedness of the gift really touched me. These soldiers all deserved so much more than some bozo buying a few pizzas. Something about that night—the dirt, the heat, that squad milling about in the grainy orange fog, and the terrible risks these young Americans were about to take—really got to me.

I clenched my jaw, as I got the familiar feeling and started to tear up. I told the kid to get the pizzas back to his buddies before they got cold. The dust was worse than ever, and I didn't want him to see the tears that were starting to spill over my eyelids. I watched his back fade into the orange fog, and he turned and flashed a brilliant smile. Maybe it just seemed brilliant because everything else was so dirty.

And that tore it; I had to get out of there. I grabbed my couple of pizzas and walked home, taking the time to compose myself and get my officer-ship back.

But I didn't know how deeply that my respect for those young troops was shared by the Iraqis. That would be demonstrated a few weeks later.

Ironically, in my respect for these young Imperialist warmongers, I was joined by many Iraqis, especially the military ones. This proof came to a bright and shining conclusion a few days after that encounter.

The day started out quite normal: me donning my armor, guns, and helmet for another day at the office. The morning passed fairly normally too. I had gone into the trailer, discussed a few things, and left to update our leadership on some of the progress, or at least lack of slippage. I was gone a few minutes and then returned.

To chaos.

Most of the guys were on their cell phones, urgently talking. Worry creased their faces as they tried to push their voices through the phones to the other party. I looked from face to face and saw the same worried look. Ahmed seemed to be the only one not on the phone, but he was paying close attention to the goings on. I sidled up to him, through the clouds of cigarette smoke, and asked in a low voice what was going on.

"There are bad things happening in their neighborhoods," he whispered, never taking his eyes off Asad and Wahid. Samir didn't seem to be involved but had isolated himself in his brother's office. He hated conflict, and there seemed to be something big going on. I saw that my presence was somewhat distracting, so I figured that I would walk across to the Ops Center, a short, gravelly journey to the small, tan building across the parking lot.

I opened that door to see much the same scene; lots of guys were on their phones, gesturing wildly, voices rising and falling over each other. That was enough; I turned around and ran back across the parking lot to the trailer, decelerating through the door. Asad had gotten off the phone, but Wahid was still calmly, forcefully directing someone. Asad looked at me, pain in his eyes, anguish on his face, and his English eloquence failed him.

"They took someone, and now Nassera says that she hears guns coming down the street." Imagine a parent hearing his young daughter describing a firefight coming her way, and being powerless to help, or even be there. This dedicated father was desperate to do something. His eyes cast about as if looking for an escape but knowing there was nothing to be done. I grabbed his shoulder.

"Sayyid, please tell me what is happening; I may be able to help somehow, but I have to know what is happening, and where. Quickly please, sayyid."

He looked at me, bushy eyebrows furrowing, considering what I said. "Mike, a bunch of men broke the door into Faisal's home." (I didn't know this man.) "They took his cousin from the house. There were many men, but no one knows who they were. We think that they are still in the neighborhood, but everyone is hiding. Can you see if your army is around to help us?" I told him I could try and ran back to my trailer.

There was an intel guy there who I knew was well connected to the army folks. I told him the neighborhood that this was happening in and he quickly made some phone calls.

The guy he talked to didn't know of any ops going on in that area. His contact would check further into it, but for now, I would take back that bit of news to my friends and see what they could make of it.

I came back into the A7 trailer to find a more subdued version of the earlier morning chaos. There was still a lot of phone conversation going on, but there was something a bit different this time. All eyes came to rest on me, as I was expected to have news that would affect the situation. The mouths kept speaking into the phones, but the faces rotated to follow the eyes to see what I had to say. There was a bit of consternation as I told them that we didn't know what was going on in that neighborhood, but the overall mood was a bit more restrained. Now it was my turn to be confused.

I asked what was going on, and Asad put his hand over the speaker, saying, "They had Hummers."

That seemed to be a bit of a relief to the guys, an indicator that at least some organization was behind whatever had taken place. The real freelance terrorists didn't have access to military hardware like the Humvee. They would've just pulled up in trucks and cars, jumped out, and grabbed people, or shot them as was their wont. They were much less predictable and much more lethal. You often didn't get your family member back from those guys.

But to have several Hummers implied that there was something official to it. It could still be officially terrorist or some Iranian-sponsored groups, which would be bad, but at this stage in the liberation, there were also some actors chartered by the Iraqi government and tacitly approved by the United States.

One of these organizations was known as the "Wolf Brigade". I think they were chartered by the Iraqi Interior Department as a desperate attempt to get some kind of organized response to the terrorist activities going on. They were a hard-scrabble Shia group, who were used to go into the rough areas of town and snatch suspects. Over time, a lot of evidence showed that there wasn't much discretion in whom they snatched or how they did it. And what happened after the snatching was a problem. So the Iraqis were terrified of them, such that Asad had told me of an encounter that his son had had with them. Apparently his son, who was eighteen at the time and attending college, had narrowly missed being pulled off the street by this bunch.

So, it was a bit better that there were Hummers involved, and that explained the lower stress level I was seeing. But the guys were still worried: having family members taken by an organized group was still worse than if they were just sitting at home, living their lives. There were still phone calls being made, but they weren't the panicked, "stay on the line" kind of calls. They were more the "call me if you find out anything" type. Samir was still really withdrawn, keeping out of the fracas. He was miserable. His small, bronze face was furrowed with worry. I think his family was far outside the city, and he felt relatively safe. But he was miserable for the others.

I was too. I felt helpless. I could very easily see a scenario where one of my guys' families would be massacred, and I would be there watching, powerless to do anything about it. I felt protective of the men that I was dealing with daily. And, now, when they needed me the most, I had turned into a spectator.

The only thing I could do was run back across the parking lot to my intel contact and give him the updated information. I waited on pins and needles as he disappeared to go make some secret intel phone calls. He was certainly trying to help, but there was only so much he could do: we weren't an operational unit that called in air strikes or anything. We were the "soft" side of the war effort. And as such, we weren't really prepared for rapid response. So I waited.

After what seemed like an eternity, he came back, shaking his head. No, we didn't have any ops running in the area, and no, we hadn't heard of anything going on there. The army would check back in a few. I steeled myself for more bad news in the trailer. Anything could have happened by now, and I didn't see things getting better anytime soon. As I walked across the parking lot again, I was mulling over what I might see: Asad screaming, perhaps, or Wahid yelling; Samir traumatized and curled into a little ball after witnessing some horror unfold over the phone. I really was worried over what might have transpired in the minutes I was gone. A lot can happen in a few seconds at the point of a gun.

So, fully expecting the worst, I opened the door and walked in. To silence.

The guys were back at work, typing on the computers, drinking tea, and chatting. It was a *Twilight Zone* episode. I literally took a step back, absolutely flabbergasted by the bizarre world that I just stepped into. I stood there for a second, trying to get my bearings.

"Asad, what is going on?" Asad returned a quizzical look as an answer. I got a bit exasperated. "*Asad*, what is going on? You were very worried for your family ten minutes ago, and now everyone is acting as if nothing happened. What is going on?"

Asad blinked as if something clicked. In that instant, I got the feeling that he realized that he had to explain something to me that was obvious to everyone else. His eyes crinkled into a soft grin.

"I'm sorry, my friend. It was the Americans."

Then he clapped me on the shoulder and returned to work.

Oh, hell no. I needed more of an explanation than that. We were the bad guys, right? We were the ones oppressing and exploiting the brown people by taking their oil. And here, in a clear-cut case of oppression or imperialism or, at the very least, racism, Asad didn't have the common decency to be mad about it.

I stopped Asad. "You said that they smashed in the door and took a relative."

"Yes?"

"Aren't you pissed?"

He gave me a little shoulder shrug and a noncommittal no. But, looking at my slack jaw, he saw that a little explanation was in order.

"Mike, at first we thought the people were attacked by terrorists, maybe from Iran, maybe from another country. They are very, very bad. They kill everyone, but first they make them tell everything. And then they get the next one and the next one…." His voice trailed off thoughtfully. "But then we thought it may be the Wolf Brigade, and that would be very bad, but not as bad. They hurt many people, but not all. There is hope if they are taken by the Wolves. Maybe one of the Shia here could call them and let them free. They don't like the Sunni, but one of our friends could talk to them. But the Americans. When the Americans take someone, they are safe. We are not worried about their safety."

"But aren't you mad that they break down doors and take people?"

"Mike…" Asad looked at me for a while. "Not everyone is good. The Americans are sometimes wrong, but it is many times that an Iraqi has given them bad information. And sometimes, if they are very wrong, they will pay you to fix what they have broken. No Iraqi would do that. But the Americans—the Americans are mostly right."

I looked around at the scene. The regular murmur of office work going on. Samir had come out of the corner where he had bravely hid. He was grinning. "It was the friendly side!" he said, as if that explained everything. And to the Iraqis, it did.

Oh, and that part where Asad's son was almost taken by the Wolf Brigade? Well, several months before, Mohammud had been walking through their old neighborhood (they had since moved), when the brigade started one of their snatch operations. As he was of the right age, they targeted him. He was far enough away that he was able to turn a corner and accelerate his gait, putting some distance between them. He called Asad in a panic. Asad was once again powerless to do anything. He was stuck on base, and the family certainly couldn't do anything, so Mohammud was on his own. He called his Dad in a panic. Asad gave him a direction to walk and instructions to walk fast—not run—and to turn corners, anything to keep widening the gap between him and the ravaging Wolves. Mohammud walked from street to street, begging his father for help, but there was nothing Asad could do (it was tough watching Asad describe this). The brigade kept closing. Asad listened to the growing panic creeping into his son's voice as he described the equipment and the men that seemed to be snatching people off the street. Mohammud let out a cry, followed by several exclamations of "Thank God!" Asad asked what had happened.

An American patrol had come around the corner. As Asad tells it, the Wolves caught sight of the patrol, burst into an orgy of good behavior, releasing those they were harassing, then slunk away. The patrol rolled by, oblivious to what they had just done. They were just a bunch of regular guys, too stupid to go to a really good school or be seen in any of the right places. They clearly couldn't have had any future so were forced to join the army and do terrible things to brown people. But, just by showing up, they saved my friend's son from…something.

Oh, and whoever you were in the turret of the Hummer, with the goggles pulled down and the dust mask pulled up, with one hand on the M-240 and that thought to use the other hand to wave at a young Iraqi man who barely raised his hand in return—you are a better ambassador than all of those swells that attended all the right schools, had a great future, and were seen in all the right places. So, for doing what you probably thought was just the "right" thing, Asad thanks you.

You gave him back his son.

16

LITTLE BIG MAN

One of the common themes I have alluded to was the Iraqi military's reluctance to make decisions or disagree with their bosses in any way. There was no "check" on a leader's decisions. Obviously, in the military, especially ours, there is an expectation of snappy salutes and going forth to conquer when given an order; but in the USAF (and I assume the other services), there was much more to it. We had an annual requirement to complete a training class on moral orders, Geneva convention expectations, and other facets of American-style warfare. A large portion of the class is devoted to hammering home the reality that you are *never* able to hide behind the fact that a superior told you to do something. You are always, no matter the rank, held responsible for your actions. Because we are Americans.

Abu Ghraib was a crime because we considered it so. By Western rules of warfare. We (collectively) turned ourselves in, to be punished by our own rules[6]. That was before the pictures of the despicable actions were published in the newspapers or the news organizations got their precious "scoop" that endangered people that had nothing to do with the tiny number of wrong-doers. And, in spite of the fact that the outrages were conducted by low ranking scumbags without a shred of honor or decency violating their own rules, the effects rippled up through the ranks to the Secretary of Defense. Some of that was media just trying to harm a Republican, regardless of the cost to the warriors; but it reflected a bit of the expectation of responsibility that we have, that other nations and cultures don't.

It also cloaked very bad people in a sheen of moral outrage, so when they committed yet another atrocity, the teleprompter sages could nod knowingly behind their carefully placed glasses, intimating "retribution" or "equivalency." The Iraqis that I worked with were a bit mystified at all the noise about it, saying that these were bad men, and we hadn't killed them all, so what was all the fuss? But the bad men, they would say, would use this as an excuse to kill and torture and kidnap all the more.

We are willing to put ourselves at risk so as not to hurt civilians, even as the enemy uses this kindness as an opportunity for killing us from the cover of women and children. Large arms caches and supplies are constantly stored in mosques and schools and hospitals, knowing we are loathe to even inspect mosques, much less engage in active combat in them. Knowing that we follow the various rules of warfare enables the enemy to exploit them, for they have no moral code. And if you have a moral code, as our services do, then not only can your boss be wrong (carrying out orders to gas the Kurds), but you have the obligation to tell them so. And, in the absence of the boss, subordinates could be trusted to make decisions along the same moral code, because another tenet of our creed is to trust your underlings but hold them accountable to the same standards. And that was the part of our example that the Iraqis were struggling with. The fact that their boss could be wrong. Because not only was the culture in that part of the world nonconfrontational to start with, under Saddam's vicious dictatorship, to say that your boss was wrong or to make a wrong decision was to invite all sorts of negative consequences, up to and including death.

---

6 Schorn, Daniel. *Exposing The Truth Of Abu Ghraib.* February 11, 2009 . http://www. cbsnews.com/2100-18560_162-2238188.html?pageNum=2&tag=contentMain;content Body (accessed August 3, 2012).

It was much the same for an absent boss. If the head man wasn't around, then no new decisions could be made. Even if they were high up in the rank structure, most Iraqis were very reluctant to step out and make decisions that weren't detailed explicitly to them. One could argue that these aren't really decisions in that case; they are just executions of decisions made elsewhere. And one would be right.

But there were some shiny spots. By this time, I had been there a few months and gotten to know everyone rather well. We had pushed through a class at IMAR so had a few graduates, brand-new lieutenants, running around. Plus the class up at Taji was in session and had gradually settled into a routine: the Americans trying to pull out of the action roles, leaving more and more up to the Iraqis. This combination of factors developed into a couple of the most memorable and defining incidents of my tour.

The following class behind the Magic Eleven had started to get a little more out of control as time went on. The combination of weak political appointees in charge at the school and the dysfunctional and adversarial Iraqi generals led to the Americans being thrust more and more into the very leadership roles they were trying to vacate. The students were feeling more and more confident and safe and so were pushing at restrictions. When they discovered weak Iraqi leadership, they did what most big groups of twenty-something-year-old men do: they pushed harder. The Americans started to get more and more worried that the tremendous strides that had been made to date were in jeopardy. Since we had almost daily communications, I decided to ratchet up the pressure on General Akram to solve his problem.

Problem number one was that General Akram refused to see that what went on at Taji was his responsibility, even though it was clearly training. Under the Iraqi construct of old, leadership was great, but the responsibility for that leadership was anathema. So General Akram wanted to be in charge of everything related to training but wanted nothing to do with it if any of it started to go wrong. And the general in charge of the school was a politically connected weakling that the base commander, General Arhem, loved because he would do anything he was told. By the base commander. So trying to get General Akram to take action to fix or fire him was next to impossible. All of these issues together resulted in conversations like this.

"General Akram, the students at Taji are refusing to go to class and misbehaving, but the Iraqi leadership won't make them behave. What do you want to do?"

"That is very bad."

"Umm, yes, but what should we do about it?"

"Bonset (many of the Iraqis had trouble with the "a" in my name), we must make them behave!"

"Umm, yes, do you want to travel to see them and talk to your subordinates about how they are going to make them behave?"

"No, maybe General Abdul Khalid will make them behave."

"But, sayyid, he is there now, and they are not behaving. The Americans think that he is perhaps not a very strong leader."

"Yes, he is not. That is bad."

"So, should you go to Taji and help him? Or make a new leader?"

"No, that is maybe General Arhem's problem; he should fix it. Yes, General Arhem must fix it."

"Sayyid, General Arhem does not work for training; he is the base commander, working for another division."

"Yes, that is very bad. I think maybe he is a bad man."

"So, sayyid, what should you do within your *own* chain of command to make *your* students behave?"

General Akram looked thoughtful for about two uncomfortably long minutes. "Maybe the 'friendly side' would help us?"

"No, sayyid, the Iraqis must solve this. You cannot have the Americans solve the problem because that makes the Iraqis look weak. The Iraqis must solve this, and you can do it by just going up there and talking to the students and the instructors."

"That is bad."

And so on.

General Akram, the self-described "number one pilot in Iraq" and possibly the best pilot ever, was powerless against twenty or so young students. He would prevaricate and stall, constantly coming up with new ways to not do anything about the situation. Asad, Wahid, and Nasser certainly understood what I was trying to do but were powerless to do anything. They cautiously tried to convince Akram, but the conversation usually ended in a flurry of Arabic with shoulder shrugs and apologetic glances at me.

But finally I had a breakthrough. At some point, General Akram was worn down. I had tried everything to get him to do something about the situation, and I was greatly surprised when he finally said, "Okay, Bonset, I will go to fix the students at Taji."

"Really? That's great news, sayyid! I will tell the Americans the great news. Make sure to call General A. K. and tell him you are coming. What are you going to tell them? What are you going to do? When are you going?"

Akram was beaming from ear to ear, as he had made me very happy, but out of the corner of my eye, I saw Asad smirking. I shot him a scowl, as I had finally won, and I didn't need his sour grapes to spoil my victory. Akram continued to look thoughtful and then made his grand pronouncement.

"Bonset, I will fix everything! I will talk to General Arnhem, and I will put General A. K. in very much trouble. Then I will tell the students to listen, because"—with a modest shrug—"I have trained approximately one hundred percent of the pilots in Iraq. So they will listen."

Yes! My patience had paid off; he was going to take care of everything. Although as time went on I would learn to listen to Akram with a more, umm, realistic ear, I was really excited about this.

"When will you go? How will you get there? Do you need any help to get there?"

"No, Bonset, my friend, I will do everything." Asad's eyebrows went up again, as Akram continued, "I will show them who is the boss, and I will make everything better. And I will do it all after I come back from *mujas*!"

Asad began jiggling, as he often did when he was overcome with laughter.

"Umm, mujas? When are you going on mujas? When are you coming back?" I knew that mujas (the term for vacation, often of indeterminable lengths) could mean anything. Some guys, a very few, never came back from mujas. But I did know that for this mujas, it meant that Akram was totally full of crap. This was yet another jink tactic from the best pilot in the IQAF. Nothing would change if I left it up to him and his initiative. Yet the delicate balance must be kept: the Americans must stay in the background but not let the Iraqis fail. Failure of the Iraqi military implied weakness, which invited more attacks, which showed a weakness in the military, which invited more attacks, which led to the Americans being here longer, with more casualties all around. We couldn't do it for them, or they would never learn proper leadership, which would breed weakness in the successive generations of leaders, which meant that the IQAF would be susceptible to the very actions that had led me there in the first place.

So I had to figure out a way to do it within the construct of the Iraqi mindset. When General Akram left for his two- or three-week vacation and the problem still hadn't resolved itself, I approached Colonel Wahid.

I caught him in the office and approached him about the problem. He totally understood what needed to be done, and he would have loved to do it but couldn't, because his boss, the goofy General Akram, hadn't authorized it. He couldn't get in contact with Akram, as his mujas was taking place in either Syria or Mosul, and he was out of comms. So it would be up to him to do something. As I continued to press him, I could see the tremendous struggle taking place within Wahid. He knew without a doubt the right thing to do but could not bring himself to do it. It was just a leap too far. To make a decision and take action in the absence of clear guidance was against everything he had ever been taught or seen around him. He had some experience with the ramifications of being out of step with his superiors, and it wasn't pleasant. But here was this American telling him to do exactly the opposite of everything he knew.

I could see the agony in his eyes, as he desperately tried to come upon a way of addressing what he knew was right and the "wrong" way in which I was asking him to accomplish it. His already worn face was furrowed in worry, as he wrestled with his integrity. He eventually became so frustrated that he tried to demonstrate to me what he was talking about.

We were out in the hall in HQ by this time, in order to talk semiprivately. In a flash of inspiration, he gestured at the folder that I was carrying.

"Mike, your folder, what color is it?"

"Why, it's blue, sayyid."

"Yes, it is blue. Now, if your boss says it's red, what color is it?" He was half smiling, fully expecting me to have to say it's "red", now that he had properly explained the question.

I looked at him like a cow staring at a new gate. "It's still blue, sayyid. If my boss is wrong about something, then it is my duty to tell him so. This is probably the most important duty one could have! It's more important than any job I do: being a good officer is more important than being a good pilot, and this is being a good officer."

His jaw dropped in disbelief. He couldn't understand how I couldn't understand. This wonderful, moral, loyal officer could not get the distinction I was trying to make, and I had no idea how to make him. Until I saw Speedy.

Speedy was one of our earliest graduates at IMAR. He was part of the first class that had made it into the IQAF at large and was actually performing duties. I had talked to Speedy several times, as most of the young officers always wanted to practice their English. He was a scrawny kid, with kind of a beak nose, and always with a smile on his face. He had been through a lot as a member of the first class. They were always getting rocketed and mortared down at IMAR, so they had been learning all we could teach them in between dodging shrapnel. And now he was assigned to personnel. The IQAF didn't really have a good personnel assignment system as yet, so when the new officers popped out, they just kinda went wherever. We were still establishing the methodology to assign students where they would be most productive, but for the first couple of graduating classes, it was pretty random. So here, at HQ, was Speedy.

He would make an excellent subject for my test. I summoned him over, his face splitting into a grin as he heard me call his name. He saluted Wahid and greeted me. I put on my stern face and began prepping the test subject.

"Speedy, you are a lieutenant, correct?"

"Yes, sir!' he squeaked.

"And I am a major, correct?"

"Yessir!"

"So I can tell you what to do, and legally, you'd have to do it, right?" (I couldn't, I didn't think, but that wasn't germane to the conversation. Besides, if people do what you tell them when you tell them to do it, then you can give them orders, right?)

"Yes, Major Banzet." This was given along with a confused look on his face. He really didn't know where this was going. But Wahid was giving me a knowing smile, assured that finally Mike would get it. He didn't realize what amazing powers of ignorance I have at my disposal. Meanwhile, in my head, I was hoping that he would give the "right" answer. I was hoping that the training that the Americans had given him would counteract the daily examples that he saw around him. There was so much that had to happen before the school could be stood up and start educating him. Many marine corps, army, navy, and, yes, air force members had given their lives to give him this opportunity. I silently prayed he wouldn't squander it.

"Well, lieutenant, I want to ask you a leadership question. Do you see this folder in my hand?"

Again the look. "Yes, sir."

"Well, what color is the folder, lieutenant?" I emphasized the word *lieutenant* to try to reinforce the rank differential.

"Sayyid, it is blue, yes?"

"No, it is not. It is red."

Speedy's head jerked back, eyebrows meeting over the protruding nose, lips pursed. He stumbled over the next few words. "I'm sorry, sayyid, my English must not be very good. I thought that was blue. How do you call that color?"

I had to clarify, as I ran into a distractor in my own test: he wasn't sure what the English word for the color he was seeing was. So I had to make sure that the English translation wasn't the problem. I pointed, like Babe Ruth picking his spot, to a blue sign on the wall, about the same shade too. "That is blue."

If his eyebrows could've crossed, they would've. His big brown eyes darted between the sign and the folder, confirming that they were indeed the same color. "Banzet is either colorblind or a dumbass" was written across his young face. He searched my face for some hint of what was going on. I remained stoic.

"Sayyid, it is not red; it is blue."

"But what if your boss thinks it is red?"

Speedy thought for a second, a bit of uncertainty flickering across his face, until his eyes locked and an internal decision had been made. He look me square in the eye.

"Sayyid, blue is blue."

I could've kissed him. I was elated. At that point I realized what a difference we were making—truly making—in this region. This kid now knew the right way, and he was always measuring the performance of his own military against the greatest force for good in the world: ours.

Wahid was clearly confused. He was taken aback by the young officer's forthright answer in spite of pressure to answer otherwise. His eyebrows furrowed as he considered what had just happened. This was a new way of operating, a way to temper power with truth, a way to tame aggression with the restraint of clarity. I looked carefully at his face, to see how he would take this. He thought for a minute.

"I will try."

I showed restraint, but I'm sure a big smile was plastered across my mug. Speedy realized something had happened, but didn't know what and did not know his part in it. I assured him that the truth was always the right answer and that I was proud of him. I scooted him on his way by reminding him that he probably had work to do for his boss and that I was sorry I interrupted him while performing his duties. He remembered that he had duties and scampered off to perform them. I turned to Wahid to see what the next step was.

"Mike, I will call General A. K. now and see what I can do." And he did. He pulled out his personal cell phone and called. Several questions followed, then a gradually louder battery of statements, followed by louder and more rambling explanations coming through the phone. Arabs conduct their business loudly and passionately anyway, but this was at the upper end of the passionate scale, even for these guys. After about twenty minutes of "earial" assault, Wahid smacked the phone closed, brushed past me, and hollered for Asad. He often did this when frustrated or felt his command of the English language was inadequate to the task. I followed into the office to get some of the barrage that Asad was now on the receiving end of.

Asad listened thoughtfully and then relayed what had happened.

Nothing.

General A. K. knew he was protected and further knew that Wahid was operating out of his lane, and so the general had slyly asked about Akram. Wahid had no patience for this dissembling and blew up. And got nowhere. Even as a highly respected officer from the old school, with the assurance that no one was going to get shot for being substandard and the realization that the Americans didn't have a lot of choices when it came to immediately staffing the armed forces, Wahid had no leverage. And now, he felt bad that he let me down. I was hoist on my own petard.

But at least he had tried. He had gone way outside of his comfort zone and been rebuffed, but not defeated. And I was determined that we would get some sort of result, or at least the appearance of a result. I asked Wahid who would be the best one to help us. He was really uncomfortable talking about it. To him it was going around his boss. So we were stumped with how to proceed. But then I remembered the little general.

I asked Nasser to accompany me, as he had been with me the first time I had gone to see the general. "Nasser, would you go with me to see General Jasham again?"

Nasser hid his obvious excitement at the thought of accompanying me to the head general in charge of all Iraqi military training by rolling his eyes and holding up his hands in sort of a "warding" motion, while moaning, "Please, Bonset." He was very clever at concealing his excitement like that. This was really way out of his comfort zone. I thought that I had established a decent relationship with the general in an earlier meeting, so would try to capitalize on that by asking him for advice on how to handle unruly cadets, which I could then use to help persuade my reluctant one-star to actually take command of something. Those cadets were worth more than gold to the Iraqi effort, although at the moment they were very unrefined and needed a lot of polishing. So I would take the risk of getting chewed out in order to get the help we needed. So I asked Nasser to accompany me, as he was with me the first time I had gone to see the General.

I had been taken to see General Jasham about a smaller matter. Nasser had taken me to the Joint Iraqi Armed Forces building, just two buildings down from where we were. I had strapped on the body armor and helmet, grabbed my clipboard, and followed Nasser, crunching through the gravel in the 110-degree heat. We went by a guard sitting in a white plastic patio chair, who reluctantly stood up, nodding as I passed. After all, I had a gun, and he didn't. I gave a cheerful greeting and plunged into the dark of the foyer, trying to keep up with the dark green flight suit of Nasser, who was trying to lose me, I thought. The corridors were filled with smoke and lots of folks passing each other, carrying sheaves of papers—all very official. I was the only American that I could see, and even though I was with Nasser, whom I implicitly trusted, there were still a lot of folks around, and I only had one pistol and one extra clip. We knew the bad guys had infiltrated all the services, so anytime I got isolated, I got a little nervous.

There was no blending, either; not only was I a good foot and a half taller than all of them, I was also a foot and a half wider—the body armor was not very flattering. Plus my helmet added another four inches or so of height. I was Willie Wonka trying to blend in with the Oompa Loompas. Potentially lethal Oompa Loompas. Regardless of how much the air force spent on the new camouflage, I stuck out. So I kept moving quickly, but Nasser was always, tantalizingly, just out of reach, so I just smiled, nodded, and kept my gun hand free. Like always (except at the Ministry of Defense), most of the faces I saw seemed to be happy to see me. The younger ones were more accepting, I thought. I kept moving, up two flights of stairs, through surprised security guards in their white plastic official "security chairs," and finally into the anteroom of the man we had come to see.

A small general sat behind his desk, talking with a couple of Iraqis in this large, well-appointed office. There were several others gathered around a computer monitor, all intently looking at something. We respectfully took a seat; soon a young Iraqi captain came over and, in flawless English, introduced himself. He was an army captain, a member of their special forces; his command of English had landed him in this office to help translate for this important general. The captain was a really nice guy, brave to a fault, dismissing the bad guys as a mere nuisance, saying that the insurgents mostly were guys without girlfriends. He said it a little less diplomatically than that, and I immediately liked him. We were interrupted when, like often happened, other Iraqis gravitated over to the American, to talk, find out about my background, where I was from, did I have a family, and so forth. America was a giant mystery to them, a dream world that they were just starting to understand. Among the questioners was one of the guys that I had seen hunched over the computer in the office.

He was kind of a goofy-looking guy, about sixty-five-years-old, with big, rheumy eyes, a florid face, and a hacking cough. I really would've preferred that he not be so close to me, but it was always tough to extricate myself from these overexcited guys. Plus, I didn't want to offend. He started asking me questions about music: Did I have any? What did I like? Why? Had I ever heard of this person? That person? I wasn't sure what this had to do with training Iraqi soldiers or sailors or airmen, but I felt like I was being tested somehow. I answered the best I could but still felt like I was failing. This guy knew most of my music, but he kept asking me if I had it with me, so he could copy it. I didn't. I looked at Nasser, and he gave me the patented Iraqi shrug, but with a gleam in his eye. I still couldn't make the connection between my music choices (and availability) and Iraqi training. I wasn't even sure that I was in the right place.

I looked around the office, and sure enough, there were certificates hailing the accomplishments of the guy who inhabited the office. Successions of Americans had praised the office occupant with helping with this, being invaluable with that, and so on. I assumed they applied to the gentleman sitting behind the desk, deeply engrossed in a conversation (or two) with a couple of Iraqi generals, who were loudly and simultaneously agreeing and/or disagreeing with each other and/or the guy behind the desk. The older, distinguished gentleman looked on with amusement. He glanced over at me while I was busy getting peppered by spittle from the music man, assessed my desperate look, and smirked. I was trying to glean some information about why the music information was important to know in the training world. But the guy didn't speak enough English to really explain. I kept looking over at the guy behind the desk and saw that now the two generals were quietly listening to him. Apparently, he demanded respect: he was indeed the right guy.

At some unseen signal, Nasser wrapped up whatever conversation he was having with his neighbor, but my guy was still tugging at my sleeve, insisting that I must have music that I wanted to give him. He kept getting closer to me as he insisted on making his point, really grossing me out. Just as my heebie-jeebies reached their nadir, Nasser lightly touched me on the shoulder: it was our turn.

The young captain shook my hand again, turned, and relayed my name to the general. The general smiled widely then came around from behind his desk to shake my hand. He was very small, around five feet, about sixty-years-old, trim, and energetic. His well-lined face reflected a lot of time spent in the sun and also a lot of smiling. I placed my right hand over my heart and greeted him. Of course I looked like a moron; he had his hand outstretched to shake mine. About the time he started to withdraw his hand, I realized it and thrust mine out. We looked like we were slap fighting. He finally chuckled, grabbed my hand, and said in a gravelly voice, "Hello, Banzet. I am pleased to meet you. I am sorry to take you away from talking to the leader of the Iraqi Military Band." He said this with a big grin. Apparently the guy that had been moistly talking to me was part of the informal security system. If you stayed through ten minutes of conversation with that guy, then you passed the test. I hadn't realized that the Iraqis had a military band, but they would become the main characters in one of the funniest things to happen in Iraq the whole time I was there. At least the guy's questions now made sense. I glanced over toward the computer monitor, and sure enough, the screen showed the Iraqi military band, resplendent in their scarlet uniforms, trimmed by white leather belts and piping. And pith helmets. White ones. Which was awesome.

I grinned widely and responded that I was honored to meet him, and he gestured to a seat. I've forgotten the topic of this meeting, but we stayed for quite some time and had multiple cups of tea; all the while the crowd of Iraqis got bigger and bigger. There was a lot of laughing and shouting and talking about general things, not really the things we had come for. Shockingly, this was really the first he had been told about the IQAF training piece, in spite of the fact that the effort had been ongoing for almost two years. Nobody thought to come over and tell the head of Iraqi military training about it. Heck, I had only gotten here because I had called Akram's bluff on whatever issue we were dealing with.

But it turned out that he couldn't have been nicer. Any misgivings I had about being here on my own dissipated as he talked. He was attentive to everything that was being said, with the captain helping out with some of the abstract concepts I was trying to get across or when I got stuck trying to explain something. Nasser would rapidly fire answers to questions that I didn't know were being asked, with the captain providing the translation after the fact. I also learned that this pleasant old man was one of Iraq's fiercest patriots. He had been involved in the Iraqi army for about forty years, fighting the Iranians, us, and us again. We had twice decimated his tanks and destroyed his army, narrowly missing him on several occasions. He said that the wars were terrible mistakes for the Iraqis, but they just couldn't get out from under Saddam. He was too powerful; they couldn't do it themselves. At this point in his story, he thrust his hand out again, grasping mine, then covering both with his other hand. His merry eyes, somber now, locked mine. The assembled men fell silent.

"Thank you, Banzet, and all your men for helping us in this. Now we can try."

I stammered out a gracious (I hoped) reply, and I was genuinely touched by his words, haltingly spoken in soft English. What do you say when a man, whom you (and your friends) have tried to kill on many occasions, who had lost friends to us and had his entire life turned upside down by us, thanks you for it? Yeah, I don't know either. But it happened to me a few times over there. I wish you could've been there.

Soon after that, we left to go back to the IQAF HQ, but I always remembered that little giant of a man. Which was why I thought of him when my advisees had reached the end of their collective ropes. Wahid, Asad, and the productive Iraqis at Taji needed some top cover that was never going to show up. Unless I pushed it. So I did.

After Nasser calmed down from how excited he was to be accompanying me on another trip down out-of-his-lane, he looked to Wahid, who gave a slight nod. Again, with the twinkle in his eye. So I geared up and repeated the earlier process to go to the Joint HQ. We stopped in a couple other offices to recruit a couple guys from upper management. After several loud greetings of "Helloooo Bonset my friend!" and a couple of man-kisses, we showed up in General Jasham's office, about six guys and me.

This time, I was ready for the band leader and swiftly defeated him with clever obfuscations and telling him that Bony-M's "Rasputin" was the perfect song to march to. I had just heard about it from one of my British comrades. So he went scurrying off to see if he could download it from somewhere. Having defeated the security system, I strode up to the general. He warmly embraced me, hollered for tea, and sat down.

"Bonset, my friend, how can I help you today?"

I briefly explained why I was there and described some of the self-imposed limitations that were preventing the IQAF from handling the cadets as cadets, not children. I explained that I was worried about the cadets getting proper discipline and education. I started to go into how valuable they were to us, when he held up his hand.

"Bonset, I think they are more valuable to us than they are to you. I am the old way, and they are the new way. They must be taught different than I was. They must be taught what the Americans think is proper for a military officer. They will still be Iraqi officers, but taught the American way."

"Sayyid, you are a very smart man. You said it much better than I could. So, do you have any suggestions on how to help us?"

He rapidly fired some stern Arabic at Nasser, then at the larger group. I didn't have the captain with me, so I missed most of it. There was about three to four minutes of intense back and forth, with Nasser looking increasingly more uncomfortable. Finally, after some consensus was reached, the general turned back to me and said, "I will go and talk to them."

That was great, and totally unexpected, news; I was sure I would have to go through about one thousand layers of bureaucracy on their side and then twice as much on our side. But as time was of the essence, I would do whatever it took to make this happen. I could see my week going up in flames as this was going to become my main job for the near future: trying to arrange movement of one of the top Iraqi generals for a day.

"Great! When would you like to travel?"

He smiled and softly said, "Tomorrow, I will go."

Oh.

Really.

And thus began my plot to kidnap a key member of the Iraqi leadership in the middle of a war.

After more pleasantries, Nasser and I took off for our building, discussing what things we each had to do to prepare everyone for his visit. Nasser was going to manage the Iraqis, whereas I would handle things on our end. This would consist of me casually mentioning to my awesome boss, Group Captain Hyslop (who had replaced Group Captain Farmer), that I was traveling up to Taji for the day, and I was taking General Jasham with me. I may have muttered that last part under my breath, but it probably wouldn't have mattered: our British leadership at that time was far more imaginative and risk tolerant than their American counterparts. He gave me permission and sent me on my way. I ran over to the operations guys who managed the Iraqi helicopters, my good friend Wahmid, one of the leadership of the Air Operations Command Center (AOCC). Wahmid was one of my absolute favorites.

He was very tall for an Iraqi, with the obligatory mustache perched over an often smiling mouth. He spoke very good English in a soft, gravelly voice and was very Westernized. He had a very soft, very precise way of speaking that just made him seem smart.

The subject of the war often came up in our conversations, and again, I was thanked for the role the United States was playing in this reshaping. He disagreed with one aspect of the invasion however; he thought we should have been tougher on them. He thought the fact that we tried to use the minimum amount of force in the invasion and occupation of Baghdad increased casualties on both sides. I tended to agree.

We often stayed late into the night in the compound, talking philosophy, military strategy, and families. He was very worried about his country, sensing the balancing act that was required to come out of the chaos as a civilized entity. But he was cautiously optimistic. He was just the kind of man to help tip the balance in the right direction: kind, insightful, honorable. He was also just the right guy for this little tasking. We hugged, shook hands, and got down to business.

"Wahmid, my friend, I need transportation to Taji tomorrow; can your Hueys help us?" The 3 Squadron flew Huey 2s, which were the workhorse of Iraqi vertical lift ops, as their Mi-171s were all grounded. The squadron was based in Taji, so I figured we could get one of our Iraqi crews to come down and get us. The squadrons flew mixed crews, so there might be an American pilot and the rest Iraqis, or an American gunner and the rest Iraqis. It was totally integrated. Wahmid asked me to fill out a request, and when I filled in General Jasham's name, his eyes bugged out. He knew General Jasham, apparently most of them did. He was extremely well thought of.

After perusing my list of passengers, he said that it was approved for airlift, tomorrow. When I pointed out that he hadn't even submitted it, he just smiled and repeated that it was approved and said that two Hueys would be at the Crossed Swords tomorrow morning at 0800. This turned out to be one of the coolest things that I was privileged to see while I was there. Nasser had made all the necessary notifications through the IQAF; given that it was General Jasham traveling, it was approved without question.

So we all met at the Crossed Swords landing zone LZ on base at about 0750 on a beautiful morning. I, Nasser, and Asad, along with one of Jasham's staffers, would be going on one helo, and General Jasham would be going on the other. If the helos showed up. The Iraqis didn't have the best track record when it came to doing things to a specific minute. Or hour. Or day. But with the constant, gentle examples during the daily exposure to the Americans, they were starting to see the benefits of dependability. I was hoping to be a recipient of that dependability.

As we made small talk in the early morning, in the back of my head, I counted down the minutes remaining to 0800. I noticed again how short the general was, even for an Iraqi. In spite of his vertical bearing, he commanded respect, and not just because of his rank. You can always tell those kind. Respect has a way of gravitating toward those who truly earn it. He was in the middle of a little group of multiuniformed Iraqis and one of my counterparts, a lieutenant colonel who was also working on the education of the military. Everyone in the group was paying attention the general. Five minutes to go. I was talking to our little group, one of the general's staff and some of my guys, a short distance away. Four minutes to go. I was discussing the immensity of the Crossed Swords complex. Most people had seen it on TV, with Saddam shooting his shotgun or pistol or whatever, and it really was huge. This was the second time I had been there, and it seemed to get bigger each time. The Iraqis had only seen it from afar, as it had been another restricted area. Three minutes.

I was really starting to sweat. Not from the heat, it was a beautiful day. I just really wanted the IQAF to look good to this man. He didn't suffer fools, so I wanted the IQAF to stay off that side of the ledger. I continued remarking on the features of the complex, bringing up the individual air conditioned seating and the Iranian helmets (some of which General Jasham may have brought home) that decorated the base of the giant forearms. I saw him glance at his watch; I hoped his was set to the same time mine was. Two minutes. Nothing but clear skies as far as I could see, totally uncluttered by Hueys. It wasn't looking good for the home team.

As the two groups started to mill together, I was wondering how I was going to spin the lack of punctuality on the part of the IQAF. Looking at my watch, given the history of the IQAF, I was getting ready to deploy some readymade aviation excuses—weather, cranky equipment, and so forth—when I heard it.

The beautiful, iconic *wop-wop-wop* of big fat Huey blades beating the air into submission. I think most people think of some sort of movie soundtrack when hearing that unique sound: in this case, "Ride of the Valkyries" was reverberating through my head loud and clear. We were all standing next to the reviewing stands, facing north, with Saddam's truncated forearms off to our right. The two little groups turned as one toward the sound of the woppers, and sure enough, through the bright morning haze, two little dragonflies appeared over the high-rises and infrastructure of Baghdad, chasing each other through the washed-out dawn. Only as they drew closer did they turn into war machines; the desert camouflage paint, along with the door guns seeking targets off each side, demonstrated the seriousness of their mission. As they came closer still, at some unseen signal, the door guns went up into the stowed position, and the helos dropped lower yet, on final to our little LZ. They came in perfect formation, slowing as they crossed a small water feature, the mist curling up over the rotor discs as one of the helo's nose came up, the tail rotor dropping low to bleed off speed, while the other continued, breaking off, to approach at a different angle. I was enthralled by the whole thing, unconsciously just grinning my fanny off. I snuck a peek at General Jasham; his face crinkled up in a smile, especially as the lead Huey flared and we could see the Iraqi flag painted on the bottom of it. I felt proud too. The skids thumped down onto the tarmac in a whirlwind of dirt, and if the thing that hit me in my helmet was any indicator, very small boulders. I stole a glance at my watch.

0800.

God, I loved my job.

The choppers wound down to idle, and the door gunners came off to escort us on to the ships. Right behind the pilots, there were two small cargo seats, but  the best seats in the whole bird were the ones facing the outside. There were about three spaces in the cargo net seats that had seat belts, with one more at the end of the row being dedicated to the door gunner. I shifted my M-4 to my other shoulder, aligning the single point sling system so the weapon hung in front of my right shoulder, muzzle down. I clipped the sling into one of the carabiners I had attached to my MOLLE vest, so in the event of a shoot-down, it would stay with me. I had seen the videos of survivors of shoot-downs by our honorable opponents. I wanted my long gun with me. I grabbed my backpack and hopped on. I was pleasantly surprised to see a buddy of mine in the right seat, playing copilot to the Iraqi colonels aircraft commander. He shot me a big grin; I smacked the back of his helmet in greeting, strapped in, and in five minutes, we were airborne.

The Huey shook like a liberal being forced to say the Pledge of Allegiance, spun on its axis, dropped the nose, and away we went, out the same way they'd come in. On some unseen signal, the door gunners put a round in the chambers of their Russian PKM machine guns and racked the bolt back. They were ready for business. I didn't pull the bolt back on the M-4 or chamber a round in the M-9; I was confident I could make my contribution to the party in a timely fashion if circumstances dictated. I saw, as we accelerated and climbed, that I was in good hands. The young Iraqi on the gun was waving to the folks on the ground with his left hand, while tracking potential shooter spots with the gun in his right. I was soon joining in, waving at all the people on the ground. They were all waving back. The women in their dark hijabs would stop and wave . On every empty dirt lot, the inevitable self-propelled dust cloud would stop, shatter into its component little kids and a soccer ball, and they would start waving their little arms off, jumping up and down until we lost sight of them. Over and over again, this was repeated on the short trip. There seemed to be a lot more waving than the previous trips.

Once again, the humbling experience of being in the American military caught up to me. Here I was, some dumb kid from Montana, one who had risen from the lowest rank and was now buzzing along over Baghdad at about three hundred feet, boots and M-4 dangling in the wind, kidnapping an Iraqi general to go talk to a bunch of Iraqi cadets. My cheeks hurt I was grinning so much. The door gunner saw me, flipped up his visor, leaned over to me, and shouted through the slipstream, "Good fun, yes?" He had to speak some English in order to be aircrew, but especially in those days, the initial cadre of non-officer IQAF members didn't speak fluent English. While he was talking, his eyes never left the blurred ground, and the gun barrel never stopped traversing back and forth. He seemed to know his business. And yes, I was having "good fun".

We flew up along the Tigris River, tracking over the lush palm trees and some very nice, painted cinder-block homes. I was surprised at the greenery, although we *were* right next to the river. Still the sheer amount of foliage surprised me, not only the palm trees, but tall grasses, stretching into the built-up areas. It must have been the "nice" part of town. Inside the helo, a whine filtered through my earplugs, as smells of old equipment and hot hydraulic fluids wafted over me: I was in heaven. I looked over my shoulder to the interior of the helicopter, meeting Asad's eyes. He met my eyes with a big grin and a sausage-sized thumbs-up. I winked, looked past him toward the other side of the helo, looking at the heads seated in the short row: a couple of American helmets and a few Iraqi ones, all tilting together, as one would talk to the other over the roar of the Huey.

I felt really good about the whole thing, as we were going to finally take some sort of action to deal with the malcontents up at Taji. More specifically, the Iraqis were going to try to take some action. Our guys up there could have easily handled the situation, but because of the implications of us stepping in again to direct operations we were really desiring an Iraqi solution. The sacrifices of the ones who had come before demanded that the training wheels start to come off a bit and the leadership of the Iraqis bloom. But as mentioned before, those same sacrifices also demanded that we not allow failure. My hopes on both of those fronts rested on the three stars that shown on the small shoulders of the little general in the other helicopter.

We broke off of the river after about ten minutes and left the built-up areas of Baghdad, now heading north over farmers working in their beautifully green cultivated fields. There were few of the circle-type fields indicating a more modern type of irrigation. Most were fairly small tracts, probably five to ten acres. Even these folks would straighten up, look into the early morning sun, and wave as the Iraqi flag pounded over them. I remember one shepherd in particular; as we passed overhead, he stood up, stretched out his arms with his staff in one hand, lifting his face to us. I thought I could make out a beatific smile on his face. In the robes he was wearing and with the job he was doing, he looked a little like Jesus. It was a beautiful thing to see.

Soon enough, the gunners pulled the bolts back on the guns, lifted the covers, and removed the ammo belts, carefully folding them back into the attached ammo cans. The barrels came up and were stowed. We had crossed the small river that defined the southern edge of Taji Air Base. We had a little compound that consisted of a newly renovated schoolhouse and several buildings that had been converted to barracks. It's important to note that it was renovated to Iraqi standards, meaning the new, freshly painted bathrooms had no conventional toilets, just the "bombsight" ones: imagine a conventional toilet that has the tank mounted on the wall, close to the ceiling, while the bowl is inset into the floor. These are not designed to be sat on, but crouched over. It was...interesting.

The two ships flared over the runway, slowing to airfield speeds, and took spacing. They "taxied" along the taxiways, hovering about three feet in the air, spinning on their axis under the guidance of the Iraqi crew chief then backing into their sandbagged revetments. We gently touched down, the turbine whine spinning down and the fat rotors slowing with rhythmic whooshing. The Iraqis drove up in their ubiquitous Land Cruisers, in various civilian attire, and swooped up the Iraqi party. I was relieved, as I was never sure of any Iraqi plan until it was actually executed. I caught on to that fairly quickly. My buddy Mike, a stern lieutenant colonel who ran the Taji location for the coalition, met me with a big smile. He had replaced the hard driving Colonel Kim that I had met the first time I came up here. He didn't smile much; he was charged with just making things work, no matter what, so he and his staff worked nonstop, coming up with creative solutions to everything from electric and fuel shortages to food supply, water availability, and so forth. He was a navigator, so there was no training in his background for any of this. But he was an American military man, so he could do anything; see Preface. And the miracles he pulled off daily—he made sure that the Iraqis got the credit. This surprised the hell out of them. Unfortunately, General A. K. counted on this false credit; he was the rooster crowing about his role in the sun coming up. Mike had kept the school on track but was counting on some sort of correction from this visit. It was the first time we had gotten such high-level interest in this little project of ours—the future Iraqi air force.

I wedged myself into the front seat of the SUV, arranging the various weaponry dangling off of me so that they didn't jab me in the eye or something, and we headed off to the base commander's HQ. This was the "bad guy" that everyone was scared of. General Arhem bullied General A. K. and did whatever he wanted with the students, even though they weren't his. Mike had run interference as much as he could, trying to be a portable spine for General A. K., if he would only use it. He didn't avail himself of it often.

We bumped over various roads, ruts, and ditches, arriving at a small building—the lair of Arhem. In front was a sagging wire fence, corralling several goats and some ducks. The general had detailed several of the *janood* (lowest-ranking military enlisted) to take care of this little herd. The general also maintained an extensive fleet of carrier pigeons that he was very proud of. I'm not sure what military things he did, except hoard people and steal supplies, but if there was a flood and we needed to jump on an ark, well, he was a guy I would want in my corner.

We jinked around the menagerie, heading for the conference room. The Iraqis were already seated, softly talking to each other. I took my seat at the corner of the room, but got up again and sat at the table in response to General Jasham's gesturing. That felt good. Mike was smirking; apparently,

General Arhem was really on his best behavior. The tea arrived, lukewarm cups of Lipton with a quarter-inch of sugar at the bottom. Everyone sipped until the little general started talking. The translator was falling behind, but the gist of the speech was that he was happy to be there and wanted to know the problems, and he praised the IQAF for its efforts so far. He thanked the friendly side for their efforts in helping to make sure the supplies got to the right place. General Arhem stiffened a bit at that one. I saw Mike grinning at Arhem's discomfort. He really hated that corrupt SOB.

After that short speech, General Arhem gave his return salvo, a whiney, rambling diatribe that Jasham soon tired of. General A. K. sat thoughtfully, trying to figure out how to take both sides of the issues. He resolved his dilemma by enthusiastically weighing in when General Jasham was talking about the issues and just as enthusiastically jumping in when his puppet master spoke. Jasham's eyes became harder as this went on. His jaw started to set, and I was trying to signal Mike to shut A. K. up. Jasham shot A. K. a disgusted look, looked at me, then smiled and rattled off something in Arabic. The assistants came in and started to clean up everything. Apparently, the meeting would be shortened, and we were going to head over to see the cadets who were making trouble.

Mike and I and another American jumped into the SUV and bounced our way back to the school. We got there first and walked down to the small classroom. The cadets had made a square around the perimeter of the room, their desks facing inward. As soon as I walked in, they recognized me, and I them. They made me smile, just seeing their brave, trouble-making faces. These were the same guys that I had visited in Al Muthana countless times at the English lab we were operating there. They always had something to complain about, usually valid, but there was usually not much we could do about it.

"Major Bonset, Major Bonset!" I felt like a rock star, although a rock star whose name was never quite pronounced correctly. The students felt very comfortable with me. I think they had known me longer than any other American; plus, I had the advantage of being able to roll in, see what was going on, and go back to the bosses and affect some change. Usually in small things, but it made me into a bit of a grandfatherly figure. I could come in, spoil the kids, and leave. Mike and his counterparts in Rustymaya, Kirkuk, and Basra were the day-to-day grownups, consistently influencing both staff and students. After a lot of handshaking and high-fiving, the students, about twenty of them, all started talking to me at once: Did I know what their jobs were going to be? Did I know how the food was? Did I know when they were getting paid? Mercifully I was interrupted from having to tell them how much I didn't know.

A bit of shouting in Arabic signaled the arrival of the General Jasham. The student mob blew apart, scattering to their chairs but remaining standing, so they could be called to attention. General Arhem made his entrance, followed by A. K., who turned to announce Jasham. The cadets snapped to attention, taking their seats as Jasham waved his hand. His interpreter sidled up to me, wanting to make sure that I got everything he was going to say. Jasham got situated in the room, cleared his throat, and began to speak.

The first part was not very memorable: a lot of standard "I'm glad to be here" stuff. After a while, he veered into a bit of the "You're valuable to Iraq" mantra; I thought it was going well so far, as I was glad to have a man of his stature telling them this. It went on for a bit in this vein, and then he opened it up for questions.

Now, Iraqis are very vocal in their complaints; surprisingly, the students didn't feel much restraint in venting to this very important officer about fairly mundane things. As the complaints were translated, I began to get a little embarrassed by the issues being brought up. General A. K. was looking positively miserable, as more and more small stuff came up that should've easily been handled at his level. General Arhem was putting on quite a show, as he furrowed his eyebrows and frowned, looking at A. K. as if to say, "If I'd only known this was going on, I would've handled it." A fairly good performance all in all, especially since he was totally, unequivocally full of crap. He was one of the main roadblocks in getting stuff resolved. But now, more and more dirty laundry was been aired. Quite literally: most of the barracks had laundry hanging everywhere.

At first, Jasham listened, but he developed a scowl as more and more seemingly trivial issues came up. It was like a time lapse series of a decaying pumpkin carved for Halloween. More and more lines appeared as time went on. I looked at Mike; he had a devilish grin on his face, as he was enjoying this student roast of their boss. I was worried about the impression we were making on this influential member of the Iraqi military; I certainly didn't want the IQAF to come off as whiney. But Mike had dealt with this spineless little weasel and his puppet master for too long not to get a sense of satisfaction when it started to all come crashing down. I should've had a little more faith in Jasham.

At some point he stopped the conversation with a chop of his hand, turned, and fired off a rapid stream of Arabic, with a distinct "Bonset" injected at the translator beside me. I thought we were screwed. I had bragged on these students, kidnapped the general, and when I finally got him here, all he had heard were a bunch of trivial complaints that should have been solved by the IQAF a long time ago. This was a disaster. I planned on walking home, just so I would have a good excuse not to show up. The man turned back to the assembled students, as the translator whispered to me, "The general wanted me to make sure that you understood this part."

Oh crap. Now he was going to call me out by name.

"Please sit and be quiet. I want you men to hear what I am saying to you." He half turned to me, his face solemn. "Under Saddam, you could trust no one. What you men are doing now would not be tolerated. We didn't have the freedom to complain." All this was said in empathetic Arabic, with the translation being whispered to me a millisecond later, producing a kind of reverb in a different language. It made my head hurt, but I was really enthralled by what was being whispered.

"I know that there are many problems here. Things are not perfect. I know that things are very dangerous for you. I know that you are worried for your security and your safety. I have heard the things you have complained about. But I want you to know that you are the luckiest men in all of Iraq. Yes, lucky; do you know why?"

"You get to work with the Americans. You are lucky to have the greatest military in the world teach you. If you are being taught, do you not want to be taught by the best? The Americans came here and freed us from one of the worst men in the world. We were slaves, and now we can be free. Saddam kept us by ourselves. We have had blinders on for more than thirty years!" He covered his eyes with his hands, then flung them open, becoming more and more animated as he spoke. "I have been in the military for thirty years, but this year was the first time I'd ever been on an airplane to another country!" (He meant a commercial flight.) "I have seen other countries; my world has grown larger. Thanks to the Americans, we can now see the other parts of the world that we have been told were bad."

"We can go to America; we can see the friendly side with our own eyes. We will never be the same. Because they came and set us free. And they were kind. Instead of a fist, they have used their hands to help us. The Iraqis should use their example to be better. You should not complain. You should behave yourselves, and learn everything that they want to teach you. You should not complain over little things; be strong, and be thankful for the friendly side. " And with that, they were called to attention , and he left.

There were a lot of moms and dads of dead soldiers, sailors, airmen, and marines who should've heard that speech.

I hope I got it close to right.

17

CAKE, ANYONE?

One of the continual bright spots of the whole deployment was the fact that our little group of primary advisors got to work directly for the Brits. Their dry wit, good cheer, and unflappable optimism in difficult times certainly served us in good stead. They often served as B.S. buffers from the HQ staff over in the embassy area. The HQ was a never-ending fountain of taskers and presentation preparation, and our Brits (group captains, O-6 equivalents) worked splendidly as crap filters. Good leaders do that.

Each one was a bit different. Colonial Oppressor number one, Group Captain Farmer brought smiles to our faces all the time with his wit and his obvious dedication to the cause. He really understood the challenges and the timeframes associated with the effort here. (England does have some experience with nation building, I'm told.)

We got along great, and the Iraqis loved and respected him as well. This was very important as he was responsible for dealing with the number two man in the Iraqi air force, General Altair.

General Altair was a very nice man who had very limited authority. He certainly tried to do the right thing, in spite of the fact that he controlled almost nothing. At one point, we were in a very small meeting, just the group captain, me, and a couple more folks, when General Altair was venting about his lack of authority. He relayed a couple of anecdotes about a trip and the system that he was stuck in.

About midtour, General Altair got to travel to the United States and flew part of the way in an air force C-17. He marveled at the mixed crew (male, female, black, white) and authority that the young pilot (a captain) exhibited. He marveled at the level of responsibility that the crew wielded, all under the command of a single captain. He watched from the jump seat as this young man directed the crew and the aircraft with such confidence and certainty. That's the standard for us. Faith in leadership tempered by certainty of our own value. Nobody on the crew was a "serf". There was certainly a rank structure, and that is critical, but each member was valued. Even though I started as an E-1, I never felt that I couldn't do something. There were limits to my authority, surely, but I knew that if I proved myself, there were no limits to my potential.

And that was what was on display on the C-17. This young team, piloting a multimillion-dollar machine over vast oceans, through sovereign countries, and in and out of weather systems, carrying the number two man in the Iraqi air force, was just accomplishing another mission. And that number two man in the IQAF marveled at it. And he felt comfortable enough around Farmer in the meeting to vent a little bit.

"Here I see this young man and his young crew flying over all the oceans of the world, and I, who have fought many battles and flown many planes, don't have the authority to buy underwear!"

He went on to say that the head of the IQAF, General Kamal, had the authority to spend the equivalent of about two thousand dollars a month without having to go to the Ministry of Defense for additional permission. Altair angrily spat this little factoid out. This was the generational burden of living in a no-trust society.

The irony wasn't lost on me that Altair felt comfortable venting to us, none of whom he had known very long, while remaining reticent about doing the same with other Iraqis. That was a testament to the groundwork laid by those that came before, most recently the good Group Captain

Farmer. The British officer's western values had had a positive effect on his principle. Trust.

But not everyone felt that way about the British. Sometimes, the US Army seemed to still be upset about the past. This reared its head one day as we attempted what heretofore had been a simple task, getting lunch. We were heading to one of the army's fine dining facilities with Group Captain Hyslop. He was one of the finest officers I've had the privilege of serving. Kind, and with a ready smile, I would really grow to admire this sterling example of leadership, even if he was wearing the wrong clothes.

Jim decided he wanted to take the group captain to lunch at a place I hadn't been to before, but Jim knew the way, so he led the two-ship to the other side of Camp Victory. We piled out of the two trucks and crunched across the gravel parking lot toward the big tent-like structure.

As we approached, there were two guard stations, one at either end of the tent, each followed by another guard station as you continued into the tent. We approached one of them, Jim in the lead, then me, then Hyslop, then a couple more of our folks. We were engaged in routine chatter as we went about the absolutely mundane task of showing our IDs and passing through to the next station.

Until the group captain tried to enter. He was stopped by the young army enlisted guy at the dusty wooden podium. "I'm sorry, no foreign militaries at this checkpoint. You have to go to the other side."

Hyslop responded, "I'm with the Americans, young man."

"You have to go to the other side and sign in with the foreign militaries."

"But I'm not a *foreign* military. I am part of the American force, attached to CAFFT, working for an American general and the USAF."

"You're a foreign military, sir. You have to sign in with the rest. Down there."

Jim and I had already gone through the double plywood doors but now zipped back to the first podium to try to assist. We knew that the kid was really only doing what he thought he was supposed to do, but this guy was our boss, every bit in our chain of command. It was already sort of embarrassing, but now both parties were sort of digging in, and I was pretty sure that the young army troop didn't realize that he was barring an O-6 from entering the dining facility. The British O-6 insignia is a bit hard to distinguish until you get used to it: a series of stripes, in contrast to our supercool eagle.

So I tried to assist. "Sergeant, this man is my boss; on this deployment he is absolutely part of our team. He represents the USAF and operates within our chain of command. He has been chopped to us."

Jim piled in and just basically said, "Yeah!"

By now, we were all talking, and Group Captain Hyslop was starting to get steamed. It was little hassles like this that seemed so unnecessary, when one considered the big picture. I'm sure there was a point to the rule, most likely some sort of accounting thing, but Hyslop was with us. And it would stay that way.

I finally said to the young man, "Look, wherever he goes, I..." I looked around. "We go. If that means that we all go and sign in at the other side, that's what we'll do."

That seemed to make an impression; we all understand camaraderie and loyalty. With logic like that, the young troop finally nodded, pointed at the sign-in sheet, and let us continue on. With our little commander in tow. Jim and I flew through the next little checkpoint and into the main area of the dining facility. Alone. Damn it.

I looked at Jim, and he looked at me. Right about that time, I heard a familiar, exasperated voice from behind the wooden swinging doors. "But, young man, I am a British officer!"

Oh crap, here we go again, I thought. Jim and I once again reversed direction and went back through the plywood doors for the fourth time. The second line of defense for the chow hall was going through the same thing, not curious at all why the guy twenty feet in front of him had allowed this heinous threat through.

This confrontation went just like the previous one. The bottom line was that this dining facility wasn't used to the CAFTT presence, so any personnel in different uniforms were assumed to be there as part of their distinct unit, not an integral part of one of ours. I couldn't blame them for getting confused; there were certainly a lot of different militaries to choose from in George Bush's unilateral effort.

We finally got through the last checkpoint, this time making sure we had the good Group Captain Hyslop in front of us. The dining facility opened before us—the culinary Promised Land. The group captain's blood pressure was finally returning to normal as he walked to the counters, behind which lay all manner of food-coma inducing delights. Because he is fairly stumpy of stature, I passed him en route, so I got to see it first.

Prominently displayed in front of the glass case, as an effort to trace army lineage and foster pride, was a giant painting. It was quite beautiful, with vivid colors and realistically depicted, historically accurate figures. It was the first time I'd seen it, and as soon as I did, I burst out laughing. For this beautiful piece of art, which my little British commander had to pass on his way to get his food, after getting tons of crap for being a "foreigner" among us, was a beautiful depiction of the Brits and the US Army joined in action at one special moment in time.

Unfortunately, that special moment in time was June 17, 1775. And the action that was captured was mostly fledgling US Army revolutionaries stabbing and shooting the hell out of the British as they attempted to take Bunker Hill.

Jim had arrived and started chuckling in the understated way that he had, by basically collapsing into convulsions. His shoulders were jiggling up and down, and he was biting his lower lip, as he struggled to control himself. I don't have that sort of self-control and was laughing my fanny off.

I will always remember the look on Hyslop's face as he walked up, glanced at the picture, and then stopped. From the back, you could see his shoulders rise and then droop as he took a deep breath. He slowly turned around and looked at us. There was a twinkle in his eye and a small grin on his face. "Bastards."

I just about died. He thought we had engineered the whole thing. I wish we were that smart. We had a great lunch.

I was able to live up to his smart-ass expectations of me on a couple occasions, and I really think that these moments helped him deal with the crap that we all had to put up with. I had to put him on the Rhino twice a week to go across Route Irish to attend the obligatory staff meetings, and it wore him down a bit. He was often cranky for a time after coming back from what he termed "Cake and Oss parties".

Translated into proper English, that really means "Cake and Ass party", from the British, meaning complete waste of time. I never did find out the relationship between cake and ass in contemporary British culture, but as a travel tip; don't eat cake in the UK.

At almost every return, he would be fuming about the silliness that emanated from the PowerPoint rangers in the Green Zone. He got it double when he got back to A7 and had to deal with the Iraqi leadership, who were so incredibly hobbled by distrust of everyone but us. To get them to take care of their own issues was very difficult; no one can be more stubborn, dodgy, prevaricating, obfuscating, and in denial of responsibility than newly liberated oppressed people. Well; Democrats, but that's outside the scope of this book.

So, if I got a chance to alleviate the pressure, I felt that I should; and if I could do it humorously, that was a two-fer. Toward the end of Group Captain Hyslop's tour, I had an opportunity.

Group Captain Hyslop soon became familiar with Akram's foibles (from the knowledge that I got from the guys and passed along to him) and able to detect his horse crap (with his fully calibrated British BS detector). As a result, it was even harder to get things done. We certainly couldn't encourage the Iraqis to violate their chain of command, merely work within it, but in this chain, the general was the weakest link. So I was very frustrated with him.

I tried to handle this in subtle (and some not-so-subtle) ways. Our communications guys had worked with their guys (A6 division) to establish a network connection for the IQAF, and the Iraqis were in absolute heaven. Once Akram figured out that the whole world could get the benefit of his knowledge via e-mail, he was unstoppable. He was even more insufferable via electrons, because you couldn't steer his thoughts—whatever came out of his fuzzy little brain went straight to his keyboard.

After enduring yet another e-mail, sent to everyone, about nothing, I decided to help him out. His signature block (yes, the A6 guys had stressed the importance of signature blocks) was "pleasure, Gen Akram."

So I approached him about the "correctness" of his syntax. He insisted that he was correct; after all, he had been to America. That was the kind of guy he was. Even with his rudimentary knowledge of English, he felt confident telling me, a native English speaker, that I was wrong. After a short argument, I came up with an alternative that he should use.

I told him that "pleasure" wasn't quite right. The phrase was "my pleasure." But there were better ways to express how happy you were to provide the information that you were sending via e-mail. He looked quizzical; he certainly didn't want to look stupid; he wanted to seem extremely conversant in English when he sent out his missives.

So, after a bit of discussion, we came upon a salutation that we thought would be a true reflection of his greatness as a pilot, lover (as I was told), man, father, pilot again, and so forth. I helped him by jotting it down on a sticky note. I finished up the daily business, then took the walk from the trailer back to the office, where I filled out the reports and updated the brass on the latest happenings with the marvelous General Akram.

The next day started uneventfully; I didn't go over to the Iraqis' trailer for a good part of the morning, instead catching up with the Americans scattered all over Iraq trying to put together coherent strategies for moving the young men through the pipeline, while keeping them safe and healthy. I didn't check my e-mails for quite some time; I figured I would at around noon; then I'd head over to see the guys.

Oh, my. General Akram had been prolific. There were quite a few posts, addressed to lots and lots of people. I wondered, as I clicked on the first one, what sort of wonderful news I would get. I don't remember what the e-mail was about, but I certainly remember the close. General Akram had finally found the signature block that captured his essence. For there, at the end of the e-mail, in big, bold, fourteen-point Times New Roman, was his sign-off: .

"Pleasuring myself,
Gen Akram."

Later that day, I implied that the group captain should really read some of the e-mails that General Akram sent out, as they were very informative. He looked like he had had a crappy day already, so he sighed and allowed that he would get around to it. He slouched his way back into his little office.

About ten minutes later, as I and the rest of the gang were diligently typing and PowerPointing and engaged in other war-winning activities, I heard a great bellow. "Bonzet!" (He couldn't really say my name either.)

The group captain came flying out of his office, sprinted to my desk, and collapsed in laughter.

"You bastard!" he gasped out.

"'Pleasuring myself'! That's bloody brilliant!" He was literally in tears. The rest of the gang that I had clued in were already giggling, while those that hadn't been privy suddenly found General Akram's e-mail to be very interesting. Pretty soon, the whole trailer was laughing.

That was a pretty good day.

I let the smug little General send his e-mails out for the rest of the day, then I went over to their trailer and started talking to him about various things, working the conversation toward his e-mails. He was very proud of them. I told him that after I got them, they did look a little funny, so maybe we really shouldn't use that as a signature line. Perhaps he had misunderstood me, I said, when I told him that it should be "My Pleasure" or "A Pleasure." He insisted that no, it was 100 percent correct.

"How do you know that it is one hundred percent correct, sayyid? There could have been a misunderstanding."

"No, Banzet, I am sure this is right."

"Oh, really? How?"

"Banzet, you wrote it down!" He triumphantly produced the sticky note that I had written it down on.

Dammit.

The sense of humor and the focus on the true essence of why we were there was never lost on Group Captains Hyslop or Farmer, or even the fourth British commander that I had over there. The advisors loved three out of the four that we had.

There were a couple of stinkers in there; two come to mind, but only one of them did any damage to the effort. It's worth noting that there were quite a few American stinkers as well; as always, when you get one of them, you work around them to the maximum extent.

When they were at my level, it really wasn't a problem; at one point I had three British O-4/5 officers working with me. Two of them, Rich and Russ, worked directly with me and were the absolute salt of the earth. The other, Guy, worked in the HQ side and was more of a salted earth kind of guy. He was a fighter pilot that disdained Iraqis, Arabs, and any "woolies." I think he just despised anyone who was not British and named Guy.

Russ and Rich hated him too, and thank goodness, he didn't work directly with the Iraqis but was kept busy doing something. The something he was doing, I never knew, but he never missed the opportunity to let us know how revolting it was to work around the woolies. Many of the workers around were Pakistanis or Indians or Nepalese. In short, there were a lot of brown people working in and around us. They were fairly easy to identify, as all the manual laborers wore bright blue jumpsuits.

Granted, their hygiene was not the best, and it wasn't enhanced by the fact that they were working in 100-plus-degree heat, filling sandbags, shoveling dirt, and other heavy labor in bright blue overalls. So they were a bit ripe. But they were always smiling and always had a friendly hello if you made eye contact with them. Which was something that Guy avoided at all costs.

He often repeated how much he avoided them and didn't want to acknowledge them, much less smile or say hi. He made it a special point to say that he had never so much as touched one the entire time he was in-country. He was quite emphatic on that point. See that? That's foreshadowing.

At some point, I had to be over in the HQ for a beating or something. When we had to go, we would usually stay for a couple days, because it was a real pain scheduling a Rhino or hopping on a helo. Plus, the embassy food was awesome. And they had the Green Bean Coffee shop. So there was a bright side.

But, in spite of the good things, being in HQ was a pain, because that's where PowerPoint came from. And all the silly stuff that went with it. Our group captain's main goal was to make them forget that the advisors existed, so we could continue to work with the Iraqis, versus wandering around leaving PowerPoint and excel spreadsheets in our wakes. But when we were over there, it was line of sight taskings.

But Guy was over there permanently, so he was double bitter, and for the time that I was there, there were major construction projects going on. This meant tons of little blue guys milling around all the time. I guess that put him at triple bitter. He was wound tighter than a Democrat explaining the Second Amendment at an NRA convention.

Rocket attacks and mortars were also coming in quite often at this time. Being attacked two to three times a day and some at night was not uncommon. We usually had some warning at least; a horn would sound, giving you a couple of seconds warning to throw on your helmet or get under a desk.

I was at the temp desk near Guy's when the horn went off again. The door from the outside went *bam*, and a stream of little blue men came running into our area. They all piled up on the floor just as the rocket hit the side of the building with a *thump* and *crack*, exploding in the bathroom. The exterior wall took the brunt of the damage, getting a hole punched through the cinder blocks and splattering the inside wall of the bathroom with shrapnel. The room instantly filled with dust and smoke.

I ran over to the outer door and kicked it open to see if anyone outside was down. There were always smokers outside, plus there were lots of workers, and I didn't know if the pile of blue guys on the floor represented all of them. There wasn't anyone hurt outside, so I ran back in to see if anyone was hurt inside. I couldn't see Guy, but I heard him.

I'm only fluent in English, know a few words in Spanish, and know a few less words in Arabic. I had no idea the meaning of all the words that I heard coming from somewhere. It sounded like Guy was buried in the rubble, but I hadn't seen him going to the bathroom or anything. And the rocket hadn't penetrated the inner wall. I was looking around, standing beside the pile of little blue men, now covered with dust and smoke, when it struck me.

Guy had dived for the ground seconds before the stream of blue men had come crashing in. And now he was gone. And where he had been, now lay a pile of little blue and brown people—especially ripe and now filthier. And he was at the bottom.

Like a drowning man, his arm broke the surface of the blue pile, followed shortly thereafter by his helmet, followed shortly thereafter by his head, which had his very busy mouth in it. I can only imagine the true meaning of the invective that arrowed out of his mouth; I wish I would have had Rich or Russ to translate. But maybe not.

I looked around and saw that no one was hurt; the one guy in the bathroom had gotten out, pulling up his pants as he went.

So I looked back at Guy, now emerging from this wriggling, smiling, chattering pile of workers. I just collapsed. It was like Count Dracula had opened his cupboard and been buried in a pile of garlic. In short; hilarious.

I just sat right down on the floor, and was laughing so hard that I started tearing up. My big gasps weren't helped by the great volumes of dust still in the air, and that made me collapse into a coughing fit. By that time, Guy had come fully upright, standing about a head taller than his new best friends. He glared at me on the floor, dust curling off his helmet and clothes.

"I hope you choke, you bastard."

He stalked off. Why can't the Brits pronounce Banzet? It keeps sounding a lot like "baastaard". Oh well; must be the accent.

The little blue guys helped me up and tried to dust me off, but I shook hands with them instead. There followed a bit of pantomime concerning explosions and stuff, and they went back to work.

Guy was furious with me the rest of the day.

He was the exception; the other Brits were fabulous. As a matter of fact, we were so enamored by our Group Captain Hyslop that, when it came time for his tour to end, I endeavored to make his going away as memorable as I could. There was another reason for trying to make this special, too. We had been getting more senior level officers in, and these USAF O-6 ladder climbers were starting to realize that the real work was being done by the advisors.

Soon, they started showing up at our meetings, which we usually had a recap in the evening; then, realizing that we were Americans, began worming their way into our chain of command. It was embarrassing to see; we were all ecstatic being led by the Brits. But these colonels just couldn't help themselves.

One of the worst of those was an acquisition colonel that showed up very late in the game and, even though he was on the HQ side and out of our chain of command, thought he would get more of a career boost if he could absorb the advisors as well. He was certainly ill prepared for this type of operation, as the first order of business for him was to immediately call a staff meeting and make it mandatory for everyone. The group captain, in his quest to placate HQ, said that we had to go.

Everything I needed to know about this guy I learned in the first five minutes that he spoke. We were all assembled around the long conference table. Combined with the HQ staff, we numbered around twenty folks, including the four Brits. He walked in, expecting everyone to leap to attention, not realizing that the British senior officer was already in the room. He was impeccably groomed, and fairly tall. He clearly was irritated that we hadn't jumped to attention and spat out a terse "Be seated." I guess we were really good staff because we had anticipated his needs and never got to our feet in the first place.

This guy didn't have a seat at the head of the table; that was for our Brit. But by God, he would have a co-chair. So he pulled up a chair beside the group captain. Two chairs at the head of the table.

We hadn't had much luck with our first couple of welcomes by the Americans; both of our senior leaders seemed to use that time-honored welcoming technique of telling us how much we sucked. This guy was different, however, and decided to use his time to tell us how awesome he was.

Now, I would expect that of a pilot, even a misguided fighter pilot; but this guy had never even deployed. He made sure that he mentioned all the special schools he'd attended, instead of, well, doing the mission. There are some folks that do that—get identified as a hard charger as a captain or something, then go to a special school and, because they go to a special school, get picked up for another special school, and so on. In this way they avoid ever actually getting real experience, merely theory and, as a nasty side effect, self-aggrandizement. They become more certain of their expertise and more disconnected from reality. I've known commanders that spent a lot of time away from their families without ever deploying, just staying at the office doing paperwork and ensuring their careers were taken care of. Who has time to deploy, when there is all that sucking up to do? The people underneath them were actually threats; they were all potential problems. And that—taking care of folks—could hurt your career.

Well, this guy couldn't tell us enough about how hard he had worked and the rewards he had reaped. He introduced himself with a callsign. Usually pilots are the ones with callsigns. I think it's kind of silly. But, then, I'm not an emotionally stunted fighter pilot. And it's even dumber for support officers to pretend to be emotionally stunted fighter pilots. He even said that, although he had never deployed, he had "taken the Triple Nickle downtown." I think this meant he was on base when aircraft would take off from Italy and fly missions (I think in Bosnia). His real focus came out in full relief during an exchange that he had with an intel officer (Major Q) that I knew, which I witnessed immediately after this stupid meeting.

Apparently, the major knew of a poor USAF captain that had shown up and fallen through the cracks. He didn't have a place to sleep and didn't have a place to work. The major, although the captain was not his responsibility, took it upon himself to address that with the guy whose responsibility it was. For an officer to have no accountability in a combat zone was absolutely unforgivable in my view. And maybe that same feeling what set this major off.

After we got finished with the "I wanted to hold this meeting to show you how important I am" meeting, we filed out, many of us shaking our heads. The intel major caught the eye of the young warrior colonel. I was walking slightly behind the major, so the colonel blew by me to take up stride next to the man. He was red in the face as he leaned into the major and hissed.

"Don't you ever f——ing do that to me again, you understand me?"

The major was taken aback but apparently knew what this guy was referring to. He apologized and started to explain why he had done this heinous thing.

"Shut the f—k up, dammit. You ever embarrass me in front of the boss like that again, and that's it. You don't ever approach me in front of him; you f——ing got that? Pull that bulls——t again, and I'll…" He drifted off as he apparently wasn't sure what he was going to f——ing do.

The major tried again.

"Sir, I wasn't trying to embarrass you, I just thought that you would want to know that one of your guys didn't have a place to sleep and no place to work and—"

"Shut the f—k up!" the colonel ground out. "I don't give a shit about where he f——ing sleeps. You f——ing embarrassed me in front of the general."

About that time, I had drawn abreast and was staring at this sterling example of leadership. Dead. In. The. Eye.

He clearly hadn't realized that I was around, kind of did a double take, and tried again.

"Well, of course I care where he sleeps, but that wasn't the place to address it. Yes, yes, the welfare of my troops comes first, of course. We'll get on that first thing in the morning."

And he accelerated away to his office.

As I stood there shaking my head, I asked the major what the hell that was all about. He said that he had known this captain was homeless for a couple days, and no one seemed to be missing him. He had mentioned it to the colonel a couple days prior, and the colonel had said to get back with him in a couple of days, so that's what he was trying to do.

He didn't interrupt the conversation between the colonel and the general, but when the situation presented itself, he thought he would see if he could get some sort of resolution. He didn't; he got an ass chewing.

Eventually the captain got place in a tent and was assigned a place to work.

I was able to go back across the base to where I slept, away from this stupidity. However, this guy took on more and more power, and soon we were having two meetings a day. Toward the end of my deployment, the advisors were probably spending two to three hours a day with the Iraqis, instead of the seven, eight, or nine that we had been.

That is what it more painful to see the Brits go. Maybe we just got lucky, and got the right guys there, or maybe most of the British officers are just that good. So it was important to me that I to do something for the group captain that he would remember. I think I did.

Russ, Rich, and Hyslop were a critical part of the momentum that had built up around the Iraqi air force, so I really wanted to make this going away special. We hadn't done much for Group Captain Farmer; although the Iraqis held a goat grab (food free for all), we just didn't do anything different. Kind of the standard stupid certificate and a see ya later.

I decided that the big contribution I could make fell, as it often does, into the smart-ass category. I was struck by a genius idea, and I enlisted the help of Brooks, a five-year-old boy dressed up like an air force lieutenant colonel. The guy had a huge sense of humor, matched only by his heart and optimistic outlook. He was a big, tall, ruddy-faced guy who ran around either laughing or smiling. Nothing seemed to rattle him. He was always self-deprecating and was genuinely concerned for those under him. He was definitely one of the kindest people I had the privilege to meet over there. In my opinion, he was a perfect officer.

He had showed up a little later than the rest of us but soon fit right in with this dysfunctional bunch. He felt the same way about the Brits that I did, so he volunteered to use his lieutenant colonel skills to help with the going away preparations.

I told him what I needed: a couple of Bundt-type cakes, a big sheet cake, and some frosting. Brooks was excited to track those war-winning materials down. Since the US Army operated the chow halls, it would have to be a joint operation. No one was better at that kind of operation than Brooks.

He only had a day to pull this together. Looking for cakes in the middle of a warzone was a little easier than you would expect; we were pretty close to the HQ, so the infrastructure was really well established. I'm sure that the real warfighters would've had a bit harder time, out on the edges of the battle, but I was impressed everywhere I went in Iraq there were really, really good army dining facilities. The Iraqi dining facilities were definitely a hit-or-miss proposition.

Brooks was going to hit up our army buddies for the needed supplies. At the end of the day, we decided to meet at his hooch in the compound to construct our delicious dessert concoction. I crunched across the gravel the three hundred yards to his hooch, which was luxurious. He only had to split his trailer with one other person, not two like I did, so he had about four more feet in his room. I felt like I was in the Taj Mahal.

In this luxurious abode, there was a dust-covered table on which rested a smattering of baking tools and a tinfoil-covered pan. He was a bit out of breath, as he had just gotten back from his scavenger hunt. He described to me how his day had gone.

He had gone from dining facility to dining facility and was told to submit an official army form to requisition a cake, three days in advance and so forth. All of his pleas fell on deaf ears as this was in no way official. That was obvious to the various specialists in the chow halls as soon as Brooks described the project. Apparently, there isn't a box to check on the official army requisition form for "ass cake."

I was a bit surprised by that, because, given the many "cake and ass" parties that Group Captain Hyslop had claimed to have been to, I figured there was a plethora of them. And the officialness of the lieutenant colonel's request lost its luster as soon as Brooks said "ass cake." So he had to rely on his charm, which apparently was in as short supply as ass cake.

He got nowhere fast with his charm, until he ran into a crusty old army master sergeant, a female apparently. At first, the master sergeant rebuffed all of Brook's entreaties, but after describing the project, the sergeant's professional interest was piqued. She agreed to provide Brooks with the requested items on one condition: she got pictures of the result.

So Brooks went down the list of his requirements. He needed two Bundt-type cakes, of course, or several sheet cakes that the budding Michelangelo, me, could sculpt the appropriate butt cheeks from. My plan was to stack up some sheet cakes, then cut away everything that didn't look like a butt.

We were in luck; they had a couple of Bundt cakes lying around. The sergeant asked him what else she could help Brooks with. A sheet cake and a big pan would be great, he allowed. She was able to scrounge up a really big sheet cake, about twelve by twenty-four inches, and a pan that could accommodate it. Did the colonel need anything else, she inquired?

As Brooks thought about it, he just needed some frosting to finish the product off. Okay, the sergeant had plenty of frosting, but was there a particular color that would be required? Brooks thought long and hard before arriving at the perfect answer.

"Caucasian."

I now had a big pan, some plastic knives and forks, a big bowl of Caucasian-colored frosting, two round cakes, and a giant sheet cake. Brooks and I started working on the cake immediately, and the masterpiece took shape quickly. I cut a very shapely waist in the sheet cake and carefully placed the two round cakes up high. Nobody wants a saggy ass cake. Our cake would be toned.

Brooks had left his door open, as it was actually not awful in the evening. Lots of army folks went wandering by, and as they casually looked in, there were plenty of double takes, especially as the cake progressed. I turned out to be such a talented sculptor that I had to maintain a close watch so that the thousands of lonely guys that surrounded us would not take advantage of the cake's good looks and sedentary nature to despoil it.

I even saw Brooks eyeing it rapaciously, and had to remind him that he would be eating it, so he had better be on his best behavior. In spite of his assurances that he would guard the honor of the seductive (no matter how it was dressed) cake with his sacred honor, I decided that since the cake would be stored in his room all night, unmonitored, I would wait until Brooks took a bite before I would touch the thing.

The cake build went perfect; there was only one redo. In order to get the tone just right, and in keeping with the theme of the "cake and ass" meetings, in which the only discernible product was more crap, I decided to get creative. I had extra Caucasian frosting, so I mixed in some instant coffee and while Brooks was outside, made a turd and placed it appropriately.

I knew I couldn't use it the moment he came back in. He actually jerked to a stop and took a step back. It takes a lot to disgust him, but I had pulled it off. He was truly horrified. Based on the violation of even his low standards, I decided that although art is in the eye of the beholder, sometimes, it's just shit. So I was compelled to remove the offending pile of frosting. It was delicious.

The appointed hour came, and we all headed out to the facility where the going away party would be held, which happened to be a contractor-owned building. That was another cool relationship that I noticed over there. Many of the contractors went above and beyond to help out or make life a little easier for us. I know a lot of money was being thrown around, but a lot of these folks seemed to genuinely care about us and honor the mission. There were certainly a lot of retired military and plain old patriotic Americans among them.

These guys had loaned us the use of their facility for the evening, no charge. Most of our unit was already there, and the staff at the place took great pains to help us hide the ass cake. Although it was shrouded in tinfoil, we didn't want any of the Brits to have any idea of the impending awesomeness.

Everyone got settled down, and we had a catered dinner, which was very good. I don't remember paying for any of it, so I think that the contractor picked up the tab for it. Or maybe one of the senior-ranking Americans did. Group Captain Hyslop gave quite a toast, and we all raised our glasses with a hearty nonalcoholic "Here! Here!" The Brits abstained from booze out of empathy their long-suffering colonial brothers who, because of General Order One, were prohibited from drinking alcohol in theater.

We tucked in to the dinner, and as I ate, I marveled at the camaraderie at the table. These guys were every bit as dedicated as we were to getting the Iraqis up on their feet and were just as frustrated by the glacial pace of the progress. I honestly thought that I was better led by these folks in different uniforms than my own service. I'm sure they have their ladder climbers too, but I didn't see them at the senior level like I saw with our own guys.

Dinner ended uneventfully, and we all drifted into the adjoining room. We sprawled on the couches and chairs that were scattered around, our Brits circulating among us. We would be sad to see them go; they were a perfect fit to the organization. Lt. Col. Chuck was the MC for the whole thing and decided that this would be a good time to start the going away ceremonies. He got up and started presenting the awards and gifts, pretty standard stuff: mini-T-walls and such. I had gotten Rich and Russ a couple of fake *Soldier of Fortune* magazine covers that integrated their pictures with headlines that me and a couple of buddies had come up with. Some of them weren't so complimentary: "Squadron Leader Richard on the Perils of 'Male Camel Toe'" (Richard hiked his pants up a bit), or "Squadron Leader Russ Loses a Pound, Disappears" (Russ was emaciated-doubled his weight when he strapped on his sidearm). Things like that. They took it in great stride, and good times were had by all. But the big revelation was yet to come, and that one was going to the group captain.

No one had seen the cake yet, except Brooks and I. So while Chuck started the intro, Brooks went out and got the pan from where it had been carefully squirreled away by the helpful contractors. The group captain was a bit bemused when it came out, all covered in tinfoil, with toothpicks supporting the foil so as not to expose the distinctive ass shape or spoil the Caucasian frosting (sans turd).

Finally, Chuck went into his intro of the group captain and did a really good job of listing the reasons why we were sad to see him leave. He understood the mission; he had perspective and scope; he stood by his troops; he led from the front—all with smile. The group captain was graceful, well spoken, and modest, as he accepted the accolades of the group. If there was ever a person deserving of a hand-crafted cake of ass, it was him.

Brooks and I threw back the tinfoil, like a couple of "Price is Right" showcase girls and the whole place exploded in laughter. The group captain collapsed on the table, laughing, and gasped (you guessed it), "Bonset, you bastard!"

The cake was delicious, I was told. I hadn't the heart to tell everyone that I had left this very shapely cake in the company of Brooks overnight.

I wasn't touching it.

18

A HERO YOU'VE NEVER
HEARD OF

Yet another example of the silent heroes that plague the military is one I'll try to out here. Chris wouldn't like it. So I didn't ask him.

Back then, I didn't know him personally, but I learned about his work early- culminating with finally meeting him in the desert outside Beyji, Iraq.

Now, I generally don't give a hoot about public affairs (PA) yahoos. They always seemed to be swarming around the VIPs, shooting photos or video and certainly getting in the good graces of the movers and the shakers. They were conspicuously absent during any of the crappy times, building sandbags, erecting tents—the hard, unsexy stuff. They seemed to be a little too much like groupies for my taste.

But the air force has a bunch of them, and as I was closer to the counter-insurgency (COIN) efforts in Iraq than I had been before, I began to realize my shortsightedness. When you have a large portion of a population that can't read or is functionally illiterate, you communicate with them via pictures or spoken language. And if they don't speak your language, well, that narrows it down. Even with the rise of picture editing software, pictures are still the universal communicator.

Therefore, if you're in a COIN fight with terrorists embedded in a population that has difficulty with the printed word, swift public affairs actions are critical to winning the soft war. If you can roll out pictures (captioned in the native language, of course) about an event before the terrorists can put their spin on it, it can help neutralize the impact. It can cause doubt about the veracity of the bad guys among their target audience, neutralizing recruiting efforts. The camera is a critical offensive and defensive weapon in the wars on terror.

After smartening up on the value of PA, I really saw a value in demonstrating to the Iraqi people the progress of their air force—progress in the schools and that sort of thing. Once again the balancing act came into sharp relief: we couldn't brag too much and compromise anyone in the school system, but we couldn't make it seem as if we were hiding anyone, either. That would project weakness and send the wrong signals to the populace. In light of that, there were articles that represented generalizations and announcements, and they were always carefully coordinated with the Iraqis.

The Iraqis that our PA guys worked with were a hoot. They only had one camera but were constantly thinking up inventive ways to reach out to illustrate the progress that was being made, without getting anyone killed. In one particularly inventive recruiting poster, they photoshopped Iraqi flags onto an American door gunner. That young man became a hero of Iraq. They then photoshopped some Russian aircraft (a type that they had formerly operated) zooming around the skies. The Iraqis just didn't have that many aircraft yet. So they used the resources they had available while bouncing ideas off our guys.

Chris worked around the headquarters, somewhere, and although we didn't have a ton of contact, we ran into each other at one of the graduations for my guys. There were always a bunch of Americans at any of those kind of events, snapping pictures like proud parents when the Iraqis completed one of their goals, or had a significant victory. He was well thought of and was considered to be very enthusiastic about his role in bringing the accomplishments of both militaries to the people of Iraq (and the United States). He had an infectious grin plastered beneath his be-spectacled vis-age that reinforced his positive attitude. His camera lens collected stories and images that reflected his take on the war around him.

Chris had noticed that the "good news" often didn't seem to be of any interest back home. This was a "big issue" for this young PA SSgt. He had come up with several stories, even sending them back home to various newspapers, but nothing. We were similar in that way; although not as skilled as he with wordology (thank you George Bush!), I too had writ-ten a similar question to my hometown newspaper called "When is Iraq Newsworthy?" about halfway through my tour. Of course, my paper, being awesome, ran it. Chris had no luck with his efforts. This was a major source of frustration for this young patriot.

He came from a family of patriots. As I came to know him, I discovered that his Dad was prior army, and his brother John was the one that actually recruited him into the Air Force. He was on his second tour of duty in Iraq when I met him. He missed his little children terribly, but little Mackenzie (about six) and even littler Mitchel (about three) got regular updates from their daddy, careful not to let them worry about where he was.

He had plenty of worries, though. Like many of us , he was worried about his little ones, he was in a combat zone, but he got to wrestle with even more; while there, his mother, Bridget, was diagnosed with cancer; proof that the Good Lord doesn't give you more than you can handle, I sup-pose. As a dutiful son, his weekly phone calls home to Mom became a bit more frequent. And conversations with Dad became promises to let him know the minute the cancer prognosis changed.

His vice was that he loved the Packers. He would stay up all night to catch the game on the other side of the world, joining the other cheeseheads in their misguided rooting. I guess it could've been worse. Apparently, New England still has a team.

The path to our formal introduction began after the Iraqis got the Mi-171medium-lift helicopters certified for flight and, after completing some safety of flight-type courses, started flying the heck out of them. At Taji, the 4 Squadron had the Mi-171 HiPs and the 2 Squadron had the Hueys that I enjoyed zooming around on. Our guys immediately embarked on an aggressive flying, training, and checkride policy. Again, there was a delicate balance to maintain: we didn't want to tell the Iraqis what to do, but we had to demonstrate why we thought our way worked better.

Iraqi thinking about continuation training (and training in general) was very different from ours. US airmen continually train, and every month, we have certain events that we have to practice, contingent on the airframe you fly. The Iraqis had a very different view: once you were a pilot, it didn't seem like you had to do a lot of training to stay current. Some of the stories the IQAF pilots I worked with relayed were pretty humorous.

For instance, one of the colonels that I worked with had been qualified on the MiG-29, then had spent the next six years flying Mirages. Nevertheless, when the invasion started, he was placed on alert status in a MiG-29 squadron. And he got scrambled. He couldn't get the plane started; he just couldn't remember how. And when he did get it started, he had trouble taxiing out of the spot. He noticed that it took almost full power to start to move. He had the emergency brake on. And this was an alert launch. Although he eventually launched, he ran into some of us; I think he walked back from that sortie. He should've kept the brake on.

So the continual training that we had inculcated into our military culture really wasn't present amongst the Iraqis. There were a couple of exceptions. Colonel Wahid said that he relentlessly trained his men, but I got the distinct impression that that was because of his nature, not because it was policy. There was also a Colonel Sammie down in Basra whose squadron was impeccable: aircraft, facilities, and people reflecting high degrees of proficiency.

But there just weren't enough Wahids and Sammies to go around. Our flying cadre really had their work cut out for them. They were making great strides, but it took constant pressure, and for some of the higher-ranking aircrew, egos were very fragile. It was a balancing act again. We couldn't ground all their pilots and just train up new cadre. Pilots take a looooong time to train. Experience is a patient but deadly teacher.

So it was a really big deal when the Iraqis took on a new mission and got all trained up to go do it. One of those new missions was a resupply mission from an Iraqi army depot to units near Mosul. This would be a good start to demonstrating the value of teamwork with the Iraqi army. A good result would encourage more missions and, hopefully, more good results.

A mission was laid on to send a two ship of Mi-171s to do the resupply, and Chris was excited to be able to accompany the flight on this important mission. He was flown up to Taji, where the mission would originate. The lead Mi-171 would be flown by an Iraqi crew, and "two" would be flown by Americans.

The Iraqi crew would have the squadron commander flying with an older lieutenant, the engineers, and door gunners. They also had a civilian Iraqi photographer on board. Chris would be flying along with the American crew to document the flight, showing progress for the IQAF, buoying up the service in the view of the Iraqis themselves. This was the part of PA that was so incredibly useful and so incredibly important. The effectiveness of those little positive nudges that great, heroic pictures can give a society can't be overstated.

Chris was pretty excited to go and document the whole exercise. He actually fought to get the assignment; this was going to be a great story to tell. Even though he hated to fly - a harrowing experience in a JSTARs (an air force surveillance plane) had caused him to leave that career field for PA- he bumped around in helicopters in Iraq fairly regularly. And this event was a mini milestone, one that he would get to relay to the Iraqis and the folks back home, but more importantly, little Mackenzie and Mitchel as he sat them on his lap to tell them what he had *really* been up to those months that he was gone. He was also pretty pumped because one of the last conversations with his Dad and Mom revealed that the cancer had gone into remission, so he wouldn't have to come home early to see his Mom. Dad gently reassured Chris that he wasn't needed at home just yet. Mom was doing OK.

So this was a great opportunity; the IQAF was struggling back to its feet, and he would be there for a small part of it, his camera lens pulling in the images that would feed the pride that was so desperately needed by the Iraqi people. A proud people don't need American scapegoats.

The day came, and the two-ship took off uneventfully. The Mi-171s were performing fine, and the weather was good. Lead did a fine job of taking the formation to their first destination, and the offload went flawlessly. The big helos hit Tal Afar for an intermediate stop for fuel, updated the weather report, and started for home. Chris' camera lens had been busy for the first couple of legs, grabbing the images of the Americans working in concert with the Iraqis; but something was wrong.

Chris thought that perhaps he could get a better story, or at least some better visuals, if he just hopped on board with the Iraqis. He certainly didn't have to, but he just thought he could do a better job, get a better angle, tell the story more effectively. I think at this time, he was about twenty days from going home: this adventure would be fresh in his mind, a bedtime story for his two little ones, and the recovering Mother when he got home. His lens would now collect another positive series of *Iraqi* images for a people desperate for them.

There isn't a safer place to be than in the hands of American flight crews. They are the best trained and equipped in the world. So when Chris made his decision to jump off of the US-crewed helo and onto the Iraqi-crewed helo, he knew full well what he was doing. But this was a great opportunity to get a positive story out about the good things happening in Iraq. The American media certainly wasn't going to do it. To me, it seemed like the only time news came out of Iraq or Afghanistan, it was calculated to make the military look bad; if the news media stateside had to make it harder for us to succeed in Iraq, costing lives and treasure, well, that was a sacrifice that the talking heads were more than happy for us to make. On their behalf. To make us look like the failures Harry Reid said we were.

That's why Chris' perspective was so important; give the public the opportunity to see the truth, even if it was just via the air force news. This twenty-four-year-old staff sergeant, making about thirty-five hundred dollars a month, would do his best to get the story out while the mainstream media would rather find ways to smear the president. Plus, Chris just loved his job.

This, then, fit right in with the dedication he had shown on a daily basis, in Iraq, on his second tour as a combat cameraman. He hopped on the lead helo, and the two-ship took off for home.

A few hours later, we in CAFTT were alerted that the second helicopter had landed safely at home, after running into a sandstorm and getting separated from the lead helicopter. But the lead helicopter was overdue. We weren't worried quite yet; a very experienced crew was flying lead. The weather had degraded fairly quickly, and since the communications gear in the Polish aircraft weren't great, there were some communications problems.

That's not a huge deal either, though. US aircrews brief for almost any eventuality; comm problems get briefed at the beginning of the sortie. As do lost wingman procedures. That's basically what each aircraft will do if it can't establish visual with the other. The most important consideration in a lost wingman situation is to get away from the ground and then get away from each other. It differs for different terrain and aircraft types, but that's the gist of it. The proper training ensures that these are just little hiccups on a sortie. No big deal.

There were plenty of places for a helicopter to land, of course. There were plenty of bad guy spots, but there were also little towns and such where the lead helo could land and wait out the storm. With the havoc that a sandstorm plays with communications and the marginal radios in the 171s that the Iraqis had purchased, we would have to rely on good intel to tell us where they eventually landed.

As the hours wore on, folks in the headquarters were starting to get progressively more worried about the crew. The Americans had been home for hours and were helping to narrow down where the lost helo could be. They knew where they had lost sight, and they knew the lost wingman procedure should have kept lead on a similar ground track to the one they took.

Allied forces along those routes were alerted to be on the lookout for a wayward Mi-171. Their patrols were alerted, as the aircraft could be sitting anywhere. That would be less palatable; if it had to set down in a hot zone, there could have been a firefight and prisoners, or something. So the eyes and ears of hundreds of GIs were put on alert for an Iraqi helicopter.

More hours passed, and then the good news came: the Iraqi A-6 (communications) had reported that the aircraft was down, safely by some little town, and that all seven were having tea in the local police station. We were all relieved at the happy outcome. It was the expected outcome, but still, not having anyone hurt was always a bonus. We looked forward to getting a full accounting of the adventure from Chris, as he was the only American on the helo.

But when we started to try to actually talk to the crewmembers, then it started to unravel. It turned out that the report was an official version of the telephone game, where at each information exchange the actual message gets a little more convoluted. Someone in a little town may have said that they saw a helicopter; by the time it got to us, it was "we have them drinking tea in a police station." That crippling desire to placate those in authority, even if only for a few moments had reared its ugly head again.

Our hopes were dashed. Dammit. Back to square one. I could see some communication procedure changes in the IQAF future. But, overall, everything was going to be fine. Given sketchy communications and the disarray that was the Iraqi command and control, they could have landed in the backyard, and we wouldn't have known about it. I'd seen silly things back in the States, where we have every form of communications, but things just get mixed up. In the middle of a war, in a very remote part of Iraq, I could certainly understand how the comms just didn't get through.

Unfortunately, I was wrong. During the night, a UAV had discovered wreckage in the desert around Beyji.

The next morning, we assembled an accident investigation team, and I volunteered, along with several other members. Since it was an Iraqi aircraft, we would be accompanying several Iraqis, a couple of whom I knew well and a couple of whom I only had a passing familiarity. It was going to be their investigation; we were there to ensure that the investigation was conducted to the highest standards. We had advisors for the safety detachment too.

Safety wasn't their strong suit. Much of Islamic culture has a lot of *inshallah* running through it, which, loosely translated, is "as God wills." It could be used as an excuse for a lot of laziness. If you don't do an inspection, and an aircraft crashes—oh well, inshallah. We were going to make sure that none of that showed up in the investigation. And, at this point, we certainly couldn't rule out enemy action.

We escorted the Iraqis over to the helipad. I was glad to see my friend Heidr, the maintenance chief for this team. He had a ton of experience in helicopter maintenance and didn't have any time for the inshallah mindset. He was a hardnosed man, who loved to try to increase his English proficiency with me at every opportunity. Mostly by asking about dirty words. He would say something in English and then ask if there was a dirty version of it. I would do my best to be his X-rated thesaurus.

If there was an appropriate (or inappropriate, in this case) term, then I would hear that ad nauseam. He would gleefully repeat whatever word that I had made the mistake of teaching him, regardless of audience. I think he considered the translation to be a success based on the horrified look on my face. He seemed to like hanging around me; I was the only pilot they had ever met that was also an "engineer," or maintenance guy. Again: no restrictions in my world, nothing but fences in his. There was one drawback to him being on the team. His best friend in the world was the pilot in command of the mishap helicopter.

The IQAF general was a man named Khalid and was really out of his depth, so our counterpart, a wonderful Colonel Armstrong, was going to be riding herd on him and would really have his hands full. Underneath Khalid was an IQAF colonel named Fahad, who was fairly westernized and had a pretty good investigative sense about him but, at this point, didn't really have the rank to truly affect the culture. The fact that Chris was involved meant that no stone would be left unturned in the quest to find out what had put this helo into the desert.

We lifted in a two-ship out of the helipad in Baghdad, winging our way northwest. The loud whine of the Blackhawk precluded much in the way of chitchat. It was a pretty somber time. Communications had been established already with Iraqi army commander and a US Army major at a little outpost in the middle of the desert close to where the helicopter had gone down. They would be waiting for us to arrive and get us bedded down for the night.

En route, it was decided to go get a bird's-eye view of the site. The Iraqi army had secured the site, but they didn't have much in the way of site discipline, so our Iraqis had to make lots of phone and radio calls to ensure that the unit in charge of site security understood how important it was not to disturb anything. We were a bit anxious to see how this was working as we arrived overhead.

Apparently, the constant communications from our Iraqi buddies made an impact. As we arrived overhead, we were able to see the Iraqi positions, in a defensive perimeter well away from the aircraft. The Iraqis on the ground waved, as we dipped our noses and departed the area.

About ten minutes later, the two ship flared to landing on the forward operating base, and we were met by the major and the Iraqi army colonel. We decided on a time to meet with the Iraqis and brief the next morning, and the Iraqis went their way, and we went ours.

We grabbed a bite to eat, then went to this unit's operations shack. And it was a shack. I think it had been a barn or something; the roof had collapsed but had been rebuilt, so at least the weather was kept out. There was the obligatory dog that everyone certainly didn't feed or pet or anything. The floors were dirt along with some elevated parts that were wood. Wisps of straw skittered across the floor, riding the little eddies of dirt that demonstrated the "hole-istic" approach to wall repair. It just wasn't that important to fix that.

The team met the major to discuss the relations with his Iraqi army counterpart, hostile action, and the plan for tomorrow. The army was going through much the same thing as we were, although on a vastly different scale. The Iraqi army training pipeline was so much shorter than the IQAF one, and they were so much bigger that quality control was an issue. Our army guys were very exposed whenever they went on joint operations with the Iraqi army. Really gutsy.

The air force flew with the IQAF as well, but there were only a few single-propeller aircraft, three C-130s, and a couple of squadrons of helicopters. We flew a lot, but the army was engaged in joint operations all the time, big and small. This major had been over here a year and some change, and had been through one bad Iraqi battalion commander. But he seemed to be pretty happy with his current counterpart. He was aggressive, smart, and apparently loyal to Iraq. I say apparently, because loyalty was more of a day-to-day thing in the field.

But the major allowed that this new guy might not get very far, precisely because of those qualities and the fact that he wasn't connected politically. Which was a ringing endorsement to me. I remember the scorn Wahid had for the ladder climbers in the Baath party. I think at some point, you were just enrolled in the party, but Wahid had a strong enough personality that he got away with not being an active member.

That sounded a lot like this guy. Maybe he was the Iraqi army's version of Wahid. Which would be a very, very good thing. His guys were the ones that were out pulling security on the helo.

We continued to get acquainted, and it was really neat to watch the interaction that the major had with various members of the team. Young guys would come in, and the major would ask about this or that, then offer some follow-up advice. It was really interesting to see the dynamic out at this remote outpost. In the air force, I had really never commanded a bunch of guys in the field. After I became a pilot, I was just commanding a few guys for a mission. And they were fairly highly trained. I hadn't had this level of responsibility with my guys before. As a lieutenant, just one hundred guys and nuclear weapons; I guess if something went wrong there, it would've gone really wrong. I really enjoyed the personal attention that the major paid to each soldier, no matter how low ranking.

After an uneventful evening spent in some sort of stable, the team met up with the rest of the army team out by the MRAPs for a premission briefing. It was pretty similar to a premission brief that I was used to giving for a formation flight: specific members of various trucks given very specific duties and sectors to watch. The major had considered all of the variables of his personnel before assigning not only which truck to place people in, but positions within the truck as well. Once he had made sure that everyone knew where they were sitting, they started talking about the response to contact.

They covered what would happen if one truck got blown up: what the other trucks do and who recovers casualties and/or vehicles. They covered the different responses to indirect fire, IEDs, or small arms fire, and it was really obvious that they'd done this before. This major ran a really tight ship. They all knew their responsibilities and roles and seemed to have had the opportunity to perform them. Then he looked at us.

He addressed the colonel. "Sir, for you air force guys, if you are in the vehicle, stay in the vehicle. If you are not in the vehicle, get in the vehicle. And stay there until we are out of contact and recovered. We'll handle the rest."

I was disappointed that there wasn't any consideration for my clear badassery. But it was probably for the best. We were to let the professionals do their work. We were to be good passengers and sit down and shut up. He also didn't want the Iraqis running around. We made sure that they knew exactly what was expected of them, strapped on our gear, and mounted the MRAPs. It was my first time in one, and they are pretty darn cool. If I become really rich, I'm going to buy one, turn it into a camper and then camp wherever the hell I want. They look like a lifted, camouflaged school bus, except shorter. Yes, I was in the short bus again. I jumped up the stairs into the cabin, which stood about four feet off the ground. There were two rows of seats, one along each wall. Each seat was mounted in a collapsible way, so if there was an explosion, the upward energy would be used in collapsing the seat structure, versus rocketing the occupant into the ceiling.

The interior was packed with communications gear, tow ropes, and some emergency supplies. The cockpit had all sorts of doodads in it, blue force trackers, moving maps, inclinometers, and the like. It was really nifty. We helped the Iraqis strap in, then strapped in ourselves, throwing on the helmets and goggles. The crew mounted up, checked us, then strapped in to their stations, one of them (I think a captain) sitting on a tree swing–type apparatus under the main gun on top. I thought that was cool; who wouldn't want to have a tree swing in the backyard that had a machine gun attached to it?

The big diesel rumbled to life; the little convoy started to move out. We slowly weaved through the base exit then stopped to lock and load. The occupants put clips in weapons but didn't chamber a round. The guns on top fired a short burst into a sand trap, until , finally, everyone was outside the base and on our own. The major had decided to "handrail" the road. Basically, since the road was Swiss cheese from the various bombings and IED attacks, we would take an offset from the road of a certain distance. The GPS navigation capability made sure that we didn't get lost, as we soon lost sight of the road.

The short column staggered through the desert; it was the surface of the moon. The captain was in his little swing, swiveling back and forth as the gun covered various clock positions. The major was on the radio constantly, giving little nudges to the various trucks: "cover that direction," "crest this ridge here," "slow down," and so forth. He was pretty cautious, so it was a good thing I wasn't driving.

We crested a small ridge, and the lead vehicle slowed to a stop. I really couldn't see why, but the major was concerned. He waved forward and said that there was an oil slick in front. I couldn't see squat except sand. As he explained, the oil bubbles up and then the sand blows over it, creating a serious quicksand trap for vehicles. It doesn't even have to be that deep. It's so slick that it doesn't take much to get even a giant vehicle like the MRAP stuck.

And bad guys like to hang out next to places where vehicles get stuck. So his sixth sense was tingling pretty steady. There really wasn't any decent way around, so the rear two vehicles started a bit down the slope, below the military crest of the ridge, setting up fields of fire for the lead vehicle that was going to try to ford the oil trap. The major gave a quick synopsis of the reaction to fire, so that everyone knew their roles as each vehicle went through.

The lead vehicle nosed gingerly into the bottom of the little ravine, and sure enough, the front wheels sank into what appeared to be normal sand. As they continued to rotate, they came up blackened with oil. Lead pressed ahead, with the determination that if it went in up to the axles, we would abort and find another way around. The major was really nervous; he didn't like sitting in one spot for so long. The captain in the swing was covering the twelve-to-six position with his machine gun, while the other half of the spectrum was covered by the gunner in the third MRAP.

The lead MRAP stopped, front axle in the gunk. The major really didn't like that. He was talking to his driver, apparently a little PO'd that the driver of the lead vehicle was a bit of a cowboy. I didn't see anything crazy, but then I hadn't been playing dodgeball with 7.62 mm rounds for a year. That makes one lose one's sense of adventure, I guess.

The major nervously authorized the lead MRAP to attempt the crossing. The big vehicle backed up a bit; then smoke belched out, and the camper from hell rocketed forward, throwing sand-encrusted oil in four rooster tails twenty feet in the air. It was awesome. The MRAP fishtailed a bit, before biting into the firm ground on the other side. The oil slick was only ten feet across and about a foot deep.

As it went up the other side, a loud "Yeehaa!" burst out of the radio.

The major looked at the radio, then at me, a big grin creeping across his face. He keyed the mike. "Radio discipline." He sounded gruff, but he was shaking his head and grinning. I think he was doing a mental "yeehaa" himself.

The rest of the little formation crossed the little obstacle with no problems and continued on to the site.

After about twenty more bumpy, dusty minutes, Iraqi HMMVs came into view. They were arrayed in a defensive posture around a darkened smudge against the light tan terrain. The MRAPs slowed a bit, spread out, and moved through the outer perimeter of the Iraqi formation. Carefully avoiding any wreckage, the major established the MRAPs into a smaller defensive perimeter. The engine rattled to a stop, and he looked back to the colonel.

"We're here. Please remember, if we do get into contact, get back to the truck. We'll take care of the threat. If there is anything you need, please let me know. I hope you get what you need."

The colonel nodded, and everyone unstrapped. I adjusted my weapons and stepped out of the vehicle. It was a fairly cool day, but the sun was extremely bright. It was a good environment to conduct the investigation. Heidr followed me out, ditching his Russian-looking helmet for a soft cover. He looked over the scene, shaking his head. There really wasn't a lot left. A fairly large helicopter had been reduced to a smear of blackened wreckage, a fairly intact tail boom, and rotor hub. Everything else was not as obvious.

Colonel Armstrong suggested to the Iraqi general that we have a little conference to get everyone on the same page as to how to proceed. The colonel wanted to ensure that no one contaminated the scene and that the investigation would be methodical and thorough. The general agreed that the colonel's idea was a good one, and for the rest of the event, that would be the case. Whatever the colonel said was what the general was just about to say. Because he was in charge and this was his investigation, because he was in charge. Plus, he was in charge.

Some of the other US airmen had already had crash investigation experience, so were well aware of what to look for. We basically moved out as far as we could within the perimeter and started documenting everything we found, without touching anything. We were just trying to get the facts, before any making any conjectures. Colonel Armstrong was riding herd on the general, who was already making sweeping statements on how it must've happened. He had a lot of theories, for sure, and he was going to start moving stuff around and walking all over everything, but the gallant Colonel Armstrong was on him like a Collie with a herd of short-attention-span sheep. Or one sheep, anyway.

After some eye-rolling exchanges between us, the rest of the Iraqis got to work. Heidr and Fahad took a very professional tack to figuring out exactly what happened. I was plotting the outer limits of debris field, looking for anything that would indicate enemy action: missile fragments or indications that the helo broke up in flight (as a result of antiaircraft fire). The other folks were doing similar actions, trying not to miss anything.

The army folks were maintaining a perimeter, with the Iraqi army spread out a little beyond them. The terrain was an unbroken visage of moonscape, cast in tans and browns. Strangely, there was a little house about two hundred yards from the main site. It had been checked out for bad guys, but I was wondering what on earth the occupants could have done for a living. It just looked so out of place. It was a nice little home, fairly new, against this hostile landscape.

I likened it to if Neil Armstrong had stepped out onto the moon thusly:

"That's one small step for Man, one giant leap for, - oh, hey, we're in someone's backyard."

It was just odd. But it did serve as an approach, so it was watched to make sure we weren't interrupted while we were working.

With our safety in very capable hands, the scene took on a very clinical aspect. We were just going around, gathering data, in preparation for later analysis. We found quite a bit that day. Heidr and his group continued to work closely with ours; Colonel Armstrong continued to keep the Iraqi general from disturbing the rest of us. He did have his hands full. The general was walking around, making pronouncements about the cause of the crash, which were met with a grain of salt, to say the least.. And sand.

"The helicopter came in very fast, at a very shallow angle—like this!" The general made a swooping motion with his hand. After seeing the looks on our faces, he added, "Or, maybe, I think, very slow, but steep!" Again, he backed up his theory with the hard evidence of the swooping of his hand, this time in a more vertical direction. It didn't help that he had replaced his hat with his kaffiyeh, and it was wrapped weird, so he was wandering around making pronouncements looking like he'd been hit in the head with a pile of laundry. Colonel Armstrong kept up with him, steering him away from any damage he could do and generally keeping him out of trouble.

To their credit, the other Iraqis on site were consummate professionals. Heidr was working with our maintenance people; Fahad was talking with the helicopter pilots that we had with us; and the other folks were accomplishing their assigned tasks.

This went on for a while, as the team was on the outer edges of the scene; but as we moved toward the center, I heard an anguished howl. I looked over at the source; it was coming from my hardnosed, chain-smoking, dirty-English-word-using friend, Heidr.

He was raising his hands up, silhouetted against the robin's-egg-blue sky. It looked a lot like the *Platoon* movie poster. I walked over to see what the matter was.

He had found his friend.

Or, more specifically, he had found his friend's flight suit, just the upper left chest part—the part that had the nametape on it. I looked on, past Heidr's agony, at his very personal discovery. That part of the flight suit had been torn from the rest of it by the impact. It lay about thirty yards from the main crater. The nametag was in pristine condition: black, with the squadron commander's name embroidered in silver thread, propped up on a small rock, awaiting Heidr's discovery.

I placed my hand on this sobbing Iraqi's shoulder, while Heidr composed himself. I wondered how many times that scene had been repeated over the last few years: an American imperialist warmonger comforting someone he was supposed to be oppressing. I bet it happened a lot. I slipped my arm over his shoulder, and we just stood there: he with the thoughts of his loss, me with sympathy for my friend. It seemed like a long time, but soon Heidr had gathered himself, shook his shoulders, took a deep breath, and re-attacked

the task at hand. Sobered, I restarted my efforts, occasionally glancing over to see if Heidr was okay.

The afternoon wore on, and darkness started to creep toward us. The army major came up to us and said we needed to mount up; we didn't want to get caught out here after dark. The Iraqi army folks were staying through the night to maintain security of the site. We weren't going to argue—that's for sure—so we loaded up into the MRAPs. The major quickly briefed, and we were off. The little convoy formed up, and we handrailed back to the base, this time using a different offset. It was an uneventful trip and evening: food, then briefings and analysis of the day's events. Then we made our way to the stable-like buildings for sleep.

It went on this way for the next couple of days, and at the end, the Iraqis came up with some very sound conclusions. It was especially telling because the findings were critical of the Iraqis. Although I knew the findings, the honesty of the final report was a breath of fresh air. I got the impression that it was unusual in its honesty. As I've mentioned before, responsibility and accountability were not the hallmarks of the Iraqi regime before we showed up. (Yet another bad habit we brought with us.)

The Iraqis had really shone. Even Heidr, working in the gravesite of his dear friend, had used his tremendous maintenance knowledge and keen intellect (well hidden by his profane tongue) to tease out some conclusions.

The helo was not brought down by enemy action but some training deficiencies in the Iraqi aviation units. The Americans had done everything they could to force the pilots to practice, practice, practice, but habits and thought patterns established over decades don't disappear over the course of a few years. Especially if there wasn't a sufficient push to change.

The interviews with the American crew were heartbreaking, as these brave, proficient professionals spoke to the utter helplessness they felt as the lead helicopter disappeared into the sandstorm, falling back on instructions that ran counter to the teaching of American helo crews. Their desperate attempts to reach through the radios to the lead helicopter to assist went for naught as that crew became more and more disoriented. The instruments on the lead helicopter were working; the Iraqi crew just wasn't very good at using them.

The helicopter crashed as a result of the Iraqi crew's actions. The crew apparently became disoriented in the sandstorm, something that can happen to even the best of pilots, but the lack of instrument flying practice was a major player in the accident. In safety investigations, it's crucial to get to the truth. That is the only thing that makes you better. There's a saying in the air force flying community: all the "stupid" rules are written in blood. Somebody did something that was ultimately preventable. Since we value each and every life so highly, safety investigations have certain exemptions, in hopes that honesty will prevail and the real root cause can be discerned. It's absolutely critical to get the truth, and therefore, the system is set up to get at the truth, as opposed to punishment. So safety investigations are sacred.

In many societies, where life is cheap, safety is an afterthought. But here was an investigation that was a reflection of the teamwork; the somewhat humbled IQAF was taking positive steps to determine what went wrong, wherever that would lead them. And some of that intensity and drive for the truth was because they had hurt someone from the friendly side: Chris.

That bright, shiny day as I stood with my friend Heidr, comforting the loss of his friend in the middle of the barren desert, something else caught my eye. A few feet away from Heidr's friend's nametag, in the outer perimeter of the broken helo, among the charred engine cases and twisted armor, lay a shattered camera lens.

The story that Chris was trying to tell would have to be told by someone else. His two little children would not hear it from him. He wouldn't be there to tell it to them as he tucked them into bed, having asked them about their day, said their prayers, and kissed them on the forehead before folding the covers over just right. He wouldn't be there to pause by the door, looking over his shoulder at his son as he turned out the light, checking in on the sleepy-eyed big sister as she drifted off to sleep. He wouldn't be cheering the Packers on again. This part of his story had ended in the deserts of Iraq.

SSgt. Christopher Frost was killed on March 3, along with all seven of his Iraqi brothers. His legacy would be unknown to many in the United States. But he is remembered in the Iraqi air force as yet another hero from the friendly side.

The stress of his death reawakened a ravaging cancer, and his beloved Mother died four months later.

Rest in peace, quiet warrior.

19

FINALLY, AMERICAN ARROGANCE

As things progressed, more Iraqi lieutenants started popping out of the various commissioning sources. Little groups started to be absorbed into the cadre of the IQAF. But their assignments were really just spur-of-the-moment. We were trying to impress upon the powers that be a systematic approach to determine their needs and plan their accessions appropriately.

But the situation was so chaotic that a systematic approach really didn't apply to much in Iraq, so they would lurch from one emphasis to another, depending on the pressure of the day. One day, they would be shouting for intel analysts, and the next it would be mission sensor operators. There were only so many ways you could slice up eight or nine guys.

Eventually, the equipment purchases that had been coordinated long before I arrived were starting to come through. And some of those pieces of equipment had to have qualified operators, or they would be useless to the Iraqis. One of the big ones was a King Air transport plane, a twin-engine prop aircraft that was going to be the basis for light airlift duties and, with some modifications, an intelligence, reconnaissance, and surveillance (ISR) platform.

That meant that we needed crews to fly, fix, and operate the sensors, and ideally we would have those things in place when the equipment showed up. This would ensure we were not stuck with a ten-million-dollar boat anchor until someone showed up that knew how to use it. For once, we were a little ahead of the game, and the Iraqis had prescreened that initial group of graduates, and had placed a couple of them into the mission sensor operator (MSO) specialty.

These graduates had English scores and physical fitness good enough to make them aircrew members, just not pilots. They would form the nucleus of the new IQAF specialty. There were a couple of veterans who also volunteered to be MSOs, but the recent graduates were the seeds of the new crop. I started to research a little about how the training was going to occur.

The hard part was getting permission from the Iraqi Ministry of Defense for overseas training, which required a six-month lead time. It was often denied or delayed just long enough for the training dates to have passed. The bureaucrats in the MOD would all shrug their shoulders, saying that it was too bad they had missed a training opportunity. Their true motivation became obvious: they didn't have to worry about someone skipping out and applying for asylum in the country of training, or worse, disappearing. That had happened several times, with the resulting loss of face and prestige. It was easier and safer to simply find obstacles until the training window had passed, and then be sorrowful. It set the progress of the country back, but at least the politicians and administrators had a safe job.

To compensate for that, we were going to send some American crews to train in San Diego, where the manufacturer of the sensor suite conducted classes. They would get trained up in the operation of the sensor suite and, upon returning to Iraq, would train the Iraqis.

That didn't set right with me. The Iraqis had bought these aircraft and sensor systems with their own money, brokered through the Air Force Security Assistance Center. I had pretty good communications there with an old B-52 guy named Swanny, who worked the Iraqi portfolio from somewhere in the bowels of a building in Texas. Swanny was a hoot, someone who really had the best interest of the Iraqis at heart. He was frustrated with the glacial pace of spending in the Iraqi portfolio: this large amount of money could bring rapid improvements to the Iraqis. We got along great. He said I was the only one to ever hang up on him because I was getting rocketed. That counted for something.

Swanny had seen it over and over; he'd made arrangements and gotten the money all squared away, but the Iraqis failed to materialize. It was easier to just have the Americans go and come back to teach. There was also an undercurrent of superiority; it would just be better training if the Americans received it first. Swanny hated that too, but it seemed like I was the first one to point it out. Swanny was very excited to attempt to schedule the Iraqis for any training stateside. They had all this money in their accounts, and get blowing the opportunities to spend it. And the worst part; blowing the opportunity to get exposure to the west.

The King Air program was a watershed for many reasons. It was a new and modern piece of equipment, with a lot of technical holes to fill: maintenance, pilots, and sensor operators. It would be a good test for the Iraqis.

Swanny felt the same way about the Iraqis receiving the primary training. With every King Air purchased, a crew of two and a maintenance guy got to train for free. With every sensor suite, a crew of two. The Iraqis had paid for it and should get it.

It was also the right thing to do. Not only was sending Americans in their stead letting the Iraqis off the hook for taking care of themselves, it was also a reinforcement of a bad stereotype; talking points of the radical left, socialists, fascists, and the rest of the Democratic base. That Americans are arrogant.

As I figured out what the Americans had signed themselves up for, I ran my thoughts to the boss at that time, to make sure that I had some backing in our chain of command. General Bash (the replacement for General Dice) was of a like mind. The Iraqis needed to attend the maximum amount of training possible; it was their money, and they certainly needed the exposure to the West.

I immediately called Swanny, stateside, and told him that we were going to push to fill all the slots with Iraqis. His jaw hit the floor. (Or, at least, that's what he told me; we were on the phone, after all.) Then he got really excited; he was going to make all the arrangements to get not only a pilot to take simulator flights in Texas (for the King Air) but clear the way for the first MSOs to go to San Diego. And after that, he'd send some guys back for C-130 simulator training. And then, we were going to get unicorn squadrons.

I immediately asked the Iraqis to figure out who from Kirkuk should attend the pilot training. Colonel Wahid asked a few questions of Colonels Ahmed and Nasser. Then they said they would call Colonel Kamil in Kirkuk to see if his recommendation matched theirs. About that same time, I relayed the request to the American counterparts at Kirkuk to get their take on things.

They all came back with the same recommendation: Major Bashir would be the one to go to the pilot qualification course at a commercial contractor in Texas. This was the same course that the USAF guys had to go through for their qualifications on that type of aircraft, and the manufacturers were really excited to have their first Iraqi attend the training. It would be the same level of training that the USAF crews went through.

The Americans at Kirkuk thought that although he was probably the best Iraqi pilot with the requisite English language skills, his instrument flying was not up to snuff. Few nations train their pilots to the levels we do, but at the end of the day, the ability to fly an approach is a binary solution set. Either you can or you can't.

The Iraqis, however, thought that Bashir was a demigod and basically invented not only the GPS satellites, but placed them in orbit with his God-like hands. They all said that he was ready to go. I talked with Wahid and the other pilots; it was clear that they thought a lot of the guy and his skills. Since I hadn't flown with any of the Iraqis as a pilot, I couldn't say. But the Americans that had said he needed a lot of work on instruments; they had even developed an instrument course for their small cadre. But we would proceed and use one of the slots the Iraqis paid for to qualify Bashir in the King Air.

At the same time, I was trying to get a selected group of Iraqi officers into the MSO training. Alhasan, Alaa, and Ghalib were the lucky three that we were pushing through the MOD to travel to the States for training on the sensor suite. Lieutenants Alhasan and Alaa were among the first graduates that came through; Ghalib was a major from the old air force. The Four Amigos were very proud of the three. Wahid took a grandfatherly tack when describing them, especially the two young lieutenants.

Alhasan and Alaa were quite a pair. They remembered me from a much earlier encounter—I think one of the trips to Taji—and they seemed to remember that I said that learning English would enable all these great things. Here they were, with their great English scores, getting ready to go to the United States.

Blind squirrel; nut.

Alaa was a tall (around six feet three), heavyset young man, with an open face and kind eyes. Unkempt hair spiked out of his head, topping off an oft-smiling mouth. He was one of the quiet ones, who had been in the back ranks of any meeting. He was the kid that everyone liked to be around: not the leader, just an indispensable part of the crew.

Alhasan was shorter, a little more refined, with sharp eyes and an angular face under a carefully groomed head of hair. He, too, was quiet but in a more calculating way. He was slender and stood about a head shorter than Alaa. His English was probably the best of the three.

Ghalib was the old head: about forty-five to fifty years old, a previous pilot who volunteered to be an MSO. He was well respected in the community as a solid, dependable guy. He looked like everyone's uncle: bald, short, with the beginnings of a pot belly; a wrinkled face hosted twinkling eyes, like two glittering lumps of coal staring out of a catcher's mitt. He grinned and laughed a lot. He was supposed to be the grown-up on this trip, and the way he looked at those two young men, smirking and elbowing each other, he wasn't going to like it one bit.

In truth, he was probably more frightened than either of them. They didn't have the history of the last few decades, when the West was always waiting to attack the peaceful people of Iraq—the Great Satan pacing at the border. Ironically, one of those minions of the Great Satan pacing up and down the border was me, the guy standing before them now. It was tough for Ghalib to override that conditioning; the younger guys didn't have all that baggage.

One of the challenges was to raise the bail money that the MOD had determined was necessary for anyone heading overseas. I'm not sure if it went by rank or whatever, but all these guys were responsible for raising about ten thousand dollars each to hold as a bond. Their families also would not be allowed to leave the country for an extended period of time. This was supposed to ensure that the guys would come back. To raise that much was at the edge of the impossible. They all collected money from family, friends, and coworkers to give to the MOD, which they would get back upon return. The challenge was getting money from relatives while having to either lie about what it was for or bringing them into the circle of trust, along with the accompanying danger.

Oftentimes, fellow Iraqi air force officers would pony up money for their fellows to go. I did the math once. I think a colonel made about twelve hundred dollars a month; obviously, lieutenants made a lot less. So the amount of money they had to raise was staggering. To add insult to injury, they wouldn't get paid for anything until they got back. The fact that they got anyone to go at all was astounding.

Bashir seemed to raise the money without too much difficulty, but the three MSOs had a lot more trouble. Over the course of many meetings, these worried young men (and one older man with a family to support) discussed their money-raising efforts. It was really touching how these fairly destitute families would scrape up whatever dinars they could, sometimes for no more defined purpose than "Alaa needs this money for something." Alaa said that some of his extended family had no idea what the money was for, but sent some in anyway. It came right down to the wire for the MSOs. I think Ghalib got his money bonded a day or two before he was supposed to leave. Bashir had a little easier time of it.

He came through Baghdad and got a talking to by Colonel Wahid. I think that was part of the process: the "old man" talked to you before you went anywhere. It was telling that Wahid did the talking, not the Iraqi general. Bashir departed on time and went to Texas, where he was accompanied by a handler to ensure that he didn't get into trouble and to smooth any problems he might have. He started his training on time, and soon it became apparent that this would be a struggle. He was way behind his contemporaries when it came to instrument and emergency procedures. But his close association with the Americans had paid off. He wasn't afraid to ask questions, work hard, and overcome his shortfalls.

In the end, Bashir did okay. He mostly graduated because the check cleared; still, the simulator operators had nothing but positive things to say about him. They spoke to his work ethic and obvious intelligence, along with the obvious preparation that the hardworking guys up at Kirkuk had given him. Bashir mentioned them all the time while going through the training course. And although he wasn't up to the usual checkride standards, what he brought back to Iraq was invaluable, culturally and professionally. His failure was a huge success. He was humbled by his performance, but instead of blaming someone else, he realized what the Americans had been saying all along was true: there is a reason we are the world's best military.

The MSOs' trip was not nearly as smooth. Ghalib had some difficulty raising the required bounty. He was already struggling to support a family; most of his relatives were too. In the end, it was his brothers in the IQAF who made it possible for Ghalib to go to America, even though they, too, had families to support, in the especially uncertain times. Ghalib explained, "Major, when I told them what I was going to do, they all tried to give what they could. They said that they could never go to the West, so I must go for them. I must represent the people of Iraq, and I must bring them the real United States."

His dark eyes sparkled over his grinning mouth. He looked away from my eyes, suddenly bashful. He paused for a moment. The sparkle died a little, as he suddenly became somber, as stoic as I'd ever seen him.

"It is a great honor to be chosen for this. There are a lot of questions about America. Some people think it's impossible."

I was a bit confused. "What do you mean—'it's impossible'? Getting there?"

He shook his head, in small movements, thinking of how to explain. He spread his hands, denoting helplessness. His vocabulary had failed him. He kind of straightened up and just murmured, shrugging his shoulders. "Just…impossible."

He eventually raised the money and deposited it at the MOD, along with the other two. Wahid wasn't around when they were scheduled to leave, so they just stopped by the personnel office in the IQAF headquarters building to see us before they left. We had just been rocketed the day before, and it had blown out some windows in the room that we were going to talk to them in. While I was waiting for the three to show up, I pulled a big chunk of shrapnel out of the personnel file beside me. It had blown through the window, a wooden crate, and about six inches of paper files. It made for a good conversation starter.

When they did show up, they were in great spirits; the departure date was just a couple of days away, their bonds were paid, the tickets were secured, and the passports were taken care of. Swanny had worked all the angles stateside, so there would be someone there to support them as soon as they stepped off the plane. After lots of greetings, they came up to where I was standing, next to the shattered window.

I'm sure I was grinning my butt off; I was so happy and proud I could've burst. We had worked awful hard to get to this point with these guys. Swanny had steered the big, ponderous bureaucracies to meet at this narrow point in time to receive these young men; we had been back and forth to the folks in the MOD and worked within the IQAF system to get these young men a chance to go to the United States to attend the training they had paid for.

And while they were there, they wouldn't be dodging shrapnel like the sliver I held in my hand.

So I thought I would talk to them, in all their nervousness.

"All right, guys, you'll be going to San Diego; it's really a nice town, but you will still have to be careful. Talk to your sponsor when you get there about what neighborhoods you should and shouldn't go into. Because you—"

"Yes, Major, we will be killed!"

Lieutenant Alaa's interjection was heartbreaking. Although I suppose there are a couple neighborhoods in the United States where that is true, Baghdad was awash with them. Hell, any neighborhood was dangerous if the wrong people rode through it. Sometimes, the bad neighborhood would come to you. But in Alaa's young life, a small misstep could very well mean death. His life had been one of unease and distrust. How very different than the life Americans lead. Again, some neighborhoods are wracked with violence, but that is a result of unwillingness to punish the guilty.

His face showed a little concern, and that gave me pause as well; he was very matter-of-fact about that consequence to any misstep. I shook it off with a laugh. "No, Alaa, you won't be killed; what I was trying to say is that if you wind up in the wrong neighborhood, you may have to ask for directions to get home! I think you'll find that most people in America are very friendly and helpful."

There were three thoughtful faces at that bit of information. So, a wrong turn may result in having to ask for directions. Being men, of course, they would rather die than ask directions.

We spent some more time talking about the particulars of who was going to meet them, when, and what was going to happen while there. Ghalib was looking more and more worried as the two twenty-two-year-olds looked more and more excited. The chaperone was not going to be getting a lot of sleep, I figured. Although I answered a lot of phone calls from Ghalib until they actually got on the airplane to take them out of Iraq, they eventually left.

I think Swanny had a heart attack. We had had two successful departures and one successful return. We were going to be on pins and needles until they got back. But in the meantime, life went on in Iraq.

Our arrogance showed up in other ways as well. Our good friends in the media seemed to emphasize the Iraqis' shortcomings, while minimizing the successes. The operation in Basra that took place in 2008 was a great example of this.

Prime Minister Nouri al Maliki launched an operation to clear Basra of the terrorists that seemed to have been ceded a lot of freedom there, creating more chaos, more opportunities to recruit bad guys, and more death and destruction. The airfield down there got hit a lot. So the prime minster decided that he had to do something, sooner rather than later. As a result, and in keeping with the whole "we're equal partners" thing, he told the American forces there a scant four days before launching the operation. That caused a ripple effect as the Americans tried to posture to support the Iraqi efforts, if needed. Hopefully, it wouldn't be needed.

The Iraqi air force swung into action. One of their C-130s was in depot status, leaving just two operational. The Mi-171 squadron sent a detachment down to Basra, along with intel people. There was a short build-up, and then the operation began.

The IQAF flew their wings off. The two C-130s lugged almost six hundred thousand pounds of material and thirty-five hundred troops over thirty-three sorties.[7] One of the problems the IQAF created was getting more stuff into the airport than the Iraqi army could process. We heard stories of aircraft returning from multiple trips to see the same guys they left on the tarmac, awaiting transport.

For the first time, the IQAF helos conducted battlefield reconnaissance, working with Iraqi army troops on the ground to conduct effective operations. They would often bring back souvenirs of their adventures in the form of bullet holes and other battlefield damage. They were working in a coordinated way with army commanders on the ground to minimize civilian casualties and maximize damage to the bad guys. Like we would.

For the first time, they actually conducted battlefield medevac, with Iraqi medics. Trained by US advisors, the Iraqis were pushing their triage

---

7 CAFTT Press release. June 2008.

abilities in the back of the Mi-171s. Those guys had come through our schools and graduated from our classes; US Army and Air Force medics had patiently taught the young Iraqis how to assess and treat battlefield injuries to a level not seen by the Iraqi army. Now, these young men treated over one hundred guys over the course of thirteen missions. Fittingly, one of the first people treated and transported was an Iraqi civilian wounded by an IED.

The IQAF also conducted ISR missions, interdicting everything from mortar trucks to oil thieves. Even as far back as that January, a Mi-171 spotted a mortar carrier, then relayed that to a CH-2000 (single-engine prop aircraft), which in turn relayed that to a British armored vehicle, which then captured the driver.

British armored vehicle driver: "Cheerio boffin! Pip pip and all that; prithee, do you know why I pulled you over?"

Terrorist guy: "Umm, no, was I speeding?"

British armored vehicle driver: "Egad, no, it was because of all the bloody mortars you have in your boot, my good man. Now, dismount from your conveyance, you damnable cad!"

All of that was said in Mary Poppins English.

Probably.

Anyway, I'm sure by now you're bored with the facts from the operation in Basra. You've heard it over and over from the media outlets, anxious to reinforce the honest good news out of Iraq, to build up both the American troops and the troops of our allies there. To only concentrate on their performance compared to American troops, the best in the world, would be, well, arrogant. And perhaps a bit dishonest—. It would be as if there was almost an agenda behind the selective reporting of the news.

I remember coming back after my tour and sitting in a waiting room somewhere. I picked up a *Time* magazine. It was from months before, but you know how waiting rooms are.

I started to read an article about the surge. It was amazing how many words were dedicated to the "inadequacy of Iraqi forces" or the "incompetence and poor discipline"[8]. For every good thing that was said, there was a devastating *but* that followed. At the same time, I remembered a

---

8 Hauslohner, Abigail. "Measuring Iraq's Security Forces." Time Magazine World. May 1, 2008. http://www.time.com/time/magazine/article/0,9171,1736725,00.html (accessed 06 16, 2012).

conversation I had with the indomitable General Jasham, a guy who truly was in the middle of trying to save his country.

I went to see him concerning an education issue. Knowing his stature in the Iraqi armed forces, I decided to show my American arrogance and give him a little crap about the performance of his army troops.

"So, sayyid, I've heard that there were some difficulties in Basra."

"Oh, Bonset? What kind?"

"Well, I understand that a lot of your army left and the police quit and there were some bad things that happened as a result of that."

His wise face became more thoughtful. He sighed and straightened up in his chair. He interlaced his fingers on his immaculate desktop. His eyes crinkled a bit in a wry smile.

Softly, he said, "Yes, Bonset, there were some difficulties. The troops that we used were very new. They were all very new. There weren't many experienced leaders. Normally, young men come into battalions that are mostly experienced men, but with the recent 'difficulties,' we've had to take many people all at once. It's difficult to have so few with good knowledge."

I'm pretty sure that he meant experience, leadership, and so forth. And he was right. In the US armed forces, it would be rare to have that much turnover in a unit. For instance, the USAF carefully monitors the mix of pilots in a squadron, ensuring that new guys can grow up on someone's wing until everyone is confident that they won't kill anyone. Then, they fly with gradually less experienced guys, and eventually, they become the guys who are keeping new lieutenants from doing something stupid.

But in the Iraqi army, there was a massive turnover in experience; there weren't enough experienced, good, Westernized senior-, mid-, and low-level leaders to go around. And you could add to that building the army in the midst of a war infested with terrorists who will slit your throat or turn their guns on you in the middle of a firefight. Armies are hard to build. They take a long time. And air forces take longer. So General Jasham had a very valid point.

He paused, gathered his thoughts, his eyes staring at a spot somewhere over my shoulder, and continued, "Bonset, you are right, many of our troops did not fight. Many of the police turned over their equipment. Some of the troops fired on their brothers. And that is very good news."

His eyes snapped to mine, his jaw flexed, and a grim smile crept across his face. I had a feeling that some Iranians had been caught in that same smile, just before they died under his tank guns.

"Now we know who the bad guys are."

I shook my head in wonder, grinning again. He was such a stud. It was true; those who had infiltrated into the units had played their cards and came up wanting. But there was no more hiding. There would be no more cowardly lying for those waiting like a cancer in the midst of a bunch of vulnerable young patriots. They played their cards and lost.

But the American press just couldn't wait to trumpet the failure. The less-than-stellar performance was proof that the mission was a failure, yet again. They couldn't stand on their own, and so we had failed. I read one mention of the performance of the Iraqi air force, and it said something to the effect that it existed.

As time went on, the Iraqis conducted more operations, and they must have been more successful, because I didn't hear much about it. But we were briefed on the status on the Iraqi operations over time. It was instructive to see the progression.

In Basra, there were desertions and pitched battles. The allies were relied upon pretty heavily. But the Iraqis pushed through. Another operation went to Mosul, a real hotspot of terrorist activity. There was resistance, but the Iraqis didn't have any major defections, and the organized terrorist resistance was stamped out in relatively short order. The next operation took the Iraqi army a bit farther north, pushing hard against the bad guys. This one was special.

This time, as the Iraqi army approached, the terrorists bravely ran away. But first, they wrote on a bridge, leaving town, "We'll be back."

Then some defeated, demoralized, incompetent Iraqi soldier climbed up onto the steel beams of the bridge and wrote, "We'll be waiting."

That still gives me chills.

But, of course, you're bored reading all this rehash of what you've already heard over and over again from the news media, who, of course, only report the news, without any agenda. But it is tough to gauge any military when the American military is in the room. They all come up wanting. The trick is to set aside the superiority and measure the effectiveness of a military against their mission.

For instance, I hate dates. I've never liked them, but that doesn't mean they're inherently bad. To me, they are basically rotten fruit. But when the damn things were in season, we were inundated with gifts of dates from all the guys (to be clear, this is the fruit; the one on the tree). I told many of the folks that I hated dates, even though the Iraqis were extremely proud of them. So, I was a bit arrogant.

One day, when I went over to the A7 trailer, Colonel Wahid came up to me, zipper unzipped, boots untied, cigarette dangling out of his mouth. He presented me with a box of dates, tied with a piece of ribbon.

"Mike," he rasped, "I have brought you these dates. They are the best dates in all of Iraq!"

"Oh? Where did you get them?"

"My father's house," he replied.

This set off an explosion from Asad, who had been laughingly watching our exchange up until that point. Now, for some reason, he was furious and launched a fusillade of Arabic at Wahid. Wahid gave several dismissive gestures, and his tenor raised to match Asad's. I think quite a few "shut your pie hole"s were exchanged, but it turned out that Asad was furious with his childhood friend for going by his father's house to get me some dates.

You see, the assassins had staked out Wahid's father's house, as they knew that Wahid would come around eventually. So Wahid had avoided it. But he really wanted to get these "best dates in all of Iraq" for me. Even though I hated dates. Eventually, Asad threw his hands up and walked off, fuming. I asked Wahid what had happened.

"Mike, Asad is very worried about me. He is like an old woman. The terrorists don't scare me. They are jackals. I'm not afraid of jackals. They are dangerous but cowardly. They sneak around, looking for weakness and opportunity." He dismissively flung his hands away. "They are cowards; but they are getting help from Iran and targeting many pilots. So I have to watch, but I am not afraid. And Asad is like a wife; he has been nagging at me since I was this high," he said, holding his hand about waist high. "But," he added after a moment, "he is usually right, so after a little while"—he lowered his voice—"I will have to go tell him that I won't do it again."

I looked down at my box of carefully wrapped, disgusting dates. Measuring them against my standards, I still hated them. Measuring them in their environment, fully informed of the facts surrounding them,

I unwrapped the ribbon, pried open the box, and with the appropriate amount of fanfare ate every damn one, right there in the trailer. As far as Wahid knew, I was a changed man. These were the most delicious dates I had ever tasted. Since I hated dates, it was a true statement. So I gobbled them all down and spent the next two days running to the crapper.

The amazingly brave Wahid was the recipient of my arrogance on several occasions; the next one was around the time I got to return home for the six-month break.

I was getting ready to leave for the other side of Camp Victory to board the C-17 to get out of theater. At about ten o'clock at night, about twenty minutes before I was going to leave for the terminal, I got a panicked call from Wahid.

"Mike," he said, "when do you have to leave?"

"About fifteen minutes, sayyid."

"You must wait for me, Mike; please, it is very important!"

"What's wrong?" I could hear a bit of desperation in his voice, something I was not used to hearing. I was starting to get worried. I asked him if everything was all right. He was a bit evasive and would only reiterate that he needed to talk to me, that very night. It couldn't wait. He then said that he was parking his car and would have to go comm out for quite a while; as he went through the various checkpoints, he would have to surrender his cell phone until he came out on the other side.

This was also a vulnerability for the guys: going in and out of the base. They never knew when someone was watching the entrances, noting who went in and out. So this was weird: Wahid calling me late at night, trying to get back on the base, and he wouldn't tell me why. And he seemed a little stressed, which was certainly out of the norm for him. I smelled trouble.

I wasn't going to leave him, but I would certainly be bummed if I missed my flight home for Christmas. I had arranged my transportation already and had the young captain who was going to drive me just establish an orbit around our office. After an agonizing wait, the phone chirped again.

"Mike!"

"Wahid, what in the hell is going on?"

"Mike, are you still there? I am on the other side, but I am coming now. Please, will you wait? I must see you."

"Dammit, Wahid! Are you okay?"

A pause.

"Yes, Mike, why are you asking?"

Arrgh. I just took a deep breath and just resolved to punch him in the face when he showed up.

Sure enough, pretty soon I heard the crunching of tires rolling over gravel, then a sliding stop. That had to be Wahid, so I went running out to see what the hell was going on.

Wahid leaped out of his car; it was unusual seeing him in civilian clothes. He was out of breath, a little disheveled, and scattered. It didn't help. He was the calmest person I'd met over there. He held up his hand in a "stop" motion as he scurried into the back of his dusty red sedan.

"Wait right there, Mike; I have something for you!"

He turned around with a triumphant smile. He had two packages wrapped up in brown paper, tied with some string.

"I wanted to get something for you to take home for your Christmas. It is something for your family." He thrust out the packages to me. "Please, Mike, open them."

I took the packages in my hands, untied the string, and, there in the dirty evening, in a dimly lit gravel parking lot, unwrapped one of the most meaningful packages that I've ever received. Nestled in the brown wrapping paper was a little plastic Christmas tree. It was about two feet tall, with bendy green limbs and removable feet. The other carefully wrapped package held the little lights that went on it. A string of little presents that lit up in different sequences or blinked all at once. Wahid was beaming.

"Wahid, where did you get this?"

"I had to go to many places, Mike," he rasped in his gravelly voice. Not very many shops have Christian things. "I had to get a lot of advice." He grinned. " I had to go all over Baghdad! Many, many places!"

So this doofus went running around all sorts of neighborhoods, asking all sorts of questions that could get him killed. Approaching Christmas, Wahid was asking where he could get this very Christian symbol for his friend. And then he did it over and over again. Until he finally got me and my family what he wanted: a Christmas tree.

In my arrogance, I asked Wahid, "Do you know what this symbol means?" What a dumbass: I know. "Do you know what the tree means to me?"

He looked over his glasses. The sharp lighting carved his grin into his face. His eyes sparkled with mirth.

"Yes, Mike, I know that this is an important symbol for Christians."

"Why the hell did you go running around town, asking questions about this Christian symbol? Sayyid, wasn't that dangerous? Aren't people looking for that sort of thing? I can't lose you, Wahid; you are too important! You can't take those kinds of risks; why did you do this?"

He let me finish my tirade then, still grinning, said, "Because it is important to you, Mike. I want you and your family to think about your friends in Iraq at Christmas."

I stood there slack-jawed. I kept underestimating the bravery and loyalty of my little group of friends.

Before it was over, Wahid would piss me off a bunch more times. He took my shoulder measurements and had a tailor friend make me a leather jacket. It took multiple trips to the tailor. Asad would just shake his head every time he came back with another story of him trying to do something for me. I think Asad had been trying to get Wahid to behave for fifty years; I don't know why he continued to try.

After I got my jacket, I arrogantly tried to pay for it. Apparently, that's not what friends do, so I got my ass kicked for that too. When Wahid gave me his combat knife that had accompanied him on all of his combat sorties—some two hundred—I could do nothing.

Wahid continued to be the steady influence on this little band, pushing the progress as best he could, always laughing, in spite of whatever was happening around him. And immediately after that, barf up a lung. A chain-smoker all his life—he couldn't even chuckle without eventually spewing out a blob lookalike. That was just part of his charm.

And I constantly sang his praises to those in my chain of command, in hopes they might influence the leadership choices the IQAF would make. This man was critical to their success. Eventually, after I left, Wahid was made a general. (It's nice to be proven right.) I wasn't the only one who thought he was critical.

I stayed in touch with the guys after I left Iraq. I would e-mail Asad, and he would relay whatever I said to the rest. I would always get some smart-ass comment from Wahid. Asad was very proud of his friend; Wahid, the general, was right where he was supposed to be, taking charge of the future of Iraq's military aviation arm. Asad would always mention Wahid's success, and whenever I would e-mail Asad, it would start off with: "Mike, it is good to hear from you!" More often than not, there would be a reference to something Wahid did. Then, one day, I got a different kind of e-mail.

"Mike, this is the first time that I am not happy to hear from you. Our friend Wahid was killed by an IED a week ago." He was killed as the general in charge of IQAF training. The cowards did their work well. The Iraqi air force was dealt a savage blow.

Asad and the rest of the Four Amigos had a lifelong friend ripped from their lives. Wahid's wife, whom I had only met through a tattered, worn, sepia-toned picture that Wahid carried in his wallet, lost her husband of forty years. His children had lost their father, and his father had lost a prize son, one who would go to his house to harvest the best dates in Iraq for a friend. Rest in peace, my friend. Wa alaikum al Arhemm.

That cheap little Christmas tree is one of my most prized possessions.

20

A FLOWER SHOP IN BAGHDAD

Samir was very upset. He didn't get a big pencil. He finally had heard that I had distributed a couple of the Big Chief pencils to some really big movers and shakers and was pretty hurt that I hadn't provided him one. He was a simple little man. Not typical in the IQAF: mostly it was very brave men. It was clear that his older brother, Abbas, looked out for him. The price for that oversight was that he took tons of crap from the Iraqis. I'm not sure what other function Samir served in our little band. Maybe that was his only function.

He was the harmless fifth or sixth wheel that never bothered anyone and, according to Asad, had really retreated into a shell since his other brother had been assassinated. I had a soft spot for Samir, with his shock of white hair, his "badger emerging from a T-shirt" chest hair, and his dark, expressive eyes. He could hurt no one. He was very aware of any exposure to the bad guys—the polar opposite of the "they can go to hell" attitude that Wahid espoused. He was a frightened, jumpy little guy.

There is a quote attributed to Napoleon (I wasn't there when he said it, so it may not be totally correct) that he "could make men die for bits of colored ribbon." But he also said "...leave the coats behind; how cold could it *get* in Russia, anyway?" So you have to take what Napoleon says with a grain of salt.

He was disastrously wrong with the second quote and mostly wrong about the first. It wasn't the ribbon's color that men would die for. It was what that ribbon represented to the most important group to a soldier—his peers. And they didn't do it for the ribbon. A ribbon or a medal is just an acknowledgment for a deed done. It's past tense. It's an acknowledgment from the right people that "you done good."

And that's why the Big Pencil was a big deal to him. He wasn't sensitive to all slights; but ones perceived to be by Americans bothered him. The constant crap he got from his brother (the general) didn't seem to affect him, but if he thought that I or Jim were slighting him, that really brought him down. So for him to not get a big pencil was a big deal.

I got ahold of my wife and ended up having some more pencils shipped to me, to carefully distribute to all those Iraqis whose dreams had been crushed by me not giving them one—namely, Samir. He was on cloud nine after I gave it to him.

Samir had equated the big pencil with respect from the friendly side, and that was worth a lot to him. He even went downtown and brought back a gift for me. He came over to our work trailer. There was a timid knock at our cipher-locked door. I opened it up to see a shy Samir standing there.

"Major Bonset, I have something for you. It is a very special gift. I had to go to many stores to get it."

I was impressed; Samir rarely left their trailer. And here he was out in the sunshine and even more bravely, knocking on the friendly side's trailer. So of course I had to go with him. He was very excited as we crossed the gravel toward their trailer. He was all fidgety and nervous. We veered away from the trailer and into another outbuilding, where there was a small paper bag on a table.

He walked up to it, picked it up, and, beaming, gave a short speech, most of which I can't remember. But the gist of it was that, in light of our eternal friendship and our loyalty to each other and so forth, I was to receive a gift from this Iraqi man to this American man. I think it was the longest sentence I had ever heard.

And with great formality, or as much formality as one can have with a badger coming out of his shirt, Samir presented me with his paper bag. There were certainly a lot of things it could have been. But I took it and, with great fanfare, whipped off the paper bag to reveal...cologne. What I got in exchange for my undying loyalty and eternal friendship and single-handed awesomeness was some of the worst cologne (bug spray) I'd ever smelled: "Paris"; by some guy in Baghdad.

He certainly had the element of surprise. He was incredibly proud of his gift; I didn't want to offend him by saying "What the hell is this?", so I acted as if I had just been waiting for the right moment to ask if someone, anyone, would go downtown to procure me a little something to make me feel pretty on those hot, dusty nights when a man needs, well, a little pick-me-up. A little splash of that stuff, and not only would you be pretty, but you would be pretty alone.

Eventually leaving Iraq's newly employed chemical offensive behind, Samir and I talked about more serious things. When there wasn't any real business to discuss, I would shoot the breeze with Samir, and learned a bit about life in Iraq before we arrived.

It was all kite flying and unicorn races. But; enough of the media reporting.

Samir had never even wanted to be in the military. But in Saddam's Iraq, it was one of the safer professions. At least you would have a job and be held in fairly high esteem. And, until we handed the IQAF their assess, Saddam was partial to the air force. Additionally, he had to keep the military happy to ensure that he stayed alive. So if you could survive the constant strife, which Saddam instigated to ensure there would always be a bad guy to distract from his own fascism (think "the rich" and Democrats), it was a decent living.

Samir allowed that there was a time; long ago, at the very edge of his memory, that he remembered walking along the river, with dancing and shops, people eating at restaurants, and other aspects of normal life. But he was young at the time; something changed, and eventually the young Samir came to realize that this Saddam guy had started to become more and more of a presence in their daily lives.

Fascists know how to boil a frog.

Eventually, Samir started truncating his dreams, as the options became more and more limited. He had his two brothers blazing a trail into the military, so he ended up joining the IQAF as well.

He had started off by attending flight training and was flying around one day when it struck him that at some point he may have to use his war machine to conduct, well, war. And he didn't want to "hurt the peoples." He was conflicted, so he went home to his wife to discuss what they should do.

Although she really wanted to be married to a pilot (and really, who doesn't), she agreed with his conscience. His life's dream had been to own a flower shop, but that didn't have the kind of security that could be had in the IQAF: not financial security, mind you, physical security. After mulling over the options, she decided that he should stay in the air force; it was just safer there. As Samir was telling me that, I noticed a marked change in his body language.

When he got to that part, his scrawny shoulders sagged just a bit—a physical manifestation of a mental burden. He really was uncomfortable with all things military, but up until now, I hadn't realized just how much. But social pressure, self-preservation, and his family determined that the course of his life would be safer if he continued to serve in the air force.

So, eventually he had walked into the commanding officer's office and announced that he had decided to change his specialty; he wanted to be an air traffic controller. I felt this was a bad choice: with his short attention span, he was just as likely to kill people; they would just be his own pilots. So that's what he had done for the previous thirty years. I'm not sure how many victims he racked up.

He looked so heartbroken as he relayed this story that I decided I would do what I could to help him realize a small portion of his dream. My mom and dad in Montana had been trying to figure out ways to send stuff to help the Iraqis. After I told them about Samir, they asked some of their neighbors, and pretty soon, I had a package full of seeds. Then another arrived, from my wife and all the neighbors in our little neighborhood. Typical arrogant, Imperialist type of behavior, even from stateside, I guess. I got all kinds of flowers, had no idea which ones, but there was the entire spectrum of flora represented in that little cardboard box.

On one of the many bright, fresh-out-of-the-oven hot days, after I got a bit of space between things I had to do, I went and got Samir. I had scrounged a shovel, rake, and hoe from somewhere. Samir followed me, questioning where we were going. There was a little plot of land behind the Iraqi Air Operation Center (AOC), about ten yards by thirty yards, on the other side of a window in the office of the number two man in the IQAF, General Altair.

We arrived there in short order; it was stiflingly hot, and I was already soaked with sweat. I showed him where I had already cut a berm into the hard soil, outlining a perimeter. He started to get very excited, and when I gave him the box of seeds, he was ecstatic.

"Where did these come from, Major?"

I explained how all of these seeds came from friends and family in the United States and how they all wanted to see his flowers grow.

"How could they all come from America? There are so many different kinds of flowers! They all come from America?"

I really can't comprehend what others, especially those who have limited communications with the outside world, must think of America. In my travels, I have always had to verify that I can indeed get any kind of food at any time of day. Gas is plentiful. People of all colors live in peace. You are in charge of your destiny. And you can get a million different kinds of flower seeds.

So I asked Samir what we should do next. He was so very excited that his schemes soon surpassed what we had available to us. He was talking about transmuting all of Baghdad into flower beds. He described his grandiose plans with wild gesturing, spinning his body this way and that, as he pointed out where to plant what. I let him wind down, allowing that what he was describing was a good plan and all, but I thought that we would

probably have our hands full right here, in this little ten-by-thirty-yard plot. His bushy eyebrows met, and he paused.

"Yes, Major, you are right. I will start small"—he made a big gesture—"and then, I will grow big!" He ended with his arms spread wide.

Our little plot of land was about fifteen feet away from General Altair's window. There was a small retaining wall with about a three-foot drop forming one side of a walkway. This walkway went around the building to the front entrance. The upshot was that our feet were about the same height as General Altair when he was sitting at his desk, which he was now. He was looking through the dirt-smeared glass at us. He had seen me earlier, scratching out the perimeter of the little garden, and just smiled and shook his head. I guess he was kind of used to me by now.

But he did watch with interest while Samir and I had our conversations, standing in the hundred-degree heat, while Samir mapped out the garden. I think he thought of Samir the same way I did: a bit off, but harmless. (Unless you were flying, and he was controlling you; but the Americans had that responsibility now.) The general went back to work.

And Samir and I finally got to it. He attacked with the hoe, and I attacked with the shovel. He would sketch down the rows, and I would follow behind, digging into the hard soil, trying to soften it up in order to plant the seeds. It was exhausting labor, and I was glad I had made sure that I didn't have much to finish at work, because I knew that I was going to be absolutely soaked by the time this was over.

We only got about two quadrants done that day; dusk fell, and although I was willing to keep going, Samir had to catch a ride with the other guys. Wahid came over and gave Samir the requisite amount of crap, but he looked at me with a twinkle in his eye. I guess he knew what I was doing. Samir gladly (it seemed to me) put down his hoe and walked off with Wahid to the waiting brown Chevy that would take the guys to where they spent their nights. Samir took the seeds with him, not letting the other guys touch the brown cardboard box.

I decided to do a little more and then tidy up. The purple dusk had settled, and it started to get quiet. The noise from the many generators never stopped, and occasionally there was a bit of gunfire, but if you weren't getting mortared and rocketed, our little spot of heaven could be pretty quaint. I was going to finish turning over the dirt and then call it a night. The temperature had fallen a bit, so it was actually fairly pleasant.

I heard a noise behind me. It was General Altair, coming around the corner and stepping up over the retaining wall.

"Salaam Alaikum, Major Bonset. I see you are trying to be an Iraqi farmer. What has happened to your help?"

I really liked General Altair. He was an honest man and as brave as they come. He was one that could really see how the fundamental lack of trust was hobbling the efforts here. (He was the one that remarked how the C-17 captain seemed to have more authority than he did. And he was right.) He was such a friendly man, never too busy to talk, and always had a smile on his face. He was in a difficult situation, as were most of the senior leaders that we were advising. We were expecting a lot of great things from them. We were expecting things on our timeline, and the rest of their society was operating on theirs. General Altair got it from both sides. Still, I had never seen him really frustrated; he always seemed fairly level.

Here he was, in the evening calm, the number two guy in the nascent IQAF. I didn't respond to his greeting right away. He was looking off into the distance. He bent and picked up the hoe and wordlessly started digging. I took that as my cue, and for a while, we just worked there, under the same stars that had shone down on the Sumerian kings five thousand years before Christ. This dirt had been tilled many times before, I suppose. In that moment, silent except for the rasp and chunk of the hoe and shovel doing their work, I felt really small.

After what seemed like an eternity, Altair asked what the hell we were doing. He was helpful like that. He had seen me out there and just came to help, not really caring why. I explained to him that this was going to be a flower garden someday. It was going to be Samir's, since he had always wanted one. I flashed him a grin and told him that he was welcome to gaze upon it from his office, if he wanted to.

He grinned back; then something caught in his throat. "It would be nice to see beauty again. I would like it very much. When the garden gets bigger, I will maybe take some home to my wife. She would like to see some flowers."

I told him as long as he cleared it through Samir, he could. We continued to dig, soft words in the soft evening describing small things, mundane things. He talked about how much he had enjoyed the friendly side and how impressed he was with his trip to the United States. We had sponsored him to come back to the United States for a leadership tour, and it had made an indelible impression on him, as intended.

He discussed the ease with which we deal with each other. He talked about how much his young son idolizes the Americans. He had shown me some papers painted in the bright colors only a child can use: disjointed aircraft flying through a bright blue sky framed by a four-color rainbow. His son had painted American aircraft flying through the Iraqi skies, through rainbows no less. We were heroes to his son.

We talked about nothing for a while longer, he in his flight suit, me in my airman's battle uniform (ABU), adorned with my pistol. I wore my aviator wings, positioned carefully over my maintenance badge, while Altair wore his silver aviator wings.

On our chests were the symbols of the different militaries we represented; but in our hands, each of us had one of the simplest, common, and yet most powerful utensils on earth: shovel and hoe. Meant for creating life, not ending it. The best my aviator wings could do in the service of my great nation was to defend life and create the conditions for life to flourish, but even the most precise drop of a bomb, shot of a rifle, or use of artillery couldn't create life.

A flower garden here, in this harsh climate, would take a lot of tending. The flowers planted would not be able to stand on their own for a long time and would require a dedicated, attentive gardener. And as this seemed to be relatively unfertile ground for a flowerbed, special care would have to be apportioned to ensure that the inevitable weeds were removed with precision and finality. If we were to take the time and effort, he and I, working in the earth to bring this glorious riot of color and vibrancy to life, well, we'd damned well better be ready to assist with the weeding, or we had no business planting anything in the first place.

I asked him about how we could get the dark water that gurgled through the manmade canal to the flowerbed. He told me about a pump and hose that was stowed around back of the AOC. He said we could use that to water this garden as much as was needed. But now, he had to go finish up reading some crazy plan that the friendly side had come up with about command and control (C2) of precision-guided munitions that the Iraqis would soon be getting. He put a giant, worn hand on my shoulder and smiled under the harsh lights now sputtering to life.

"Thank you, Major Bonset."

He turned his heel in the now soft earth and disappeared around a corner, reappearing sometime later in his dimly lit office. He picked up his glasses, perched them down his nose, grabbed the C2 proposal, and began to read.

I picked up the tools and headed back to the advisor's trailer, where a couple of people were still working on various efforts. The advisors put in a ton of hours trying to make sure the opportunities purchased at such high costs by the young men and women of the US Armed Forces would not be squandered. So there were quite a few folks still there. It took a bit of explaining as to why I was so wet and dirty.

Nobody thought it was stupid. Some of the folks there would try some of these kinds of things to better connect with their principles or the folks that were around them. There were English classes being conducted all the time; an amazing SMSgt Jeff, spent hours and hours after his normal ten to twelve hours, teaching the Iraqis language and computer skills. Toward the end of our tour, Jeff was damn near killed by a rocket that hit just on the other side of a concrete barrier. The blast caused an intense ringing in his ears, and he was off balance for quite a while afterward. He planned to retire after his tour and set off on a cross-country bike ride with his family. I hope he did.

And I have it on good authority that a certain rotund General from the Iraqi finance department and I make a hell of a singing duo for "In the Year 2525", and especially, "Everyone was Kung Fu Fighting", or as Brigadier General "K" would call it, "Everyone Kung Foo Fight Me". There were, I am proud to say, actions associated with those lyrics, but my performances are limited to strict engagements in Iraq or other combat theaters.

So it wasn't unusual that I was doing this kind of stuff. Most of us did something. A lot of our care packages went to the Iraqis too; I was hoping to give something to Wahid that would give him the same epic squirts that his stupid dates had given me. In spite of my aunt's best efforts (I have some that can cook and one that cannot), I failed in that endeavor. I consulted the computer spreadsheets. The English language test results were finally coming in. More people were scoring well. My wife had donated some little pins that denoted a couple of different levels of English language proficiency. I had passed them out to the various units, and after many of the young lieutenants scored well on their ELTs and started sporting the pins, I started seeing a demand to be tested by the older guys. And pretty soon, we would see these pins being worn by the highest-ranking generals. Most of them were full of crap though; I think there was a lot of "rounding" in their scores. The first, cautious stages of belonging to a different kind of organization were starting to take hold.

The spreadsheets also indicated that each following class for induction into every class (pilots, MSOs, ELT, everything) was bigger than the one preceding it—and high-quality cadets, too. The IQAF had come up with some pretty interesting ways to advertise, seeing as how they still couldn't just go down to the local schools yet. They were airdropping leaflets out of their Mi-171s and Hueys buzzing over Baghdad and even airing TV commercials. One particularly gutsy one showed the IQAF CH-2000s in action, and the actual guys from that unit were in it. Awesome.

As I clicked and scanned through the data, I couldn't help feeling a bit satisfied. The work that had gone on before us, the seeds that were planted by those preceding me—this ground that was made fertile by better men than I was starting to bear fruit. America had come reluctantly to this fight. If you think there was a rush to war, you are either having to have someone read this to you, or are a bristlecone pine tree and may have a different scale of time.

Plus bristly cones.

Once in the fight, great restraint was used in order to preserve the ground for a new crop. A couple of schools of thought exist on this methodology. Some would say that if my neighbor has lots of weeds in his garden and year after year refuses to do anything about it, I must act. Eventually, those weeds will infest mine. It's the basis for every damn covenant for every neighborhood that I've lived in. What you do affects your neighbor. I can treat my garden to the best of my ability, but unless my neighbor takes care of his weeds, they will get into mine. If my neighbor is actively encouraging his weeds to grow, then my garden is in definite peril. Knowing that eventually the cost and constant pressure of defending my garden, plus the law of averages, means that my lawn will be fundamentally changed and much of what I took pride in my garden for will be gone.

But what to do?

We chose to hand-select just the offending plants and individually remove them. This is the equivalent of taking that little pokey metal rod with the fork at the end of it and popping the weeds out one by one. It's backbreaking work and costs a lot of time and resources. But doing this, you only remove the obvious weeds. You don't get the ones that haven't opened yet. And this takes the cooperation of the neighbor himself, helping to point out where they may be; after all, he knows his garden better than anyone. Unfortunately, he's also the one who has created the problem in the first place. The neighbor and all the groundskeepers who allowed this problem to flourish.

You could also spray the whole garden. It's safer and easier for me to just pray and spray, but only if you have a spray that clearly and effectively only targets the weeds, and not innocent flowers that are similar in appearance to weeds. And in the context of this metaphor, that's the equivalent of having munitions that only kill bad guys, not the guy next door, not the guy that is not obvious in their support, and not the guy that is almost a bad guy, but not quite. Only the really obvious bad guy would be hit. Since we don't have that technology yet, then our "spray" doesn't exist. That requires less cooperation from the neighbor, but unless you change the neighbor's (and groundskeeper's) practices, the weeds will be right back, and who knows, the broad based killing might make the newly emptied soil a fertile ground for even more weeds, more toxic than the last.

Or you could set fire to the neighbor's garden. You'll get everything, including the lush flowers you were trying to encourage to grow. But, this approach mandates that you have absolutely intense oversight of the garden for the next few seasons, as its going to be incredibly vulnerable. And that garden will be yours to tend for a long time, as it's pretty clear that the neighbor had nothing to do with this solution other than create the conditions necessary for you to act. This is very rarely, if ever, the American way.

We chose the first, and at first blush, it may seem the most humane way to conduct garden care. But things are not always as they seem. There are consequences to that approach that are not inherently obvious.

During one of the spates of bad behavior there, I think it was pretty early in my tour, an Iraqi colonel, (not Wahmid) whom I had never seen before, came up to me to discuss what was going on. It may have been the alleged museum looting or some other malfeasance by the Iraqis. Apparently, our guys were not supposed to take offensive, especially deadly action.

This guy had a different take on that. He put his arm around my shoulders and, in a lowered voice, said, "You should have jumped on us with *both* feet. You should shoot the looters and thieves."

I responded that the international community wouldn't like that, because the news would show wailing and sad people and the Americans looking like they are killing everyone. That would help the bad guys recruit. I was well into my speech that we needed the cooperation of the Iraqis to make this a joint effort when he cut me off.

"By not being strong, really strong, you are hurting the Iraqi people!" His arm convulsed a bit. His voice had gotten a bit louder. "You are here:

you must be in charge. You shouldn't care what your TV says; when you stand by, you make bad behavior easy. And it makes more bad behavior. And that hurts the Iraqi people. You must be in charge! If you don't tell the leaders what to do, they will do what they have always done."

In other words, he was going for the old "MacArthur in Japan" look. And that had worked. It was a sharp pain to the Japanese people over a relatively short period of time, but it resulted in a staunch ally, an honorable people, and a nation that is a respected citizen of the world. Same goes for Germany. But now, sensitive to the ways any sort of "disrespectful" action would get played in a hostile press, we had castrated ourselves and joined the New Age movement. Everyone is right, really. Dandelions are just misunderstood. The garden must learn to coexist with the weed. Right up until you have a field of weeds.

This guy was trying to make sure I understood that our reluctance to tell anyone what to do at risk of sounding culturally superior was resulting in the death and continued misery of the very people that we were trying to help. Letting bad behavior (some behavior is not just "different," it's bad) occur with the justification that its "cultural" hurts the group around that behavior. So here we were with a giant case of Iraqi affirmative action. With the same predictable results. Increased misery, poor results, and a lowering of the behavior bar.

After a bit more in that same vein, the colonel wound down, his passion spent for now. It wasn't the first time I had heard this theme. As mentioned before, often times, when I was over at the Iraqi AOC just shooting the breeze with Wahmid, we would get into very candid conversations about the proper way to conduct post–major combat actions. To a man, the guys favored the hard approach. Many of them thought that a lot of senior leaders should be replaced, with people the Americans thought were good, with little to no consideration for what the Iraqis thought.

I tended to agree. But as a good soldier, I was doing my best to work within the system that I was given. And after such a long time, it was bearing fruit.

I saw that the MSOs were getting ready to come back, and thankfully, they were *all* coming back. No desertions. Whew. They would be back in a few days, and Swanny had relayed that the sensor company reported back that they did very well indeed. English was rarely a concern; the "young ones" (Alhasan, Alaa) would explain things to the "old one" (Ghalib). They were prompt and professional. I couldn't wait for them to get back, so I could debrief them on their experience.

In the meantime, I would be working with Samir to get this flower garden to bloom. He wasn't feeling well one day, so I spent my time coordinating further Iraqi excursions to the United States, Britain, and Italy; we had a C-130 simulator training session that we were trying to fill, and Swanny was being his usual self, juggling eighteen different things, trying to make it happen.

It always amazed me, the help we got from the stateside organizations. Everybody I dealt with back home, whether from the DOD or a private corporation was so helpful. When they found out that whatever I was calling about was for the Iraqi air force, people just couldn't do enough. And we were always treated with respect too.

I shouldn't have been surprised. Way back in the beginning of this book, I told you that this country breeds good people like flies; they don't all wear uniforms. With that in mind, I couldn't wait to talk to the MSOs about their experiences. What happens when you drop a group with the experiences of this one into the maelstrom of freedom and happy chaos that is the United States? I wondered what Ghalib would look like after having to be responsible for a couple of twenty-two-year-olds who had just had their shackles pulled off (or in the words of giant General Jasham, "blinders" off).

In my mind, it was the equivalent of trying to make my sixteen-year-old son behave (a dicey proposition in the best of times) after giving him a bottle of whiskey, a bag of M-80s, a .22 rifle, the keys to the Porsche, and tickets to Wally World. So I was very interested in what Major Ghalib would look like.

Eventually, I walked across to the IQAF HQ building, where the sensor operators would be coming in from the airstrip on the other side of base. While waiting, I had a chance to catch up with Mr. Hadi, the retired army general of Big Chief pencil fame. He had finally moved his operation to the HQ building, out of the smelly basement of the MOD. He was excited to see me; I hadn't been by in a while, and we got along well. When he saw me come in, he booted out whoever was in his office, stood up, and came around the desk, hand out for a handshake.

"Bonset! How are you, my brother; please, come in! We must talk. How is your family?"

I fended off the first barrage of questions and asked how his family was. He barked a salvo of Arabic, and one of the guys scooted off to get me some sort of beverage. I sat down in the white plastic lawn chair that he had had to pay for out of his own pocket. He went back around the desk to get into the lower left drawer. A shallow crystal bowl filled with the expensive chocolates appeared in his slender hands, accompanied by a mischievous grin. It was his very fancy candy dish. His grin widened as he presented it to me.

"Major, would you like some chocolate?"

"Sayyid, everyone knows you have the best chocolate. That's why we come here."

His wizened little face broke into a big grin. He leaned back in his chair. I would've done the same, but it would've resulted in me being flat on my back, skewered by shards of plastic lawn furniture. He started talking about a couple of official type things, but soon, we veered off into his personal life. He was very proud of the fact that his daughter and granddaughter were back in Baghdad. He had them in Syria during the "trouble," and since things in Baghdad had become relatively calm, he had brought them back. About this same time, however, the stateside newspapers were trumpeting the exact opposite.

But here was this grandfather that was bringing back his daughter and two-year-old granddaughter to a city that the major media outlets said was exploding. Why? Was it possible that the bias of the media runs so deep that they would pick and choose the most dire news to report? Even when (not if) that would result in the deaths of more Iraqis and Americans? I don't know. It seemed like it to me.

They could certainly provide news, but in context, and on balance, the situation would look fairly positive. And those positive reports would buttress a burgeoning confidence in the Iraqi people and our GIs. And that in turn would lead to less violence, lower casualties, and faster transition to normalcy. But that might also reflect positively on a president that they weren't partial to. I really hope that's not what was going on.

Hadi and I continued to talk for a bit, when there was a commotion at the entrance to the room. The three MSOs had returned, like conquering heroes. I could hardly recognize them. They seemed bigger, somehow. Not fatter (although I think Alaa snuck an extra few pounds in), just bigger. Larger in life than they were when they left. I'm happy to say that their eyes lit up when they saw me there. Then the room really got noisy.

The three of them were just pounding on my back, circling me. Ghalib was trying to formally report to me but had no chance against the jabbering twenty-somethings. In the middle of this chaos, I saw Mr. Hadi retreat back into his office, fleeing the noise. I lost visual with him, but he soon came back. Armed.

He was going to get control of this noisy situation, I guess; it was, after all, his place of work. And in order to get accomplish that, he had decided to come after me.

With the big pencil.

The wizened old man came out of that office, the Big Chief held in his thin hands like a cross to ward off evil spirits, and I was sure which evil spirit he was trying to control. Me.

He pushed through the MSOs and brandished the pencil in front of me. He was grinning like crazy. I'll be damned if the pencil didn't work. We were all laughing, but it quickly subsided into a dull roar. He looked at Ghalib and, in his reedy, gravelly, thin voice said, "Major Ghalib, now that I have disciplined Major Bonset, I would like to hear your adventures."

Ghalib launched into his report and was halted by Hadi.

"In English, please, Major." Hadi looked at me, a twinkle in his eye. A lot of the Iraqi leadership was shy about their English-speaking abilities. Mr. Hadi was one. But he had been working on his English and proudly listened while Ghalib relayed his adventures.

The trip out was an adventure, mostly because none of them had ever flown on a commercial airline. I remembered that I had received several panicked phone calls on the way out; Ghalib had been really nervous. I could tell, though, as he relayed that part of the adventure, the lieutenants thought he was being an old woman. A lot of eye rolling and elbow nudging.

But he got stateside and picked up a sponsor to help. Swanny had done his work well. The training went fabulous. They were ready to not only go operational with the sensor suite, but train the next crop of MSOs as well. Ghalib would probably be handling most of those duties, and the lieutenants would be getting experience in the fight.

But the report devolved from a formal dissertation into a "what I did over the summer" report. Ghalib talked about how nice everything was. He mentioned several times the brightness and cleanliness of everywhere they went. All work in the office had stopped; everyone was listening. He must've gone to a Wal-Mart or something, because he was talking about heaps of oranges and apples and then clothes and candy. Apparently, the candy was a big hit with Alaa, because that little tidbit of information got him a lot of elbow nudges and a couple bursts of Arabic. Which resulted in more laughter.

Ghalib was very relaxed and smiling, totally different than when he left. He remarked on the kindness everywhere. Everyone was happy in the United States. People offered to help them wherever they went. And it wasn't just the people at the sensor company, either. Just normal folks. Just like I told him.

Alhasan and Alaa gave similar reports, but after Ghalib drifted off to go talk to Mr. Hadi about some other things, the two lieutenants stories took on a slightly different focus. Apparently the fun began mostly after Ghalib drifted off to sleep. Then the two would sneak out and go to bars. Or a bar. I couldn't tell. There was a lot of jabbering going on. But they reiterated that everyone was so nice and so accommodating to them.

I asked if anything bad had happened to them; they couldn't conceive of anything bad happening in the whole damn country.

Alaa talked faster and faster until the big young man just ran of words. He stopped, frozen with his arms outstretched as if he were going to catch a beach ball. He strained for that culminating thought that would summarize his experience.

"Major, everyone in America is so beautiful!"

I think the mission was a success. This young crop of lieutenants had seen things that 99 percent of their peers could not. No one would ever be able to tell them that the Great Satan was within our borders. They had been here. And the truth had set them free. Once the blinders come off, they cannot go on again.

Ghalib finished up what he was doing with Mr. Hadi and came to collect the lieutenants. We shook hands again, and I slapped them all on the backs in farewell. As Ghalib herded the boys out past me, he swooped in toward me to whisper something only to me.

"Bonset," he said, his eyes glittering, wrinkled in amusement, "I still think America is impossible."

That was a great day.

A couple of days later, I found Samir, and we decided to finish planting his garden. We finished marking out the plot; he would create the rows, and I would follow along, churning up the soil. On that hot day, we just finished the layout and decided to come out the next day and plant the seeds. We had done the prep work. Samir was very excited, but trying to be very somber, acting like this was no big deal. He just couldn't wait for the next day.

I saw General Altair in his office, and that reminded me to ask Samir about his plan for watering the flowers. It came as no surprise to me that he didn't have one. He thought maybe buckets from the canal would work. I thought that the big water pump and hose would be a better solution.

He was very excited that General Altair would let him use it; I told him that General Altair suggested it. I saw Altair working and gave him a little wave. He waved and smiled, returning to his mound of papers. I turned to Samir and said that the price for using the pump was that he would have to let General Altair take a flower or two home to his wife and family.

Samir thought that would be wonderful, and everyone could take flowers home to their wives and their families.

Have I mentioned that Samir is very excitable?

The next morning, about 1000 hours, we ended up out there again, this time taking the next step of a good gardener. We had prepped the battlefield, accomplishing the destruction of the weeds and removing the obstruction of the rocks that lay just under the surface. We had prepared the soil for new life. And now, we were going to plant the seeds.

Someone, sometime in the night had watered. The soil was moist and warm. It didn't take much to see that Altair, after burning the midnight oil, had come out here in the peace of the evening to do what he could to try to make this little piece of desert bloom.

Samir had brought his precious box with him, and he opened it grandiosely to start planting. He took the ceremonial first couple of seeds, and then we both started carefully placing this precious cargo that had come all the way from America into the Iraqi soil. (There were like a million seeds, though, so pretty soon I was planting them a whole lot less carefully.) Eventually, we stood up in the early-morning sun, stretching our backs. It was done. Phase two was complete.

The next phase is the most complex, taxing, and least rewarding. Now we had to water and tend the young plants as they struggled to break through the crusty soil and avoid getting plucked by a bird, eaten by a grub, or choked out by a weed. For that, they would need a dedicated gardener. Someone to water and weed diligently over a couple of weeks with no visible reward. Indeed, the reward wouldn't be evident until very late in the flower's life. Most of the time would not be spent looking at a beautiful bloom, but a scrawny stem, struggling to reach its potential. Only late in the timeline would we get to gaze on the beauty that we had in mind those many weeks before. And only then do you know if your mission was a success or not.

I looked at the neat pattern in the soil. General Altair had come out, stood there, and clapped Samir on the shoulder. Samir looked as proud and confident as I'd ever seen him. For a bit, he wasn't the failure. He had *done* something. A couple more of the senior leaders came out too; pretty soon there were five or six of us standing around, shooting the breeze. Samir looked like a proud father. Everyone agreed that this would be a beautiful thing, this flowerbed. I swear, Samir glowed.

The next morning, Samir went and watered the beds. I wasn't able to help much; we were really busy. I snuck out after work to do a bit of weeding when no one was looking; I wanted this to be all Samir's show. I did a bit of watering too. I couldn't wait for the results.

Unfortunately, Samir's calling was not farming. His short attention span hardly let him put on two of the same shoes, much less raise a crop. His attention to the project waned, and the earth became harder and harder, as his watering occurred more and more infrequently, eventually ceasing altogether. The nurturing environment that we had built with so much effort was reverting back to the chaos we had pulled it out of. The crust of the earth became impenetrable for most of the fragile plants.

The ones that did struggle through were set upon by the weeds that grew unchecked. Chaos always arrives faster than order. Samir's attention became focused (so to speak) elsewhere, not on the project he had started with such promise. The few stems that remained were set upon by birds. A couple of times, I went out in the evening to pull a couple of weeds or put some water on a quadrant of soil, but this was Samir's garden. I couldn't change Samir; he was set. The path of his life, his habits, his expectations, and his perception of responsibility were fixed in his psyche. But that new crop would suffer for it.

In the end, though, we gave Samir what no one else did: an opportunity. He had had the opportunity to accomplish his dream. No one told him that it wasn't the right dream or that there were too many florists already and the government didn't need any more. He wasn't worried. The Americans were here, and things were getting better. They always do when Americans are around. His success or failure was his alone. Because you and I, we gave this squirrely little guy, the butt of every joke, the scared little brother, the assassin's target, a gift that cannot be unmade.

You did that. You do that. The kindness demonstrated by us (and by extension the Tongans, Brits, Aussies, Czechs, Georgians [the European kind] Japanese, Korean, Danes, Slovaks, etc) to the citizens of Iraq is often unappreciated or unknown. The kindness that your military shows to combatants, especially noncombatants, is the stuff of legend. In spite of the fact that Democrats accuse the military of costing too much, accomplishing too little (unless they are singlehandedly leading a SEAL team to kill Bin Laden), and being a haven for stupid, backward nobodies who are "air raiding villages and killing civilians".

For a brief shining few days, Samir was in charge of his destiny. I will always remember him standing there in his dirty, chocolate chip camouflage, sweating in the bright sun. Gripping his hoe in his hand like the hammer of Thor, he owned a ten-by-thirty-yard patch of promise.

Because of you, he had his chance to fulfill his childhood dream. Courtesy of the kindest, most generous people on earth, he had a chance to own a flower shop.

A Flowershop in Baghdad.

About The Author

Michael Banzet served twenty-two years in the United States Air Force. He started at the lowest rank, E-1, then rapidly got promoted to E-6 in seven years. While enlisted, he was a crew chief on the mighty F-4G Phantom, F-16 Falcon, and the F-117A Nighthawk. He completed his bachelor's degree, graduating cum laude, then was selected for Officer Training School. Upon commissioning, he became a nuclear maintenance officer, earned his master's degree, then was selected to attend pilot training. He eventually accumulated over twenty-five hundred hours. He served in Desert Storm, Desert Fox, Southern Watch, Enduring Freedom, and Iraqi Freedom.

He has written several newspaper articles, one entitled "When is Iraq Newsworthy" and the other entitled "Why I Quit."

He lives in Ohio with his family.

7/14

DISCARDED

Lucy Robbins Welles Library
95 Cedar Street
Newington, CT 06111

26042770R00196

Made in the USA
Charleston, SC
22 January 2014